Effective Managerial
Communication

Note to the Student

Dear Student,

   If you winced when you learned the price of this textbook, you are experiencing what is known as "sticker shock" in today's economy. Yes, textbooks are expensive, and we don't like it anymore than you do. Many of us here at Kent have sons and daughters of our own attending college, or we are attending school part time ourselves. However, the prices of our books are dictated by the cost factors involved in producing them. The costs of paper, designing the book, setting it in type, printing it, and binding it have risen significantly each year along with everything else in our economy. You might find the following table to be of some interest.

Item	1967 Price	1984 Price	The Price Increase
Monthly Housing Expense	$114.31	$686.46	6.0 times
Monthly Automobile Expense	82.69	339.42	4.1 times
Loaf of Bread	.22	1.00	4.6 times
Pound of Hamburger	.39	1.48	3.8 times
Pound of Coffee	.59	2.45	4.2 times
Candy Bar	.10	.35	3.5 times
Gasoline	.35	1.20	3.4 times
Men's Dress Shirt	5.00	25.00	5.0 times
Postage	.05	.22	4.4 times
Resident College Tuition	294.00	1,581.00	5.4 times

   Today's prices of college textbooks have increased only about 2.8 times 1967 prices. Compare your texts sometime to a general trade book, i.e., a novel or nonfiction book, and you will easily see significant differences in the internal design, quality of paper, and binding. These features of college textbooks cost money.

   Textbooks should not be looked on only as an expense. Other than your professors, your textbooks are your most important source for what you hope to learn in college. What's more, the textbooks you keep can be valuable resources in your future career and life. They are the foundation of your professional library. Like your education, your textbooks are one of your most important investments.

   We are concerned, and we care. Please write to us at the address below with your comments. We want to be responsive to your suggestions, to give you quality textbooks, and to do everything in our power to keep their prices under control.

Wayne Barcomb

Wayne A. Barcomb
President

Kent Publishing Company
20 Park Plaza
Boston, MA 02116

Effective Managerial Communication

Robert W. Rasberry
Southern Methodist University

Laura Fletcher Lemoine
Louisiana State University

KENT PUBLISHING COMPANY
Boston, Massachusetts
A Division of Wadsworth, Inc.

Associate Editor: Rolf Janke
Production Editor: Carolyn Ingalls
Interior Designer: Janice Wheeler
Cover Designer: Harold Pattek
Manufacturing Manager: Linda Siegrist
Art Studio: Boston Graphics, Inc.

KENT PUBLISHING COMPANY
A Division of Wadsworth, Inc.

Printed in the United States of America
1 2 3 4 5 6 7 8 9 — 90 89 88 87 86

Library of Congress Cataloging-in-Publication Data

Rasberry, Robert W.
　Effective managerial communication.

　Includes index.
　1. Communication in management.　I. Lemoine, Laura
Fletcher.　II. Title.
HD30.3.R37　1986　　　　658.4'5　　　85-23177
ISBN 0-534-04554-5

Dedication

To *Jenni*, whose love, support, and encouragement made the long hours of this writing much shorter.   R.W.R.

To *Ashley*, in loving appreciation of her enthusiasm, encouragement, and inspiration.   L.F.L.

About the Authors

ROBERT W. RASBERRY, Ph.D. (University of Kansas), has been teaching in the Edwin L. Cox School of Business at Southern Methodist University in Dallas, Texas, since 1974. He is the director of communication services, and is a professor of organizational behavior. His major areas of research and teaching include communication skills, organizational communication, and corporate social responsibility—especially as it relates to ethics. Bob has written over 25 articles and professional papers. In addition to being a coauthor of this text, he is the author of *The "Technique" of Political Lying* and the coauthor of *Power Talk: How to Win Your Audience*. He has extensive training and consulting experience. Since the early 1970s he has participated in over 200 supervisory, middle management, and executive-level seminars. His client list numbers over 50 organizations and associations, among them IBM, Sun Exploration, Arthur Young, the United States Chamber of Commerce, Lomas and Nettleton, Rockwell International, AT&T, and Southland Corporation.

LAURA FLETCHER LEMOINE, Ph.D. (Louisiana State University), has been dean of the Junior Division at Louisiana State University since August 1984. Previously she was associate dean of the college. Her experience includes acting as supervising lecturer and director of the Comprehensive Public Training Program, a managerial and career enrichment program at LSU, for Louisiana state employees. She has taught oral and written organizational communication skills, personnel management, public speaking, group discussion, problem solving, conflict resolution, mediation, time management, counseling and discipline, interpersonal communication, and broadcasting. She has designed core curricula and training manuals, coordinated communication programs on the graduate and undergraduate levels, and conducted over 250 training programs for the public and private sector. Among her clients are the U.S. Civil Service Commission, the Ethyl Corporation, and Gulf States Utilities.

Preface

The Importance of Communication

Communication is one of the most important tools in a businessperson's arsenal—it is the means by which all organizational activity is managed. With both a well-designed communication plan and effective communication skills, a manager can be highly successful.

Proof of the importance of effective communication emerges from interviews with numerous employees in various business settings. When the authors of this book asked employees what they most liked about their bosses, the most common responses referred to communication situations. The following are some examples: "I like my manager because he listens to me." "Anytime I have a problem I can go and talk to my boss." "Staff meetings are a joy because of the positive communication climate." "My employer is a fantastic communicator. I can listen to her speak for five minutes in the morning, and I'm on a 'high' all day long." "My manager not only tells me clearly what he wants me to do, he also instills in me a belief that I can do it."

The Plan of the Book

The topic of this book is communication as it applies to management within an organizational setting. We realize that not all readers are or will be managers; however, everyone in business, even those in staff positions, must perform various managing tasks, and to do this effectively requires communication skills. Furthermore, managers agree that their job is made easier when those they supervise understand the role that managers must occupy. A basic understanding of the principles and techniques of good communication will improve the process among all participants. This book is designed to help the reader develop three essential types of communication skills: *technical skills,* or the process and techniques of communication in the work environment; *human skills,* or how to communicate interpersonally on the job; and *conceptual skills,* or the ability to communicate effective decisions designed to accomplish organizational goals.

The techniques and principles of organizational communication are conveyed through our experience in the field. We have examined communication from advisory roles in actual business practice, from managerial roles in public and private settings, and from consulting roles that range from needs assessment to training and program evaluation. We feel this array of experience gives us a perspective of communication as an event within an organization that few other business communication authors have. Thus, we feel this textbook will be unique in meeting the needs of those who anticipate a future in the business world—especially those who believe they will one day be managing other people.

The book contains five major parts, each of which begins with a review of the forthcoming chapters and insights into the philosophy of the material. Each chapter starts with an introduction and concludes with a summary. Following the summary are a list of key words, a group of review questions, and a variety of exercises that can be worked alone after completion of the chapter or in groups in the classroom.

Part 1 examines the importance of communication in business. We describe the many ways businesspeople communicate, and then we introduce a theoretical yet practical model of communication that will be used throughout the book. The elements that go into communication are defined within the framework of the model.

Part 2 describes three potential hurdles that can limit the development of effective communication skills: people, language, and organizational structure. This section focuses on perception and its impact on the way people understand and communicate with other people. Words mean different things to different people. Thus, a knowledge of language and a comprehension of language barriers will help cultivate common understanding and avoid misunderstandings with other people. The climate, networks, and channels in which communication occurs in an organization either facilitate or deter understanding. As this section shows, perception and language both influence and are influenced by the organization.

With a model of the way in which communication works and an awareness of three key barriers that can minimize effective communication, the reader is ready to examine five communication skills that are vital in business. Part 3 contains chapters that cover these areas: nonverbal communication, listening, speaking, conducting group meetings, and writing. Chapter 6 examines the many nonverbal ways a manager understands and communicates in the business world. Chapter 7 looks at listening—one of the most used, but least discussed, communication skills. Chapter 8 describes a four-part process of presentational speaking that looks at ways to organize, construct, practice, and conduct a business presentation. Chapter 9 focuses on characteristics and functions of small groups and describes specific steps that can be taken before, during, and after a meeting that will make the process more productive and enjoyable. The final chapter in this section provides the specific ways that business writing skills can be improved and presents a simplified style for report writing—the inverted style. The editing process and guidelines for writing letters and memos are also covered.

Making use of the material in the first ten chapters, Part 4 illustrates that recognition of the importance of effective communication, comprehension of potential communication barriers, and development of particular communication skills are significant factors in establishing effective management. Then, explored in full are the various concepts of a manager as interviewer, leader, motivator, conflict resolver, and change agent.

While Part 5, consisting of only one chapter, is short, it is, however, one of the most important sections of the book. By interlacing every chapter and concept detailed in the preceding chapters, Chapter 16 presents an overview of the entire text. It concludes that a clear knowledge and understanding of the communication process and potential communication problems, coupled with practiced communication skills, will enable a person to become an effective communicator in business.

Two appendices follow the main text. Appendix A presents the outlines of eight sample speeches, each with a different pattern of organization, thus providing a variety of types of verbal supporting material. Appendix B contains material helpful in developing writing skills, including examples of typical writing assignments, checklists for letter construction, and exercises for polishing the editing process.

Suggestions to the Student

It is our hope and belief that mastery of the material presented in this text will lead to the development of effective communication skills. In order to enhance the success with which this task is accomplished, we offer some ideas on how to approach this book. Following these suggestions while you are reading this book will make your job easier and more efficient, and will improve your retention of the material.

First, *preview* the entire book by looking at its various parts: the title page, contents, body of the text, appendices, and index.

Second, when a chapter is assigned, quickly *skim* each page of it before you start reading. Start with the chapter title, and then look at the number of pages in the chapter. Next, go through the chapter and note the main headings and subheadings in order to form a mental outline of the chapter. Look at all the figures and illustrations; doing this will help improve your ability to relate these items to the text when you read it in detail. Read the chapter summary in its entirety, and note important words that are briefly described. Ask yourself how these words fit into the organization plan that you have been building in your mind. If you have some confusion about the chapter outline, skim quickly through the chapter again and reread the summary.

Third, *review* the list of key words and the review questions at the end of the chapter. Seeing the words before reading the text will reinforce the words and their definitions as you read the chapter. Treat the review questions in the same way. If a review question requires that a concept, definition, or idea be stated in a brief and clear manner, look for that information as you read. Avoid reading the *exercise* questions because some of these questions give answers to quizzes presented within the chapter. Reading the exercises before reading the text will detract from the learning that you will experience later.

Fourth, *read* the chapter in its entirety. As you read, remember to relate the concepts and ideas to the mental outline that you developed during the skimming stage. Note the important items that you will want to talk about in the classroom. After you have read the chapter, answer the discussion questions and complete the exercises.

We wish you enjoyable reading, and we hope this book will help you to understand communication theory and to apply communication skills effectively as an employee and as a manager.

Our Thanks

Writing a book is a tremendous undertaking. Although we are responsible for the contents and design of the material, we acknowledge that without the help of others the book would have been much more difficult to complete.

We would like to thank our families for the steady support, encouragement, and especially "alone time" that they gave us. To Jenni, Paul Michael, John Robert, and Ashley, our special love and thanks.

A number of individuals contributed to the writing of the text. The manuscript was read and edited by Tim Riggins, Sally Rawlings, Kim Feil, Connie Johnson, Alan Tompkins, David Radman, Don Nichols, Kirk Blankenship, John Grinaldi, and Sarah Sams. Their input and ideas were invaluable.

We would also like to thank the following reviewers for their time and significant comments: Timothy R. Cline (College of Notre Dame), John L. DiGaetani (Harvard University), Myron Glassman (Old Dominion University), Florence Grunkemeyer (Ball State University), Julie Indvik (California State University, Chico), Frank Jaster (Tulane University), Elizabeth Larsen (West Chester University), Nick Nykodym (University of Toledo), Lois Ann Poag-Rhodes (University of the District of Columbia), James Suchan (University of Alabama), and Max Waters (Brigham Young University).

The chapters were typed and retyped by Beth Robinson, Georgia Harper, Ruth Day, and Nell Golden. The final draft was completed by the pleasant and encouraging staff of the Word Processing Center in the

Edwin L. Cox School of Business at Southern Methodist University: Edith Benham, Madelon Gafford, Wanda Hanson, Bess Vick, and Mary Kesner. Their extra push at just the right times helped us make all our deadlines. And finally, the book would have never been completed without the steady encouragement and support of our editors at Kent, Dick Crews and Rolf Janke. To all of you, our warmest thanks.

Robert W. Rasberry

Laura Fletcher Lemoine

Contents

see

Effective Managerial Communication

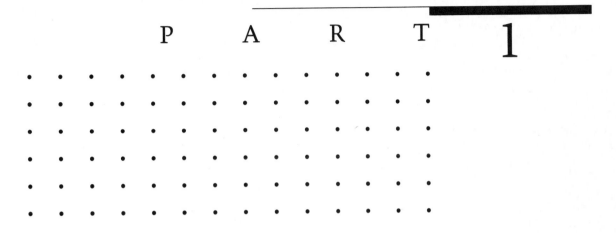

P A R T 1

Using Communication in Business

Communication is the lifeblood of business. Many employees, and most managers, spend a large part of their workday involved in some form of communication. Chapter 1 introduces the important role that communication plays in the business world. Interviewers and managers look for strong communication skills in the new employees that they hire. Communication also has played an important role in the development of management theories. Chapter 2 introduces a model of communication that will be used throughout the book. This model presents both theoretical and practical approaches to the way that managers can increase their effectiveness by improving the way that they communicate with others.

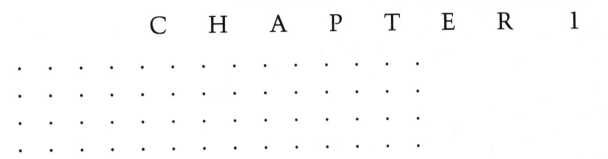

C H A P T E R 1

The Communication Role of Management

Introduction

The communication demands placed on today's manager continue to grow. A quick glance at a series of courses offered in a continuing education program for adults reveals that 75 to 80 percent of those courses deal with communication: They teach students how to read, write, communicate with computer operators, resolve conflict, upgrade interpersonal skills, learn group leadership skills, organize quality circles, learn computer languages, develop public speaking skills, coach and counsel, and train for television appearances.

In order to engage in each one of the activities listed above, a manager must master specific principles and skills. In addition, a manager must know what form of communication to use in a given situation. Since the goals of management are accomplished through the worker, it is the manager's job to communicate the goals of the organization to the worker in the form of coordinated tasks and to eliminate barriers or problems that might prevent goal attainment. Robert Katz specified three basic types of managerial skills that are important to accomplishing these ends: technical, human, and conceptual.[1]

Technical skill is the means by which the worker accomplishes a specialized activity and may include methods, processes, techniques, and procedures. For example, technical skills set apart the electrical engineer from the mechanical engineer.

Human skill is the ability to work interpersonally with other group members. Human skills include self-knowledge, communication, motivation, and understanding. A doctor's ability to relate to patients is often referred to as the doctor's bedside manner; it is recognized as an essential ingredient of effective medicine. Managers too must develop human skills.

Conceptual skill may be defined as the ability to identify and analyze problems and implement effective decisions. Conceptual skills include perceptual, creative, coordination, and integration skills that help lead the organization toward a common goal.

The ability to communicate requires a mastery of each of Katz's skill areas. Technical skill is important for managerial success, but human and conceptual skills are essential.

Research on Communication Skills

The last twenty years of research have shown repeatedly that communication skills are of primary importance to business graduates. In 1959 two simultaneous studies sponsored by the Ford and Carnegie foundations made a tremendous impact on business education and research. These studies declared that the educational objective of business education in colleges and universities should be to prepare students for personally fruitful and socially useful careers in business and related types of activity. They argued that business students must be able to assimilate and apply specific knowledge in areas of finance, accounting, and economics based on a broad educational background in nonprofessional areas. Complementary skill areas that were recommended for study included problem solving, organizing, maintaining interpersonal relationships, and communicating. Those influential in business school education felt that these skills should be acquired in appropriate disciplines in a standard sequence of study.

A decade later Clark surveyed the importance of communication skills in private and governmental organizations. She found that business school graduates lacked sufficient preparation in oral communication.[2] Ranked high in importance by business people were (1) effective interviewing, (2) giving oral orders and instruction, (3) telephoning, (4) listening, and (5) leading informal conferences. Formal speech making was ranked lower in importance.

While a variety of studies conducted in the 1960s through the 1980s have supported the need for more communication training, a study by Penrose found that "The more specific and traditional . . . topics of business writing and business speaking remained fairly consistently in the top half of the list of twelve abilities."[3] In the 1972 Summer Conference on Career Communication, representatives from a variety of professions responded to the question, "What speech communication competencies are required in your business, industry, agency, or profession?"[4] They agreed on the need for competencies such as the ability to:

- Facilitate small group discussions in an organization in order to accomplish an assigned task in a cooperative spirit;
- Interview an individual in order to determine whether he or she has the capabilities necessary to advance with the company;
- Solve problems and make decisions using a variety of strategies and evaluate the effectiveness of a decision;
- Use public relations in order to maximize credibility between the organization and the public sector;
- Apply good listening skills;
- Use persuasion effectively with clients or employees to inform, convince, or accomplish a course of action;
- Motivate employees to accomplish the objectives of the organization;
- Resolve conflict within the organization;
- Speak effectively;
- Utilize a team approach to problem solving and goal achievement by building productive relationships among members of the organization; and
- Ask questions that elicit the information that the organization needs in order to function well.

Understanding which communication skills are needed by managers requires an understanding of how communication occurs in an organization and which key theories of management have made those skills necessary.

Communication in the Organization

Most organizational charts are quite different from the one on page 6. Since this book focuses on communication in the organization, however, we want to emphasize that organizational structures are made up of people performing specific tasks. For instance, Henry, at the top of an

Figure 1.1 · The Organization

organization, might appear delighted with all he surveys, but it's difficult to tell what he is thinking. From the perspective of the other members of his organization, he has a challenging job. Henry is a new graduate in business, but because of his technical skills, he was promoted quickly to head of his section. Six months later he was made director of personnel in a medium-size organization of approximately 500 employees.

One of the first things that Henry did as director was institute a goal-setting program. He worked meticulously on the design and then called his supervisors together and explained his expectations. He asked employees to submit job goals by a given date.

All Henry's attempts to have employees participate in the goal-setting program failed. He had received no feedback by the date that employees' job goals were due. Old-timers rejected his goal-setting entirely. Henry observed reoccurring lateness in many employees; others avoided his presence. Sick leave increased. Despite his planning attempts the program failed.

Interviews with the organization's employees revealed a common belief: Henry couldn't communicate. As this book will demonstrate, communication problems can lead to a variety of low productivity results.

To help shed further light on this problem, let's define an organization. An organization consists of several people in interrelated roles who coordinate their work through communication. An organization, then, is two or more people who work together to accomplish a common goal.

One person can decide to manufacture clay pots alone. She can purchase the clay, pottery wheel, and glazes and then personally sit down and proceed to turn the pot on the pottery wheel, glaze the pot, bake it in a kiln, and put it on display. Just that one person does not comprise an organization. If, however, she relies on someone else, or on a number of people, in the glazing, finishing, or marketing of the wares, her need for organizational interdependence, coordination, and communication would be obvious.

Studies show that the average business professional spends 40 to 60 percent of his workday in one type of communication or another. Such findings represent only a sampling of the data that scholars produce to emphasize the importance of business communication. Chester Barnard, in his book *The Functions of the Executive,* emphasized that people, not boxes, make up a formal organization. Barnard stated that "The first executive function is to develop and maintain a system of communication."[5] In the next section we will review different theories of management and their effect on the organization—particularly on the communication process.

Key Theories of Management

Since the turn of the twentieth century much discussion and controversy have focused on the issue of how to manage an organization. "Management" style affects our productivity, employers, leaders, foes, or the success of a family: It molds society. While we recognize its importance, we find it difficult to define its essential parts. Its history is vague.

The earliest managers were probably the heads of families living in caves. As families became interdependent in gathering food and providing assistance or protection, they developed into small communities. Those communities then developed into villages, civilization evolved, and the skills necessary to lead and manage an increasingly more complex organization also developed. Strategies for waging war, collecting taxes, overcoming plague, or amassing resources to prevent starvation took skill and coordinating effort.

Some modern management practices can be traced to ancients such as Solomon, the famed biblical ruler. Written documents containing evidence of control practices are found in Sumerian documents written 5,000 years ago.[6] Priests managed wealth in the religious organizations, and their documents recorded inventories and listed debts.

Complex structures such as the Egyptian pyramids testify to the managerial abilities of the ancients. Cheops, pharoah of Egypt, oversaw the building of the great pyramid that covers thirteen acres and contains 2,300,000 stone blocks, each weighing an average of two and a half tons.[7] Babylonian writings include laws governing property, trade, business, and the family. Their content covers sales, loans, contracts, partnerships, agreements, and promissory notes. The laws of Moses provide one of the most common and earliest philosophies and plans for organization. The ancient records of China indicate an awareness of principles of organizing, planning, directing, and controlling. Principles of management were recognized by the Greeks, particularly specialization of labor. Xenophon, one of Socrates's disciples, described the principle of universality of management in a Socratic discourse.[8]

While principles of management existed in early civilizations, little was written describing them for succeeding generations. Because one civilization failed to learn from the successes and failures of others, continual relearning of principles was required to reach specific management goals.

Not until the end of the nineteenth century was management recognized as a science. Standards of production were subjectively established, with persuasion and coercion the prime motivators and decisions based on experience and intuition. Since that time several key theories of management have been developed. Each of the theories revolves around a particular way of viewing an organization, its people, and, ultimately, communication.

Classical Management Theory

Managers established standards of production subjectively until the end of the nineteenth century. At that time, Frederick W. Taylor began to espouse a philosophy of work. His approach, labeled *scientific management*, focused on the systematic observations of production and shop operations. His definition of management, widely accepted today, is the process of getting things done by others, either independently or in groups.[9]

Taylor's two essential elements of scientific management were *cooperation* and *scientific knowledge*. He employed many mechanisms to accomplish these ends, including time study, functional foremanship, standardization of tools and implements, differential rates, and modern costs systems.[10]

Making a contribution at the same time was Henri Fayol, a managing director of a French industrial and mining company. Fayol was the first to advocate management as a body of knowledge that could be taught. He defined its functions as (1) forecasting and planning, (2) organizing, (3) commanding, (4) controlling, and (5) coordinating. Of these five functions, *planning* was the most important.

Other writers also had an impact on the classical school and the development of scientific management. Frank and Lillian Gilbreth focused on the human side of management and used time and motion studies. They believed there was *one best way* to work, and they analyzed jobs to determine the most efficient movements for performing a particular task based on the standardization of tools and processes, the study of motion, the impact of fatigue, and the skill of the worker. They contributed to the current ideas of job simplification, work standards, and incentive wage plans.[11]

Inherent in all three of these contributions are the ideas that (1) there is a human side of management, (2) management and labor must cooperate, and (3) communication is an important tool. Fayol noted in his writings the difference between oral and written communications, the importance of explaining complicated problems, and the need to give instructions face-to-face. Taylor recognized the importance of providing recognition and rewards to keep the "human machine" running. And in his studies of time and motion, Frank Gilbreth emphasized studying the impact of fatigue and skill on performance. Lillian Gilbreth never wavered in her belief that the worker needed attention and recognition.

New methods of communicating with workers evolved. Rather than the directive or authoritarian approach, theorists espoused cooperation between worker and management. Greater emphasis was placed on new forms of communicating: on recognition, evaluation, explanation, and information gathering. As the classical approach to management became more widely accepted, however, a new theory, which emphasized the human factor, emerged.

Human Relations Theory

Mary Parker Follett made major contributions to shifting management focus from the scientific approach to the human relations approach. She criticized the "old fashioned theory of leadership" professed by psychologists of the day and proposed that leaders should possess a thorough knowledge of their industries and the ability to remember that different situations call for different leaders. She also felt that managers should be able to grasp complex situations, organize work groups, find creative solutions, direct management power, and develop leadership skills in employees.[12] Follett's writings in the area of coordination are filled with practical ideas and examples and remain relevant today. She set forth three principles of coordination in business:

1. *Using integration* and finding alternatives that all employees can live with, as opposed to compromise or domination by managers as a method of working out differences;
2. *Cross-functioning*, or the manager's ability to confer and solve problems at various levels of the organization instead of being limited to upward and downward communication; and
3. *Sharing collective responsibility*, or the ability to integrate knowledge and experience in order to produce effectively.

The human relations school was primarily interested in experimenting with working conditions and people. One of the most famous series of these experiments was conducted by Elton Mayo at the Hawthorne Plant of the Western Electric Company in the Chicago area. Mayo found that productivity seemed to be affected more by attitudes and feelings than by job conditions and environment. He observed that *informal systems* within the organization determined employee output. The importance of *social networks* surfaced as well as the role of formal horizontal communication and employee-oriented management.

The human relations movement encouraged recognition of employees' needs such as first-name status with all co-workers, employee parties, suggestion boxes, and benefit packages. Increasing employee involvement in this type of program often led to happy employees but, since these were superficial advances, led also to unproductive work forces.

X and Y Theory

The findings of proponents of the human relations school have been enhanced by the work of Douglas McGregor. In the 1950s he began to explore leadership and the way that employees respond to their superiors' actions and developed a theory of the X and Y style of management that is now considered a classic. He looked at earlier, classical schools of management thought and described, in his theory X, how those managers viewed employees. In theory Y, McGregor elaborated on his earlier theory X contentions and established a foundation for furthering the examination of human behavior in management.[13]

Theory X

1. People don't like work. They are inherently lazy, will avoid work if they can, and usually work for the basics of life: food, shelter, and clothing.
2. Because of their dislike for work, people must be forced to work or, at the very least, coerced. Consequently, they must be directed, controlled, and monitored closely.
3. People don't like responsibility unless forced to take it. By keeping employees anxious about their security, they can be induced to take responsibility and work toward organizational goals.

Theory Y

1. Work is as natural as play or rest.
2. Exercising external controls and threats is not the only way to direct people. Managers can help employees exercise self-direction and self-control and still accomplish organizational goals.
3. Commitment to objectives is directly related to the rewards associated with their achievement.
4. Under the proper work conditions the average person learns to accept and seek responsibility.
5. Most employees, not just a few, can exercise a high degree of imagination, ingenuity, and creativity in solving organizational problems.
6. Under the conditions of modern industrial life, the intellectual potentials of the average worker are only partially utilized.

Systems Theory

In March 1979 an accident at Three Mile Island (TMI) Nuclear Plant threatened the lives of thousands of area residents. Because information about that accident and the degree of danger that it caused was never made clear, the President's commission on the accident at Three Mile Island formed the Public's Right to Information Task Force consisting of fourteen communications researchers and information specialists. The task force examined media coverage, actions of officials, and the public's knowledge of TMI. They found that only four professionals handled public relations for the entire Metropolitan Edison (Met Ed) system, which included TMI. Deluged by calls during the crisis, the small, inexperienced Met Ed staff could not respond effectively to the public's need for information, and errors committed by top-level executives resulted in public distrust and loss of credibility.

Engineers staffed the public information program at TMI but had little contact with Met Ed specialists. Proud of their weekly news releases to the public, they felt they had kept the public well-informed about the facility. In analyzing these news releases, the Task Force concluded that they had been unsuccessful:

> Unfortunately, however, the weekly releases were written by engineers who had little comprehension of what the public could understand or what the media could use. They used technical jargon throughout the releases, including such terms as deenergized power distribution buses, automatic actuation, and redundant valves. Most science writers, let alone general assignment reporters, would have trouble with such terminology. The releases also failed to describe what the events reported to the NRC meant for the plant or area residents and, in some instances, appeared to purposely avoid such description. They were positive and upbeat, emphasizing startups, not shutdowns. While they did list problems at the plant, they described them as minor and part of the effort to get commercial operation under way. Almost every release described such events as not affecting "the health and safety of the public."
>
> Cumulatively, however, the weekly press releases revealed a serious pattern of sloppy operational discipline and consistent equipment problems. But these harbingers were largely ignored by local reporters, who frequently discarded the releases, condensed them for filler stories, or printed them verbatim.[14]

The Three Mile Island Nuclear Plant crisis is a vivid example of the importance of how an organization interacts with the public and its environment. An organization is affected by many interrelated influences: environment, customers, competitors, labor organizations, government, suppliers of available resources, and employee interaction. Each interrelates with others and contributes to the overall purpose of the organization. The systems theory of management emphasizes these interrelationships and views the organization as a set of subsystems.

Organizational systems are either *open* or *closed.* An open system interacts with its environment, while a closed system functions without environmental interaction. Few systems have no interaction with the environment. A computer, for example, can perform a series of very complex functions but requires interaction with the programmer before it can perform those functions. The organizational system is influenced by several factors: input, output, and feedback (see Figure 1.2).

Input

Input can be money, raw materials, information, data from opinion polls, or economic conditions. The primary functions of input are to determine the characteristics of the environment, identify trouble spots that might affect organizational output, reflect the organization as others see it, provide information for effective decision making, and improve output. Input is then analyzed and evaluated to determine if current organizational procedures should be altered.

Transformation

The organization consists of a complex network of subsystems that transforms inputs into outputs, and the organizational design plays an integral part in the logic of the network that results in tangible outputs. Compared to the smaller United States Senate, the House of Representatives' sheer size vastly increases the complexity of its communication channels. The number of House contacts necessary to gain support on an issue affects both the form of a representative's message and its content.

Output

Organizational output occurs in the form of products, public relations, information, and public service. While the primary forms of output are products and face-to-face communication, other types of output imple-

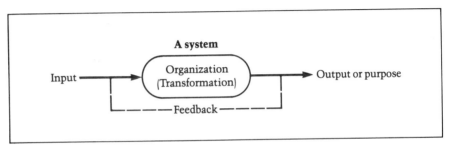

Figure 1.2

ment telephone messages, public appearances, letters, and the mass media.

Feedback

The final element of the systems model is feedback. Once decisions are made and the organization transforms input into output, consumers react to the finished product. Their reactions are feedback for the organization, and that feedback occurs in several forms: Product consumption may increase or decrease; survey results may uncover product weaknesses or strengths; complaints, lawsuits, or letters of support may become organizational barometers of success. Feedback allows the organization to evaluate its output.

The systems theory emphasizes interrelationships among workers and managers, the environment and technology, input and output, consumers and competitors. Because it functions in a dynamic environment, an effective organization seeks to maintain a balance between input and output. Few organizational systems can operate without interacting with the environment. Systems theory does not attempt to evaluate the interrelationships between environment, specific organizational structure, and job functions.

Organizational Structure

The structure of an organization helps it meet its goals in an effective and productive manner. Early classical theory teaches that the *organizational structure* includes line and staff positions (see Figure 1.3). The line organization is easily identified on an organization chart. *Line positions* carry

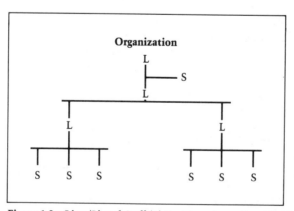

Figure 1.3 · **Line (L) and Staff (S) Positions in an Organization**

authority and responsibility over personnel and serve the direct flow of formal organizational communications. *Staff positions* assist or advise the line organization. Staff members rarely have authority or responsibility over other members of the organization. They can, however, achieve some power due to their positions in the organization. For example, an assistant to an organizational head might assume some of the power of the head, which happened when the organizational structure approach was taken from the business world and applied to the political staff of President Richard Nixon. White House Chief of Staff H. R. Haldeman, acting to control access to the president, actually assumed presidential power and authority.

The fewer the number of employees working for a manager, the greater the control he or she can have over them. The number of subordinates assigned to a manager affects the shape of the organization (see Figure 1.4). If *span of control* is limited to two or three employees, the organization will be tall. If, however, the manager has a span of control of five to fifteen subordinates, the organization will be flat.

The shape of the organization influences personal dynamics, especially communication, within the organization. A tall organization will have more levels through which communication must pass. These multiple levels increase the possibility of distortion but, nevertheless, result in the manager's exerting greater control over employees. The flat organization, in contrast, reduces the number of levels through which communication must flow. It also limits the manager's opportunities to have one-to-one contact with employees and increases the amount of communication that the manager must handle.

Span of control within an organization also determines whether centralized or decentralized decision making will be used. With a narrow span of control, decisions can be made quickly because fewer people are involved. Participative decision making, however, can lead to higher morale and is facilitated by a flat, decentralized organization. In the example that opened this chapter, Henry made decisions without involving the rest of the work force; the result was apathy and low morale.

Another aspect of management theory is the *division of labor*, the object of which is to produce greater quantity and better quality output. Labor can be divided according to either the nature of the work and its corresponding responsibility (*functional* division of labor) or the authority of the person involved (*scalar*). Often an organization combines both forms. For example, scalar division related to the allocation of authority in an organization would include the board of directors, president, vice-president, directors, and department heads. Functional divisions might include engineering staff, clerical staff, janitorial staff, and administrative personnel.

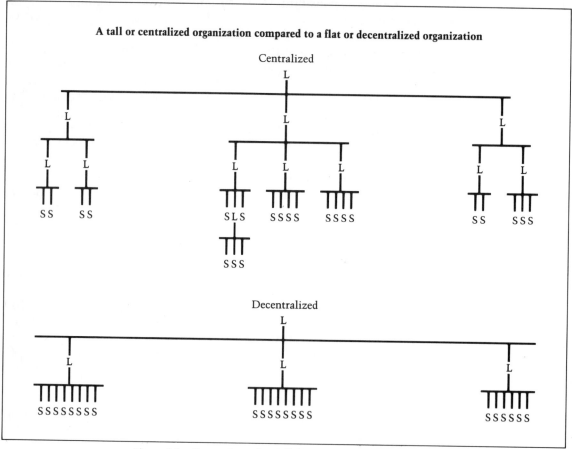

Figure 1.4 · **Comparison of a Tall Organization with a Flat Organization**

Theory Z

Since the late 1970s, management theorists have developed a new theory that enhances all the others and especially affects the human side of management. Theory Z is the name associated with the best of the Japanese management styles that are viable in the United States. It assumes that people who engage in socioeconomic activity are tied together by a variety of bonds and that a culture is established where individuals cooperate to reach common goals.

As the level of productivity in the United States falls and that of Japan increases, theorists examine and compare the organizational and management concepts of both countries. Most would agree that in the United

States, managers have been less than totally successful, while Japanese managers have made great headway. Although it will be years before a final assessment can be made of how well theory Z can be applied to U.S. organizations, management theorists have discovered eight areas in which the Japanese have been successful:[15]

1. *Organizational direction.* Organizations in the United States have long had clearly defined goals and objectives, but in their Japanese counterparts, the philosophy and values of the organization are clearly stated, understood, and shared by all employees. This creates commitment and cohesion. Top management shares information about all parts of the organization with all employees so that all have a "big picture" of the direction that they and the company are taking.

2. *Rational process.* Managers take a systematic and objective approach that emphasizes planning and problem solving. They make decisions based on plenty of information, accountability of employees, and careful monitoring and evaluating of work progress.

3. *Adaptability and innovativeness.* The organization anticipates change and is sensitive to internal and environmental needs and trends. Instead of the short-range perspective that many United States companies tend to have, the Japanese perspective is both short- and long-range. Management seeks to be tolerant of unknown possibilities, flexible in examining them, versatile in its approaches to problem solving, and always open to new ideas.

4. *Resource allocation.* Instead of placing the greatest emphasis on financial results, the Japanese focus on human resource management. The Japanese organizations seek generalists, not specialists, and make use of each employee's full range of expertise and capabilities. When new skills are needed, training is provided. The reward system is based on achievement and competence.

5. *Distribution of authority.* Participation and input into decision making are not based on position or status but on competence and knowledge of information that can be shared. This means that the lowest-level employee is invited to the highest-level meetings if he or she has information that can be used by others. The Japanese system of supervision operates on delegating not only assignments but authority and responsibility as well.

6. *Organizational climate.* The Japanese atmosphere is conducive to productiveness because management communicates a sense of respect for employees and interest in their well being. This, in turn, generates in employees a trust of management. Status barriers like dress and office locations are not used, and the superior/subordinate relationships are based on the informal power of mutual respect.

7. *Structure.* The Japanese organizational chart is not the chart well known in the United States. It is a structure that is integrated, flexible, and either temporary or permanent. It often incorporates small groups that have overlapping membership for greater information sharing.

8. *Communication.* Management listens to employees, and information successfully flows upward, downward, and horizontally. Communication is open, direct, and accurate.

Summary

Each business person needs to master the ability to communicate. Even the definition of an organization requires that goals be accomplished by a cooperative effort through the use of communication. The *type* of communication used may vary according to the particular managerial theory used within a given context, but communication itself will be the foundation for practicing any and all theories.

The key management theories are classical management theory, human relations theory, theory X and theory Y, systems theory, and theory Z. Many variables, from context to culture, may determine which theory will be most effective in practice. The most important variable is communication style, and particular styles may be more successful than others within the practice of a given management theory.

Regardless of which theory governs a given business practice, decision making within that practice includes effective communication skills. These skills will be effective only if they suit the situation at hand. To achieve maximum effectiveness, a manager must first consider (1) the goal, (2) the receivers (superior, subordinate, or peer), (3) the form (external-operational, internal-operational, or personal), (4) the structure (formal or informal), (5) the type (one to one, one to few, electronic, written, or oral), (6) the situation (environment, span of control, or structure), and (7) the feedback.

As the environment becomes more dynamic and unpredictable, the structure of the organization should become more flexible. In turn, integrating mechanisms (such as coordination and communication) should increase. Chester Barnard argued in 1938 that "In an exhaustive theory of organization, communication would occupy a central place, because the structure, extensiveness, and scope of the organization are almost entirely determined by communication techniques."[16]

During the last century, communication techniques have increased dramatically. The specific techniques that managers should use, and the manner in which they should use them, are the focus of this text.

Key Words

organization	human relations	organizational
communication	theory	structure
classical management	X and Y theories	theory Z
theory	systems theory	

Discussion Questions

1. What are the key theories of management, and how do they view communication?
2. Using one of these key theories, describe an organization to which you belong.
3. How can communication knowledge and skill help you be a more effective organizational person?
4. Explain the concept of span of control. How does it apply to communication in the organization?
5. What is the difference between the human relations approach and the classical approach to management? How does communication differ in each approach?
6. How does the Japanese style of management differ from the other key management styles?

Exercises

1. As you read the section of this chapter that describes the communication skills that employers look for when they hire individuals, you undoubtedly thought about your skills and qualifications. In the space provided below make a quick inventory of your communication skills. Which skills do you feel are adequate at the present time to help you qualify for the business world? Which do you need to improve?

My communication skills that are sufficient:

My communication skills that need improving:

After you identify the skills that need improvement, look through the contents of this book. Make special note of the chapters that cover these areas. Write a contract with yourself that highlights some things that you can do during the course of this semester or year, with the exception of reading the chapter or the book, that will help you improve those skills. If you have trouble deciding which methods you should use outside of your classroom, consult with your instructor about possibilities.

Things I will do to improve my skills:

2. In reading through the Key Theories of Management section of this chapter you probably remembered managers or supervisors whom you have known or observed who had characteristics described in the theories. Make a list of these characteristics so that you can discuss them in class.

3. Have you heard or read about any United States companies that are using the theory Z approach to management? If you have, write a simple description so that you can share that company's experience with your classmates. If you have not, spend some time in your local library and research some articles on theory Z and the Japanese style of management. The *Periodical Index* would be a good place to start.

References

1. Robert L. Katz, "Skills of an Effective Administrator," *Harvard Business Review* (Jan./Feb. 1955), pp. 33–42.

2. Kathryn Bullington Clark, "Oral Business Communication Needs as a Basis for Improving College Courses," Ph.D. dissertation, University of Michigan, 1968.

3. John M. Penrose, "Survey of the Perceived Importance of Business Communication and Other Business-Related Abilities," *Journal of Business Communication*, 13:2 (Winter 1976), p. 23.

4. Diane Lockwood and Sara Boatman, "Marketability: Who Needs Us and What Can We Do for Them?," unpublished paper presented at Central States Speech Association Convention, Kansas City, 1975, pp. 2–7.

5. Chester Barnard, *The Functions of the Executive* (Cambridge: Harvard University, 1938), p. 226.

6. V. G. Childe, *Man Makes Himself* (New York: New American Library, 1951), p. 143.

7. Claude S. George, Jr., *The History of Management Thought* (Englewood Cliffs, N.J.: Prentice Hall, 1960), p. 4.

8. *Ibid.*, p. 15.

9. *Ibid.*, p. 138.

10. *Ibid.*, pp. 89–90.

11. Frank B. Gilbreth, "Science in Management for the One Best Way to Do Work," in Harwood F. Merrill, ed., *Classics in Management* (New York: American Management Association, 1960), pp. 245–91.

12. M. P. Follett, *Freedom and Co-ordination* (London: Management Publications Trust, Ltd., 1949), pp. 61–76.

13. Douglas McGregor, *The Human Side of Enterprise* (New York: McGraw-Hill, 1960).

14. Sharon M. Friedman, "Blueprint for Breakdown: Three Mile Island and the Media Before the Accident," *Journal of Communication*, 31:2 (Spring 1981), p. 118. Reprinted by permission.

15. Evan Peelle, "Motivating People for Better On-the-Job Performance," (New York: Dun & Bradstreet, 1982), pp. 31–35.

16. Barnard, loc. cit., p. 91.

Theories, Models, and Elements of Communication

Introduction

It is Tuesday, 8:00 A.M., and Sue has a project due for her company's president Friday morning. She realizes that John has some information that she must have to complete the job and finds him at the coffee pot. She asks, "John, will you give me the information on the Smither's budget by Thursday?"

John responds, "Sorry, Sue, I can't get that to you by Thursday. Would Monday be all right?"

The verbal messages in this scenario are brief, but the information relayed is important to the people involved. Sue needs help from John. Is his response a refusal? a delaying tactic? an indication of a bigger problem? What Sue and John communicate and how they communicate it influences their behavior and, in turn, the resolution of their problem.

Our ability to develop and use effective communication skills is demonstrated when we visit with colleagues, purchase equipment, or operate a computer terminal. In the organization, communication skills have special importance. The complexity and dynamics of even a small organization involve the recording, storage, dissemination, and evaluation of ideas, information, directions, policies, and rules to accomplish specific goals. To this mix must be added human capabilities and experiences, modern business machines, and the explosion of current knowledge. Effective communication must exist if complex organizations are to be productive.

This chapter defines communication, describes its important elements, and presents a model that is developed in succeeding chapters.

The Elements of Communication

Communication can be defined as sorting, selecting, forming, and transmitting symbols between people to create meaning; it can best be understood by examining its elements. Two common elements are necessary in every communication situation: a source and a receiver. In the opening scenario of this chapter, as John listens to Sue, he sees and hears her message. Likewise, as Sue is talking, she sees and hears John's reactions. In order to understand the communication process better, we can examine this situation and identify its elements:

> It is Tuesday, 8:00 A.M., and Sue finds John at the coffee pot. She wants to convince John to give her information and sends the message, "John, will you give me the information on the Smither's budget by Thursday?"

Source. Sue is the source since she initiated a message, a complex process that includes several steps: (1) A stimulus creates a thought and a desire to communicate; (2) these thoughts are encoded into a message; and (3) they are transmitted through a channel to John.

Encoding. Sue's central nervous system ordered her to select symbols to form the sounds and actions that convey her message.

The message. The message includes everything that conveys meaning to the listener. With Sue, this includes words, facial expression, vocal expression, and appearance. Contrast her message by considering the following possibilities:

1. With hands on hips, in a stern tone and with a serious expression, Sue demands, "John, will you give me the information on the Smither's budget by Thursday?"

2. Holding papers in disarray and dropping some, Sue stoops to pick them up, appears embarrassed, and uses a hesitant, questioning tone: "John, will you give me the information on the Smither's budget by Thursday?"

In these two situations, Sue vocalizes her message differently and thereby conveys different meanings to her listener.

Transmission. Sue's message is sent into the environment and is made available to John. Her brain orders her muscles to react, and they produce sounds, gestures, and movement.

Channel. The channel is the means chosen to convey the message. Sue could have chosen a variety of modes of transmitting her message, such as a letter or telephone call, but she selected face-to-face interaction.

Receiver. John's response depends on a number of factors: the fidelity or acuteness of his senses, his competing needs, the environment, his understanding of the message, and his knowledge of Sue. Let's continue our scenario:

> John is pretty busy. Besides, Sue has had a recent promotion for which John was also considered, and she has a number of new responsibilities and tasks. To John, she appears nervous, disorganized, and less relaxed and informal than she used to be. John decides that Thursday is too soon to give her the information she wants and asks for a later date. He responds, "Sorry Sue, I can't get that to you by Thursday. Would Monday be all right?"

John's response to Sue's message provided feedback. He decoded and interpreted Sue's message and then encoded his response, which acted as feedback for Sue.

Decoding. To decode a message, the receiver must determine the meaning of the symbols used by the sender. When John said, "I can't get that to you by Thursday," did he mean (1) it was physically impossible, (2) he had other priorities, or (3) he didn't want to?

Interpreting. When John interpreted Sue's message, he put it through his mental filter. At that point his knowledge, attitudes, experience, culture, and the social system interacted to help him give meaning to the message. John interpreted Sue's message on the basis of his previous experiences with Sue. For instance, if Sue consistently asked for work before she needed it, his action might be to purposely delay this job. If she is usually late with projects, he may suggest alternatives or decide not to get involved. After interpreting her message, John decided to give Sue the information but to ask for a few extra days to prepare it. When we filter a message, applying our knowledge and experience, we give a thinking response. John reacted to Sue's request only after he considered his knowledge of Sue and his own personal needs.

Feedback. Feedback is the response of the receiver that can be perceived by the sender as a new stimulus. John's response to Sue gave her feedback that might require her to alter her plans for preparing the report unless she can manage to find the information sooner. John's vocal tone, expression, and appearance during their encounter enhanced the feedback concerning her message.

Utilizing feedback properly has become the subject of many treatises on improving message accuracy. Berlo discusses its usefulness in his text, *The Process of Communication*, and gives the following examples:

> Advertisers control the reasons given to the public for buying this or that product. But the consumer affects the advertiser—through feedback. If the public buys more (positive feedback), the advertiser keeps his messages. If the public quits buying the product (negative feedback), the advertiser then changes his messages—or the stockholders get a new advertising manager.[1]

As the exchange process continues, numerous opportunities arise for miscommunication. The speaker's purpose may not be clear, his or her attitude may be condescending, the words selected may be too technical, background noise may interfere with the listener's ability to hear, or divergent backgrounds and interests may cause misinterpretation of the speaker's message by the listener. These aspects of communication may be mapped and objectively analyzed, and it is in the interests of more effective management to do so. In the words of Wendell Johnson:

> The ability to respond to and with symbols may be the single most important attribute of great administrators. . . . Mr. A talking to Mr. B is a deceptively simple affair, and we take it for granted to a fantastic and tragic degree. . . . We have yet to learn how to use the wonders of speaking and listening.[2]

Characteristics of Communication

Several fundamental characteristics are inherent to communication: Communication is dynamic, irreversible, proactive, interactive, and contextual.[3] Because of the nature of these characteristics, they are difficult to depict in model form. Nevertheless, our model must accommodate them.

Communication is dynamic. When you speak to another person, you engage in an activity that involves ongoing behavioral changes. From the moment you utter the first word of a sentence, this continuous series of changes begins and may include varying facial expressions, body movement, gestures, or eye movement. More than likely, you will join together a series of words to form one or more sentences. Once you finish speaking, your listener begins to respond using a series of gestures, movements, or spoken words. Responses to a message may occur weeks, months, or even years after the sender originates the message. Communication is dynamic as it evolves through an ongoing process.

Communication is irreversible. Have you ever said something you wished you could take back? Communication, once it begins, cannot be reversed. You may amplify, modify, apologize, or attempt to explain something, but you cannot take it back; you can only go forward (see Figure 2.1 below).

Communication is proactive. Communication involves the total person. How we select words or react to another's words will be affected by our uniqueness. All that we have learned and experienced helps us select the words, movements, and vocal patterns that communicate our messages. These factors become part of how we analyze the message and how it affects our behavior.

Communication is interactive. Communication also involves two or more parties. When two people communicate, they symbolically link their behavior, and this interaction conveys meaning from one person to another.

"I'LL PROBABLY KICK MYSELF LATER FOR SAYING THIS, BUT...."

Figure 2.1 · Communication Is Irreversible

Source: Jim Borgman, *Cincinnati Enquirer*, King Features Syndicate, 1983. Reprinted by permission.

Communication is contextual. Communication does not occur in a void. Taking notes at a high-level meeting or talking to a client over the telephone are behaviors that are affected by the environment. A person taking notes may be surrounded by eager and attentive employees or be distracted by interruptions or arguments. Relaxed or harried, the climate alters people's reactions to message importance.

A Managerial Communication Model

Given the above elements and characteristics of communication, we can now develop a model that fits interpersonal and organizational settings (see Figure 2.2). One disadvantage of a model is that it depicts a process as if it were static. During communication, everything is in constant mo-

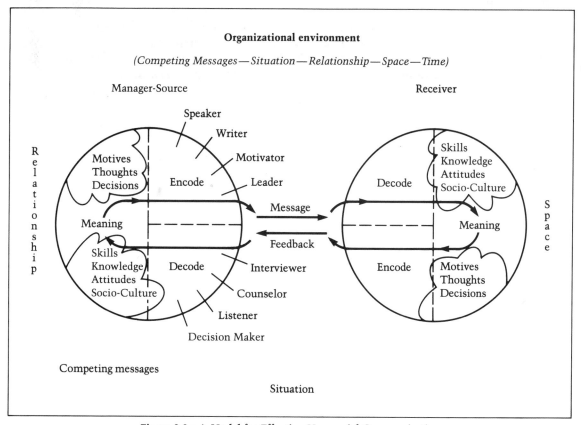

Figure 2.2 • A Model for Effective Managerial Communication

tion—the events in the environment, relationships, time, and the situation. We even receive and decode messages at the same time we are encoding and sending other messages. Imagine a situation where a worker is explaining a problem to a supervisor only to catch nonverbal signs of inattention and lack of interest. The boss proceeds to shuffle papers, look up a telephone number, and check the time while the worker is talking. A very clear message is sent: "I'm too busy to bother with this right now!" The sender and receiver are communicating simultaneously.

If it were possible to do so within a textbook, everything in this model would appear in constant motion: the arrows would move to indicate the constant selection, decoding, and interpreting of stimuli from the environment; stimuli would constantly change and interrupt or compete with the message; even the shape of the environment, source, and receiver would change to demonstrate growth and development. Time, space, and the receiver form a communication set and can affect interaction in a variety of ways, as will be demonstrated in the following chapters of this book.

While the sender and receiver are represented in our model by two circles, remember that within each of them many factors interact to affect the accuracy of the message: communication skills, knowledge, attitudes, and position within the sociocultural system.[4]

Factors That Affect the Accuracy of the Message

Communicators have varying skills as writers, speakers, readers, listeners, thinkers, and problem solvers. These skills affect their abilities to analyze motives, mediate conflict, act as change agents, and be leaders or decision makers because they affect their ability to encode the message.

The knowledge that communicators have about subject matter affects the content of the message. If a person does not understand what he or she is talking about, the message may be distorted before it reaches the listener. Conversely, when the communicator is well-informed, he or she must be careful to avoid using highly technical language that might not be understood by the receiver.

Attitudes—or the way that a person tends to respond to situations, ideas, values, objects or people—may prevent us from speaking to someone we feel hostile toward and again may distort our message.[5] In an organization, people form attitudes toward their jobs, bosses, and co-workers and react positively or negatively toward them. A boss who repeatedly encounters problems with an employee may avoid the employee. The reaction may become so intense that the employee's office is physically "out of sight."

Finally, sociocultural backgrounds also affect the communicators in the model. A person's role, group associations, functions, and prestige determine many aspects of both sending and receiving the message, which is why retailers usually survey potential social and cultural needs of an area before marketing a product.

These factors act on the source and receiver to increase or decrease the accuracy of the message. Without communication skills, knowledge about the subject matter, consideration of the receiver's attitude, or understanding of the receiver's place in the sociocultural system, the source is at an immediate disadvantage and will more than likely initiate message distortion during the encoding stage of the communication process.

Factors within the source and receiver affect the message intrapersonally—how it is interpreted in our heads—and the relationship between the source and receiver affects the message interpersonally. Wilbur Schramm stressed that the essence of communication is getting the sender and receiver "in tune" for a message.[6] The accumulated experience of the sender is present during each interaction. Unless there is an overlap between the experiences of the sender with those of the receiver (that is, they speak the same language), communication is limited, if not almost impossible. Neither party can send or receive an understandable message. Conversely, the more experiences they hold in common, the greater their ability to communicate the fully intended meaning of the message.

Finally, the intrapersonal and interpersonal factors interact to affect how the source and receiver perceive the message. Both parties will select the parts of the message that reinforce their experiences and relationship.

The Organizational Environment

The model depicts a sender and receiver in an organizational environment in which there are many competing sources and receivers. Messages continually are sent to us, whether we are convening in meetings, receiving memoranda, letters, and reports, hearing directives, or participating in interviews. Our physical space, the timing of the message, the particular situation, and the surrounding activity or noise all affect the way we perceive, decode, and interpret the intended message.

The Process

Although the communication process is continual, the model depicts the process beginning at the point when something in the environment gains our attention and acts as a stimulus. The nervous system transmits the stimuli to the brain, which decodes the message and assigns meaning to it based on personal experiences. We then encode our thoughts into words and actions, so that the message again becomes part of the environment.

A receiver hears, sees, tastes, smells, or touches parts of our message. Depending on the fidelity of the receiver's senses and predispositions (alertness, attention, interest), he or she will transmit the message through sensory receptors to the brain. The receiver decodes and interprets the message and then sends a response in the form of feedback.

Feedback informs the sender how the message is being interpreted— for example, a frown on the forehead of the listener, a letter to the editor, or the applause of an audience. We even get feedback to our own messages. We can correct misspellings, modify style, and correct typing errors. A person playing a video game receives immediate feedback in the form of a visual message whenever he or she makes an error in timing or judgment: The video "player" may disappear, explode, or in some way lose ground.

At each stage in this communication process some distortion takes place. The receiver may have a hearing or sight impairment; perhaps someone or something blocks vision so that the receiver cannot see the sender's facial expressions. The receiver may minimize or disregard the sender's actions or use technical words that the sender does not understand during the feedback stage. Given the seven stages at which communication can be distorted by either the sender or receiver, it is no wonder that communication is difficult: Distortion can occur when the participant (1) selects stimuli from the environment, (2) experiences sensory receptors and nervous system fidelity or infidelity, (3) decodes the message, (4) assigns meaning, (5) encodes the response, (6) transmits the message, or (7) is interfered with by factors in the environment.

Despite these distortions, at least four conditions can be identified as conducive to successful communication:[7]

1. The message must be easily perceived or made "available." We must be loud enough, clear enough, visible enough, and so forth. This means that we must time, place, and equip our messages with cues that will appeal to the listener.

2. We must be sure that we are speaking a "language" that the other person understands. Our message must be consistent with the other person's experiences. We will reject their message if we don't understand the words or if they do not fit in with our knowledge, experience, needs, or interests.

3. People act because of needs, and their actions are directed toward goals that satisfy those needs. A person's message is more likely to be accepted and understood if it considers the other person's needs.

4. Response to communication is often made within groups. The response must be approved by the group and will succeed if it fits accepted behaviors.

Communicating effectively as a manager takes more than making a good impression and knowing the mechanics of the job. It requires understanding multiple forces: The manager's message must be easily perceived and consistent with the receiver's experiences, needs, drives, attitudes, and organizational or group relationships.

Summary

Communication is the sorting, selecting, forming, and transmitting of symbols to create meaning in another person's mind. Communication skills are especially important in an organization because people must communicate to coordinate work efforts.

Communication is dynamic or ongoing. It is irreversible; you cannot take it back, even though you can modify or amplify it. Communication is proactive and involves the total person. It links two or more people in some form of interaction that conveys meaning and occurs in a context involving time, place, and space.

Common elements can be identified in any communication situation. The source or sender is stimulated by some need, motive, or drive to send a message to a receiver. The source must encode the message by sorting and selecting symbols through a channel such as a face-to-face encounter, written message, or telephone call. The receiver decodes the meaning of the symbols used by the sender and interprets the message. Knowledge, attitudes, experience, and sociocultural background act as a filter in giving meaning to the message. Finally, the receiver responds to the message and thereby provides feedback to the sender.

Key Words

source	decode	feedback
message	transmission	interpersonal
receiver	channel	sociocultural system
encode	noise	

Review Questions

1. Describe how a prominent politician uses television as a communication channel. What does he or she understand (or fail to understand) about the nature of communication?
2. What characteristics of the receiver/decoder should the sender consider? Why?

3. Give an example of interpersonal communication in the business environment.

4. Describe a recent situation in which you had difficulty communicating with another person. At which stage of the communication process did a breakdown occur? Why?

5. Why is communication at the supervisory level complex? Give an example, and design a model to amplify your discussion.

Exercises

1. Record your communication activities for one day by tabulating in fifteen minute intervals the number of times you speak, listen, read, or write. When you have completed your record, calculate the percentage of time you spent in each communication activity.

2. Select a word that has special meaning for you, such as a technical term, the name of a pet or friend, or a word from a song. Ask several people what the word means to them. You might ask them to describe their feelings about the word. How did their responses differ?

3. Analyze a communication situation in which you participated. Identify the elements. What did you know about the receiver that affected your message? What did the receiver know about you that affected his or her response to your message? How would you alter your message for another receiver?

4. Observe a communication situation and analyze the behaviors of the source and receiver. How did vocal patterns, body movement, gestures, facial expression, and context affect the message?

5. Using ten lines one inch in length, make two different drawings. Without showing the first drawing and giving only oral instructions, ask a friend to draw it. Do not allow questions. Repeat this exercise with the second drawing but allow questions. Which drawing was more accurate? Why? How does this exercise relate to the manager's role in the organization?

References

1. David K. Berlo, *The Process of Communication* (New York: Holt, Rinehart & Winston, 1960), pp. 113–14.

2. Wendell Johnson, "The Fateful Process of Mr. A. Talking to Mr. B.," *Harvard Business Review*, 31 (Jan./Feb. 1953), pp. 49–56.

3. C. David Mortenson, *Communication: The Study of Human Interaction* (New York: McGraw-Hill, 1972), pp. 13–21.

4. Berlo, *The Process of Communication*, pp. 113–14.

5. Winston L. Brembeck and William S. Howell, *Persuasion: A Means of Social Influence*, 2nd ed. (Englewood Cliffs, N.J.: Prentice-Hall, 1976), p. 84.

6. Wilbur Schramm, "The Nature of Communication Between Humans," *The Process and Effects of Mass Communication* (Urbana, IL: University of Illinois Press, 1972), pp. 7–53.

7. *Ibid.*

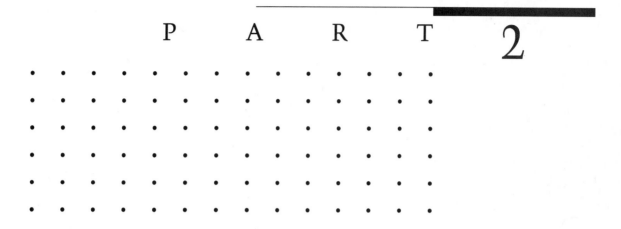

P A R T 2

Overcoming the Hurdles to Effective Communication

Three major elements can limit the development of effective managerial communication skills: people, language, and organizational structure. These elements are examined in the next three chapters. Chapter 3 focuses on *perception*, or the filter through which we take in stimuli and understand the world. The way that we perceive people is the starting point for how we communicate with others.

Language is the theme of Chapter 4. Humans are unique because they can use symbols, or words that stand in reference for items and events within society. Symbols, however, can become a barrier to effective communication among people who do not share a common understanding.

Chapter 5 examines the final potential barrier: *organizational structure.* The climate, networks, and channels in which communication occurs in an organization help either to facilitate or to deter meaning and understanding. Perception and language both influence, and are influenced by, the organization.

C H A P T E R 3

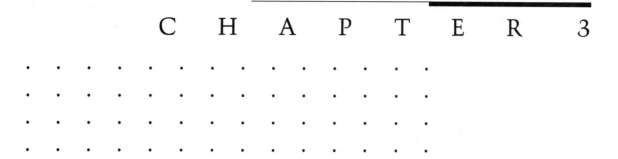

Perceptual Behavior:
The First Hurdle

Introduction

Before a recent football season started at Southern Methodist University, a story circulated about a walk-on hopeful fresh out of a local Dallas high school. The young man was making his first visit to the athletic department's impressive weight room and was eager to make a good impression on his potential coaches. He was appalled when he glanced about and saw what he later called "huge dudes lifting houses, trucks, and trees" and at the same time heard them talking nonchalantly about their physical prowess. The young man feared that he would be killed during the first day of scrimmage. Bravely he sauntered over to one of the bulging-bicepped bragging behemoths and asked, "Are you guys upperclassmen at SMU, or are you walk-ons like me?" The giant replied that he was neither: "I play for the Oilers, that fellow is with the Rams, and those two are with the Dolphins." The young man's sigh was heard by everyone in the room, including the pros using the facilities to get in shape before reporting to their pro football camps.

Perception Defined

Perhaps you have never felt as that young man did, that you were a midget in the land of giants. All of us, however, have had similar problems. We have had people evaluate, judge, and mistakenly think things about us and consequently communicate to us in error. Likewise, we have been guilty of the same type of behavior. Perception is the process of gaining insight and knowledge about the world through any of our senses, especially through seeing and hearing.

As shown by the model presented in Chapter 2, communication is the process of sharing ideas, information, and knowledge. When one person wishes to share an idea with another, he or she formulates ideas into words or symbols that the other person can attach meaning to and understand. In this formulation process we use references that are constructed from past events, experiences, expectations, and current motivational states. When a receiver sees or hears the message, he or she relies on a particular frame of reference for decoding and understanding. The more similar the frames of reference are between people, the more easily they can communicate.

Misunderstanding often occurs in communication. Sometimes the perception process is responsible for the misunderstanding, and for that reason, understanding perceptual behavior can be an important hurdle to effective communication. This chapter describes ways that perceptual problems can be resolved. It starts by examining how people perceive things, and then moves on to look at the problems involved in how people perceive other people. Since human behavior is at the heart of how people get along with others, the chapter looks at how attitudes and values influence the stages of development that people pass through. Finally, the chapter focuses on methods that can be used to correct perceptually based problems. These methods start with a self-examination and move to disclosure of information to others.

Problems in Perception

We gather information about the world by looking at and observing things around us. All too often characteristics or facts about objects are inferred based on mere visual or tactile exploration. Although we take information from things that we can see, we also infer and use information based on what we can't see but assume to know. Using this type of information can lead to problems for four reasons.

Multiple Levels of Meaning

An object like a tree, a car, or a building is visible to the naked eye, yet each of these is composed of certain elements that can't be seen. While the outer layer is observable, the layer beneath the surface can be detected only with x-rays, a microscope, or a scanning device. When seen with such an aid, the object takes on new shapes and colors. Yet a level exists beyond the observational powers of such sensing devices, and this level also can convey new meaning and definition to the object. Some technical jobs require such minute internal understanding of objects. As large high-rise buildings are built, they must appear sound to the outward eye and must pass stress tests to indicate internal soundness. Following a May 1979 crash of a DC-10 plane in Chicago, the Federal Aviation Administration ordered a close inspection of all DC-10 engine mounts. Special scanning devices revealed hairline cracks invisible to the unaided eye on several engine mounts of planes that were in use. The mounts were immediately replaced and further accidents were prevented.

Indirect Gathering of Information

By observing the world, we gain knowledge on a daily basis. Yet most of our knowledge comes from television, radio, magazine, and newspaper accounts in which others interpret the world for us. Wars that involve hundreds of thousands of people and negotiations that involve only three or four are both reported in short one- to three-minute editions on radio and television and a few short columns in newspapers. Often the communicated words and the pose of the picture selected to support a reporter's words are staged by the communicator so that the reader or viewer will perceive and accept the message as reality.

Distortion

The oldest and most complete study of perception was conducted in the early 1900s by individuals who held that the world we perceive is a composite of simple and elementary experiences or sensations and the memory of past sensations in various combinations. The school of structural perception used a variety of figures to show that people receive meaning in several ways when they view objects. A typical example is Figure 3.1, in which some immediately see a vase, others the profile of two face-to-face people. In Figure 3.2 many see a sad old woman, yet others see a very beautiful young lady with a large head covering.

Figure 3.1

Figure 3.2

Look at Figure 3.3. Are the lines the same length? In almost all cases people answer *no*. However, when told that these lines represent two telephone poles that are standing in the desert the answers quickly change from an emphatic *no* to *maybe* or *probably* and even *yes*.

Figure 3.4 is similar. Are the lines parallel? Again, most people answer no, but when told that the lines represent the rails of a railroad track that are receding into the distance, most agree that they could be parallel.

Today perception is studied within the schools of behaviorism, gestalt psychology, and functionalism. Structuralism remains important, however, because most of the knowledge about perception has been discovered through the structuralist approach.

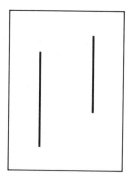

Figure 3.3

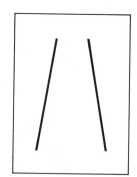

Figure 3.4

Varying Perceptions

One reason that problems and conflicts arise in the area of perception and how it affects human communication is that people see different things in the objects they view. In the Peanuts cartoon, two of the characters interpret the clouds overhead in dissimilar ways, just as in real life, people perceive objects and events differently.

Source: © 1960 by United Feature Syndicate, Inc. Reprinted by permission.

Problems in Perceiving People

Research in the area of human perception has uncovered much about what goes on during personal interactions. For instance, the way we perceive others guides our behavior toward them. Some dispositions or states are more important than others (such as warm versus cold or loud versus soft). Just as in perception of things, much of how we perceive people is the result of inference or analogy instead of facts. We often share similar experiences and consequently can make what we hope are accurate predictions ("because of . . . therefore"). While this type of inference can accurately give us some information about others, it fails to account for factors such as transitory moods or the thought processes of others, especially if we have not had the same experiences that others have had.

Most research on human perception has centered on the sources of information available to the perceiving party. These sources are external to the beholder and include factors like feelings, attributes, and intentions. We use common characteristics, cultural differences, and social pressures in the process of gathering information. Our world takes on the framework of reality because others share our views and give us feedback on the accuracy of our reality.

How the Person Perception Process Works

1. *Physical proximity.* When we can be close to and interact with others, we formulate a first impression—a mental image drawn with certain attributes and qualities attached to the image. In developing impressions, we usually group or stereotype people into categories as a result of reactions or a transfer of thoughts, such as "You remind me of. . . ." The result of the first impression can take such forms as disillusionment, liking, disliking, or desire to increase or decrease interaction. Generally, similarity encourages interaction, and differences discourage it.

2. *Self-esteem.* The perception process continues and takes on a different twist as we react to others and how they seem to perceive us. We seem to be more attracted to those whom we perceive to *agree* with our perception of ourselves and others.

3. *Rewards and costs.* Further interaction usually takes place only when one or both individuals perceive it to be worthwhile.

4. *Discrepancies.* When discrepancies occur between self-image and how one is viewed by others, information gathering is affected and further interaction can be threatened. Future contact will be limited unless the wrong information is cleared up or the impressions are balanced.

5. *Perceived intent.* Generally, people can forgive and forget if they feel another's behavior was not intentional.

6. *Accurate perceptions.* As we get closer to interpreting correctly the information we perceive about others, our relationships grow. When that occurs people become better managers, the workforce is productive, and all involved are rewarded.

Stages of Development

A frame of reference is as necessary for perceiving people as it is for perceiving things. As the six requirements above illustrate, trouble arises when the symbolic realities of two people are different. This occurs because each individual's frame of reference is a direct result of major influences in several areas of life: family, social interaction, politics, geography, life expectancy/lifestyle, work, communication/media, music/dance/books, and travel.

Psychologists tell us that we pass through distinct developmental stages from infancy through maturity and later life. While the ages of these stages vary according to the various researchers, they normally cover the following ranges:

1. Infancy and early childhood (birth to 6 years)
2. Middle childhood (6–12 years)
3. Adolescence (12–18 years)
4. Young adulthood (18–35 years)
5. Middle age (35–60 years)
6. Older life (60 + years)

Certain developmental tasks must be learned at every stage, but the most important stages for tasks dealing with "people perception" occur during the middle childhood and adolescence periods. Starting around years four and five, we observe and imitate the activities of adults. As we move into the school years, we start modeling heroes, observing from our peers, and making decisions that will serve as the foundation for the rest of our life. This foundation is a set of operating values and attitudes that governs our behavior and shapes our view of the world around us. By the time we become adults, we are so locked into that foundation that our attitudes and values seldom change during the rest of our life, except for "significant emotional events."[1] Such events can be the death of a parent or friend, financial failure, foreign travel, the reading of a book, or a personal experience. Whatever the event, it makes a lasting impact on our lives. The charts that follow show some of the developmental tasks that are established during those formative years.

Middle childhood (6–12 years)

• Building attitudes about oneself
• Getting along with playmates
• Developing fundamental skills in reading, writing, and calculating
• Building conscience, morality, and a set of values
• Developing attitudes toward social groups and institutions

Adolescence (12–18 years)

• Developing intellectual skills needed for social relationships
• Achieving socially responsible behavior
• Selecting and preparing for life's occupation
• Refining and aligning conscious values for one's place in the world

---

The Programming Makes the Difference

We are programmed with certain attitudes and values, and our foundation serves as a filter through which we see and evaluate people and things. One way to examine this foundation is to look carefully at the decade in which segments of the American public received its programming. This examination of decades is important because each period has unique events, individuals, and philosophical thoughts that cause people to think and behave in particular ways. When two people, representing two different decades, communicate regarding issues that reveal their attitudes or values, true differences become apparent. Table 3.1 (pages 44–47) outlines some of the influencing factors for the past seven decades. Starting with the 1920s and running through the 1980s, the chart shows the current age of a person programmed during that decade.

Results of the Programming

People think differently as a result of their programming. For example, Ed Bush is president of a small town bank. Ed's bank has many services for its customers. Over the past few years he has noticed a real age difference in certain customers' participation in the bank's programs. Older customers, those in their 60s, keep their money fairly liquid. Most put large sums in savings accounts, government bonds, and certificates of deposit. When Ed pushes them to take more risks in their investment program in order to make higher gains, most do not listen. Ed believes that several have money buried around their houses. Regarding their ultraconservative behavior, they comment, "You never know when another depression can hit. I'm going to be ready. I'm saving for a rainy day." They are referring, of course, to the Great Depression of the 1930s. For those people who lived through, and were programmed by, the events of the 1930s, the possibility of another depression is very real. No amount of information or persuasive talk by others can change their minds. Contrast that older group with those who are in their twenties today. They were programmed in the 1970s when inflation was running rampant and interest rates were high. Ed worries about some customers in that category because he knows they have borrowed money to invest in get-rich-quick schemes. Many in that group are living today on what they hope to earn tomorrow.

People behave differently as a result of their programming. In the 1920s there were economic reasons for women to stay at home and be housewives. Many were uneducated and lacked business skills, especially management skills. Consequently, women comprised only 23 percent of the workforce and worked at jobs that primarily required few skills. During World War II women were needed in the workforce because most men were in military service. But in the 1960s and 1970s many women received the same education as their male counterparts, proved themselves in the work world, and wanted the opportunity to reap the benefits of their education and ability.

One of the most pressing conflicts in the workforce of the 1980s is created by biases that exist against women in top-level management positions. Some men who received their programming in the 1920s and 1930s still believe that a woman's place is in the home and in the kitchen. Only a "significant emotional event" of seeing a truly capable woman manager can change their behavior; sadly enough, their biases often prevent this from occurring.

People view work differently as a result of their programming. Employees programmed during the 1920s and 1930s were introduced to the eight-hour/five-day a week work schedule. As unions gained power, the schedules and specification of work became more firmly established. Most people during this period tended to work best in routine, scheduled types of jobs. Contrast this to the currently growing popularity of flextime, nontraditional work schedules, and at-home work in the "electronic cottage." The people programmed for this type of work are motivated by jobs that provide latitude in time, space, and working conditions and would be frustrated in an old-style work environment.

People even display different purchasing behaviors as a result of their programming. A midwestern pork sausage manufacturer surveyed his purchasing audience and found that most grew up in the 1930s to 1950s. Those individuals had been served pork sausage by their parents, and so they included it in their own diets. The manufacturer found that younger buyers preferred other meat products. Such information helped him design a new marketing strategy and create new products attractive to the younger purchaser.

By learning to understand programming categories that workers, buyers, and the general public fall into, we come closer to removing the perception barrier that impedes management communications.

Table 3.1 · Major Influencers of Attitudes and Values[2]

Decade: Age in 1985:	1920s (70s)	1930s (60s)	1940s (50s)
Family	Close families the basic social/economic unit Women were 23 percent of work force	Every member contributed to welfare of family during Depression	Women were 26 percent of workforce (40) Rosie the Riveters hit 37 percent (42) Baby boom (46)
Social Influence	Beginning of Flapper age (20) Scopes trial on evolution (25) Stock market crash (29)	Great Depression (30) 1,300 banks closed in first months of Depression (30) Social Security start (36) Works Progress Administration (WPA)	Nylons replaced silk stockings (40) Young girls called Bobby Soxers (42) Nation/economy focused on war Religion in school violates first amendment (45) WPA stopped (42)
Politics	Nineteenth Amendment (women's right to vote) passed (20)	Roosevelt and the New Deal (33)	Pearl Harbor (41) War with Japan, Germany, Italy (41) U.S. Savings Bonds (41) Atomic bomb on Japan (45)
Geography	First time in U.S. history that urban population exceeded rural, although agrarian community still thrived		

1950s (40s)	1960s (30s)	1970s (20s)	1980s (Less than 10)
Members started spending more time with peers	43 percent of households with only one working spouse 48 percent married women work (68)	More divorces than marriages ½ eligible U.S. females work, 20 percent in blue-collar jobs (78) 58 percent of women with schoolchildren work (78)	Only 7 percent of U.S. population in traditional nuclear family (working husband, housekeeping wife, 2 children) More singles, marriage postponed, childbearing delayed to late 30s Shift from child-centered to adult-centered homes
Juvenile delinquency problem (54) School racial segregation unconstitutional (54) Voting Rights Bill (57)	Racism concern (63)/ sexism concern (69) Crime rate doubled Ecology concern (62) First U.S. astronaut (62)/ moon walk (69) Public school prayer unconstitutional (63) President Johnson's Great Society program (65) Use of LSD/marijuana (66) Civil rights legislation (66) Medicare for aged (66) Campus revolts (68) Hippies, liberal sex views	450 colleges/universities closed by students (70) 18-year-olds vote (71) Long hair worn in revolt, later became style Switch to sexism/racism concern Environment issues more important than civil rights (73)	Narcissist "me" generation 15 million in U.S. belong to 500,000 self-help groups (82) Do-it-yourself kits of every kind Concern with ageism "Live Aid" concert to prevent starvation (85)
Korean War (51–53)	Bay of Pigs (61)/Cuban missile crisis (62) President Kennedy assassinated (63) Troops in Vietnam changed from 200,000 to 190,000 (65), 300,000 (66), 475,000 (67) Martin Luther King and Robert Kennedy assassinated (68)	Environmental Protection Agency established (70) Illegal corporate contributions to Nixon election campaign Watergate (72–74) Vietnam War ends (73) Nixon resigns (74) Bicentennial celebration (76)	ABSCAM/BRILAB Decentralization from national to state-local community involvement
	Western states population boom; California had 6.9 million in 60, 16 million in 61, most populous state in 64	More in U.S. move to South and West Celebrate geographic diversity ("I love NY")	Few farms, each farmer produces for 75 people Decentralization of people from city to small towns

Table 3.1 *Continued*

Decade: Age in 1985:	1920s (70s)	1930s (60s)	1940s (50s)
Life Expectancy/Life-style	U.S. life expectancy 54 (20) 60 percent in U.S. with income $2,000 or less (bare minimum to survive)		U.S. life expectancy 64 (40)
Work	Henry Ford introduced 8-hour day, 5-day week (26)	Unemployment at 13 million (32)	40-hour work week (40) Worker's compensation laws (48)
Communication/Media	30 radio stations, 60,000 radio sets in the U.S. (22) 2.5 million radios in U.S. (24); 7.3 million by 1927.		30 million radios (40) Television sets sold in U.S. (47) 38 U.S. magazines with circulation of over 1 million (47) 2,079 radio stations, 76 million radio sets (48)
Music/Dance/Books	"Look For the Silver Lining" (20) The Charleston (23)	"Gone With the Wind" (36) "Brother Can You Spare a Dime?" (32)	"This Is My Country" (40) "Remember Pearl Harbor" (41) The jitterbug (43)
Travel	Federal Highway Act passed for improving highways (21)	1 of every 4.9 Americans owned auto (30) Streamlined trains (34)	Public gasoline rationing (42)

1950s (40s)	1960s (30s)	1970s (20s)	1980s (Less than 10)
Middle class more affluent Prosperity, productivity, distribution jobs (50)	Retirement villages start, first in Sun City, Arizona (60) Physical fitness program started by President Kennedy (61), ¼ population exercises First heart transplant (67)	Fast food	Life expectancy 74+ Half U.S. population regularly exercising (82) More wine consumed than hard liquor (80) 500 U.S. companies directed fitness programs Wellness programs More equality in workplace
More white-collar jobs than blue-collar (56) End of industrial era (56–57) 17 percent had information processing/distribution jobs (50)	Theory Y style of management introduced Congress passed "equal pay for equal work, regardless of sex" bill (63) Mass use of calculators "Big-is-better" philosophy Bigness in companies, 4 or 5 in each field produce 80 percent of goods	Unemployment hit 30-year high at 8 percent (75) Quality consciousness Multinationals making drastic changes in big corporations	Participatory decision making Generalist instead of specialist Work at home ("electronic cottage") "Small is beautiful" 13 percent of labor in manufacturing, 60 percent information processing, 3 percent farmers (82) 75 percent of all jobs involve computers
First commercial color television telecast (51) Coast-to-coast dial telephone service, nonoperator assisted (51) Three of five homes have a television set (54) "I Love Lucy" favorite television show (54) Sputnik marked globalization of information revolution (57)	Kennedy/Nixon television debates (60) *N.Y. Times* best paper in U.S. (61) Lee Harvey Oswald shot on nationwide television (63)	Televised Watergate hearings (73–74) CB radio craze (76) Decline of radio and television audience starts (77) Big papers/magazines dying; small thriving	Cable television, video games, allow viewer participation
190 million recordings sold in U.S. (51) "Hello Young Lovers" (51) Elvis hits it big (56)	The Twist Beatles popular (64) Hard rock music "Mrs. Robinson" (68) *Games People Play* (69)	"Bridge Over Troubled Water" (70) *Rocky* (75) *Saturday Night Fever* (78) Punk rock	Country/western music Boy George, Cyndi Lauper, Madonna *One-Minute Manager* *In Search Of Excellence*
Interstate highway construction started (56) 70 million cars (59)		Smaller cars Gasoline exceeded $1.00 per gallon	City-to-country shift made possible by highways, mass transit

People Wear Different Hats

Another perceptual problem arises because we usually know our co-workers in only one role or facet of their lives. When we examine the different hats that they wear, or the other roles that they play in their lives, we find more than just the one-sided personality from which we formulate our impressions.

Bill Tucker worked in the commercial loans department of a bank. Frank Wills, a colleague of Bill's, worked in the same department. They had worked together for four years and often ate lunch together. Bill thought he knew Frank well. One Saturday the bank sponsored a picnic for its employees, and both Bill and Frank attended with their families. There Bill saw a part of Frank that he had never seen before: This normally good-natured person was overbearing with his wife and children and even snapped at Bill during a conversation.

If you could see Frank Wills, you would draw an immediate impression about him. You have probably conjured up a picture of Frank, but your perception of the man is only a part of the person that he is and the many roles that he plays. All his roles are influenced directly or indirectly by his earlier programming. The social, environmental, and political conditions under which he lives and works also influence his personality and behavior. As we list Frank's many roles, try to develop a clear mental picture of the different requirements of each role.

At work he is an *employee* for the company, a *boss* to his secretary and staff, and a *service representative* to his depositors. At home he is a *husband* to his wife, a *father* to his children, a *son* to his parents, and a *brother* to his sister. When he relaxes, he is a *viewer* of the local television stations, a *fan* of his local baseball team, and a *subscriber* to magazine publishers. He is an *appointment* to his barber, a *patient* for his doctor, and a *policy holder* for the insurance company. At church he is a *teacher* to the class and a *member* of the congregation. Frank wears a different hat for each of the above roles; he also behaves differently in each role. Misunderstandings can occur when we know people in one role but observe them in a completely different role. We need to prevent initial impressions from becoming lasting impressions. Managers must constantly allow for a personal latitude that gives them freedom to change impressions as they gain new information about others.

Effective managers not only allow for the differences in people; they seek out the differences. As you read the following case, consider the different ways in which the characters perceive their subordinates and, in turn, are perceived by them.

The Different Supervisory Styles of Debbie and Sue

Debbie and Sue are supervisors for a microprocessor production plant. Both started as supervisors five months ago and have ten employees reporting to them. While their jobs and responsibilities are similar, their management styles are drastically different.

Debbie knows each of her subordinates on an individual basis. She prides herself in talking or checking with them every two or three days. She is always available for discussing problems and seeks to help her workers find solutions that fit both the job and their personalities. During the past five months, Debbie has promoted two people out of her department because the employees developed their skills to the point where they also became supervisors. An additional person moved laterally to another position that required someone who enjoyed working with minute parts. Debbie was able to help the company fill the spot because of her in-depth discussions with her people about things that came easily for them.

To an observer, Debbie's department might seem unorganized. People talk and laugh, work at a seemingly casual pace, design their own work style, and come and go as they please. But Debbie's department almost doubles its production quota on a weekly basis, and its quality control inspection reveals only a 1 percent defect ratio.

Sue's department is different. An observer might see little talking, people continually working, and the entire group starting and stopping for breaks and lunch at the same time. The department is a perfect example of rigid control. Sue prescribes for her workers the method of production and the quota that must be met. Her department meets its quota, but in five months has never surpassed the required goal. No workers have been promoted, although five have quit the company and two were fired.

As you can imagine, morale is extremely low in Sue's department. Perhaps one person's statement about Sue best sums how her people see her: "She could not care less about me as a person. There are a lot of ways my colleagues and I could tell her about doing this job better, and our department would be more productive, but she doesn't want to sit and listen to us. She sees us as things, not as people."

Sue's supervisor observed her problems and called Sue in for a conference. In the course of the conversation she learned of Sue's hidden feelings about herself, her job, and her workers. The manager helped Sue see herself better, gave her some useful tools, and promised to work with her in establishing some new goals for her department. Within two months the morale in Sue's department had improved tremendously, and output quotas were being exceeded on a regular basis. The methods for making similar changes are discussed in the following pages.

Methods for Correcting Perception-Based Problems

Perceptual behavior problems must be understood before managers can become effective communicators. This section discusses five major ways to correct perception-based problems. First, we must examine ourselves and how we feel about our self-image. Second, we must go through a period of self-discovery to see ourselves clearly and not in light of how we wished we were. Third, we must learn to share what we think and feel with others through self-disclosure. Fourth, we must realize the perceptual dimensions that exist when we communicate with others. Fifth, we can help others change by becoming a "positive Pygmalion."

The Self-Concept

Research conducted on self-perception reveals several interesting findings:

1. *The self is a product of interaction.* Need satisfaction is fulfilled in a developmental process.
2. *The self is unique—one of a kind.* Just as no two sets of fingerprints are identical, each individual is unique in a variety of physiological and psychological ways.
3. *The self is composed of attitudes that determine action within society.*
4. *The self grows in stages.*
5. *The self needs favorable regard.* Since we are products of interaction, we need to be seen and treated respectfully.
6. *The self prefers reciprocal behavior.* We respond best to others when we feel positive reciprocation.

The growth of personal relationships is initially determined by our perceptive impression of others and their impression of us. At the core of the perceptive process, however, is our view of ourselves. We all are able to recognize certain things about ourselves, but some have delved more deeply than others into self-analysis.

The concept of self is fundamental in every interpersonal relationship, every social interaction, and every working atmosphere. In the business world, a healthy concept of self is essential. Success at each level of the organization—no matter how high one climbs—is based on a belief in the self that breeds confidence and determination. It is the start of self-assertiveness which enables communication, personal growth, and improved self-image to occur.

A person's self-image is a complex and ever-changing phenomenon. It adjusts daily to factors such as feelings, personal relationships, interests, and the working environment. As we go through major transition periods in life, most people experience deep self-concept changes. People are like giant receptors that receive thousands of impulses daily. Each day feedback from supervisors, subordinates, fellow workers, family, and friends is transmitted to our psyches, and we, in turn, transform these impulses into a unique self-concept. Impulses, verbal or nonverbal, personal or social, make up impressions. The individual must turn these different impulses into a workable knowledge that can be used to change and strengthen his or her self-image.

Self-Discovery

Understanding and controlling our perceptive behavior is a major step in learning to communicate effectively, and it requires that we gain a better understanding of our self-concept. We do this by examining three different aspects of who we are.

The me that I know. This is the image of ourselves that we derive from all the information (both positive and negative) that we accumulate from the world around us. For relationships to grow effectively, both parties need to be able to perceive themselves realistically. People with a healthy self-image do not harbor fears, resentments, or other "not-OK" feelings of self that are constantly used against others. This position is demonstrated by managers who can see or admit to their subordinates that they have both strengths and weaknesses. A person with this self-image may reach a point of not having an immediate answer to a problem; he or she will develop an answer because that is part of the job.

The me that I wish I were. All of us have areas of our lives where we wish we were different. For some it may be the fantasy of being a movie star or the chief executive officer of an organization; for others it can be an unclear goal. Those types of images are healthy parts of our daydreams. For some people "the me I wish I were" is an unhealthy, "not-OK" position from which they combat the world.

In the case of Debbie and Sue, Sue, who faced many personality problems within her work group, could have easily possessed an "I wish that I were an effective supervisor" image. If she had compared her relationships and performance outcomes with those of Debbie or other supervisors, she would have constantly felt that she was coming up short. The more she tried to change and be the person she wished she were, the more difficult she found the behavior and the more impossible the results. By sitting down and determining new managerial goals and new skills that she needed to develop, the "I wish" position shifted to one of "I think it is possible to be a different type of person."

The me that I want others to see. Occasionally "the me that I know," and "the me that I wish I were" become mingled to the point of becoming "the me that I want others to know." This may be the calm, cool, and collected image of a speaker making a presentation to a large group. On the outside the smile and mannerisms say, "Nothing ruffles my feathers," but on the inside the person is slowly falling apart.

Some people project such good images of themselves to others that the real person is never displayed or known. On one end of the continuum, this position is effective and a part of the manager's public and professional appearance. Control to the extreme, however, hides characteristics about the real person that we fear to let others know.

Self-Disclosure

One of the best ways to achieve self-discovery, and to help others learn about us, is to practice self-disclosure. Since communication is a two-way process, information must travel between both senders and receivers.

The Johari window, conceived by Joseph Luft and Harry Ingham, examines different areas of life and people's awareness of them.[3] The window is like a large framed picture of you. Inside is everything there is to know about yourself: wants, needs, likes, dislikes, goals, fears, etc. (Figure 3.5). The frame can be divided into vertical and horizontal halves. The vertical halves contain what is known and not known to each person. The horizontal halves contain what others know about us and what they do not know. When the vertical and horizontal halves are overlaid we have the Johari window. The four quadrants are displayed in Figure 3.6.

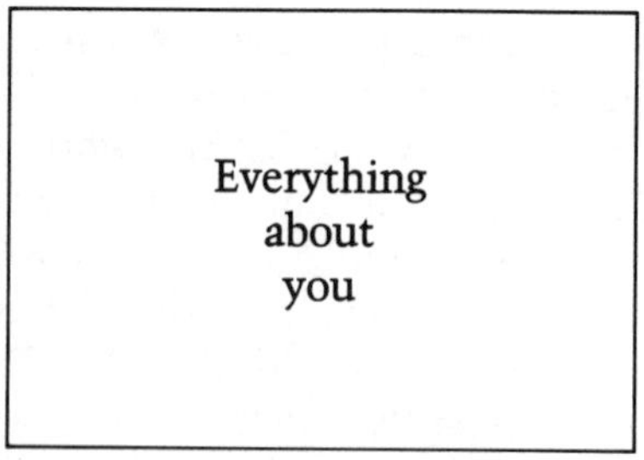

Everything
about
you

Figure 3.5

From *Group Processes: An Introduction to Group Dynamics* by Joseph Luft, by permission of Mayfield Publishing Company. Copyright © 1984, 1970, and 1963 by Joseph Luft.

	Known to self	Not known to self
Known to others	1 Open	2 Blind
Not known to others	3 Hidden	4 Unknown

Figure 3.6
From Luft, *Group Processes.*

Quadrant 1 is the open area that is known to ourselves and also to others. It is a public area where questions can be asked freely and answers given unthreateningly. This area concerns attitudes, feelings, and behavior that we understand and that others see and interpret.

Quadrant 2 is the blind area of our life. Here others see and know things about us that we do not know about ourselves. A simple example might be nervous habits. Others see them, yet we never realize they exist. A more complex example might be attitudes, biases, anger, and fears that we have toward people or events. Others observe these attitudes in our behavior, but we easily ignore them.

Quadrant 3 is the hidden area and contains those secret thoughts, fears, desires, and motives that we have and realize but conceal from others.

Quadrant 4 is the unknown area that is full of deeply hidden and programmed attitudes and knowledge. We are often motivated to behave in certain ways where unknown responses prevail, yet we are uncertain why we behave as we do. As information within this area becomes known, we then understand our thoughts and behavior.

Figure 3.7 shows the Johari window for two individuals. Which one tends to share more personal information? If these two people shared a relationship, their communication patterns would probably lead to problems and conflicts. Since A has a large open area and a very small unknown area, we can infer that he has done some introspective examining of his life and talked a lot about himself with others. We call such talk *disclosure.* As he shared information with others, they told him things

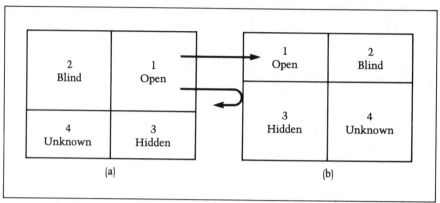

Figure 3.7

that had been blind to him before. As he grew comfortable in the relationships, he found that there was less that he wanted to hide from people. Consequently his unknown area became smaller as new things about his life were uncovered.

For B there is a hesitancy to share hidden information, and consequently his unknown area is large. When A and B communicate, their range is limited, and A will soon feel unfulfilled if his communication is ignored and unanswered.

Several possibilities exist for A and B's relationship: (1) They can settle on simple communication in a limited scope; (2) they can feel unfulfilled and stop talking; (3) they can become more open with each other, share more information, learn more about themselves and the other, and let their relationship grow. If a commitment to growth is made, the potential for a large open area exists with both people. Figure 3.8 depicts the outcome.

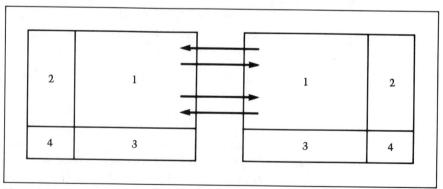

Figure 3.8

Three Perceptual Dimensions of Each Person

Information about self-concepts and perceptions of other people is collected from three distinct perceptual dimensions that exist for each person involved in the communication act. Since communication involves two people and each person has three dimensions, six dimensions are involved each time two people communicate:

- My perception of me
- My perception of you
- My perception of how you are perceiving me
- Your perception of you
- Your perception of me
- Your perception of how I am perceiving you

Why is the uniqueness of the person important in business? Many would say that it is not, and others feel that business must minimize the differences among people, especially in their styles of work, and try to have everyone look and act alike. Japanese management style, however, suggests that this misconception is partially responsible for the recent low rate of productivity in the United States. Americans have specialized jobs, while typical Japanese employees tend to be generalists. In the United States, job specialization and specific job descriptions have limited potential employee performance.

Because the workplace is filled with people from all avenues of life, managers must understand that their programming and life experiences make each person unique. What is a wise decision for one individual may be foolish for another. One author expressed it this way:

I act in a way that is *cautious* to me, but *cowardly* to you.
You act in a way that is *courageous* to you, but *foolhardy* to me.
She sees herself as *vivacious*, but he sees her as *superficial*.
He sees himself as *friendly*, she sees him as *seductive*.
She sees herself as *reserved*, he sees her as *haughty and aloof*.
He sees himself as *gallant*, she sees him as *phoney*.
She sees herself as *feminine*, he sees her as *helpless and dependent*.
He sees himself as *masculine*, she sees him as *overbearing and dominating*.[4]

The uniqueness in people makes them real people who have value: They are not mechanisms that can be manipulated and treated without respect, nor are they embodiments of concepts or definitions. For many years business has spent enormous amounts of money on its machines but ignored its most valuable resource — its people. Current management theorists extoll managers to "prize the human resource."

Psychologists have long known that much of what people are is a direct result of the influence of others. Children model their behavior on that of parents and peers. Workers follow the examples of mentors and prodigies. Managers and supervisors can have an extraordinary amount of influence on the people they lead. This influence phenomenon is called *the self-fulfilling prophecy*, or the *Pygmalion effect*, which means that the prediction or expectation of an event can actually cause it to happen. People can become what other people expect them to be.

In Greek mythology, Pygmalion was a King of Cyprus who carved an ivory statue of the ideal woman and then fell in love with his beautiful creation. Aphrodite interceded and brought the statue to life for him. Years later the playwright George Bernard Shaw used the concept in his play, *Pygmalion*, which was made into the musical comedy *My Fair Lady*. In these plays and in the myth, one person, with desire and patience, transformed the behavior of another. Professor Henry Higgins proved it was possible through hard work and positive expectations to change Eliza Doolittle from a rumpled, impolite, and loud flower girl into a gentle, soft-spoken, and attractive lady.

Becoming a Positive Pygmalion

A Short but Shaggy Morality Story About Suggestion

Back when Robert T. Hill was employed at Pennsylvania State University, a graduate instructor in the education of exceptional children asked him to approve production of a highly unstructured instructional videotape. "I went into my development act," recalls Hill, who currently is training manager at Poppin Fresh Pies, Inc., Minneapolis. "I tried to pry behavioral objectives and a content outline out of him. All he would say, however, is that he wanted to bring an eight-year-old child into the studio and tape some activities. Although this sort of unstructured program is the instructional television producer's nightmare, I finally relented and we taped a program of a young boy playing with some toys and taking a psychological word test."

A few months later, Hill happened to meet the instructor and asked him if he was using the videotape. The instructor said he was and had been very pleased with the results.

"How do you use it?" Hill asked. "Well," he said, "I have two classes of graduate students with a good background in psychology. I show one class the tape and tell them that they will be observing a child with a genius-level IQ and that they should write down the characteristics that demonstrate this. I show the same videotape to the other class and tell them that the kid is mentally retarded and that they should write down the characteristics he displays that indicate this. Every time I do it, I get what is a normal young boy written up as either a genius or a retarded child. I then tell them the truth and hope they profit from the experience."

While research on the Pygmalion effect has been instrumental in helping managers develop staff members, the initial tests on the effect were conducted in the educational system. Rosenthal and Jacobson told a group of teachers that tests showed that certain of their elementary students were "intellectual bloomers."[5] In reality the children labeled "bloomers" were picked randomly. When retested after eight months, the so-called bloomers had improved in overall IQ by four points over other children in the teachers' classrooms. Controls showed that there was no difference in the amount of time the teachers spent with the regular and bloomer children, nor did the type of classroom make a difference in the test scores. The important denominator was the *quality* of the interaction between the teacher and the students. When questioned about their impression of the students, they stated that those designated as bloomers were smarter, more appealing, more affectionate, and adjusted better and more quickly than other students. Those not classified as bloomers were seen as less bright, less interesting, less affectionate; they also were said to not adjust as well. A teacher's expectations of his or her students is a key factor in their growth and success.

Principles of the Pygmalion Effect

1. Employees act as they believe they are expected to act.
2. A manager's treatment of each employee is influenced by what the manager expects of the employee.
3. If a manager's expectations are high, productivity will likely be high.
4. If a manager's expectations are low, output will likely be low.
5. A subordinate's performance rises or falls to meet a manager's expectations.

In business the same principle applies. A manager's expectations of his or her subordinates is a key factor in the growth and success of the organization, the employees, and management. Just as Professor Higgins did in the play *Pygmalion*, many managers play Pygmalion-like roles in developing successful and productive subordinates and encouraging their growth.

J. Sterling Livingston introduced the business community to the Pygmalion effect in a 1969 *Harvard Business Review* article in which he recounted the story of a Metropolitan Life Insurance Company district office. In that office, management grouped superior salesmen with highly productive assistant managers. That group became known as the "super staff." Average salesmen were grouped with average assistant managers, and low producers were grouped with low assistant managers. The superior and poor groups both performed according to management's expectation. The superior staff exceeded their production quota; the lower group's performance rate was lower than expected, and its attrition rate higher. The real change occurred with the "average" group. According to Livingston:

> Although the district manager expected only average performance from this group, its productivity increased significantly. This was because the assistant manager in charge of the group refused to believe that he was less capable than the manager of the "super-staff" or that the agents in the top group had any greater ability than the agents in his group. He insisted in discussions with his agents that every man in the middle group had greater potential than the men in the "super-staff," lacking only their years of experience in selling insurance. He stimulated his agents to accept the challenge of out-performing the "super-staff." As a result, in each year the middle group increased its productivity by a higher percentage than the "super-staff" did.[6]

The assistant manager became a positive Pygmalion, and his expectations of his staff produced an effective change in their behavior. But what about the poor producers? The unsuccessful salesmen had low self-images and sought to prevent further damage to their egos by avoiding situations where potential failure was possible. They made fewer calls and avoided trying to "close" sales where rejection might result: "Low expectations and damaged egos lead them to behave in a manner that increases the probability of failure, thereby fulfilling their manager's expectations."[7]

Livingston explains how the pattern of failure leads to a self-fulfilling prophecy:

> Not long ago, I studied the effectiveness of branch bank managers at a West Coast bank with over 500 branches. The managers who had their lending authority reduced because of high rates of loss became progressively less effective. To prevent further loss of authority, they turned to

making only "safe" loans. This action resulted in losses of business to competing banks and a relative decline in both deposits and profits at their branches. Then, to reverse the decline in deposits and earnings, they often "reached" for loans and became almost irrational in their acceptance of questionable credit risks. Their actions were not so much a matter of poor judgment as an expression of their willingness to take desperate risks in the hope of being able to avoid further damage to their egos and to their careers.

Thus, in response to the low expectations of their supervisors, who had reduced their lending authority, they behaved in a manner that led to larger credit losses. They appeared to do what they believed they were expected to do, and their supervisors' expectations became self-fulfilling prophecies.[8]

Managers communicate both high and low expectations to their subordinates and do so through both verbal and nonverbal behavior. Even unintentional feelings are transmitted through facial expressions, eye contact (or lack of eye contact), tone of voice, physical touch, and body posture. In fact, the importance of the message is not so much in what is said as it is in how it is conveyed. Indifferent, "cold," or noncommital behavior by managers communicates low expectations and leads to low performance. Although most managers want to communicate positively, they are generally most effective in communicating low expectations.

While the Pygmalion effect occurs both positively and negatively at all levels of the organization, studies show that young workers who are new to a job are the ones most influenced by the process because they are eagerly ready to develop in the direction of an organization's expectations. The first supervisor is likely to be the most influential person in their careers. Although the Pygmalion process can have positive application to all individuals in the organization, older employees with seniority often possess a hardened self-image, see themselves in light of their career record, and have set expectations and perceptions of management.

Summary

Understanding perceptual behavior is the first step on the way to becoming an effective communicator. Because perception is defined as the way we take in information about our world, and because each person gathers information differently, problems arise in the way each individual perceives things and other people. Many of the differences among people can be explained by the programming that occurs during formative stages of childhood and adolescence. Other differences occur because wants and needs vary from person to person.

Perception-based problems can be corrected. First, we must examine our own self-concepts and discover some reasons why we behave the way we do. Second, we must learn how to share information with other people about how we think and feel in order to nurture our relationships. The Johari window illustrates this process. Third, managers can become positive Pygmalions and learn to develop high expectations for those that they supervise. Once the self-fulfilling prophecy track opens, managers' perception and communication styles can be sharpened by praising or reprimanding subordinates immediately and specifically. As positive Pygmalions, if we constantly look for the best in people, we will find it.

Key Words

perception	significant emotional	self-disclosure
levels of perception	event	Johari window
distorted information	personal programming	self-fulfilling prophecy
lifestyle development	self-concept	Pygmalion effect
	self-discovery	

Review Questions

1. Describe perception, and relate your description to a real-life situation (for example, you developed a first impression about someone but later changed it).

2. Describe the four main problems that occur in perception, and use examples from your own life to illustrate. These illustrations may be instances when you allowed your perceptions to be guided by information given by others, and so forth.

3. Describe how your attitudes and value system were shaped as a result of early programming events.

4. List several ways in which negative or erroneous perceptions of others can be changed. Cite examples of times you have taken some of these steps in repairing relationships with others. Cite examples of times others have done the same for you.

5. Describe the Johari window and its four quadrants. Relate the window to relationships in your life at the present time. How would you like to see the quadrants changed?

6. Describe the principles of the Pygmalion effect. Has anyone acted as a Pygmalion for you? Describe that person's characteristics.

Exercises

1. Here's a nonthreatening exercise that can show you and your classmates how first impressions are formulated, how accurate they are, and how, with additional information, they can be changed. Team up with a classmate you have never met or talked with, and find a quiet place where you both can work. Complete the following first impression questionnaire. As you look at each other, write down answers about the other that you imagine to be true. Do not talk with your partner until you both have answered all questions. After you have finished writing, share your answers, and find out which person gave the most accurate responses.

   First Impression Questionnaire

   a. What is your partner's name? _____

   b. What city do you think he or she is from? _____

   c. What kind of car (specifically) do you think he or she drives? _____
   _____

   d. Is he or she married? _____ engaged? _____

   e. How many children does he or she have? _____

   f. What political party does he or she support? _____

   g. What kind of music on tape or album do you think he or she would buy?
   _____

   h. What book (specifically) do you think he or she is now reading? _____
   _____

   i. What is his or her main hobby? _____

   j. What athletic activity do you think he or she enjoys? _____

   k. What does he or she enjoy doing in free time? _____

   l. What subject area do you think he or she is majoring in? _____

   m. What kind of job do you think he or she wants or has? _____
   _____

   n. What three adjectives would define how he or she feels right now? _____
   _____

   o. What three adjectives would best describe his or her personality? _____
   _____

   p. How many of the above questions did you answer correctly? _____
   _____

2. First impressions either become lasting impressions or change as more information is gathered. On the following questionnaire, write the initials of people that you know who fit each category. Next to their initials, write words that describe the image you have of these people. You may want to do this exercise in small groups and share your impressions with others. It is not necessary to use names.

	Person's Initials	Person's Image to You
a. A person you really like who is the same age and sex as you		
b. A person you really like who is the same age but opposite sex as you		
c. A person you dislike		
d. Someone who openly accepts others		
e. Someone who rejects others		
f. A teacher you like		
g. A teacher you dislike		
h. A successful person		
i. An unsuccessful person		
j. An ethical person		
k. An unethical person		

3. Between the time you read this chapter and meet for your next class, note the different roles that you play and the specific expectations that people have of you as you play those roles. Use the following space to record your findings, and report them to class.

4. In the space below, draw two Johari windows. In the one on the left, draw quadrants that represent how you feel about your relationship with someone close to you (a friend, parent, etc.). In the one on the right, draw quadrants that represent how you think that they feel about their present relationship with you. Do the two windows match? How are they different? If a difference exists, should you and how can you make adjustments?
   a.

   b. Form a small group to talk about people who have been positive Pygmalions in your life. Use your answers to the following to help begin the discussion: "I have done my best work for teachers who _____."

References

1. The term "significant emotional event" is used by Morris Massey in his program, "What You Are Is Where You Were When." Those interested in additional research and investigation into the area of attitude and value programming can benefit from a reading of Massey's book, *The People Puzzle: Understanding Yourself and Others* (Reston, Va.: Reston Publishing, 1979).

2. Demographic information used in these charts was pulled from several sources. The most valuable were Paul C. Murphy, *What's Happened . . . Since 1776* (Oklahoma City: Journal Record Publishing, 1980); John Naisbitt, *Megatrends* (New York: Warner Book, 1982); Alvan Toffler, *The Third Wave* (New York: William Morrow, 1980); David Wallechinsky and Irving Wallace, *The People's Almanac* (Garden City, N.Y.: Doubleday, 1975).

3. Joseph Luft, *Group Processes: An Introduction to Group Dynamics* (Palo Alto, Calif.: Mayfield Publishing Company, 1984), pp. 11–12.

4. John Stewart, *Bridges Not Walls: A Book About Interpersonal Communication* (Reading, Mass.: Addison-Wesley, 1977), p. 209.

5. Robert Rosenthal's work on the Pygmalion effect is found in two separate publications: Robert Rosenthal, "The Pygmalion Effect Lives," *Psychology Today* (Sept. 1973), and Robert Rosenthal and Lenore Jacobson, *Pygmalion in the Classroom* (New York: Holt, Rinehart & Winston, 1968).

6. J. Sterling Livingston, "Pygmalion in Management," *Harvard Business Review* (July/Aug. 1969), pp. 82–83.

7. *Ibid.*, p. 83.

8. *Ibid.*, pp. 83–84.

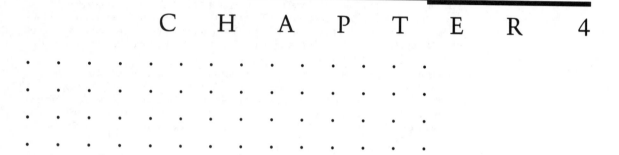

C H A P T E R 4

Language Barriers:
The Second Hurdle

Introduction

Before, during, and after the act of communication the communicator's cognitive view of the world influences what is communicated. People never come into direct contact with total reality, however, because everything experienced is filtered through the nervous system. As this chapter shows, individual perceptions can vary considerably from person to person: Perception is how people create meaning out of experiences. To create meaning, language barriers must be overcome.

Social Semantics Defined

Language—and its effect on perception, communication patterns, and interpersonal behavior—is an important facet of effective communication. Social semantics—as this field is called—evolved from research in four disciplines: science, linguistics, psychology, and sociology. *Science* contributed knowledge of the biological stimulus-response process and the physical sciences; *linguistics* contributed knowledge of how symbols are used as patterns of thought for languages; *psychology*, the mental process of using symbols; and *sociology*, the relationships between groups of people.

S. I. Hayakawa, long considered the contemporary father of general semantics, explains the grammar-to-general semantics journey:

> Grammar deals only with word-to-word relations. It teaches how to put words together into a sentence. It is not interested in how sentences are related to each other or how they are related to facts. Logic goes further. To a logician, sentences are assertions, and he is interested in relations between assertions (if this is true, then that is true). But for the logician, words need not have any meaning except as defined by other words, and the assertions need not have any relation to the world of fact. The semanticist goes further than the logician. To him words and assertions have meaning only if they are related operationally to referents. The semanticist defines not only validity (as the logician does) but also truth. The general semanticist goes the furthest. He deals not only with words, assertions, and their referents in nature, but also with their effects on human behavior. For a general semanticist, communication is not merely words in proper order properly inflected (as for the grammarian) or assertions in proper relation to referents (as for the semanticist), but all these together, with the chain of "fact to nervous system to language to nervous system to action."[1]

Social semantics derived its conceptual core from general semantics and added relevant materials on the social consequences of semantic habits, particularly as those habits are displayed in human interaction. Social semantics also influences managerial behavior, and certain semantic tools are available for managers to use.

The word *semantics* comes from the Greek word *semantikos*, which means *significant*. Today it is defined as the study of meanings between *symbols* (words, signals, and so forth) and the objects that they refer to, or the *referents*. The term *general semantics* was coined in the early 1930s by Alfred Korzybski, whose major work was *Science and Sanity: An Introduction to Non-Aristotelian Systems and General Semantics*. Korzybski studied cognitive perception and in doing so explored new territory. The work of those he gathered around him (Wendell Johnson, Irving J. Lee, Stuart Chase, and S. I. Hayakawa) has greatly advanced this field of study. Hayakawa and his writings, particularly his influential book *Language in Thought and Action*, gave the field credibility and introduced practical tools that are taught and used today.

The entire study of semantics is based on a relationship between a symbol and its referent (see Figure 4.1). The referent is the object, and the

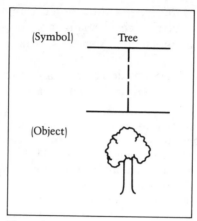

Figure 4.1

symbol is the word that represents the object. A gap always exists between the world of reality and the world of symbols. Before we can understand that gap, we must learn more about symbols.

The Symbol-Using Process

For humans, communication occurs in two ways: verbally and nonverbally. Nonverbal communication includes environmental signals, social symbols, human gestures, and signs that are used in the transfer of message and meaning. We examine the area of nonverbal communication in Chapter 8.

A profound difference is found between the use of *symbols* and *signs*. The human use of signs is evidence of the first manifestation of the mind. This is the beginning of intelligence and mentality, since signs are learned by trial and error. Animal mentality is built on sign usage because a sign is something to act on—a means to command action. Signs stand in a one-to-one relationship with an experience.

Animals have evolved in stature by using signs as signals. When their environments are small (a dog in a backyard), the learning is limited. When the environments are large (eagle on a mountaintop), the variety of available signals increases. Learning also increases as a result of long experience and reactions to many signs.

The uniqueness and superiority of human beings over other animals are attributed to their wider range of signals, greater power in integrating reflexes, and quicker learning by trial and error. Most of all, humans have the ability to use signs to indicate things and to represent them. With people, signs do not announce things; they are reminders. They serve not as vicarious stimuli to action but as references to things removed; they serve as symbols.

Signs do not limit people to using them in the here and now. They serve as symbols for the past, present, and future of something. A wet street is a *sign of rain*, the patter on the roof is a sign that *it is raining*, greenness of vegetation means that *it has rained*. These are all natural signs. The development of language documents a gradual accumulation and elaboration of verbal symbols.

The human mind can be compared to a telephone exchange. Messages can be relayed, answered by proxy, stored if the line is busy, sent over lines that didn't exist when first used, and even jotted down and kept if no desired recall number is given. Words are the plug put into the superswitchboard that connects impressions of ideas, information already stored, and the total functioning of the entire system. Sometimes these lines become crossed in humorous or even disastrous ways.

A significant difference between humans and other animals is that humans can survive because they can think. Animals learn to respond to signs, but only humans can use symbols. Through the use of symbols (or the word-using communication skill process), people can learn from the past, adapt themselves to new and changing conditions, learn new skills, and create the type of living environment that they want. The symbol-using process makes us human.

In her autobiography, Helen Keller describes the point when she became "fully human." Born blind and deaf, she communicated as a child through grunts, groans, and growls. She had used signs, had formed associations, and had learned to identify people and places. But sign learning was finally eclipsed by the miracle of symbols and a word. The months of teaching paid off one day with the help of her tutor, Anne Sullivan.

As they walked down the path toward the well-house together, someone was drawing water. Anne placed Helen's hand under the waterspout. As the cool stream of water gushed over Helen's hand, Anne spelled into the other hand the word *water*, first slowly, then rapidly. Somehow the mystery of language was revealed to Helen. She understood that *w-a-t-e-r* meant the wonderful cool something that was flowing over her hand. Helen left the well-house eager to learn. Everything had a name, and each led her to a new thought and understanding.

Helen Keller's experience shows the difference between *signs* and *symbols*. Signs are things to act on; symbols are instruments of thought. *W-a-t-e-r* was a sign that previously could be acted on. But as a word it became an object that could be communicated, remembered, and mentioned at a later date.

Aristotelian Logic

General semanticists started their study of language and meaning by rejecting three premises of Aristotle's framework on thought. Aristotle used a certain technique of definition—classification—that has three parts: identity, excluded middle, and contradiction. When Aristotle used his classification premise, he placed people in categories and grouped all people together. General semanticists classify by operational definition on a one-to-one basis, which makes classification more accurate.

1. *Law of identity.* According to Aristotle, "A is A." In application this could be stated, "Grass is green," or "Henry is dumb." But when we attempt to analyze what *dumb* means, we suddenly realize that we are referring to Henry's behavior. Consequently, Henry is not dumb; he does dumb things.

2. *Law of the excluded middle.* Aristotle stated this in a right or wrong, one or the other, dichotomy: "A is B or not B." Statements are often made in good/bad or true/false terms. For instance, some feel a person is either a conservative or a liberal, motivated or unmotivated. The world is not this black and white; it contains shades of gray.

3. *Law of contradiction.* This is stated as "A is not A." Things cannot be "good and bad" or "right and wrong" at the same time. Is the water hot or cold? If it is one, it cannot be the other. For Aristotle, language defined the world and the way of thinking. Our language influences our thinking and defines our world.

Linguists have shown that language is more than vocabulary and terminology or a way of identifying something as one thing or another. It reflects culture and gives insights into the world. Languages are different; they are not synonymous. A person who learns a language also absorbs certain predispositions of the culture that produced the language and certain ideas that can be verbalized. Each language has symbols that have been derived for its vocabulary. When people speak two or more languages, they therefore can experience more than one view of the world. Semanticists have established three basic steps for drawing order into the communication process:

1. Establish facts and characteristics of life of which communicators are aware.
2. Be aware of the language habits that represent reality inadequately.
3. Find specific, usable, and teachable devices that can make language habits produce a proper evaluation of what is being discussed.

Social semanticists have examined the way that language symbols are used and, as a result, have discovered several "bad" language habits. These habits have been analyzed and systematized along with techniques and devices for correcting them. Also, these bad language habits can be used to evaluate how we communicate with others.

Words

The symbols most used by humans are words. Words serve as pointers, indicators, and representatives of things in the world. Communicating messages requires that we implement several different characteristics of words.

Basic Characteristics of Words

One word can have several meanings. There would be fewer communication problems if each word that we used had only one meaning, but that is not the case. The examples below give us ten different meanings for the word *case*:

1. Harold has a *case* of mononucleosis. (occurrence of disease)
2. The *case* Dr. Jones is working on concerns a small boy. (a client)
3. State the *case* for increasing corporate taxation. (a set of reasons for or against an action or thing)
4. Sue's a real *case*. (a peculiar or eccentric person)
5. Type the letter with upper *case* characters. (style of type)
6. The thieves *cased* the store before the break-in. (planned observation)
7. The engine is housed in the metal *casing*. (a cover or framework)
8. Please put the books in their proper book*case*. (wooden structure)
9. I and you, respectively, are in the nominative and objective *case* in "I like you." (a linguistic pattern)
10. Please take the papers out of my brief*case*. (a carrying object)

One meaning can have two or more words. The cultural and social sources of language make it possible for one symbol to have more than one word that can describe it. Eskimos have several words for that cold.

wet substance that English-speaking people call snow. They use distinctive terms for falling snow, snow on the ground, snow drifts, and so forth.

Words sometimes have no meaning. While it doesn't often occur, a word can be coined before a meaning is assigned to the word. Pluto, the ninth and farthest planet from the sun, was named before it was ever seen. Astronomers knew it was there because only the presence of another planet in that part of the solar system could provide an explanation for the orbits of other heavenly bodies.

There are technical and nontechnical words. According to Don Fabun, "There are believed to be 600,000 words in the English language today. The number is constantly growing, as we add new human experiences to be reported upon . . . or as we coin new expressions to describe present experiences. . . . The number of words . . . that an educated adult uses in daily conversation is about 2,000. Of these, the 500 most frequently used have 14,000 dictionary definitions."[2]

Technical words tend to have restricted and limited usage. Take, for example, the technical term *sodium chloride*. The definition of this technical term leaves little room for confusion. It is a colorless or white crystalline compound. But its nontechnical name, salt, can have many uses and meanings.

Words have regional meanings and usages. People who travel from place to place in the United States and around the world become accustomed to the different regional meanings and usages of words. In England a *tonic* is a bottle of pop and a *soft drink* is mineral water. In the United States we might use the words *pop* or *soft drink* for a refreshment or call it by its brand name. If you order a *soda* in New York, you'll get a soft drink, but in Ohio you would get an ice cream soda. The Amish refer to vacations by saying, "He's on his free and his free is almost all." In the north, candy on a stick is a *lollipop*, but in the south it's a *sucker*. At some hotels people want to carry your *suitcase*, or *grip*, which also is the term used to describe a person who handles sound equipment in movie productions.

Words in Transition

Words are added. In this age of rapid change, new words are added on a regular basis. When the second edition of *Webster's New World Dictionary* came out in 1977, it contained more than 1,000 new entries, including: antsy (meaning fidgety), bumper sticker, idiot card, Peter principle, head shop, victimless crime, and xeroradiography (a new x-ray technique). Each year some 250 to 300 new words are added to our language. Several find their way into dictionaries, some drop out, others change meaning.

Words are deleted. Some words remain in the dictionary even though they are rapidly becoming obsolete. One such word is *bamboozle*, meaning to deceive or cheat by trickery. The word began more than 200 years ago as a slang word and then became an informal word. It probably will be dropped soon because most people twenty years old and younger don't know its meaning. To linguistic purists the dropping of a word or the change in its meaning is regrettable, but language is in a constant state of flux: To think that words are static is like saying that life cannot change.

Answer for 58 Across No Longer Operable

WASHINGTON (AP)—State Department officials doing Tuesday's *New York Times* crossword puzzle found themselves in trouble; the answer for 58 across is no longer in their vocabulary.

The clue was "a truce-like period." The answer was "detente."

The problem is that President Ford abolished that word from his lexicon on grounds it does not reflect the true state of affairs between the United States and the Soviet Union.

No formal orders went down after Ford eliminated the word, but like the court members who saw the emperor's invisible clothes, the State Department bureaucrats say the word no longer lives.

Robert Funseth, the department's main spokesman, was asked Tuesday if *detente* is still allowed. Well, he answered, "We will follow his (Ford's) wishes in that regard. . . . I will be guided" by the President.

"I will make every effort not to use it," Funseth said.

Ford revealed his "coup detente" in an interview Monday with Miami television station WCKT: "I don't use the word *detente* anymore because it doesn't adequately describe the policy of 'peace through strength.'"

The only real question left, according to one wag at the State Department, is fitting "peace through strength" into the seven blanks allotted for 58 across.

At the White House, press secretary Ron Nessen said earlier that American foreign policy, minus the word *detente*, will be the same American foreign policy. Nessen said the word has lost its meaning and has been misunderstood. The word was used during the Nixon administration to describe a policy of seeking to lessen international tensions.[3]

Words change meaning. As society changes, the words it uses and the meanings of words also change. The word *dynamite* has long been listed in the dictionary as a noun and defined in terms of a power explosion caused by compositions of chemicals and absorbant materials. But a few years ago the meaning expanded to be used as a slang adjective, as in "That was a dynamite presentation." Other terms like *genetic engineer-*

ing, information processing, and *citizen's band* are combinations of words that mean more than the sum of their parts.

Problems in Using Words

Social semanticists have examined a variety of language problems and have devised solutions that make communication easier.

Allness

Chapter 3 noted that people perceive only a portion of what is going on in the world. Noted semanticists Irving J. Lee and Laura L. Lee used a diagram (see Figure 4.2) to illustrate how little of the available world we select and how much is omitted. The large circle contains everything that is available to discuss about any subject; the small circle contains the limited details that are selected for discussion. Whenever we talk, we always omit more than we can say. We also have the option of making factual statements or inferential statements.

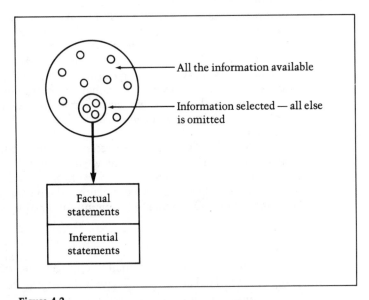

Figure 4.2

Source: Irving J. Lee and Laura L. Lee, *Handling Barriers in Communication* (New York: Harper & Row), p. 136. Copyright © 1956, 1957 by Laura L. Lee.

When people forget about the selection process, and that certain things are always omitted, they have what semanticists call "allness illness." These people think it is possible to know and say everything about something. Comments that reflect this position are "It all happened because . . ."; "The problem with that is . . ."; "I'll tell you exactly what is wrong. . . ." People who have the allness illness are intolerant of others' viewpoints; they think they know all there is to know about something; they ignore information that could change an outcome; they judge people by one small action or a particular event; and they will not listen to additional information that others want to give.

An example occurred in a recent factory accident in which four eyewitnesses saw an employee fall off a two-story scaffold. Each witness reported "factual" detail about the incident, yet all four gave different accounts. Even firsthand observation doesn't allow us to see and know *all* that there is to know. Statements that include the word *all* can often be wrong: "All minority members are lazy"; "All Southerners are rednecks"; "All managers cover their own hides before helping their subordinates."

People with allness problems tend to be close-minded. Their use of language has locked them into a mindset that excludes and never considers many possibilities. Fish in marine life exhibits and elephants in circuses are programmed to be close-minded. Humans often allow themselves to be programmed in the same way. A large fish in a natural environment eats small fish. But in commercial exhibits these fish are trained with a clear piece of glass between themselves and the small fish. When they attempt to eat the smaller fish they hit the glass and soon give up trying. Soon afterward they can be placed in the same aquarium with the smaller fish, and the earlier programming will prohibit their eating the small ones.

The Word Is Not the Thing

Semanticists use the word *bypassing* to distinguish miscommunication patterns that occur when senders and receivers miss each other with the meaning of words they use. Supervisors and subordinates can use the same words, but the intent of their communication can fail because they each attribute different meanings to the specific words. This was disastrously displayed in 1969 when four English Royal Air Force jets were involved in an accident. As the four pilots flew in formation, the rear pilot noticed a fire in the plane in front of him. He radioed, "You are on fire — eject!" Two of the first three pilots immediately ejected, and their planes crashed. Only one of the planes was on fire.

ZiGGY™

"Clean Up the Mess"

Cecil Mead was working hard at his station in the machine shop
when his supervisor, Ed Jones, turned the corner and asked him to "clean
up the area." "I'm trying to finish this piston job." "Finish it when you
clean up," Ed said.

Thirty minutes later Ed came hurrying up to Cecil as he was cleaning
grease off a machine. "What do you think you're doing, Mead?" "I'm doing
what you told me—cleaning up." "My gosh, delivery is waiting for the
piston to be bored, and you're wiping grease off that machine." "You told
me to clean up this whole area," justified Cecil. "I only meant for you to
sweep up some of the filings from the middle of the floor. I didn't say the
'whole' area. You could have swept up in a couple of minutes."

The problems in these examples occurred because the individuals
involved thought that they knew what common words meant. They
didn't stop to question whether the other person's meaning was different
from their own.

The fallacy is, "Words have meaning." When a word leaves its symbolic use, it serves as the object. But words are not the object. Managers
must remember that people have meanings; words don't. People use

words in an attempt to convey ideas between themselves. Words are different than the things they represent; they are only symbols, arbitrarily chosen to stand in reference for certain things. Words are the product of our experiences (that's why the first automobile was called a "horseless carriage").

Managers can resolve the bypassing problem by concentrating on the person instead of the words, asking people what they mean when their statements are not completely clear, and realizing that a single word can mean numerous things:

- X is the Roman notation for ten.
- X is the mark of illiterate men.
- X is a ruler removed from the throne.
- X is a quantity wholly unknown.
- X may mean xenon, a furious gas.
- X is a ray of similar class.
- Xmas is Christmas, a season of bliss.
- X in a letter is good for a kiss.
- X is for Xerxes, a monarch renowned.
- X marks the spot where the body was found.

The misinterpretation of words is one of the biggest communication problems we encounter. The following real-life example illustrates the importance of realizing that the meaning of words is in people and not the words themselves. People are the containers of meaning, and words only direct others to what we mean.

A Japanese word, *mokusatsum*, may have changed all our lives. It has two meanings: (1) to ignore, (2) to refrain from comment. The release of a press statement using the second meaning in July, 1945, might have ended the war then. The Emperor was ready to end it, and had the power to do so. The cabinet was preparing to accede to the Potsdam ultimatum of the Allies—surrender or be crushed—but wanted a little more time to discuss the terms. A press release was prepared announcing a policy of *mokusatsum*, with the *no comment* implication. But it got on the foreign wires with the *ignore* implication through a mix-up in translation: "The cabinet *ignores* the demand to surrender." To recall the release would have entailed an unthinkable loss of face. Had the intended meaning been publicized, the cabinet might have backed up the Emperor's decision to surrender. In which event, there might have been no atomic bombs over Hiroshima and Nagasaki, no Russian armies in Manchuria, no Korean war to follow. The lives of tens of thousands of Japanese and American boys might have been saved. One word, misinterpreted.[4]

Incompleteness

Words are in a sense the map of the territory that we wish to share with others. A geographical map serves as a representation of a territory, with many details and facts omitted or distorted. When you compare major landmarks to the map that represents them, they fail to agree in size. On a map a river is a blue line no wider than the hatched black lines of a railroad track. Words, likewise, fail to accurately represent objects, events, feelings, and ideas. It is impossible, in fact, to say everything about anything. We can describe much, but we cannot exhaust all of the events and their minute particularities.

The semanticist would tell us to say, "The map is not the thing." Think for a moment about a map for your city. It probably shows streets, blocks, and outlines of parks. It does not give the position of houses, trees, cars, gravel on streets, or potholes in the road. It is impossible to develop a map that can tell everything about your city.

Just as a map cannot give a truly exhaustive view of a city, language does not give a complete view of reality. As individuals we can never see all there is about our city, and so we cannot describe it as it is but only as we perceive it. Since language and reality never conform, we must mentally practice using *etc.*: There is always more that can be said about anything.

Language barriers arise when we become *intentionally* instead of *extensionally* oriented. People who are intentionally oriented are more absorbed in their own subjective maps of the territory than they are in the territory itself. Intentional orientation is based on personal perception and definition instead of real-world observation. When people are extensionally oriented, they first perceive and inspect the territory, and then they construct verbal maps that correspond to the territory. Verification of facts is important to the extensional person. People who practice this orientation have less tendency to take what others say for granted. When people become extensional in their reactions, they look at and observe the territory and life facts first. Then they construct maps (words) that closely correspond to those facts. Look at an object, close your eyes, and then describe the object. That is intentional meaning. Now put a hand over your mouth and point to the object. That is extensional meaning.

Levels of Abstraction

The human nervous system is incapable of getting all possible details on or about any item. We must abstract some details and omit an infinite number of others. The words we use on various levels of abstraction depend on how easily we can see, understand, and then communicate about the object. A typical ladder of abstraction shows the different levels that emerge as we move from specific details to general information.

Managers must be conscious of abstracting, since any given object or event has multiple levels of meaning. When communicating with others, the manager must mentally define from what abstract level the other person is speaking.

Inference Versus Facts

Often in the process of observing the world we draw inferences before we have all the necessary facts. Inferences are constructed so quickly that we seldom reflect on whether they truthfully represent an object or represent it as we would like for it to be.

Read the following case about Joe Zoe, and then answer the questions following the case without referring back to the story. If the answer is true as it relates to the story, check T; if false, check F; if you don't know an answer or need more information, check ?.

A man and wife had their small house thoroughly redecorated—walls, windows, woodwork. At 5 P.M. the decorators left. The man and wife cleaned up the house, locked up their cabinet that contained silverware, and then went to bed. The next morning, they found a window open, the cabinet open, and all the silverware missing. The police were called and subsequently found a set of fingerprints on the window sill. The fingerprints were sent to police headquarters for identification. A reply from headquarters said that the fingerprints on the window sill exactly matched those of a notorious criminal named Joe Zoe.[5]

Questions About the Story

1. The silverware was stolen.	T	F	?
2. Joe Zoe took the silverware.	T	F	?
3. Between the time the house was painted and the window found open, Joe Zoe was in the house.	T	F	?
4. Joe Zoe left his fingerprints on the window sill.	T	F	?

Declarative statements of this nature are made on a regular basis in business: "She didn't return the file"; "He didn't complete the work because he's lazy"; "If you would just listen to me, you would understand me." These sentences give no grammatical indication of whether they are factual or inferred. If we do not have the facts to prove these allegations, and we infer the judgment instead, disagreements in communication will follow. There are five basic ways in which we can distinguish between statements of fact and statements of inference:[6]

Factual Statement	*Inference Statement*
1. Made *following* firsthand experience	1. Made *anytime*—before, during, or after experience
2. Made by the observer	2. Made by anyone
3. Must be limited to what one experienced	3. Can go way beyond what is experienced
4. Statements of fact are limited by experience	4. Statements of inference about experience are unlimited
5. Approaches maximum certainty	5. Approaches only a degree of probability
6. Calls for agreement with those involved in the experience	6. Calls forth disagreement with those involved in the experience

In light of the above information, do you want to change your mind on any of the four questions about the Joe Zoe case? Each of the questions should have been answered with a question mark. They could be true or they could be false; but you did not have enough factual information to answer them. Incidentally, this case is based on the famous Marlboro Jewel Case of Scotland Yard. It is regularly used in police training to make officers sensitive to gathering all facts and not jumping to conclusions. When the crime was finally solved, police found that two criminals were involved. Joe Zoe's partner killed him, cut off his hand, committed the theft, and left Joe Zoe's fingerprints at the scene of the crime.

The Shipping Department Case
Assume that you are a new plant manager touring the factory and you pass by the Shipping Department. As you walk by, you see the scene shown in Fig. 4.3. List both the factual and inferential statements you can make about the picture. After you have recorded several statements, discuss the scene and statements with your classmates.

Factual Statements	**Inferential Statements**
_____	_____
_____	_____
_____	_____
_____	_____

Figure 4.3
Source: Lee and Lee, *Handling Barriers in Communication*, p. 15.

Some inferential statements you could make are: "The young man is whittling wood and not working"; "The employee is lazy"; "The man must not have much to do." We can make several factual statements: "The man is sitting on a box"; "He is whittling wood"; "Boxes are around him"; "A truck is pictured in the doorway"; "The word *straw* is on the barrel."

The Shipping Department Case Facts
It may interest you to know the actual details of this case. It's something that really happened in a shipping department. The boy's job was to pack straw in and around some castings to prevent breakage during shipment. One day a new plant superintendent was making a tour of the plant. He observed young White whittling on a stick. The superintendent immediately walked up to the boy and fired him. The *inference* was that the boy was wasting time whittling on the job. The *fact* was that the boy had discovered he could do a better job of packing if he tamped the straw down with a sharp stick. And that's what he was doing—sharpening a stick to use for the tamping.[7]

To avoid drawing inferences, managers should:

1. Realize that all statements about the future are inferential; anything that deals with hopes, predictions, plans, or prophecy is an inference;

2. Realize that anything that cannot be observed—attitudes and motives of others and information we hear secondhand, even though that information may be a fact for the person telling us—is an inference;

3. Realize that factual statements are based on what we see, know, or experience with all our senses;

4. Ask for more data, if we need it to make factual statements;

5. Label our inferences as such, and try to get other people to do the same.

Summary

Language affects perception, communication patterns, and interpersonal behavior. This process is called social semantics and is the study of meanings between symbols and their referents.

Word usage is the foundation for accurate communication because words are the primary symbols used by man. Each word has basic, complex characteristics that cause some words to have several meanings or two or more words to have one meaning. Some words have no meaning at all. There are technical and nontechnical words and applications for words and specific regional connotations for words.

Major communication conflicts can result from the way we use words. Conflict is frequently the result when people assume that a word can say all there is to say about an object, or when people associate the word and the thing that word represents as being one and the same. A word in itself is incomplete. The meanings of messages are shared by two or more people when words are added to other words and framed within a context.

Many levels of meanings are available for any particular object. Managers who learn to properly abstract items can use words to approximate an accurate description of objects. Word usage is a particular problem when we infer meaning from objects, events, and statements instead of obtaining all the necessary facts and then interpreting them.

Managers should not take words and the symbolic process for granted. Communication will be accurate only when it is preceded by a great deal of thought and reflection.

Key Words

semantics	Aristotelian logic	inference
social semantics	allness	fact
sign	bypassing	intensional
symbol	abstraction	extensional

Review Questions

1. What is the difference between general semantics and social semantics?
2. What is the precise difference between symbols and signs, and what importance do both play in human communication?
3. Describe the three parts of Aristotelian logic and how it affects language.
4. Describe with examples the six basic characteristics of words.
5. Cite a personal example of the "allness" problem and how it interferes with communication.
6. What does it mean when we contend that "the word is not the thing"? How can a person prevent this misconception from occurring?
7. Use words to draw a verbal map of your campus or workplace. Is the picture complete or incomplete? Tell why.
8. Often in arguments and general statements, we base opinions on inferences instead of facts. Give an example of how this occurs and how it can be prevented.

Exercises

1. In your public or school library conduct a search for material that describes linguistic and semantic problems. The information may be found in stories or articles like the ones used in this chapter or in cartoons. Take the material to your next class, and share it with the instructor and your classmates.
2. Think for a few minutes about the problems that sometimes develop because of word usage or the assumed meaning of the words. Share results of the following instructions with your instructor and classmates.

   • Make a list of problem situations you have been in where misunderstanding occurred because there were two words with one meaning or two meanings for one word.
   • Give some examples where the use of technical words caused problems in understanding something about people.
   • In your travels or experiences you have probably noticed regional differences in word usage. Cite some examples of regional words that can cause misunderstanding.

3. While you are at the library, look up the yearbooks for several encyclopedias. Those yearbooks often list new words that have recently been added to various dictionaries. Make a list of several words that have only recently been officially recognized as dictionary words. Share this information with your instructor and classmates.

References

1. Anatol Rapoport, "What Is Semantics?," in *Et cetera*, Vol. X, No. 1, International Society for General Semantics. Reprinted by permission.
2. Don Fabun, *Communication: The Transfer of Meaning* (Beverly Hills, Calif.: Glenco Press, 1968), p. 27.
3. *Dallas Morning News*, March 3, 1976, p. 76. Reprinted by permission.
4. Stuart Chase, "Everybody's Talking," in *Power of Words* (New York: Harcourt, Brace & Co., 1953), pp. 4–5.
5. Irving J. Lee and Laura L. Lee, *Handling Barriers in Communication* (New York: Harper & Row, 1957), p. 11. Copyright © 1956, by Laura L. Lee.
6. *Ibid.*, p. 13.
7. *Ibid.*, p. 15.

C H A P T E R 5

. . . .

. . . .

. . . .

. . . .

An Organization's Communication Climate, Flow, and Loops: The Third Hurdle

Introduction

Structure helps an organization meet its goals productively. Those goals are accomplished by employees who have been directed and motivated by management. The high degree of understanding required for successful direction and motivation is best achieved through a sound two-way communication policy that is developed and supported by all management.

The AT&T Story
In the early 1900s Arthur W. Page, as the vice-president for public relations at American Telephone and Telegraph Company (AT&T), established a management philosophy of corporate employee communications that became a model for the organizational world. He based this philosophy on five essentials:

1. The top management of an organization has responsibilities to analyze its overall relationship to the publics it serves and to constantly look for changes in the desires and needs of the publics.

2. Every organization needs a system to inform employees about the general policies and practices of the company.

3. The organization needs a system to equip contact employees with the needed skills to function politely and efficiently with the public and continued incentives to reinforce these qualities through pay and promotions.

4. Each organization needs a system that ensures that employee and public questions and criticisms flow through the organizational levels and reach top management.

5. Each organization needs to tell the public frankly about its operations, practices, and policies through advertising, official statements, speeches, and other forms of communication.[1]

With the help of the model established by Page, AT&T developed a system to help it communicate with employees and the public. This system was the foundation of AT&T's corporate communication program and existed until its reorganization in 1983–84. In the early 1900s the Bell System employees interfaced frequently with the public as telephone operators, installer repairmen, and service representatives, and the AT&T image became synonymous with communication. AT&T operators were taught to smile when talking over the phone with a customer; soon they became "the voice with a smile."

AT&T also showed the business world that informed employees have high morale and are thus good ambassadors to the public. As Page put it, "People who believe in their organization are proud of what they are doing when they touch the public. . . . [They] are the best advocates they can be."[2]

In the typical organization, communication occurs in a variety of oral, written, and nonverbal ways: daily meetings, sales forecasts, manuals and documents, letters, and telephone conversations. Even titles, signs, and office locations communicate messages.

In defining organizational communication Greenbaum uses a broad approach and states that "it is important to look at communication in organizations as a process by which people work with and through others to mutually accomplish organizational objectives. According to this theory, organizational communication is considered to be the sum of a group of communication networks with each network being related to one or more of the major organizational goals."[3] He places communication activities into four major networks (the types of activities and the numbers of participants involved are outlined in Table 5.1):

Table 5.1 • Internal Verbal Communication Activities Classified by Number of Participants and Communication Network Objectives

Number of Participants	Regulative Network	Innovative Network	Integrative-Maintenance Network	Informative-Instructive Network
Interpersonal (2 persons)	Supervisor directions and requests Supervisor-subordinate appraisal meetings Job descriptions and standards Annual appraisal Special problem sessions Reports on operations Memoranda	Ad hoc problem resolution Supervisor-subordinate idea development meetings Annual goals determination in work-planning program Informal get-togethers as in-house lunch meetings Reports on visits to other organizations, conventions, seminars	President's welcome letter to new employee Grievance discussion Progress review in work-planning program Annual appraisal Informal meeting of two organization members Superior-subordinate informal conversation on personal matters	Hiring interview New employee orientation Memoranda Oral and written reports Cross-functioning
Small-group (3 to 10 persons)	Meetings: directors, executive committee, departmental; crisis-type meeting as in fire, flood, strike	Meetings: directors, executive committee, departmental, inter-departmental, problem-solving sales development, crisis-type, budget, group lunch	Meetings: participative work-group, interdepartmental, coffee-break, group lunch	Meetings Training in small group
Organization-wide	Organization plans Policy statements Standard procedures Regulations Union contract Chart of organization Staff memos	Suggestion program Problem-finding program Operations audit reports as to general and specific areas of the organization	In-house publications Holiday social function "The grapevine" Literature available to personnel concerning plans, etc. President's talk to all employees Supervisory staff meeting	In-house publications Bulletin-board notices Staff meetings Employee information booklets Benefits brochure Statements of standard procedures Union contract Organization policy statements "The grapevine"

Source: Howard H. Greenbaum and Noel D. White, "Biofeedback at the Organizational Level: The Communication Audit," *The Journal of Business Communication* (Summer 1976), p. 8. Reprinted by permission.

1. *Regulative or task-related networks* allow for goal accomplishment through coordination of plans.
2. *Innovative networks* allow problem-solving, idea-sharing, strategy-development, and implementation processes to be discussed.
3. *Integrative-maintenance networks* encompass employee morale and social factors within the organization. The flow of communication is often informal yet highly visible in its activity and rewards.
4. *Informative-instructive networks* deal with the regular information that employees need to properly complete their jobs.[4]

Communications can be labeled according to their network functions. Communication barriers can be limited if the various network activities and their functions can be identified, if the level at which the form of communication occurs can be determined, and if the effectiveness of the message can be evaluated. Examining the communication climate is one of the first places to start breaking down communication barriers.

The Communication Climate

The communication climate is the degree to which an organization allows and encourages a free flow of ideas and information between employees. What is the communication climate like in your organization? The answers you give to the following questions will help you determine whether it is healthy or unhealthy:

1. Do you generally get enough information from the other people at work (including superiors, subordinates, and peers) to do your job properly?
2. Do you generally get more information than is needed to do your job?
3. Does the information usually come when you need it, not when it's too late to be fully useful to you?
4. Is information generally clear, relevant, accurate, and consistent?
5. As a rule, do you know where to turn for information?
6. Can you get information from other people easily, without having to press them for it?
7. Do other people at work usually give you information directly and officially, or "through the grapevine"?[5]

There are three key components to a healthy climate: the *quantity* of the information shared between employees, the *quality* of the content, which determines how well it accomplishes the purpose, and the number and nature of *channels* available for relaying information.

Quantity of Information

The climate is usually considered favorable if the quantity of information is adequate for people to perform their jobs with sufficient knowledge, understanding, and confidence.

Too little information exchanged between employees can be frustrating and confusing and can lead to errors and incomplete results, which, in turn, can generate mistrust of superiors and colleagues who one feels are sending nonverbal messages by withholding information. If this occurs between departments, it produces feelings of isolation and generally leads to an "us against them" rivalry. In areas of production and finance the lack of information leads to extremely costly errors.

Too much information is also a problem. If needed but given in abundance, it produces feelings of mental overload. If the abundance is delivered sparingly instead of evenly it contributes to the same feelings of overload. If the information arrives in the form of company propaganda, it can tarnish an employee's perception of the company and make him or her wonder why the organization is "wasting" so much money.

Exchanging information too late can create costly errors, require work to be redone, is frustrating to the receiver, and can tarnish the sender's credibility. If this is a habitual problem, the receiver, who needs the information, may alter work behavior to the point that other individuals and departments are affected and the entire organization suffers.

Quality of Information

Sources of quality information can be found from the top to the bottom of an organization. From an employee's perspective, however, the most important sources of information are the following: subordinates, colleagues, immediate supervisor, top management, middle management, department meetings, and the grapevine.

Channels of Information

Information is exchanged in organizations through two channels: vertical (downward and upward) and horizontal (from side to side, peer to peer, and department to department). Two requirements must be met for channels to successfully support the quantity and quality of information

Source: Cartoon based on cartoon that originally appeared in *Systemation*, January 15, 1959. Published by Systemation, North America, Denver, Colorado. Used by permission.

needed in a thriving organization: They exist where they are n
necessary; employees who need to use them have easy access to them.[6]
Employees who need information or want to send information but cannot
find channels through which to do so become threatened and fearful, lack
trust, and look to others (often inappropriate people or the grapevine) for
help.

Effective channels of communication that exist directly between individuals are called *formal channels*, as opposed to the indirect, underground, *informal grapevine*. As the cartoon shows, the channels that a
company believes exist are not always the ones that employees use.

Formal Communication Flow

Communication flows in three directions within the typical organization: downward, upward, and horizontally.

Downward Communication

Messages and information sent from top management to subordinates
comprise the downward flow. On organizational charts the flow normally
follows the formal lines of authority downward from position to position.

The downward flow is the strongest of the three directions. Management has the power to put messages in motion and start them on their
downward journey. Yet messages are sometimes not received, arrive distorted, arrive too late, or are not sent at all.

When asked to define the objective of business communication
within their organization, most managers respond with, "keeping employees informed on issues that pertain to our company." With such a
system in place, management can spell out company objectives, change
employee attitudes, mold opinions, help adjustments to change, and diminish employee fears and suspicions. A study by the consulting firm of
Towers, Perrin, Forster & Crosby (TPF&C) indicates the many things
that employees want to hear from their company:

> The kinds of things that modern, multi-faceted people want to know
> about reflect an awareness that they and their jobs are parts of larger
> things. They want to know how their firm is doing financially; what
> profits mean and how they relate to the economy as a whole; why layoffs
> occur; what their organization's product or service means to consumers,
> the environment, and the economy; what the firm is doing about equal
> treatment for different age, sex, and racial groups; how pay is determined;
> why improved productivity is important to them; and how to respond
> when their firm is attacked by outsiders.

If the information supplied by the organization is unsatisfactory in quality, amount, or timeliness, today's employees will find out what they want to know from other sources: the grapevine, the union, the mass media. Then they'll act in one or more of their guises. They may buy more stock, or sell what they have; they may buy a case of the company's product, or boycott it; they may write letters to the editor supporting the firm's position on public issues, or call for a government takeover; they may dismiss a union organization attempt, or they may sign the organization card and return it promptly to the union. But they *will* act, and management's communications philosophy and expertise will have a lot to do with the way they act.[7]

According to Katz and Kahn downward communication in an organization usually encompasses the following:

1. Job descriptions and instruction regarding specific employee tasks and methodology;
2. Policy rationale that explains why and how the tasks fit the company's overall objectives;
3. Straight information on the company's past, present, and future along with explanations about policies, practices, and procedures;
4. Job performance evaluations that focus on how well a person is doing the job;
5. Company ideology designed to make employees respect, support, and work for continued company and product success.[8]

Reasons for Poor Downward Communication

There are five common reasons for poor downward communication.

Growth causes isolation. Many companies at their start-up are small enough for face-to-face contact between management and subordinates. With growth, however, more formal lines become established, and soon individuals isolate themselves. Messages go to the wrong people, are late in being sent, and sometimes are not sent at all.

Clearly defined objectives are missing. Management is sometimes confused over information that it thinks that subordinates need and want to know. This confusion is seldom audited or clarified by useful communication. Most companies constantly update both long-term and short-term goals, yet they pay little attention to clarifying their objectives about how to communicate these goals, useful information, and important issues to all people in the company.

Management never audits present communication techniques. Habits are established when people communicate in the same way for long periods of time. Management may never audit its style of communicating with subordinates and so will never learn whether its communication is received, is understandable, or is adequate and timely. A written memo may be automatically issued when a face-to-face conversation would be more appropriate.

Confusion arises over who is responsible for communicating. Top-level management may feel that middle-level or first-line supervisors should be responsible for issuing certain information, while those in lower positions may feel that it is top-level management's responsibility to communicate downward to all the employees.

Segregation exists between supervisory and nonsupervisory personnel. Unspoken norms can segregate management and nonmanagement personnel. This usually starts when management is held responsible for making decisions that affect the entire organization. A nonparticipatory management style may isolate management from the wants and needs of subordinates.

As the formal leader of an organization the chief executive officer is responsible for making sure that the internal communication lines are open and working. Another report by TPF&C indicates that the problems of poor downward communication often start with the person at the top of the organizational chart—the CEO.

- CEOs usually have limited direct, personal contact with employees of their organizations; generally, they communicate regularly only with those who report directly to them.
- Although CEOs and top managers usually blame breakdowns in downward communications on middle managers and/or supervisors, the problems usually start—through distortion, delay, omission of information—at the higher levels and mushroom at each successively lower level.
- CEOs, top managers, and middle managers usually acknowledge a need for improved downward communication to employees, but they are not usually as aware as first-line supervisors of how inadequate communication to employees often is.
- CEOs believe that upward communication from their top managers is good but emphasize that too many problems are withheld from them until situations reach the "disaster" stage.
- CEOs generally consider the communication of hard facts, particularly financial information, and the creation of a favorable public image to be their most important and attainable communications goals. Most haven't thought much about a philosophy or a set of objectives for employee communications.
- Upward communication to the CEO level tends to be most effective when managers at each organizational level are held responsible for effective communications performance.[9]

The same TPF&C report reveals that the most credible source of information within an organization is the organization's lowest-ranking employee. The report cites examples of the different perceptions between management and employees:

Management says:	1. We are concerned about employees.
Employees say:	1. Management couldn't care less.
Management says:	2. Our employees believe us.
Employees say:	2. We don't believe a word they say.
Management says:	3. Profits haven't been high enough to warrant any unnecessary frills.
Employees say:	3. This outfit is really swimming in dollars. The president makes $300,000 a year, and we just built a lush headquarters building.[10]

When employees of an organization hold such beliefs, the programs of pay, benefits, and communications do not work. The burden of the problem's solution must be placed on the CEO and top management:

Employees at all levels want to hear from you. They want to hear your views, hopes, and aspirations, just as much as they want you to hear theirs. Employee communication really is *everyone's* job—but the tone and substance of that communication must come from the top.[11]

Methods for Improving the Downward Flow

There are three ways that favorable downward communication can be implemented. First is the establishment of *objectives* for both the intended message that a manager wishes to communicate and the overall flow of communication downward within the organization. Second, the *content* of the message is important. Chase lists six content qualities of a manager's message:

1. *It must be accurate.* That is, the message must be a true report, be it good or bad concerning information about the company. . . .
2. *It must be both definite and specific in meaning.* . . .
3. *It must be forceful,* i.e., the message must be stated in a way to show that management carries a firm conviction for any actions taken which may affect the company. . . .
4. *It must suit the occasion and must be receiver-oriented.* The message must be stated in such a way that subordinates will have no trouble understanding how it directly affects them. . . .
5. *It should not contain complexities, but be stated as simply as possible.* The contents of the message should be transmitted in such a way that the recipient will understand and be able to grasp it quickly. . . .

6. *Finally, it should contain no hidden meaning.* A message may have one meaning under certain circumstances and another under different circumstances.[12]

The third way in which favorable downward communication can be implemented is to consider the *technique* with which the message is sent. Is individual face-to-face contact better than small group meetings, telephone conversations, or written forms?

Management does have a responsibility for keeping employees informed on issues, for building pride in the organization and its products, and for gaining employee acceptance and support of organization policies and goals. This downward flow of communication is nevertheless only one-third of the communication needs that a manager must oversee and nurture. To complete the organizational communication loop, upward and horizontal flows must also be established and working.

Upward Communication

Bruce Harriman, a former vice-president of New England Telephone, makes an interesting point about downward communication:

> Communications in a hierarchical society or organization work according to the principle that governs gravity. Downward communications are usually better than anyone realizes and frequently more accurate than those at higher levels want them to be. Conversely, upward communications have to be pumped and piped, with a minimum of filters, in order to be effective.[13]

Upward communication flows from subordinates to superiors. In a study of seventy-five companies in the United States and Canada, Harriman found the following disappointing information about upward communication: "We encountered no experts, studies, or programs on upward communication. Most corporate communications programs dealt with downward communications, and the few that were aimed upward were individual techniques, such as employee suggestion plans, methods for answering questions, or ways of letting off steam."[14]

Curley explains the importance of establishing an "upward" communication loop in management:

> An effective business communication program is not only one which "speaks," but also one which "listens." . . . [I]t has a two-way orientation. Employee publications, defined procedures, speeches to the work force, orientations and effective day-to-day work direction can handle the

"speak" half of the communication loop; but how about the "listen" half of the loop? Is it really necessary? If so, how can it be accomplished? The "listen" dimension takes on considerable importance if the organization wants the loyalty and complete support of its people.[15]

Reasons for Poor Upward Communication

Size and complexity of an organization. The larger the organization the more common the barriers to upward flows of communication. This is especially true at the ground-floor levels of the organization.

Unrealistic assumptions. Often, assumptions about the organization, employees, and the in-place communication process create enormous problems. Eisenmann and Hughes comment on this factor:

> We often send messages out through the organization with the assumption that all people are listening and understanding exactly the way we intended. Many managers presume their communiques are penetrating the minds of their employees but never bother to check. In reality, there is often a serious gap between the message sent and the one received. The amount of time and money spent on employee communications, directed from management to the people, generally exceeds tenfold the amount spent on listening to people and getting feedback about the effectiveness of the management process as perceived by the members of the organization.[16]

Filtering and distortion. Each step in the upward flow of communication within an organization allows for a filtering and consequential distortion of messages. Such filtering easily occurs when management perceives that everything is positive but in reality there is tremendous employee unrest.

Fear of presenting bad news. In some companies middle management has learned to respond promptly and effectively to actions they perceive to be of personal interest to top management. Sometimes this is inadvertent; sometimes it is self-serving. There is a tendency to delay sending bad news in hope that the problem will be resolved or eliminated before those above must be told or involved.

Step-loss sequence. As information flows upward from one level to the next, meaning is distorted and filtered intentionally and unintentionally. This is partly due to limited knowledge of the total organization and its specific problems. Added to this are managers who are fearful of having subordinates receive credit for ideas and accomplishments that could make the manager look weak, unproductive, or uncreative.

Superior-subordinate relationship. Two factors discourage upward communication in the superior/subordinate relationship:

1. *Fear of punishment* can cause subordinates to conceal or distort their feelings, important information, or disclosure of problems and potential solutions. Gemmill comments on the ramifications of this action:

> Decisions by subordinates not to disclose such information results in a superior being unaware of how his actions affect them. This lack of feedback may prevent him from changing his managerial style or from correcting misconceptions on their part. Similarly, he is put in a position where he is unable to share knowledge with them that might lead to improvements in their performance. Perhaps most important, however, from a manager's perspective is that this lack of communication may cut him off from some essential information.[17]

2. *Belief that emotions should not be displayed* can cause a subordinate to hold back feelings, opinions, and matters that he or she would otherwise like to talk over with a superior. If such emotions are aired, the person expressing them will probably experience some feelings of guilt and anxiety regarding the superior's perception of his or her strength and ability to do the job.

Bottlenecks. Several types of bottlenecks to the effective flow of information have been discovered:

1. *The gatekeeper* is usually the second in command. This person can be a secretary or administrative assistant. They filter the information they receive and pass on only what they think their superior should know. In the illustration the subordinates have to trust the gatekeeper to pass their information upward.

2. *The status seeker* hordes information that he or she receives and uses it for personal benefit. This person is fearful that divulging it would make others his or her equal.

3. *The promotion rival* keeps information that could help others receive faster advancement in the organization.

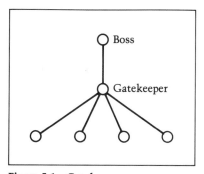

Figure 5.1 • Gatekeeper

4. *The department competitor* wants his or her work group to look better and be more productive than other departments. Consequently he or she withholds information that might help other departments.

Ice jams. The blockage problems in the upward communication flow have also been referred to as an ice jam:

> What can be done about the blockages? Not a great deal, unless the main effort to break up the ice jam comes from the same source that started it.
>   The breaking of the jam can be accomplished by some or all of the following techniques: empathetic listening, question-and-answer columns in employee publications, small group meetings, suggestion systems, real "open door" policies, ombudsman programs, participative decision making, attitude surveys, and communication audits. The common denominator among all of these should be a managerial attitude that is *actively* cognizant and supportive of employees' innate desires to know, to participate, to understand, and to contribute.[18]

According to a study by Elizabeth and Francis Jennings the basic remedy for unfreezing the flow requires a manager to gain insight into his or her own thoughts and feelings before attempting to gain insight into an employee's thoughts and feelings:

> It may be that the executive does not understand his function; it may be that he fears the responsibilities he has assumed, that he does not value people and so misuses them, that he is afraid he will lose his power, that he needs training—but any of these statements can be reduced to this: he is unaware of himself. If the executive were aware of himself in relation to others, he would make an attempt to alter his behavior.[19]

Methods for Improving Poor Upward Communication

While each company must determine the best upward communication techniques that can be implemented to meet employee needs, several suggested methods are used today:[20]

1. *Cracker-barrel sessions* are conducted periodically so that employees can ask for information and their supervisor can provide it.
2. *Operational reviews* occur when managers visit the work stations of the people they manage and review problems and hindrances for successful completion of the work.
3. *Suggestion boxes* are still found in many companies and ideas are forwarded to the appropriate persons.
4. *In-company educational courses* are often designed where written assign-

ments allow employees to express their thoughts and ideas to instructors, who then channel them to appropriate top-level officials.

5. *Task teams* consist of nonmanagement personnel who serve on panels to identify problems and possible solutions. This information is then forwarded to management for responses.

6. *Employee annual meetings* resemble stockholder meetings where top management solicits and answers questions asked by company employees.

7. *Junior boards of directors* are made up of several middle managers and subordinates who develop policy recommendations that are presented to the corporate board.

8. *Corps of counselors or ombudsmen* are often located throughout an organization and are accessible to employees as liaisons.

9. *Subordinates are included in meetings* when information is needed that only a specialist might have. Those subordinates should be included in management meetings to answer questions and serve as resources.

10. *Subordinates make presentations to top management* and describe the responsibilities of their jobs.

11. *Employee audits* reveal how employees feel about their jobs and the company.

Horizontal Communication

Communication in a lateral or diagonal manner within the charted organization is referred to as *horizontal*. This is the most frequent flow of communication because individuals at the same level talk to each other constantly about work-related events, management, and personal matters. Lewis estimates that two-thirds of the organizational communication flow is horizontal.[21]

Work-related communication revolves around formal tasks and goals that are vital to the organization. The personal, informal communication is part of the social/emotional needs that all people must maintain while working closely together for long periods of time.

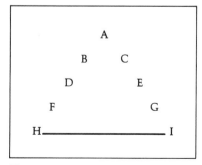

Figure 5.2 • Horizontal Communication Distance in an Organization

The shape of the organizational structure symbolizes that employees at the bottom have a greater need for information and a wider gap to fill than those at the top. Henri Fayol described this in his bridge for horizontal communication. We can also see the wasted time and energy if H had to communicate to G or I but had to go up through the different levels and then have the message go back down from A through G before the sending was complete.

When the types of messages passed among individuals on this plane are task related, they encompass ways to coordinate work, solve problems, share information, and resolve conflicts, and they cover such areas as production, sales, personnel, purchasing, and finance. Kelley describes a study of a textile mill where supervisor communication patterns were influenced by technology.[22]

Professor Richard L. Simpson, a sociologist at the University of North Carolina, conducted a survey of eight supervisors in the spinning department of a synthetic textile mill in order to test the hypothesis that "work-related communications between officials are more often vertical than horizontal."

The method employed by the researcher was a structured but open-ended interview procedure. The question put to the supervisors was: "About how often do you talk with ——— on business? Don't include times when you just say hello or pass the time of day; just the contacts needed to get your work done. . . . What kinds of things do you talk about with him?" Some of the findings and interpretations were:

The contacts of the three men at the higher levels—A, B-1, and B-2 (see Figure 5.3)—were overwhelmingly vertical, but they could hardly have been otherwise. A, being the only man at his level, could not possibly have any horizontal contacts. B-1 and B-2 could communicate horizontally only with each other, but they could communicate downward with several foremen and upward with A. They seldom had to communicate with each other, since the work relations between their sections were coordinated mainly through horizontal contact between their subordinates. . . .

On the C-foreman level most contacts were horizontal except those of C-3. . . . Three of these five foremen—C-1, C-2, and C-5—had markedly fewer vertical and more horizontal contacts than would have occurred on the chance expectations that every man communicates equally with every other man. The contacts of C-4 were mainly horizontal, in about the same proportion as would be expected on the basis of chance. . . .

The preponderance of horizontal communications reported by four of the five first-line foremen (level C) is understandable if we examine the content of the communications they reported. Very few communications involved the issuing of commands or the reporting of results—the stan-

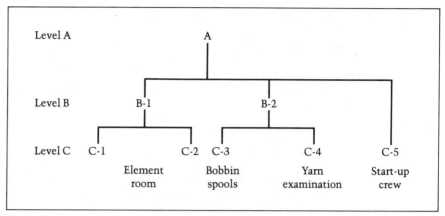

Figure 5.3 • Organization Chart of Spinning Department Supervisors

Source: R.L. Simpson, "Vertical and Horizontal Communication in Formal Organizations," *Administrative Science Quarterly*, Vol. 4 (September 1959), pp. 188–196.

dard types of vertical communications. Most contacts of men at level C involved either (1) joint problem-solving or (2) coordination of work flow between sections. These were mainly horizontal communications. . . .

It is noteworthy that they [the level-C men] worked out these problems without consulting or informing their superior.

The findings neither confirmed nor rejected the hypothesis but led to a modified hypothesis:

Mechanization reduces the need for close supervision (vertical communication), since instead of the foreman the machines set the work pace; but automation (i.e., extreme mechanization) increases the need for vertical communication, to deal with the frequent and serious machine breakdowns.

The horizontal flow also is a place where subordinates evaluate their superiors in areas of skill, attitudes, values, personality, problem solving, planning, and organizing. Messages transmitted at this level are important to a supervisor because they serve as feedback on how well he or she is managing. The information, however, is rarely given in person and is usually transmitted through the grapevine.

Reasons for Poor Horizontal Communication

Departmentalization is the biggest barrier to horizontal communication. There are increased numbers of people and messages to deal with on this plane, so departmental rivalries develop and vibrations from the created friction can be felt even at the top of the organization.

Personality clashes and conflicts between employees are common and are more often felt in the horizontal flow of messages. These clashes and conflicts may be the result of suppressed facts, of one person's possession of material that another person needs, or of one person's general dislike for another.

Methods for Improving Horizontal Communication

1. *Construct realistic organization charts.* The organizational chart that shows both the formal and informal structure can enhance the flow of communication. True authority relationships should also be noted. This saves guesswork on the part of employees.

2. *Individual job descriptions should be accurate.* Each employee should know precisely what he or she is to do and how it is to be done. Such descriptions should also list the authority that is delegated to each employee and supervisor and the vertical and horizontal channels of communication that should be followed.

3. *Organize and utilize interdepartmental projects.* Individuals in groupings and departments should communicate before their communication is sent to others. Such projects cut down on interdepartmental competition and open the flow of communication within the entire organization.

4. *Encourage regular meetings and communication.* If departments and divisions within an organization establish regular times for meetings, there is less use of the grapevine and a greater sense of organizational loyalty. While it is not practical to demand that each subordinate communicate regularly with every other subordinate, it is vital that access to other employees be available and that needed communication be adequate.

5. *Model proper communication usage.* As Strickland et al. describe, there are several skills that can be taught:

> Conflict management is certainly a valuable one. Considerable time and energy can be wasted through conflicts which are not resolved effectively. If managers and supervisors can model effective conflict resolution, subordinates can pick it up without much difficulty.
>
> In addition, managers and supervisors can teach subordinates management skills, planning skills, and so on. The point to remember is that subordinates learn the most from you by what is demonstrated in addition to what is said. Consistent good modeling is the best way to teach skills of any kind.[23]

Informal Communication Flow
The Grapevine

While communication flows formally in a vertical and horizontal manner within an organization, there is also an informal manner in which it can be charted. Some say that it starts in the rumor mill, which implies that rumors, or gossip (which is unconfirmed and generally not based on knowledge), is processed like grain in a mill on a regular basis. Does this occur? According to Lewis, "Managers should be aware . . . that a number of organization studies show that almost five out of every six messages are carried by the grapevine instead of the official organization channels."[24]

The *grapevine* is "an unofficial, confidential, person-to-person chain of verbal communication."[25] The term originated during the Civil War when telegraph lines were hung from trees and resembled grapevines. The messages sent over them were usually garbled, and so all rumors were said to be from the grapevine.

The grapevine is an informal, underground network that channels communication both within and outside an organization. A message may start in the rumor mill, but the grapevine keeps it alive. Whenever people come together, a grapevine develops. Many managers prefer that it be destroyed; they consider rumors to be untrue, malicious, and harmful to personnel and the organization. They view the grapevine with considerable caution and discount much of what they hear from it.

According to Keith Davis, however, whose research has given us much of the knowledge that we currently have on the corporate grapevine, the grapevine is "a natural, normal part of a company's total communications system and is no more evil in itself than pain or the weather. It is also a significant force within the work group, helping to build teamwork, motivate people, and create corporate identity."[26]

Facts About the Grapevine

1. *The grapevine spreads information faster than most formal systems.* With the help of the grapevine, messages can be received before they are formally issued or even prepared. The fast pace is uncanny, as the following example shows:

> One company . . . signed its labor contract at 11:00 P.M. and had to keep its publications staff busy all night in order to have a suitable bulletin ready for employees arriving at work the following morning. It was the

only way that the company could match the grapevine's speed and forestall undesirable rumors about the agreement.[27]

2. *The grapevine can complement the formal flow of communication.* Both the formal and informal flows of communication allow information to be sent and received in ways that meet the needs of all employees.

3. *The grapevine can destroy the effectiveness of the formal system.* If employees elect to use the grapevine because they distrust formal channels or because they believe that their message will not be conveyed accurately or the receiver will not listen, the formal system will eventually be rendered inoperative.

4. *The grapevine does not follow the official channels.* While the formal communication flow significantly follows the organizational chart and the chain of command, the grapevine does not follow official channels. As Korda states:

> There are various ways in which news, or rumor, travels. It works something like a river system: there is invariably a headwater of mysterious origin, then a mainstream from which tributaries branch off to every department. Once you have traced the main river to its source, it is perfectly possible to pick up whatever news you want from the tributaries—the water is the same.[28]

Informal Communication Chains

Like the river, the grapevine is considerably more flexible than the formal flow. In his research Davis found four paths for informal communication (see Figure 5.4).

The single-strand chain. In this chain **A** talks to **B**, who then tells **C**, who tells **D**, and finally each person in the system hears the message. Most people picture this type of chain when they think of how the grapevine distorts and filters information beyond the point of being recognizable. Indeed, the statement that **K** will receive will probably be completely different from that started by **A**.

The gossip chain. Here **A** shares the message with everyone available. The length of the lines, however, will vary. This indicates the degree of trust, gullibility, or interest on the part of either **A** or the various receivers. If **A** believes **C** wants more explanation of the story than **B**, **A** will spend more time giving **C** the story or will add more to the story.

The probability chain. Because of the law of probability it is conceivable that when **A** tells **F** and **D**, they will then pass the message on to a

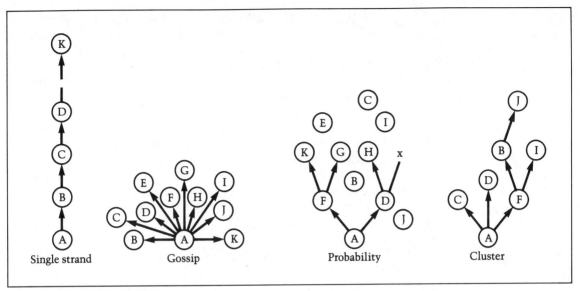

Figure 5.4

Source: Keith Davis, "Management Communication and the Grapevine," *Harvard Business Review* (January/February, 1953), p. 46. Reprinted by permission.

select group. Organizations often use this method to test the response of employees regarding new policies or changes the company may contemplate making. Knowing that several individuals will hear and respond, they can then wait for an indication of how best to proceed.

The cluster chain. This chain contains a degree of surety that the probability chain does not have. **A** tells two or three select individuals who in turn tell others. According to Davis's research this chain is probably the most used in organizations. Here a company can use the grapevine in a productive way. A supervisor can plant a rumor to person **A**, knowing that **A** takes coffee breaks and eats lunch with **C**, **D**, and **F**. Since **F** carpools with **B** and **I**, they will usually be told as the message is discharged throughout the cluster.

Methods for Controlling Grapevine Influence

In seeking to make the organizational communication system as effective as possible, there are several things a manager can do to combat the grapevine influence:

1. *Do not try to suppress the grapevine.* Since the grapevine often flourishes because employees feel they cannot exchange information freely, seek to destroy the ice jam in the formal flow of communication. This will lessen the pressure on the grapevine.

2. *Control openness.* Some managers try to control the grapevine by being "completely open" about problems or situations the company is encountering. This is not always practical. If information cannot be shared until tough decisions are made or remedies are found, be honest about it. This may not cut the amount of talk in the grapevine, but it is better than indiscriminate sharing that can increase employee speculation.

3. *Limit the attempt to seek subversion.* A company can often successfully fight a rumor by disproving it and turning it back on itself. But the task is also time consuming, and obvious fighting tends to give more credence to the rumors.

4. *Tell the truth as soon as possible.* Davis found that the greatest spread of information occurs immediately after it is known and that more people feed the grapevine when their friends and work associates are involved.[29] For this reason, on matters of firings, promotions, layoffs, and so forth, employees need to know the true story as quickly as possible. If they don't receive it from the company, they will fill in the gaps with rumors.

5. *Effective formal communication systems, good subordinate/superior relationships, and a healthy climate prevent the grapevine's destructive tendencies.* The supervisor must get to know his or her employees and understand their needs and problems, their attitudes and values, and their perceptions of the company and job. If a supervisor sees gaps in what employees want and need to know, and in what they are receiving, he or she should move quickly to supply the information.

If you question why the grapevine flourishes, examine the communication that takes place within your own office. Davis found that the relationship between secretary and boss is a major indicator of the extent of fuel for the grapevine: "[T]he secretary plays a key role as liaison agent in the grapevine. Since she processes her boss's correspondence, greets visitors, makes appointments, and often acts as her employer's confidante, she is strategically located as a communication center in the work system and is the one most likely to feed the grapevine."[30]

6. *Educate employees to the deleterious effects of the grapevine.* You can maximize the potential benefits of the grapevine and minimize its deleterious effects by educating employees to the care and cultivation of the grapevine. Freeman describes the process taken by Xerox:

a. *Begin by setting up a one-day workshop* consisting of 10–12 first and second line managers from different work units. These are the people furthest away from "what's really happening," yet usually called upon first to validate or debunk information.

b. *Use an external resource as a workshop leader* to minimize the appearance that is just another attempt by "management" to control the news.

c. *Start off by acknowledging the existence* of the grapevine. Review both its positive and negative effects. Explain its function and purpose.

d. *Develop examples of its use and abuse* in the organization. Have specific instances available as case study material for initial review. Then undertake a workshop exercise which assures that each individual describes personally how he has used the system.

e. *Establish an action plan* which will allow these managers to communicate about the grapevine with their people on the job. Particular attention should be given to techniques which will allow the grapevine to function in a controlled, constructive fashion.[31]

Communication Loops

Formally, the vertical dimension of communication within an organization flows downward and upward; the horizontal dimension also fits into the formal category. Informally, each organization has a variety of grapevines. Another aspect of organizational communication is the communication loop. Unlike the available directions in which information can flow, communication loops depend on personalities and the working conditions of small groups for their existence.

The term *communication loops* originated in the work of DiSalvo et al.: "When we talk about communication loops existing in the organization, we are talking about people being linked together in permanent or temporary loops as the organization works toward achieving multiple goals. Many times the effectiveness and efficiency of a loop will be determined by the people that make up the loop."[32] Katz and Kahn developed five characteristics of communication loops:[33]

1. *Size.* The size of a loop is determined by the number of people in an organization, the amount of distance between people, and, most important, by the number of individuals who need to receive and pass particular types of information. See Figure 5.5 for an example. According to DiSalvo, "Many are operating simultaneously, some operate continually, and others operate at different times throughout the work day. The makeup, size, and shape of the communication loop depends on the task at hand and the employees involved in the task."[34] Managers sometimes

can incorrectly perceive the "real" communication loop. In Figure 5.5 Mary never gets her message either to Ed or to Linda. The reason? Bill forgets to tell Ed, and William thinks Linda doesn't really need the information.

2. *Transmission technique.* When messages are passed between people, the information is either echoed or modified as it passes through the loop. In the *echo approach* the same message is given to each person; these messages can be notices on bulletin boards, printed policy statements, reports, memos, etc. In the *modified approach* information is changed somewhat as it is given, usually verbally, to different individuals: "[W]hat typically happens is that as the message passes through the multiple links in the loop, through different people, the message changes so that when it reaches its destination, it is no longer the 'same' message that was sent."[35]

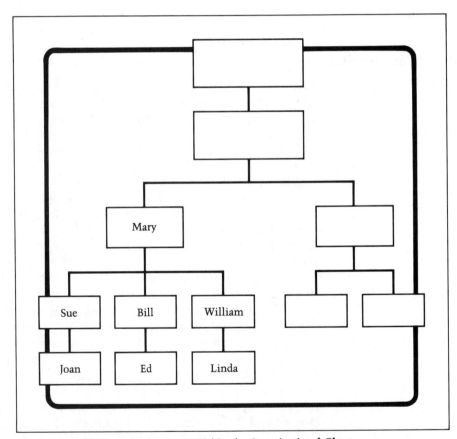

Figure 5.5 • A Communication Loop Within the Organizational Chart

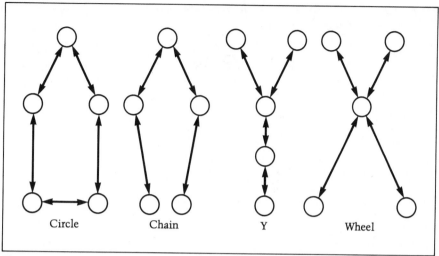

Figure 5.6 • **Communication Loops**

3. *Immediate or delayed closure.* Immediate closure occurs when a message is sent but the process for providing feedback is closed or blocked immediately after the message is delivered. For instance, Mary calls Sue at 4:50 P.M. with a question about dates for a new promotion campaign. By the time Sue checks with Joan and calls Mary back, it is 5:10 P.M. Unfortunately, Mary's secretary has left for the day, and she transferred Mary's phone to another desk so that her boss would not be disturbed as she finished her day's work. Delayed closure would occur if Mary calls Sue and asks her to check the dates. She tells Sue that she will stay and wait for her answer. The feedback loop is open, but closure of the message is delayed until Mary receives her answer.

4. *Efficiency and satisfaction.* Research on communication loops has tended to examine the various effects of freedom and restrictions on an employee's ability to freely communicate. In a classic study Leavitt tested four loops: circle, chain, Y, and wheel (see Figure 5.6). By making certain adjustments these loops can be rearranged to fit a typical organization chart. What did Levitt find? (1) The *wheel* loop was the most efficient in terms of fewest errors and fewest messages needed to accomplish a task; (2) the *circle* had the highest level of job satisfaction, followed by the chain, the Y, and the wheel. Leavitt found two extremes between the circle and wheel: The circle is active, leaderless, unorganized, and erratic, and yet in it a deep cohesion exists among members; the wheel has a distinct leader, is well organized and less erratic, but its members are unsatisfied.[36]

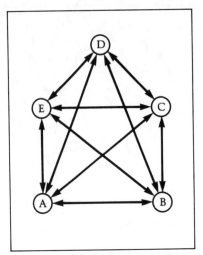

Figure 5.7 · All-Channel Network

The circle can be expanded to an all-channel model that allows two-way communication to flow between each person within the loop (see Figure 5.7). Greatest satisfaction is found between employees in this type of loop, and a strong leader generally must emerge to orchestrate a free-for-all communication flow into a dynamic, purposeful, task-accomplishing process. Without this direction the communication is overcomplete, and a great deal of time is wasted.

5. *Matching and mismatching.* Hierarchical levels within organizations are shaped by the tasks that must be completed and the skills and personalities of persons within the organizations. The formal vertical and horizontal channels of communication that were examined at the beginning of this chapter allow information to be communicated to the right

Table 5.2 · Communication and Organizational Structure

Characteristic	Circle	Chain	Wheel	All-Channel
Speed	Slow	Fast	Very fast	Slow/fast
Accuracy	Poor	Good	Good	Poor/excellent
Morale	High	Low	Very low	Very high
Leadership stability	None	Marked	Very pronounced	None
Organization	Unstable	Emerging stability	Very stable	Unstable
Flexibility	High	Low	Low	High

Source: Philip Lewis, *Organizational Communications*, 2nd ed. (Columbus, Ohio: Grid, 1975), p. 86.

people at the right time. Ideally people receive the precise information they need, when they need it, and they do not receive information that is not needed. Communication loops, however, may or may not fit the ideal. If they fit, a match is declared. If they do not, a mismatch occurs. Findings from most of the research on communication networks and loops are summarized in Table 5.2.

Auditing Organization Communication

As was demonstrated in the last section, the communication that takes place in an organization is not always the same as that intended by management. When management senses that communication problems exist, a thorough examination of the process is in order. Numerous studies show that senior management often incorrectly assumes that it knows what employees want and need to know and hear, and that it does not know what employees actually hear. Organizations, and especially organization consultants, have developed several tools for locating the weaknesses in communication systems and for prescribing corrective action.

Employee Surveys

Specifically designed and sharply focused surveys can tell management a great deal about employees' attitudes regarding an existing communication system. Many companies use the survey as the starting point for diagnosing improvement processes. The best surveys allow employees to explain such things as how much information they receive and how much they need.

Generally, such surveys are followed by small group meetings where employees talk freely and honestly about how they perceive needed changes. A company should use objective interviewers, and often employ out-of-company consultants. Employee comments are then analyzed and weighted for intensity before being summarized to both employees and management. Surveys also give valuable demographic information based on sex, age, loop location, job responsibilities, pay categories, and so forth.

Gildea and Emanuel found that the initial survey provides a good tool for maintaining long-term two-way communication:

The initial survey, in fact, provides a model mechanism for maintaining two-way communications over the long term. A survey conducted to include employee group discussions can be logically followed with periodic small group meetings. These provide for effective and ongoing upward communication of employee suggestions for improving productivity. Employees' suggestions should, of course, be acted upon, with feedback—positive or negative—provided to the appropriate employee(s). We have observed that most employees want to know management's reaction to their proposals and why they will or will not be adopted; simply rewarding employees with cash for suggestions is a short-lived motivator.

Employee participation through two-way communications discourages the belief that management's ideas are dominating the program, or that management has a free hand to manipulate measurement standards. Another formal survey at the end of the time frame initially established by management can provide data to be compared with the findings of the first survey.[37]

Communication Audits

An audit is somewhat analogous to a physical checkup. When properly handled it can provide an organization with valuable information regarding the health of its internal communication. Three different audit techniques are currently in use: ICA, OCD, and ECCO.

The ICA Audit

This audit instrument was established in the early 1970s by the International Communication Association, a professional society composed of communication researchers, practitioners, and teachers. The tool is considered to be the most complete auditing system and utilizes substantial research and documentation.

The ICA audit uses a standardized system of five instruments and incorporates both computer analysis and feedback methods. In addition, the ICA has a data bank that can be tapped for comparisons among communication systems of various organizations. The audit's five measuring tools are questionnaire survey, confidential interview, network analysis, diary of specific communication activities (conversations, phone calls, meetings, and written materials) for a one-week period, and a description of critical communication episodes that represent typical incidents that occur in the organization.[38]

The OCD Audit

The Organizational Communication Development (OCD) Audit system was developed at the Helsinki Research Institute in the early 1970s and is used extensively in Europe. It implements an attitudinal and perceptual questionnaire and then statistically evaluates that questionnaire to see if the results correspond with norms from the test bank. The advantages of this tool are that it is inexpensive, easy to administer, brief, and provides quickly obtainable results. Its disadvantage is that the test norms for the data bank are based on twenty-four Finnish organizations.

ECCO Analysis

The Episodic Communication Channels in Organizations (ECCO) analysis was designed by Keith Davis in 1952. The tool was created to map communication networks, measure rates of communication flow, indicate redundancy, and pinpoint distortion of messages. This tool is fast, convenient, reliable, and inexpensive. It deals with concrete messages rather than perceptions or attitudes. It has limited use in large organizations, however, since answers assume that a respondent knows everyone in the organization.

Summary

Managers must effectively exercise organizational communication—the passage of messages and meaning by people within an organization. The communication climate determines how successful managers can be in sending and receiving information. Three factors affect each climate: quantity of information, quality of information, and the channels of information.

An organization's communication climate further defines the specific ways that messages flow: in formal patterns (downward, upward, and horizontal) and in informal patterns (the grapevine). In addition, a variety of communication loops, or the numerous interpersonal groupings, are established within every organization.

Several auditing tools have been constructed to aid in examining organizational communication, including employee surveys and audits (ICA, OCD, ECCO analyses). Using the appropriate communication audit technique can significantly enhance both the accuracy and effectiveness of management communications.

Key Words

regulative network	informative network	information quantity
innovative network	communication	information quality
integrative network	climate	information channels

formal	step-loss sequence	grapevine
communication	bottlenecks	informal
flow	ice-jam	communication
downward	horizontal	chains
communication	communication	communication loops
upward	informal	communication audit
communication	communication	
filtering	flow	

Review Questions

1. What is the "communication climate" in an organization, and what are three factors of information that can be analyzed in determining the climate?
2. What are the precise differences among the three formal ways that communication flows in an organization?
3. What are some specific reasons for the poor downward flow?
4. What are four ways that the downward communication flow can be improved?
5. Cite six reasons for a poor upward communication flow.
6. What are some ways that the upward flow can be improved?
7. Name two reasons for poor horizontal communication flow.
8. Cite five ways to improve the horizontal flow.
9. What is the common name for the informal communication flow of information in business?
10. Draw out and explain the four informal communication chains.
11. What are some ways to control the grapevine influence?
12. Describe what is meant by "communication loops."
13. Describe the advantages and disadvantages of and the differences between the employee survey and communication audits.

Exercises

1. Read the following story regarding organizational communication, and then answer the questions that relate the story to this chapter. Discuss the story and your answers with fellow classmates.

Don't Let the Grapevine Trip You Up
As Oliver Manzini drove home, he was deep in thought about the news he had heard that day and what he was going to do about it. Because the

government space program was being phased out, Manzini's company had lost a major contract—one that had called for the production of integrated circuits for computers.

But things were not as bad as they had seemed at first because the marketing department had anticipated the loss more than a year before. To head off the bad effects of a drop in sales, the sales manager had contracted with two major computer manufacturers to provide the two with the same integrated circuits, only slightly modified, that the company had been supplying to the government. The modification required a change in two machines that were used in producing the circuits, and so the machines would have to be shut down for two weeks while the maintenance department made the necessary adjustments. During the shutdown, thirty workers—all of them under Manzini's supervision—would have to be temporarily laid off.

As he approached his house, Manzini was pondering the best approach for telling his subordinates about the change so that they would understand and accept the layoff as well as possible. He knew that if the employees were not properly informed, rumors would circulate, and the situation could turn into a real problem.

As Manzini entered the house, his wife hurried to greet him. "Oh, honey," she said. "I just heard. It's so terrible! Will it affect you?" Manzini ran through several events of that day to try to figure out what his wife was talking about but finally had to ask her to explain.

"I'm talking about the big layoff," she said. "Jane heard about it at the beauty parlor and called me right away. She was so worried that they would let you go. It's all over town now that your company has lost all of its government contracts and will have to close down most of its operations at that plant. The way you looked when you came up the walk, I just knew you had been laid off."[39]

---

a. What type of organizational communication process does this story fit?
b. How do you think that the notice of the shutdown/layoff left the company so fast?
c. What methods would you have used if you were Oliver Manzini, or an executive of his company, to ensure that a rumor of this type would not circulate?
d. What would you do now?

2. The following statements pertain to your personal use of the upward, downward, and horizontal communication flow as a manager. If you have had, or now have, supervisory experience, respond to the statements from that framework. If you have never had a supervisory job, respond from the position of what you think should be done to correct the communication problems. After you have written your solutions, look up the suggested solutions. The numbers in parentheses indicate the suggested solutions.

Upward Communication

a. Your communication does not inspire your superior's confidence in you as a communicator. (1)
b. You do not receive the desired results from your writing. (1)
c. You have difficulty getting your messages to the right person. (2)
d. Your superiors seem to not have the time to listen to you. (3)
e. Your superior does not respond to your written memos until it is too late for effective action. (3)
f. You are often confused over which communication method to use. (4)

Horizontal Communication

g. Those on your horizontal level do not have confidence in your communication. (1)
h. Those you communicate with receive so much communication that yours does not receive needed attention. (1)
i. People misunderstand your communications. (1)
j. You are often puzzled as to which communication method to use. (4)
k. Those on your level question your authority to issue communications. (7)

Downward Communication

l. Your written communications are often ignored and do not produce the desired action. (1)
m. Your communications are often resented. (1)
n. The accuracy of your statements is often doubted. (1)
o. Your subordinates feel that your position on issues is on the other side of the fence. (1)
p. You are often confused over which communication method to use. (4)
q. Rumors and information leaks affect the results of your communication. (5)
r. You have trouble reaching every person you wish to communicate with. (6)

Possible Solutions to the Communication Flow Statements

The following possible solutions address some common managerial communication problems. The number before each response corresponds with the number following each statement above. One solution may be applicable to several problems.

1. Work on improving your communication techniques. Plan your meetings and organize your thoughts ahead of time. Make sure that written communications are accurate, are timely presented, are concise, and communicate your exact message. Be sure that messages do not leave out necessary information.

2. Make sure that your messages are directed to the specific person you wish to reach. If that person does not receive your message, find out why. Perhaps someone is blocking the reception. Is there a person who is intercepting messages between you and the intended person? If it is important for this

interceptor to have the information, send it to him or her first. Stress the importance of the date and when the message must be received. If blockages continue to occur, carry the message to the intended person.

3. Perhaps you have sent too many messages or have not stressed when you need a reply. Perhaps the person is busy and has not had an opportunity to read your message and respond. Try setting up a few minutes when you can see the person. Also try developing the message in a form that can be responded to in short written answers. Follow-up memos may also be advantageous, but be careful not to offend.

4. Consider the objective of your communication. What do you wish to accomplish? Do you want to share information, instruct, issue a directive, or receive a response? After you decide your objective, make decisions about how to accomplish it. A directive might be best received with a memo or on a bulletin board or may be mailed to each person. Instruction or transfer of certain types of information may be more easily exchanged at a meeting.

5. Find out if there is a definite leakage. A leak may indicate that you need to send additional information to your subordinates. Instruct them to disregard unofficial messages that do not come from you or another authorized source.

6. Be sure that a summary of each meeting is prepared and distributed. Have a routing slip designed that each person can initial when he or she receives your information.

7. Attach an informal note explaining why you issued the communication.

References

1. Noel L. Griese, "The Employee Communication Philosophy of Arthur W. Page," *Public Relations Quarterly* (Winter 1977), p. 8. Griese summarizes the five points that Page made in two speeches. Points 1 to 4 are from Arthur W. Page, "Fundamentals of a Public Relations Program for Business," a speech to the Seventh International Management Congress, Washington, D.C., Sept. 20, 1938. Point 5 is from Arthur W. Page, "Some Remarks on Public Relations," a speech to members of the Institute of Life Insurance, New York, Dec. 2, 1942. Page had formulated the elements in his five-point philosophy well before he delivered the two speeches just cited.

2. Griese, "Employee Communication," p. 8.

3. Howard H. Greenbaum and Noel D. White, "Biofeedback at the Organizational Level: The Communication Audit," *The Journal of Business Communication* (Summer 1976), p. 6.

4. *Ibid.*, p. 6.

5. Corwin P. King, "Keep Your Communication Climate Healthy," *Personnel Journal* (April 1978), p. 204.

6. *Ibid.*, p. 206.

7. "Face Values," *Communications & Management* (Spring 1975), p. 2 (a publication printed by Towers, Perrin, Forster, and Crosby, New York). Reprinted by permission.

8. Daniel Katz and Robert Kahn, *The Social Psychology of Organizations* (New York: John Wiley & Sons, 1966), pp. 239–43.

9. "The Cheese Stands Alone," *Communications & Management* (Winter 1974), pp. 1–2 (a publication printed by Towers, Perrin, Forster, and Crosby). Reprinted by permission.

10. *Ibid.*, p. 3.

11. *Ibid.*, p. 4.

12. Andrew B. Chase, Jr., "How to Make Downward Communication Work," *Personnel Journal* (June 1970), pp. 480–81.

13. Bruce Harriman, "Up and Down the Communication Ladder," *Harvard Business Review* (Sept./Oct. 1974), p. 97.

14. *Ibid.*, p. 97.

15. Douglas G. Curley, "The Other Half of Employee Communication," *Personnel Administrator* (July 1979), p. 29.

16. Charles W. Eisenmann and Charles L. Hughes, "Have Your People Talked to You Lately—Candidly?" *Personnel Administrator* (October 1975), p. 13.

17. Gary Gemmill, "Managing Upward Communication," *Personnel Journal* (Feb. 1970), p. 107.

18. "Fear and Trembling in the Workplace," *Communications & Management* (Fall 1973), p. 2 (a publication printed by Towers, Perrin, Forster and Crosby).

19. Elizabeth Jennings and Francis Jennings, "Making Human Relations Work," *Harvard Business Review Supplement* (1970), p. 66.

20. Driver, "Opening the Channels," pp. 26–29; John B. McMaster, "Getting the Word to the Top," *Management Review* (Feb. 1979), pp. 64–65.

21. Philip Lewis, *Organizational Communications*, 2nd ed. (Columbus, Ohio: Grid), p. 68. Reprinted by permission.

22. Joe Kelly, *Organizational Behavior: An Existential-Systems Approach*, rev. ed. (Homewood, Ill.: Irwin, 1974), pp. 616–17. A case condensed from R. L. Simpson, "Vertical and Horizontal Communication in Formal Organizations," *Administrative Science Quarterly* (September 1959), pp. 188–96.

23. Ben Strickland, John Arnn, and Edna Harper, "Communicating to Motivate: How Good Are You?" *Magazine of Bank Administration* (March 1980), p. 39.

24. Lewis, *Organizational Communications*, p. 69.

25. Peter Drucker, *Management: Tasks, Responsibilities, Practices* (New York: Harper & Row, 1974), p. 124.

26. Keith Davis, "The Care and Cultivation of the Corporate Grapevine," *Dun's* (July 1973), p. 44.

27. *Ibid.*, p. 46.

28. Michael Korda, *Power: How to Get It, How to Use It* (New York: Ballantine Books, 1975), p. 104.

29. Davis, "The Care and Cultivation of the Corporate Grapevine," p. 46.

30. *Ibid.*, p. 47.

31. Jefferson Freeman, "The Grapevine: Bane or Boon?" *Xerox Xchange*, 2 (1975), p. 2. Reprinted by permission.

32. Vincent DiSalvo with Craig Monroe and Benjamin Morse, *Business and Professional Communication* (Columbus, Ohio: Charles E. Merrill, 1977), p. 252.

33. Katz and Kahn, *The Social Psychology of Organizations*, p. 240.

34. DiSalvo, *Business and Professional Communication*, p. 254.

35. *Ibid.*, p. 255.

36. Harold J. Leavitt, "Some Effects of Certain Communication Patterns," *Journal of Abnormal and Social Psychology* (Jan. 1951), p. 46.

37. Joyce Asher Gildea and Myron Emanuel, "Internal Communications: The Impact on Productivity," *Public Relations Journal* (February 1980), p. 12. Copyright 1980. Reprinted by permission.

38. Gerald M. Goldhaber and Donald P. Rogers, *Auditing Organizational Communication Systems: The ICA Communication Audit* (Dubuque, Iowa: Kendall/Hunt Publishing, 1979), pp. 9–19.

39. Jack Danner, "Don't Let the Grapevine Trip You Up," *Supervisory Management* (Nov. 1972), pp. 2–3.

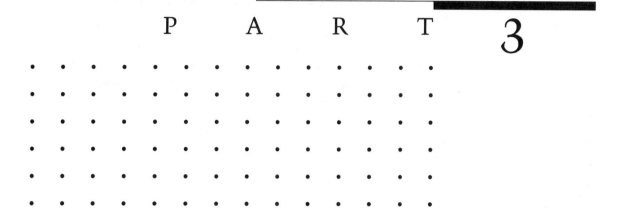

P A R T 3

Communication Skills That Managers Must Develop

Using our model of how effective communication works and knowledge of the three barriers (perception, language, and the organizational structure) that can minimize effective communication, we can examine five specific communication skills that are of particular importance to managers: nonverbal, listening, speaking, group leadership, and writing.

Chapter 6 examines the many *nonverbal* ways that a manager understands, and communicates in, the business world. Because nonverbal communication either augments or contradicts verbal messages, managers must learn how to interpret and use nonverbal communication in environmental, social, and physical settings.

Chapter 7 looks at one of the most used, but least discussed, communication skills—*listening*. It describes specific ways that managers can listen better and improve their interpersonal listening behavior.

Chapter 8's four-part process for *presentational speaking* describes specific ways to organize, construct, practice, and perform in a business presentation.

119

Chapter 9 focuses on the types, characteristics, and functions of *small groups* and describes specific steps that can be taken before, during, and after a meeting that make the process more productive and enjoyable.

Chapter 10 provides specific ways that business writing skills can be improved. Part A focuses on the *inverted report writing* style, a time-saving, "upfront" approach to telling the reader at the outset what you want him or her to know. Part B focuses on the *editing process of writing* and gives specific ways that average writing can be turned into polished, professional writing. Finally, Part C presents some quick and easy steps to *writing letters and memos.*

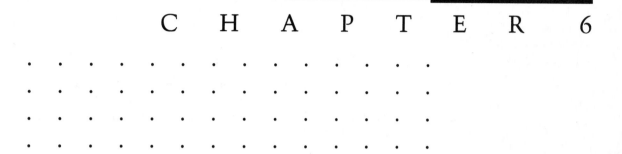

C H A P T E R 6

Nonverbal Communication: Augmenting or Contradicting the Verbal Message

Introduction

Nonverbal Communication Defined

If someone asked you to list the various ways that a manager communicates, you would probably start your list with several acts associated with words: listening, talking, and writing. These acts are considered *verbal* because they use verbal symbols, or words that stand in reference for facts, ideas, and things. Another form of communication is more predominant than verbal, however.

Nonverbal communication refers to human action and behavior and the corresponding meaning that is attached to behavior. A subordinate may want to say, "Boss, I'm really frustrated and I'd like to talk to you." If the words are hard to express, however, the person will try to send the message by way of gestures, facial expressions, vocal pauses, and body movement. Much nonverbal communication is unconscious or subconscious and can represent a major portion of our mental capacity: We send, receive, and decipher thousands of bits of nonverbal information every day.

The Relationship Between Verbal and Nonverbal Communication

When we communicate with other people, we usually use words. Those words, however, are spoken within a nonverbal context that is more meaningful than the words. According to Mark Knapp, nonverbal behavior relates to verbal in six ways:[1]

1. *Repeating.* Someone says, "She walked toward the Student Union," and points in that direction.
2. *Contradicting.* Someone says, "I'm not angry," in a loud voice with face flushed and hands clenched.
3. *Substituting.* Someone makes a statement that you do not believe, and you say nothing but peer at them with head down and eyebrows raised. This clearly says, "Oh, come on!"
4. *Complimenting.* Someone says, "I love you!" with bright eyes and a big smile on his face.
5. *Accenting.* Someone says, "I don't want you to do that again!" and slams a hand on the table when saying *don't*.
6. *Relating and regulating.* Someone raises her hand indicating that she wants to speak.

Why Study Nonverbal Communication?

Although numerous research projects have examined the communication process, no simple formula has been developed for interpreting the specific communicative meaning of behavior. Each act must be examined within its setting and culture. Examining nonverbal communication from a managerial perspective is important for at least six reasons:

1. *No universal communication messages exist.* Each message is created by a unique person, in a unique setting, within a unique cultural background. The more we observe the actions and words of others, the better able we are to understand the messages being sent.
2. *We draw hasty conclusions about the messages sent by others.* As soon as verbal and nonverbal messages are sent, our minds rapidly start the process of deciphering the intended meaning. Without some prior knowledge of nonverbal messages, we draw hasty, and often improper, conclusions.
3. *We grow insensitive to the behavior of others.* When we work side by side with people for a long time, we tend to become insensitive to their words and actions. We ignore messages that are communicated with emotion or feeling. By

observing nonverbal behavior, we heighten our sensitivity to others and enrich the communication procedure.

4. *Nonverbal messages are stronger than verbal ones.* When verbal and nonverbal messages clash, the nonverbal is most often accepted. As the words from an old song say, "Your lips are saying no-no, but there's yes-yes in your eyes." Posture, facial expressions, and vocal utterances can outweigh words and help the observer determine the true meaning of a message.

5. *Nonverbal messages clarify verbal messages.* Such things as gestures, movement, and demonstrations help to clarify and reinforce verbal messages. For example, a manager can tell a new employee how a product can be assembled, but the manager can better communicate the process by demonstrating it.

6. *Nonverbal messages are sent more frequently than verbal ones.* According to research conducted by Albert Mehrabian, only 7 percent of the meaning we receive from messages is transmitted through words; 93 percent comes through nonverbal cues such as voice, inflection, gestures, and facial expression.[2]

This chapter examines three major divisions of nonverbal communication: the *environmental* (buildings, room design, and time); the *social* (space, status, and symbols); and the *physical* (gestures, facial expressions, eyes, voice, color, clothing, and touch).

Environmental Communication

Think about the business offices you have visited recently. How did you feel about those offices? Were some more comfortable than others? If you haven't ventured into many business offices, consider the offices of professors or health care providers or the homes of friends. Each territory conveys a message about its occupant. Some are so neat that you feel out of place when you sit down; others are so dirty and messy that you dislike the thought of having to find a seat. As Sussman noted, an environment often influences the communication that takes place within it:

> Objects in our environment often indicate the status and image of the people who are in possession of those objects. A key to the executive washroom, a large corner office with windows, a nice view, a carpet on the floor, a mahogany water pitcher, an original oil painting, and a private, marked parking space are objects we normally associate with high status in the organization. The use of some common objects, such as an executive dining room or a faculty center at a university, can also be indicative of our position or status.[3]

Within the environment, time, territory, and design and arrangement all contribute to the communication of messages.

Time

Business is time-bound. Consider the work day at a typical automotive plant in the United States. Assembly-line workers must report to the job on time. They punch in on the time clock, work in shifts, and meet specified production quotas that have been determined by time and motion studies. They have a designated lunch hour and two coffee breaks. When they punch out, they hurry to their cars in order to avoid the rush hour traffic jams.

Types of Time

Time can be viewed from several vantage points.

Business time uses the 24-hour clock and the 365-day calendar; it is vital in the smooth planning and operating of a business.

Relaxed time uses few specific guidelines. A supervisor's saying, "I'll drop by to review those papers in a little while," or "We'll worry about that next week," indicates a relaxed attitude toward time.

Technical time is a precise measurement process used in some businesses, especially manufacturing, where minute time periods are extremely important. For example, brick manufacturing requires that the amount of time that the product remains in the firing, ripening, and drying stages must be noted to the fraction of a second.

As the popularity of time management seminars indicates, time is one of a manager's most valued possessions. To be kept waiting for even a few minutes is frustrating; to be "stood up" for an appointment is outrageous. Managers observe and draw impressions about employees from the way employees use time.

The Value of Time

Rosenfeld and Civikly give three reasons why time is seen as one of our most valued possessions.

Time is money. Psychiatrists, lawyers, plumbers, and repairmen are paid by the hour. An American's value of time may even supersede his value of money. When asked to donate time to a charitable cause, for example, people frequently back off, offering to donate money, food, or clothes instead.

Time is power. People with busy schedules are perceived as more important than those who have time for social niceties and preliminary chit-chat. The person granted an hour-long meeting with the President of the United States is looked upon as more powerful and important than the person granted only two minutes.

Figure 6.1
Source: AP/Wide World Photos. Reprinted by permission.

Time is status. While the employee must make an appointment to see the employer, the supervisor can "drop in" on the worker without notice or explanation. Status is also communicated by the amount of time a person is kept waiting.[4]

Which of the above reasons best describes the time messages found in Figure 6.1?

Territory

Humans, like animals, are territorial creatures: We have places and spaces that are uniquely ours. Archie Bunker has "his chair," a mother "her kitchen," a scientist "her laboratory," and a professor "his office." Each designs, maintains, and uses the territory for safety and pleasure and guards and defends it from invasion.

Territorial behavior also pervades business and underlies many non-verbal messages. Usually we consider our work space our territory; it may be a table and chair on an assembly line, a piece of machinery that an individual has run for several years, or the private office that others cannot enter without permission. In organizational territory we arrange the materials we use, place odds and ends where we want them, and generally establish a work place that is conducive to our mental and physical needs.

Animals growl, hiss, or snarl when their territory has been invaded. Employees do the same. If someone rearranges the parts on an assembly line table, the line worker will probably be distraught. Touching or using machinery without the operator's permission might draw a verbal warning. Opening a door and walking into another's office without first knocking could generate a reprimand. Managers must be sensitive to the territory of others and regard it as an important and privileged place.

We define territory as a place that a person can claim, whether it is an office or a piece of machinery. That place usually remains definable, unchanged, and stationary. In organizations we constantly make reference to territory: "my office," "my chair," "the president's parking

We expect others to respect our territory.

Figure 6.2

Cartoon by Tony Hall, from *Communicate!*, 2nd ed., by Rudolph F. Verderber. © 1978 by Wadsworth Publishing Company, Inc. Reprinted by permission of Wadsworth Publishing Company, Belmont, California 94002.

space," "the sales territory." We also manipulate this territorial urge to our advantage. Consider the following example.

Home Field Advantage

In one organization a female manager from the training department agreed to meet with several production managers to discuss her training goals. One of the production managers was her most outspoken opponent and made it clear to others in the organization that "this woman is trying to destroy the management system that the company has successfully established." The meeting was called by the male manager and was to be held in his office.

On the morning of the meeting the trainer called several of the managers who were to attend and asked if they had any objections to meeting in her office—so that she could use the stack of charts she had constructed. Each manager approved of the change in meeting place. The trainer then called her opponent and related that she knew it would be inconvenient to change the arrangements, but would he mind? "Incidentally," she said, "I have touched base with the other managers, and they don't mind at all." The opponent, of course, relented, and the training manager was able to sell her program successfully to all the other managers. Afterward she stated that "having the home field advantage" really paid off.

One of the most highly publicized challenges of territoriality occurred in 1968, during the discussion on the size and shape of the negotiation table at the Vietnam peace talks in Paris. Eight months were spent before an agreement was reached. The diagram in Figure 6.3 shows the first five seating proposals and the one finally chosen. McCroskey describes the discussions:

The United States (US) and South Viet Nam (SVN) wanted a seating arrangement in which only two sides were identified. They did not want to recognize the National Liberation Front (NLF) as an "equal" party in the negotiations. North Viet Nam (NVN) and the NLF wanted "equal" status given to all parties—represented by a four-sided table. The final arrangement was such that both parties could claim victory. The round table minus the dividing lines allowed North Viet Nam and the NLF to claim all four delegations were equal. The existence of the two secretarial tables (interpreted as dividers), the lack of identifying symbols on the table, and an AA, BB speaking rotation permitted the United States and South Viet Nam to claim victory for the two-sided approach. Considering the lives lost during the eight months needed to arrive at the seating arrangement,

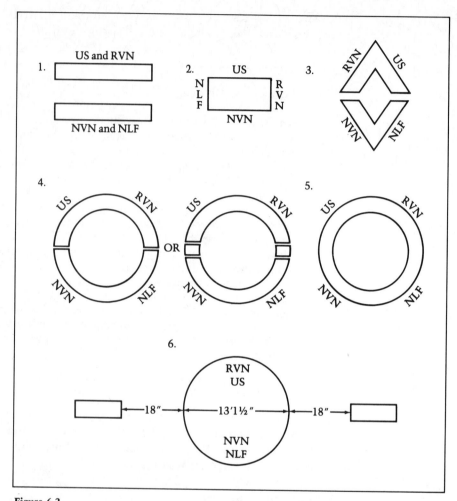

Figure 6.3

Source: Based on a figure in McCroskey/Larson/Knapp, *An Introduction to Interpersonal Communication*, p. 98. © 1971, reprinted by permission of Prentice-Hall, Inc., Englewood Cliffs, New Jersey.

we can certainly conclude that territorial space has extremely high priority in some interpersonal settings.[5]

Design and Arrangement

We are constantly influenced, sometimes without realizing it, by the design and arrangement of the environment. Managers should be familiar with five elements of that environment: building design, office space design, room design, room color, and desk arrangement.

Building Design

According to Alder and Towne, the design of an entire building can shape the type of communication among its inhabitants:

> Architects have learned that the way housing projects are designed will control to a great extent the contact neighbors will have with each other. People who live in apartments near stairways and mailboxes have many more neighbor contacts than do those living in less heavily traveled parts of the building, and tenants generally have more contacts with immediate neighbors than with people even a few doors away. Architects now use this information to design buildings that either encourage communication or increase privacy, and house hunters can use the same knowledge to choose a home that gives them the neighborhood relationships they want.[6]

Office Space Design

As you look at existing office buildings and also the more contemporary facilities under construction, you probably would never guess that a debate is currently raging over the design of office space. The debate is between proponents of the conventional office versus those who support the open office.

The conventional office has a basic quadrangular configuration and is familiar to everyone. Outer perimeter offices usually have windows. Hall space separates these offices from the inner offices that run parallel to those with windows. Sometimes the center part of the floor is called the "bull pen." Posner describes the pecking order for the conventional office.

- *The perimeter offices are for the honchos.* And if you've got *two* windows, you're really special. This is the senior executive turf. A corner office with windows on two walls is usually claimed by a chief executive officer or a partner.
- *The inner offices are for the junior executives.* No windows, but at least there's a door, and an area you can call your own.
- *The bull pen is for the lower echelon and support personnel.* It's like having your desk in the hallway. No privacy. It's tough to swear or sulk out here, because you are utterly visible.[7]

The open office concept originated in Germany in the 1950s and arrived in the United States in the late 1960s. Instead of enclosed offices it consists of free-form groupings, or work clusters, that fill the space in a way that optimizes the flow of human traffic and work. Proponents claim that this concept establishes a democratic atmosphere and increases communication, flexibility, and even productivity among office personnel.

The open concept is gaining popularity. Over ten thousand offices "opened" between 1976 to 1983, and by the mid-1980s over 45 percent of the office space was estimated to be open space. The concept, however, is not without its opponents. Without walls there are no nonverbal signals of hierarchy or status, and many corporate officials find it hard to part with their status offices. Consequently, the modified norm is to have private offices for upper-level executives, several conference rooms, and the rest of the space open for staff personnel.

Room Design

Robert Sommer, in his book *Personal Space: The Behavioral Basis for Design*, describes the thought process that underlies the design of restaurants and bars. Patrons tend to stay longer in places with dim lighting, subdued noise, and comfortable seats. An owner who wants to have a fast turnover will need a restaurant with brightly shining lights and little soundproofing.

Furniture also plays a role in how long people will stay in an environment. The Larsen chair, designed for restaurant owners in Copenhagen, is intentionally constructed to be uncomfortable by applying pressure to the back of the occupant who stays in the chair for longer than a few minutes. Makers of expensive automobiles apply the reverse technique. They construct car seats that contour to the driver's back. Some seats even have a lumbar device to prevent back pains caused by long trips.

Room Color

A former political leader once commented that a lifetime of participating in conference meetings convinced him that conferences conducted in cheerful, bright-colored rooms were more successful than those held in duller surroundings.

Color is also used as a motivator. Red is considered aggressive, exciting, and stimulating and related to emotions and passion. Blue is cool, clear, and serene and has a calming effect. Green is light, fresh, and peaceful, unless of course it is the "hospital" green of the 1950s that many business halls still display. Other demotivating colors are prison gray, high school yellow, and occasionally the heavy dark brown of executive wall panels.

Desk Arrangements

The two scenes shown in Figure 6.4 are from a typical office; they are common to all of us. If you had to enter this office, which desk arrangement would make you feel more at ease? Your desk and its size, shape,

(a)   (b)

Figure 6.4

Source: Redrawn from Fig. Two "Semifixed Space" in Sara A. Barnhart, *Introduction to Interpersonal Communication*, (Thomas Y. Crowell Co.), p. 92. Copyright © 1976 by Harper & Row, Publishers, Inc. By permission of Harper & Row, Publishers, Inc.

and position affect the impression that you make on people and can determine the degree of open communication that takes place in your office.

There are four common desk arrangements (see Figure 6.5). Preston uses illustrations to show the possible participant interaction in each.[8] In the *standard placement* (a) the occupant stays seated behind the desk and controls the office space. The position stresses power and gives the visitor little freedom. Such positioning is sometimes necessary to establish roles as in disciplinary situations.

The *friendly arrangement* (b) removes the desk as a barrier and allows more personal communication. The interaction is still in a social zone, and the occupant still is in full control.

The *back-of-the-desk* (c) position totally removes barriers and places the visitor and occupant on the same level. Usually this arrangement is reserved for those people who share close personal contact.

The *neutral site* (d) is an informal place in the office where the occupant conducts the conversation. It can be a couch, lounge, or conference area that is away from the desk. Normally only people with status have this kind of office space available.

Appropriate office arrangements coincide with the purpose of the intended communication. For instance, the standard placement might be inappropriate for giving employees good news but quite appropriate for

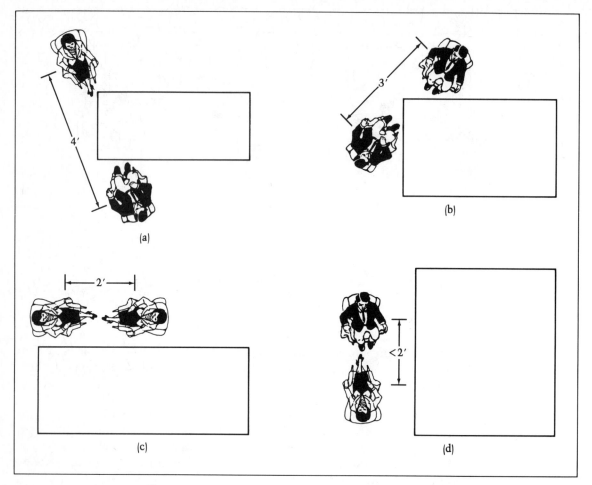

Figure 6.5

Source: Based on figures in Paul Preston, *Communication for Managers*, p. 127. © 1979, used by permission of Prentice-Hall, Inc., Englewood Cliffs, New Jersey.

reprimands. Likewise a neutral setting can reinforce the goal setting process or any personal counseling that might be needed. Going to an employee's office can be significant, for it can show recognition of valued performance and encourage interaction.

Social Communication

Working and living environments influence how we communicate and can be examined in terms of how they affect social behavior. Verbal and nonverbal behavior is most easily recognized, understood, and controlled in small groups. This section examines social aspects of nonverbal communication that send important messages: space, status, and symbols.

Space

In the business world, almost everything that people do involves space. Our idea of space synthesizes all human sensory inputs: visual, auditory, kinesthetic, olfactory, and thermal. Each of these constitutes a complex system and at the same time is molded and patterned by culture. Since people grow up in different cultures, they learn to live and operate in different sensory worlds and are often aware of how their world differs from those of people around them. Remember that space is similar to territory but it is also different. Although people establish fixed territories that do not change, their ideas of space are flexible and changing. Edward T. Hall coined the term *proxemics* to refer to the study of human behavior in relation to space[9] and identified four distances most frequently used by Americans in business and social transactions. These distances are culture-bound and are determined by an individual's attitudes, feelings, and relationships (see Figure 6.6).

Intimate distance is reserved for people to whom we feel extremely close. This space starts with physical contact and extends out to about eighteen inches; it is reserved for lovers embracing and close friends discussing secrets. In business this distance is rarely used, although there are times when thoughts are shared as one person whispers to another. Occasionally a reprimand can be given by a manager speaking softly and directly into the ear of the subordinate (which sounds more like a threat than a reprimand).

Personal distance extends from one foot to four feet away from the body. Within that space we entertain casual and friendly relations. This space is often referred to as an invisible bubble that surrounds each person; it is variable in size and can expand or contract according to particular situations.

Social distance, between four and eight feet away from the body, is used for impersonal and businesslike conversations.

Public distance extends from twelve feet to the limits of hearing. This space is used mostly for public speaking because it is not suitable for interpersonal communication.

When individuals invade the personal space of others, adverse effects can arise. When people are in an elevator, for example, it is common for each person to feel uncomfortable. Since Americans dislike having their personal space invaded, in elevators they become almost inhuman objects. As more and more people crowd into an elevator, less and less space

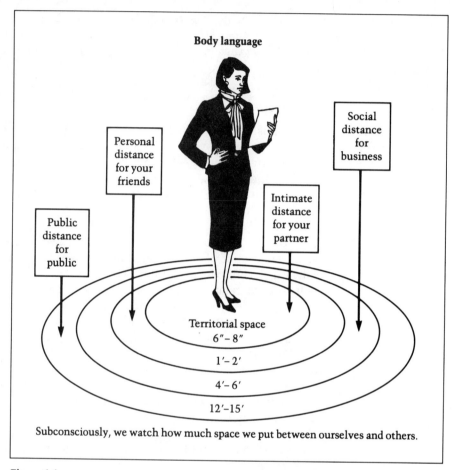

Figure 6.6

Based on a drawing by Jack Halloran in *Applied Human Relations: An Organizational Approach*, 2nd ed., p. 46. © 1983, used by permission of Prentice-Hall, Inc., Englewood Cliffs, New Jersey. Information for the original drawing was taken from Julius Fast, *Body Language*, (New York: M. Evans and Company), © 1970.

is available. Each person faces forward, folds hands in front, does not make eye contact, watches the floor numbers, doesn't talk to strangers, stops talking to acquaintances and avoids brushing against bodies.

In cramped office situations, desks placed extremely close together induce people to watch others work and to overhear telephone conversations. In those cramped situations even the aisles become subject to property rights. Workers whose desks border the aisle often assume ownership rights to aisle property. One worker described becoming anxious and hostile when neighboring office workers used his wastepaper basket.

He felt that his territory was being invaded and that his ownership rights were challenged.

Status

There are many ways to detect status within organizations. Titles, of course, are one of the best, but nonverbal signs and signals also convey messages of power and position. For instance, the use of space says much about the status of individuals.

Fast, in *Body Language*, gives an example of space and distance factors between a boss and visitors. Fast found significance in the time elapsed between knocking at the door and entry:

> The quicker the visitor entered the room, the more status he had. The longer the executive took to answer, the more status he had. . . . How far into the territory the visitor penetrates, and how quickly he does it, in other words how he challenges the personal space of the executive, announces his own status.
>
> The "big boss" will walk into his "subordinates" office unannounced. The subordinate will wait outside the boss's office until he is permitted in. If the boss is on the phone, the subordinate may tiptoe off and come back later. If the subordinate is on the phone, the boss will usually assert his status by standing above the subordinate until he murmurs, "Let me call you back," and then gives the boss his full attention.[10]

According to Goldhaber, territory in an organization says three things about the status of individuals who occupy the space:[11]

1. *The higher up you are in the organization, the more and better space you have.* The officers of a company (i.e., president, vice-presidents, and department heads) will have large and attractive offices. Their offices have high-quality furnishings and more windows than subordinates' offices.

2. *The higher up you are in the organization, the better protected your territory is.* A person with high status often is assigned the services of a secretary or assistant. The job of that person is to protect the time of the boss and to filter out individuals that he or she does not want to see.

3. *The higher up you are in the organization, the easier it is to invade the territory of lower-status personnel.* A manager may walk into the office of a subordinate at will, even if the door is closed; the subordinate, however, does not reciprocate.

Symbols

We respond to symbols without realizing we are doing so, as when we see long-established international symbols for rest rooms and no smoking

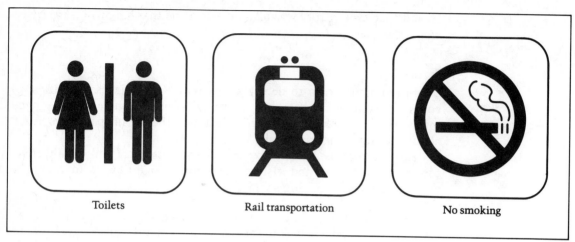

Figure 6.7 · Symbols

(see Figure 6.7). A message can be quickly and accurately transmitted and received through symbols. Preston describes the importance of symbols to the business world:

> Corporations, foundations, trade associations, and government agencies also use symbols (logos) to identify themselves or their products. Once a symbol has been firmly placed in our mind, we think of the organization every time we see the logo. Such symbols help to create recognition that is useful in helping sales and in maintaining a visible public image. In one well-publicized search, the NBC television network spent $1 million on its new logo, and Exxon spent $100 million and three years converting to its new name. (Its original name was Standard Oil of New Jersey, and later the name was changed to Esso.)[12]

Physical Communication

The social aspects of space, status, and symbols send out nonverbal messages. The most personal, often the most unconscious, but easily the most controllable part of our nonverbal world is physical behavior. This section examines the body, gestures, facial expressions, eye movement, voice, clothing, and touch.

Body

The body is constantly sending messages, such as whether we are happy, sad, angry, or confused. Some characteristics, like height and skin color, remain relatively permanent throughout adulthood. Other factors, like posture and weight, can change. In fact, status has been known to influence a change in the posture of individuals, and posture often can influence the status obtained. Three things must be remembered about interpreting the signals that the body sends:

1. *A precise meaning cannot always be obtained from body position and movement.* Arms crossed around the chest are usually interpreted to mean the person is closed to interaction with others. Yet nonverbal behavior combined with a verbal explanation and a certain amount of intuition might lead the observer to realize that the other person is physically cold and is attempting to stay warm.

2. *Body language differs from culture to culture.* Every culture has its own body language. Italians talk and move in Italian; British movements differ from those of Americans. Fiorello LaGuardia, a former mayor of New York City, delivered political speeches in Yiddish, Italian, and English and mastered the appropriate gestures for each language group. His gestures were so clear that some people could tell from newsreels which language he was speaking without ever hearing the sound.

3. *Interpretation of body language messages is more accurate when they are received over a period of time and not in one observation.* In 1957 anthropologist Ray Birdwhistell began a systematic study of human nonverbal communication.[13] *Kinesics*, the name now applied to the study of various movements of the mouth, the eyebrows, and the hands, supports his findings that accurate interpretation of messages is cumulative.

Interpretation of messages is often best discovered through the congruence or incongruence of the verbal and nonverbal. *Congruence* occurs when words and actions complement each other. Americans, for example, generally raise their head slightly at the end of spoken statements to which they expect an answer. This is a nonverbal signal to other Americans to give a reply. Response to these signals is intuitive and unconscious.

Incongruence is perhaps best illustrated by the employee who is sitting back in a chair, with arms folded and knees together. Verbally she is telling her employer that she is pleased with the $50-a-month raise she has just received. The nonalert employer would probably accept the employee's seemingly pleased response; but the employer with an awareness of body language might realize that the employee's withdrawn position, folded arms, or shrug of the shoulders indicates complete or partial dissatisfaction.

Gestures

In 1826 Noah Webster, author of *Webster's Dictionary*, wrote a book on speech entitled *Webster's Reader and Speaker*. Webster, one of the first to discuss the importance of nonverbal expression, contended that expressed sentiments should be accompanied with proper tones, looks, and gestures. Facial expressions reveal our inner emotions and passions, while gestures are the movements of our hands and body.

In business settings congruent meaning often is found in situations that call for multiple gestures. When a manager has to discipline a subordinate, the manager's head is held high, the shoulders are pulled back, and eye contact is directed straight at the subordinate. The dominant posture signals: "I am the boss, and I want you to listen." The subordinate's posture signals acceptance or rejection of the manager's power. Acceptance is seen in a submissive pose, with shoulders held down and eyes lowered. The opposite reaction to a reprimand would be a posture that mirrors the supervisor's and says, "I defy you."

Nierenberg and Calero, in *How to Read a Person Like a Book*, offer a complete analysis of nonverbal behavior in business settings (see Table 6.1).[14]

Cultural Context

An American business executive who was flown to Ethiopia to interview nationals for his company's branch suddenly found that he had offended the interviewees. He did so by entering the waiting room following each interview and pointing with his finger to the next person in line.

Table 6.1 · People-Reading Index

Movement	Description	Possible Meaning
Smiles:		
Simple	Lips together, teeth unexposed	Person is not participating in any outgoing activity, is smiling to himself
Upper	Upper incisors exposed, usually with eye-to-eye contact between individuals	A greeting smile when friends meet or when children greet their parents
Broad	Both upper and lower incisors exposed and eye-to-eye contact seldom occurs	Associated with laughing, commonly seen during play
Holding hands	Two women gently hold each other's hands and with congruous facial expressions communicate their deep sympathy	Woman's expression of sincere feelings to another woman during a crisis
Open hands	Palms up	Sincerety and openness
Crossed arms	Men—arms crossed on chest Women—arms crossed lower on body	Defensiveness, defiance, withdrawal

Table 6.1 *Continued*

Movement	Description	Possible Meaning
Leg over chair	Sits with one leg up over chair arm	Indifference or hostility to other person's feelings or needs
Leg kicking	Legs crossed with foot moving in a slight kicking motion	Boredom
Hand to cheek	"The Thinker" position with hand on cheek	Involved in some sort of meditation
Stroking chin	Hand strokes chin, man strokes beard or mustache	In process of making decision
Removing glasses	Very slowly and deliberately takes glasses off and carefully cleans the lenses or puts the earpiece of the frame in the mouth	Procrastination—pausing for thought, gaining time to evaluate
Pinching bridge of nose	Closes eyes, pinches bridge of nose	May signal self-conflict, quandry about a matter
Sideways glance	Often takes a sideways position, body turned away	Associated with distrusting attitude—a gesture of rejection
Hands on hips	Standing—both hands placed on hips Sitting—body leaning forward, one hand on knee	Individual is goal-oriented—is ready and able
Leaning back, hands supporting head	Seated, leaning back, one leg crossed in figure-four position, both hands clasped behind head	Gesture of superiority, smugness, and authority
Jingling money in pocket	Jingling coins in pocket	May be much concerned with money or the lack of it
Locked ankles	Ankles crossed tightly, hands may also be clenched	Holding back strong feelings and emotions—apprehension—tension
Tugging ear	Raises hand four to six inches, hand goes to earlobe, gives a subtle pull, then returns to its starting point	An "interrupt gesture"—a signal of a wish to speak
Steepling	Joins finger tips and forms a "church steeple"	Communicates idea speaker is very sure of what he or she is saying

Source: Chart "Body Language" in John W. Drakeford, *Do You Hear Me, Honey?* pp. 56–57. Copyright © 1976 by John W. Drakeford. Used by permission of Harper & Row, Publishers, Inc., New York. Chart condensed from Gerald I. Nierenberg and Henry H. Calero, *How to Read a Person Like a Book* (New York: Pocket Books, 1975).

In the United States the pointing gesture is acceptable, but in Ethiopia it is for children—and the beckoning signal is for dogs. The correct method for calling someone in that country is to extend the arm and hand, hold the hand out with the palm down, and close the hand repeatedly.

Gestures must be interpreted in the context of their meaning. Winston Churchill made famous the V formation of the index and middle fingers and used it as a sign for *victory*; in the 1960s and 1970s the same symbol stood for *peace*. In fact, the handshake, which is the initial gesture of friendliness in business, originated as a symbol for peace. People who extended the right hand showed that they had no weapon, were approaching in peace, and were inviting the other person to do the same.

Facial Expressions

The human face is a valuable instrument of communication; the mouth, eyes, and brow can sensitively convey specific emotions, thoughts, or intentions. The face is the primary way of expressing feelings of anger, joy, fear, sadness, happiness, surprise, concern, worry, embarrassment, contempt, hurt. The face is capable of producing over 250,000 different expressions, even though we use only a few words (for example, smile, grin, frown) to describe general facial expressions.[15]

The face is also one of the most rapid means of conveying meaning. Other nonverbal factors, like gestures or posture, take time to change and use. Facial expressions can be changed instantly, even without detection by the eye. Managers, in fact, sometimes stop a confusing, irrelevant, or undesired message by squinting in a particular way, raising an eyebrow, or setting the jaw. In the business world facial expressions are the first physical conveyors of nonverbal expression.

Although facial expressions are used frequently, the emotions that they express are not always easy to read. The face can convey several emotions simultaneously and is adept at hiding expressions. For example, men culturally are taught to act "tough" and sometimes mask feelings of hurt or disappointment. Our cultural programming can lead us astray if we assume that everyone should, and will, act in the same way.

The Misread Facial Expression

A supervisor observed four subordinates eating lunch together one day and noticed that at least three of the men had cans of beer. Because drinking alcohol was strictly forbidden while on the job, after lunch he called each of the men into his office and fired them. The fourth man, several colleagues argued, was innocent, and although he was eating with the other three, he did not drink. The fourth man was questioned by the supervisor, and, even though no hard evidence against him existed, he was suspended. As the supervisor explained, "He wouldn't look me in the eye. He dodged the question. He had guilt written all over his face."

Later that day, when sharing news of the situation with another supervisor, he learned why the facial expressions had indicated guilt: "You misread the man's 'body language.' What you took for guilt was the man's way of showing respect. He is Puerto Rican, and Puerto Rican culture teaches people not to look into the eyes of those in superior positions. To do so would be disrespectful."

Facial expressions tell us when others are confused. For instance, a manager in a problem-solving meeting may suddenly turn from the podium to the chalkboard to draw a flow chart of the procedure she is discussing. Nonverbal cues from others in the room told her that the group was confused and needed more information.

Eye Movement

The eye moves an estimated 100,000 times during the average day. It is one of the most expressive parts of the body, and the meanings that can be attached to various eye movements are limitless.

Researchers have found a correlation between the eyes and social space. In the Middle East people hold conversations in small, tight circles. They tend to stand about two feet apart (instead of the five feet customary for Americans), a distance at which they can see the size of each other's pupils. Because a person's pupils usually dilate when he or she is interested and excited and contract when the person is bored and uninterested, pupil size is used to indicate how one person responds to another. Until recently the factor of pupil size had little bearing in business, but studies have shown that nonverbal messages conveyed by the eyes of models in pictorial advertisements can play an integral role in what is communicated to viewers.

Voice

Paralinguistic messages relate to vocal factors like tone, quality, style, rate of speech, or accents. Research supports the belief that the voice is revealing and can mask feelings. What does a voice disclose? A quaking voice reveals nervousness; stridency shows an uncertainty; and a smooth, full voice indicates confidence. The way we speak certain words carries many meanings. For example, consider the different meanings conveyed in these sentences by the emphasis of different words.

- *You* did an excellent job on the report. (not just any person, but *you* in particular)
- You *did* an excellent job on the report. (past tense, regarding when you did the report)
- You did an *excellent* job on the report. (not just a good job, but one that was excellent)
- You did an excellent job on the *report.* (not a project or presentation, but a report)

The sensitive manager strives to use a voice that complements and emphasizes the words that he or she speaks.

Clothing

It used to be said that "Clothes make the person"; in some circles the phrase has been changed to "Clothes make or break the person." Books on dress and clothing have emphasized that our clothing influences how the people around us think about us. John Molloy, a clothing consultant for large corporations, was one of the first wardrobe engineers. He combines the elements of psychology, fashion, sociology, and art and teaches salespeople how they should dress to sell more insurance; trial lawyers, to win more cases; and executives, to exert more authority. Molloy believes that the way people dress communicates a variety of messages to others in an organization. In his first book, *Dress for Success,* he describes how types of dress affect corporate executives:

> I showed them [100 executives] five pictures of men neatly dressed in obvious lower-middle-class attire and asked if these men were dressed in proper attire for a young executive. Forty-six said yes, fifty-four said no.
> I next showed them five pictures of men dressed in conservative upper-middle-class clothing and asked if they were dressed in proper attire for the young executive. All one hundred said yes.
> I asked them whether they thought the men in the upper-middle-class garb would succeed better in corporate life than the men in the lower-middle-class uniform. Eighty-eight said yes, twelve said no.
> I asked if they would choose one of the men in the lower-middle-class dress as their assistant. Ninety-two said no, eight said yes.[16]

The clothing we wear communicates three different things about us: It reveals something about our *emotions* (how we feel affects what we wear, what we wear affects how we feel); it discloses information about our *behavior* (wearing a uniform, for instance, may cause us to stand or walk more rigidly and to even talk in a different tone); it *differentiates* us from other people (casual attire suitable for a college campus, such as jeans, sportshirts, or warm-ups, differentiates you from the business world of pin-stripe suits, wing-tip shoes, and silk ties).

Touch

Infants know touch before other senses: The order of sensory development is tactile, auditory, and finally visual. But as we grow older the order of usage reverses: visual, auditory, and tactile. Ashley Montague, in his book *Touching*, stresses the important need humans have for tactile satisfaction: "[A]dequate tactile satisfaction during infancy and childhood is of fundamental importance for the subsequent healthy behavioral development of the individual."[17]

Psychologist Sidney Jourard studied the amount of physical touching that takes place during exchanges of confidences. He discovered that touching, outside of sexual relationships, occurs on a minimal basis among Americans and English. In fact, both men and women touched mostly the other's hands, arms, and shoulders. According to Jourard, an almost "touch taboo" exists:

> I think it is part of the more general alienation process that characterizes our depersonalizing social system. I think it is related to the same source that underlies the dread of authentic self-disclosure. When people are committed to upward mobility, in competition with their fellows, everyone masquerades, and keeps his real self concealed from the other who is a potential enemy. You keep others at a distance and mystified by withholding disclosure, and by not letting them get close enough to touch, not letting them know how you feel.[18]

Physical contact with other human beings is essential for healthy development. Even in the world of business, touch is an important clue to liking and acceptance. Marketing departments have read the human need for touch, and they have used that knowledge to improve sales.

The importance of touch is often underestimated: A gesture can be used where words are not possible or socially acceptable. For example, in an interview between two men, a simple pat on the back may convey significant emotional support that could not be easily conveyed in words. Touch can also be misunderstood; a female who places her hand on a male's shoulder may be perceived as flirtatious. As managers we must recognize the impact touch can have, and yet we must be sensitive to the proper time and way to use touch.

Summary

Nonverbal communication in business can either augment or contradict what we say verbally. Managers therefore must learn to coordinate both their verbal and nonverbal messages and at the same time be sensitive to what their peers, subordinates, and supervisors convey nonverbally.

The three major divisions of nonverbal communication are environmental, social, and physical. *Environmental* aspects of communication include how people select, protect, and utilize territory to their advantage. Building and office space is designed, arranged, and painted with certain objectives in mind. Desk and seating arrangements affect the degree of open or closed communication that occurs within offices.

From a *social* standpoint humans operate within flexible and changing personal space by establishing distances between themselves and others that coincide with the situations they encounter. Work space, job titles, and other nonverbal signs and signals convey status. Symbols, too, such as logos, deliver social messages as they replace words in business.

The most unconscious yet easily controllable part of our nonverbal world lies in *physical* behavior. People constantly send messages with their bodies, facial expressions, gestures, eye movement, voices, and touch. Clothing style, quality, and color convey messages of credibility and class. Physical nonverbals combine with environmental and social ones to send many messages on a daily basis. Managers must become sensitive to the way in which these nonverbal messages are used.

Key Words

nonverbal
business time
relaxed time
technical time
territory
conventional office
open office

standard placement
 desk arrangement
friendly desk
 arrangement
back-of-the-desk
 arrangement
neutral site desk
 arrangement

space
proxemics
intimate distance
personal distance
social distance
public distance
status
kinesic

Review Questions

1. What is the precise difference between verbal and nonverbal communication?

2. Words are spoken within a context of nonverbal communication. Describe the six different ways that nonverbal behavior relates to verbal.

3. One reason for managers to study nonverbal communication is that only 7 percent of the meaning we receive is through words. Tell where the other 93 percent comes from, and list five other reasons for studying nonverbals.

4. Three different divisions of our environment influence us nonverbally. What are they?

5. We often take time for granted, but there are three different types of nonverbal time. Describe them, and also list the three ways we value time.

6. Territory is defined in this chapter as a place that a person can claim, whether it is an office or a piece of machinery. Describe some ways that territory helps messages to be communicated in business.

7. Describe and contrast a conventional and an open office.

8. Name the four different desk arrangements, and tell which ones are the most controlled and the most informal.

9. Name the four different zones of personal space, and describe the distance each covers and the type of communication that occurs in each.

10. How do you describe status within an organization?

11. Why are symbols an important tool for society? Describe their importance.

12. Name the eight ways described in this chapter that we physically communicate with others.

13. We interpret body messages through their congruence or incongruence. What does this mean?

14. Seventeen different gestural movements were listed in Figure 6.7. List and describe at least ten of them.

15. According to Birdwhistell how many different expressions can the face produce?

16. Why is touch between people important?

Exercises

1. For the next few days observe how you, and people around you, use and abuse time. How much of your time is "relaxed" and how much is "business" related? Do you find yourself mentally employing one type of time when you are physically employing another? In meetings, classes, and at work make a list of how people act nonverbally when they arrive early or late. How do the people who are waiting act?

2. Make an informal survey of the offices where you attend school or work. Examine the waiting rooms, secretarial facilities, managers offices, faculty offices, and other types of public and private space. Keep a list of spaces that are designed for formal and informal use. How many fit the open and conventional office designs? What kind of nonverbal messages did you receive from the designs and the people that work in them? In how many ways were people defending their territory? You may desire to make some simple drawings in order to share this information with your class.

3. In an informal survey make a list of the various colors and color schemes that are used to decorate the walls of your classrooms, administrative buildings, offices, dormitory rooms, and so forth. Did one or two colors dominate? Which colors were they? What kind of feelings did you receive when you examined the different rooms? Did any particular colors give you pleasant or unpleasant feelings? Share your findings with others, and then describe them to your class.

4. Try this simple "invading space" exercise and describe the results to your class. In a library, cafeteria, or other public place pick out a person who is seated alone surrounded by empty chairs. Sit in the chair closest to the person. Describe his or her response. (You may also wish to explain afterward that you were conducting an experiment.)

5. Make a picture collage with different slogans and symbols that you find in magazines and newspapers. How many of your friends are able to give the names and meanings of the symbols? What kind of nonverbal messages do these symbols denote?

6. Visit a friend, and sit down in his or her favorite chair. Don't offer to move, but note the person's nonverbal actions.

7. Set aside thirty minutes or an hour to observe other people. Select a space where other people are constantly interacting, such as a sidewalk, a student union, a hallway, or the door of a building or cafeteria. Observe the gestures, facial expressions, and body movement that people use. What kinds of meanings do you draw from these behaviors?

8. Design your ideal office space. Compare it with a classmate's and discuss the differences between the two. How would you modify your classmate's? Why?

References

1. Sara A. Barnhart, *Introduction to Interpersonal Communication* (New York: Thomas Y. Crowell, 1976), p. 116. Barnhart condensed the work of Mark Knapp's *Nonverbal Communication in Human Interaction* (New York: Holt, Rinehart & Winston, 1972), pp. 9–12.

2. Albert Mehrabian, "Communication Without Words," *Psychology Today* (September 1968), pp. 53–55.

3. Lyle Sussman and Paul D. Krivonos, *Communication: For Supervisors and Managers* (Sherman Oaks, Calif.: Alford, 1979), p. 87.

4. Lawrence B. Rosenfeld and Jean M. Civikly, *With Words Unspoken: The Nonverbal Experience* (New York: Holt, Rinehart & Winston, 1976), p. 197.

5. James McCroskey, C. Larson, and M. Knapp, *An Introduction to Interpersonal Communication* (Englewood Cliffs, N.J.: Prentice-Hall, 1971), p. 97. Reprinted by permission.

6. Ron Adler and Neil Towne, *Looking Out/Looking In*, 2nd ed. (New York: Holt, Rinehart & Winston, 1978), p. 276.

7. Mitchell J. Posner, *Executive Essentials* (New York: Avon, 1982), p. 497.

8. Paul Preston, *Communication for Managers* (Englewood Cliffs, N.J.: Prentice-Hall, 1979), p. 127.

9. Edward T. Hall has conducted extensive research on proxemics—or space. A review of that work can be found in "Proxemics," *Current Anthropology*, 9 (2–3) (1968), pp. 83–108. A more detailed description is contained in Hall's book, *The Hidden Dimension* (Garden City, N.Y.: Doubleday, 1966).

10. Julius Fast, *Body Language* (New York: M. Evans & Co., 1970), p. 48.

11. Gerald Goldhaber, *Organizational Communication* (Dubuque, Iowa: William C. Brown, 1979), pp. 150–53.

12. Preston, *Communication for Managers*, p. 150.

13. Ray Birdwhistell, *Kinesics and Context* (Philadelphia: University of Pennsylvania Press, 1970), p. 176.

14. Gerald I. Nierenberg and Henry H. Calero, *How to Read a Person Like a Book* (New York: Pocket Books, 1975).

15. Birdwhistell, *Kinesics and Context*, p. 176.

16. John T. Molloy, *Dress for Success* (New York: Peter H. Wyden, 1975), pp. 27–28.

17. Ashley Montague, *Touching: The Human Significance of the Skin* (New York: Perennial Library, 1971), p. 334.

18. Sidney Jourard, "Out of Touch: The Body Taboo," *New Society* (Nov. 9, 1967), p. 660.

C H A P T E R 7

. . . .
. . . .
. . . .
. . . .

Listening:
Hearing and Understanding
What Other People Say

Introduction

Listening Defined

Listening and hearing are not identical. We can hear and not listen, and we can listen and not understand. In fact, listening is made up of four separate stages. The first stage involves hearing, which uses the physical *sensation* of sound waves, is often a passive process, and also uses the usual sensing of nonverbal messages (discussed in Chapter 6). Next, we *interpret* the sounds and sights that we receive, which leads to knowledge and understanding or misunderstanding. Third, we *evaluate* what we hear and decide how to use the information. Finally, we *react* to the entire process.

Listening Dominates Communication Time

According to a folk saying, we are born with two ears and one mouth because we were meant to listen twice as much as we talk. Regrettably,

148

although listening is the first communication skill learned by infants and is the one most used by adolescents and adults, it is also the least-taught skill in the educational process. In the past few years, however, listening has been studied as an important communication skill needed by business professionals. Today it has become the fourth member of the reading/writing/speaking triad.

The first study on listening was conducted in 1926 by Dr. Paul Rankin. He found that people communicate seven out of every ten minutes, or 70 percent of their waking time. Studies since then, conducted on blue- and white-collar workers, salespeople, housewives, college students, and others, have increased that figure to 80 percent of waking hours. As Table 7.1 shows, more time is spent in listening than in any other of the four communication modes.

Since businesspeople spend 80 percent of their workday engaged in communication activities, then 6½ hours of an 8-hour workday are spent listening to others. Just think of the many listening situations one encounters during a business day: staff meetings, sales meetings, instruction sessions, telephone calls, conversations with superiors, discussions with peers, counseling subordinates, making decisions, and listening to speeches of others.

Since we spend so much time listening, it is crucial that we learn to listen well. This chapter examines reasons for improving our listening, types of poor listeners, ways to improve the skill of listening, the important interpersonal dimensions of listening, and ways to give proper feedback to others.

How Well Do You Listen?

In 1979 the Sperry Corporation was looking for a new advertising slogan. The old slogan—"Making machines do more so man can do more"—had worked well but lacked the impact that Sperry needed. Through commissioned research studies, Sperry learned that as a company it was

Table 7.1

	Listening	Speaking	Reading	Writing
Learned	First	Second	Third	Fourth
Used	Most (45%)	Next most (30%)	Next least (16%)	Least (9%)
Taught	Least	Next least	Next most	Most

Source: This material is from "Your Personal Living Profile," a brochure prepared by Dr. Lyman K. Steil, President of Communication Development, Inc., St. Paul, Minnesota, for the Sperry Corporation, New York. Reprinted by permission of Dr. Steil and the Sperry Corporation.

different because its employees would listen. These studies led to a long-term advertising campaign centered around the slogan "We understand how important it is to listen."

Since the campaign's inception in 1979, Sperry ads on listening, like the one in Figure 7.1, have been seen in the *New York Times*, in the *Wall Street Journal*, in other business publications, and on television. More than 90,000 instructional pieces of listening material have been sent to Sperry employees, over 10,000 employees have attended a company-sponsored listening training program, and hundreds of thousands of listening brochures have been mailed to the general public. Sperry is showing people, both inside and outside its organization, that listening is an important communication skill.

Thanks to Sperry it is possible to gain insight into how well you listen by answering the questions to three tests that will give you a personal profile of listening behavior. This profile was developed by Dr. Lyman K. Steil, a special consultant to Sperry, and is printed in a Sperry booklet, *Your Personal Listening Profile.*[1] After you complete the tests in Table 7.2, turn to pages 171–172 to see how you compare with others who have completed the profile. There are no right or wrong answers.

Listening Skills Can Be Improved

As the findings of Sperry's listening analysis reveal, most people listen poorly. Tests show that the average listener retains only 50 percent of what he or she hears immediately following the remarks. Within twenty-four to forty-eight hours the retention level drops to 25 percent. There are several reasons for this poor showing.

Reasons for Poor Listening

Lack of Proper Education

As Figure 7.1 explains, we receive little instruction on how to be better listeners and consequently develop poor listening habits and inadequate skills. While most people have taken at least one course where they were taught to write, read, and speak, few have had a course on listening.

Poor Perception

Each person's perception of the world—of its objects, events, and people—is different. If a listener uses this perceptive filter to preevaluate a

THERE'S A LOT MORE TO LISTENING THAN HEARING.

Most of us have perfectly good ears.

So why, then, are we such perfectly awful listeners – listening on the average at a 25% level of efficiency?

The fact is, there's a lot more to listening than hearing.

After we hear something, we must interpret it. Evaluate it. And finally, respond to it. That's listening.

And it's during this complex process that we run into all kinds of trouble.

For example: we prejudge – sometimes even disregard – a speaker based on his appearance or delivery.

We let personal ideas, emotions or prejudices distort what a person has to say.

We ignore subjects we consider too difficult or uninteresting.

And because the brain works four times faster than most people speak, we too often wander into distraction.

Yet as difficult as listening really is, it's the one communication skill we're never really taught.

Well, as a corporation with more than 80,000 employees, we at Sperry are making sure we use our ears to full advantage.

We've set up expanded listening programmes that Sperry personnel from our divisions worldwide can attend. Sales representatives. Sperry Univac computer engineers. Even the Chairman of the Board.

We're convinced that effective listening adds a special dimension to what we can do for our customers. And when you speak to someone from Sperry we think you'll be equally convinced.

It's amazing what more than two good ears can do.

1. HEARING   **2. UNDERSTANDING**

3. EVALUATING   **4. RESPONDING**

✦ SPERRY

WE UNDERSTAND HOW IMPORTANT IT IS TO LISTEN.

Figure 7.1

Source: Sperry Corporation, New York, from *The Economist*, European Edition.

Table 7.2

Quiz 1

A. Circle the term that best describes you as a listener:
   Superior
   Excellent
   Above average
   Average
   Below average
   Poor
   Terrible

B. On a scale of 0 to 100 (100 = highest), how would you rate yourself as a listener?

   _____
   (0–100)

Quiz 2

How do you think the following people would rate you as a listener?
Your best friend _____
Your boss _____
A business colleague _____
A job subordinate _____
Your spouse _____

Quiz 3

As a listener, how often do you find yourself engaging in these ten bad listening habits? *First,* check the appropriate columns. *Then* tabulate your score using the key below.

Listening Habit	Almost Always	Usually	Some-times	Seldom	Almost Never	Score
1. Calling the subject uninteresting	_____	_____	_____	_____	_____	_____
2. Criticizing the speaker's delivery or mannerisms	_____	_____	_____	_____	_____	_____
3. Getting over-stimulated by something the speaker says	_____	_____	_____	_____	_____	_____
4. Listening primarily for facts	_____	_____	_____	_____	_____	_____
5. Trying to outline everything	_____	_____	_____	_____	_____	_____
6. Faking attention to the speaker	_____	_____	_____	_____	_____	_____
7. Allowing interfering distractions	_____	_____	_____	_____	_____	_____
8. Avoiding difficult material	_____	_____	_____	_____	_____	_____

Frequency (column group heading spanning Almost Always through Almost Never)

Table 7.2 *Continued*

Listening Habit	Frequency					Score
	Almost Always	Usually	Some-times	Seldom	Almost Never	
9. Letting emotional words arouse personal antagonism	___	___	___	___	___	___
10. Wasting the advantage of thought speed (day-dreaming)	___	___	___	___	___	___
Total score						___

Key

For every "Almost always" checked, give yourself a score of	2
For every "Usually" checked, give yourself a score of	4
For every "Sometimes" checked, give yourself a score of	6
For every "Seldom" checked, give yourself a score of	8
For every "Almost never" checked, give yourself a score of	10

Source: Dr. Lyman K. Steil, "Your Listening Profile," pp. 3–4.

speaker, for example, and assumes that the speaker is going to be boring and the topic uninteresting or unimportant, then the listener cannot accurately hear and understand that speaker's words.

Lack of Agreement on the Meaning of Words

Semantic problems can serve as barriers to effective communication (see Chapter 4). Speakers who assume that their words carry meanings that everyone understands are doomed to let technical jargon and company lingo block full understanding by their listeners.

Gap Time

The mind functions like a high-speed computer that is capable of processing more than 500 words per minute, yet the average person talks at a rate of 140 words per minute. This results in "gap time" on the part of the listener. To fill this empty time the mind skips to other thoughts at the same time that it listens to a speaker. During your next class meeting, listen for a few minutes and then make a list of the different thoughts that raced in and out of your mind while you were listening to the instructor. This doesn't necessarily happen because the speaker is boring. The process seems to be a psychologically healthy one but also one we can control.

Passive Versus Active Behavior

Because we don't learn proper listening techniques, and because we are lazy about filling our gap time, we develop passive behavior. Passive listeners sit, almost in a trance, and let words and actions pass in and out of their ears and minds. One Sperry executive explained the passive listening response like this: "I think it is one of our basic human tendencies that when someone talks we turn ourselves off. We let his or her mouth move and we try to respond with some non-action kind of comment and we don't want to pick the problem up and work on it."[2]

Descending Order of Efficiency

Problems can occur because of the vertical and horizontal flow of communication in an organization (see Chapter 5). Directors tend to hear 90 percent of what other directors say. But, as Field tells us, less listening takes place as communication descends the organizational ladder:

> A vice president, talked to by a chairman of the board, retains 67% of what the chairman said. A supervisor, chewed out by a VP, remembers about 56% of what he is told. A foreman listening to a manager hears with 30% to 40% efficiency. And a worker, tuned in to a foreman, can be expected to hear only about 20% of what was said.[3]

Poor listening also occurs on the way up the organization ladder. Many senior executives and supervisors are so conditioned to giving orders that they shut themselves off from what subordinates have to say; some are in love with the sound of their own voices.

Poor Listening Is Costly

Because we take listening for granted and are passive about this important skill, the value of proper listening is cheapened, and listening mistakes develop that are extremely costly to the organization. Assume that you communicate 80 percent of your workday and that 45 percent of that time is spent in listening activities. The chart in Table 7.3 shows what your listening time costs your organization. As the table shows, the organization that employs you is paying a high premium for your listening time. Assume that each employee in the company commits one listening error within the space of a month: A simple $10 listening mistake can cost a company with 100 employees $1,000; a company with 1,000 employees will pay out $10,000; and an organization with 10,000 employees will lose $100,000. In the United States there are over 100 million workers. A minor $10 listening error by each person would cost $1 billion, and most workers make numerous listening mistakes each week. Listening errors cost money, but in addition they cause the scheduling of new meetings and appointments; loss of orders; reshipping of problem shipments; retyping and recopying letters, memos, and reports; apologizing to

Table 7.3

Salary	Cost of Communication Time	Cost of Listening Time
$ 15,000	$12,000	$ 5,400
25,000	20,000	9,000
35,000	28,000	12,600
50,000	40,000	18,000
100,000	80,000	36,000

and damaging relationships with customers; and handling countless telephone calls. Much of this unnecessary effort can be minimized by improving listening skills.

Reasons for Improving Listening Skills

Understanding

Understanding occurs as we hear what others say, observe the way they say it, and relate that information to our own knowledge. The listener, not the speaker, is primarily responsible for the learning that takes place. By clearing the hurdles of ineffective communication (see Chapters 3 to 5) and observing nonverbal behavior (see Chapter 6), listeners can fully understand a speaker's ideas and feelings and can accurately judge the information. Their ability to instruct, supervise, manage, lead, and counsel is enhanced.

Accuracy

Accuracy results when we understand clearly. Accuracy requires that we ask questions when the words and actions that we hear and see are unclear or incomplete. When your boss tells you to be at a meeting with clients on Monday morning at the Holiday Inn in Columbus, you better know whether she means the Holiday Inn in Columbus, Ohio, or the Holiday Inn in Columbus, Georgia, before you make your travel arrangements.

Coping

Coping is something we all do when, for instance, distracting background noise, unusual accents or dialects, static on the telephone line, or a non-working microphone interfere with our receiving and comprehending abilities. These distractions can be frustrating at the least and ultimately can distort entire messages. Even highly technical or unfamiliar words can block understanding. Speakers can help their listeners by minimizing these factors. Listeners can improve their listening behavior by practicing and learning to cope with distractions.

Remembering

Remembering what other people say is a hard task for many listeners. We have all been introduced to an important person, only to realize a few minutes later that we didn't retain the person's name. Paper and pencil can be used to record what is said at meetings, but we often need to remember points of discussions when we have nothing to write on. Later in this chapter is an explanation of a method for remembering a speaker's words by the continual mental manipulation of their content.

Emotional Feelings

Emotional feelings are not usually stated in a speaker's words, yet the ideas that speakers verbalize to others are colored by the emotions they feel. If a customer service representative says, "I don't have time to talk with you," to a customer, it could mean that she is busy helping five other people and there are two calls waiting; or the statement could mean that the customer and his problems are a bother to her; or perhaps she is really saying that the customer bores her. Interpreting the "real message" behind what she says requires that you listen to her words and interpret the nonverbal emotions that shape her message. Mastery of both these areas can help you become more sensitive to "totally hearing" others.

Types of Poor Listeners

There are several types of poor listeners in the business environment. As you read the descriptions below, decide if you—or anyone you know—fit into the categories.

The Faker. This is a pseudo listener—a person who pretends to be doing the real thing. The faker displays head nods that seem to confirm or reject what is being said and adds comments like, "I see," "That's interesting," and "Yeah."

The Continual Talker. This listener never seems to run out of things to say. He takes a stand on every issue, interrupts conversations, and loves to hear himself talk. If you give this person the opportunity to talk, you may never be able to get another word into the conversation.

Goosemyer   by parker and wilder

Source: *Goosemyer* by Parker and Wilder. © 1980 Field Enterprises, Inc. Courtesy of Field Newspaper Syndicate.

The Rapid-Writing Note Taker. This listener thinks it is important to record every word a speaker utters. Unfortunately, she finds herself placing a period at the end of the first point as the speaker introduces the third: She is so involved in the accuracy of note taking that she completely misses the second point.

The Critic. The critic can take any of several forms. This listener calls the subject uninteresting, demeans the speaker's delivery style and lack of supporting ideas, and listens so hard for the facts that he misses the speaker's underlying feelings. A personal bias sometimes arouses his antagonistic emotions.

The "I'm in a Hurry" Listener. This person never slows down long enough to look you in the eyes and finish a conversation. She talks and listens while opening mail, talking to others on the telephone, or shuffling through papers on her desk. Typically the speaker wants to shake this listener out of her busyness and force her to listen. But more often than not, the speaker's typical response is to hurry, finish the words, and walk away.

The "Hand on the Door Knob" Listener. This listener reminds us of physicians, college professors, and many businesspeople. He ordinarily keeps his office door closed. When he decides the talk is over, he gets up from his desk or chair and moves toward the office door. There he stands with his hand on the door knob, nonverbally indicating "Time is up."

The "Make Sure It Is Correct" Listener. She can be found in every office. In meetings and conversations this person listens carefully for facts and is the first to signal when an error has been uttered. While the type of information this person remembers is often important, the method she uses—interrupting the conversation or making the speaker look bad—can become obnoxious.

The "Finish the Sentence for You" Listener. This person seems to be impatient, is always in a hurry, and feels as though he knows exactly what the speaker will say next. He can be helpful when the speaker is actually stuck and is searching for facts or lost words. But usually he intrudes when a momentary pause is taken or the speaker stops to get her breath.

Supervisors may feel that they know what their subordinates are going to say next. But they must be careful not to program the listening/discussion sessions by constantly finishing another person's sentences. This process can cause a pattern to develop where the subordinate starts talking and will automatically stop mid-sentence to let the superior finish. Needless to say, this can distort good communication relationships.

The "I've Done One Better" Listener. This type of listening is a typical form of one-upmanship. It is a variation of the fish story, where each time the catch is reported the fish grows in length. This listener, in order to obtain psychological strokes, consciously or unconsciously responds to activities and events in the lives of others with, "That reminds me of the time I. . . . " His story, of course, always demonstrates more difficulty, harder trials, worse conditions, and/or better results.

We all fall into the role of poor listener from time to time. But effective listeners work to change their ineffective behavior before it becomes a hard-to-change habit. The next two sections discuss how to actually improve your listening skills and your interpersonal listening behavior.

Improve Your Skill as a Listener

Although listening is a seldom-taught skill, it is one that can be improved. To improve your listening, however, you need instruction. By practicing the following six steps on a regular basis, you can improve your listening behavior and your overall communication effectiveness. The second part of this section describes three ways that you can improve how you listen in public speaking situations. As you will learn in Chapter 8, the ability to accurately listen to speeches helps speakers better construct and deliver their talks.

Steps for Improving Your Skill

1. *Try to create an interest in the topic.* At the outset of a speech or meeting, when you hear the discussion topic, mentally brainstorm for a few moments and think of all the things that you would like to know about that topic. By starting the listening process with an open mind and a positive attitude, you will find it easier to follow the speaker. Throughout the speech, even if you become disappointed in what is being said, strive to constantly listen for the positive and interesting information. Ralph Nichols, the forefather of listening improvement instruction, put it this way:

> The key to the whole matter of interest in a topic is the word *use.* Whenever we wish to listen efficiently, we ought to say to ourselves: "What's he saying that I can use? What worthwhile ideas has he? Is he reporting any workable procedures? Anything that I can cash in, or with which I can make myself happier?" Such questions lead us to screen what we are hear-

Source: By permission of Johnny Hart and Field Enterprises, Inc.

ing in a continual effort to sort out the elements of personal value. G. K. Chesterton spoke wisely indeed when he said, "There is no such thing as an uninteresting subject; there are only uninteresting people."[4]

2. *Start by constructing your mental outline.* Outlining will be discussed in detail in Chapter 8. For now, remember that listeners need to be aware of the thesis or theme of a talk and the major points that will support the thesis. For instance, a representative from an office product company comes to your office to give a presentation regarding the purchase of word processing equipment. If the representative is wise, she will thoroughly research your company and its equipment needs prior to the presentation. Let's assume this takes place. She knows of your needs and your interest. At the start of her presentation she introduces the word processing model that she wants you to consider. (Her thesis will revolve around the model.) Next, she states that her talk will cover four primary areas: the equipment's ability, ease in operation, cost, and the maintenance process.

If you are tuned in at the start, and you will be if you have a vital *interest* in obtaining such equipment, you will start with an empty outline in your mind (Table 7.4). As the representative talks, mentally fill in your outline with her key points (see Table 7.5). By starting with an empty outline you can "actively" participate in the listening process and retain in your mind the speaker's main points after she has finished.

Table 7.4

(Thesis) _____

(Main point) _____

(Main point) _____

(Main point) _____

(Main point) _____

Table 7.5

(Thesis of speech)	The word processing equipment
(Main point)	Capability
(Main point)	Operation ease
(Main point)	Cost
(Main point)	Maintenance

3. *Continually review your mental outline.* Speakers, like listeners, can change their minds and the content of their speeches while they are talking. If you constantly go through a memory review process, you can use your "gap time" for the review and summary process. Remember, the computer in your mind is constantly running. Discipline your mind to work for you by selectively deciding what you will allow it to think.

4. *Use key words in your mental outline.* Remember the pitfalls encountered by the rapid-writing note taker? Don't be guilty of mentally committing that same mistake. Our educational process leads us to feel that we must make extensive notes of everything that is said in speeches. In so doing we fail to discipline our minds and our ears, and, like the note taker, we sometimes miss what is said.

Your mind is capable of handling much more work than you give it. Test it; discipline it; rely on it to work for you. In Table 7.5 only one word or term is entered in each main point division. Using only one word per main point can save you a great deal of work. When you ask yourself, "What kind of capability?" your mind naturally knows you are referring to the machine, and it will in most instances recall several facts that were stated about the machine's capabilities.

5. *Judge between important and unimportant information.* Not everything that the speaker says is important or even relevant. Be critical of the content, but not the person, and attach only the important information to your mental outline.

Our word processing representative described several aspects of operation ease, including ease of entering information into the system, ease of retrieving information from the system, and comfort in using the equipment. All of this information is important. In fact, key words can again be used to enter the ideas into the mind (Table 7.6). Most presentations contain unimportant information that listeners do not need; these are often facts. Don't memorize facts. Facts are meaningless unless you connect them to the talk's main principles and concepts.

6. *Tackle distractions head-on.* At times nothing can hinder the act of listening as much as distractions, such as the noise from office or

Table 7.6 • The Word Processing Equipment

	Capability	
	Operation Ease	
E	R	C
N	E	O
T	T	M
E	R	F
R	I	O
I	E	R
N	V	T
G	I	
	N	
	G	

production machines, low-flying aircraft, automobiles, radio and television programs, crying babies, or whispering adults. All of these and more serve to disrupt the meaning of the words we hear and cause us to shift focus to the distraction or the person causing it. Sometimes the shift is necessary. A quick glare at those who are talking, or a polite request to "Please turn down the radio," can eliminate the interference. At other times distractions are not that easily overcome.

Some people listen better when distractions exist. They have learned, usually from first-hand experience, to listen through the disturbance, to hear what is said, and to process and use what they have heard.

Distractions can take forms other than surrounding noise. The accents and dialects of the speaker can be a hindrance. Perceptive speakers with distracting problems of this nature usually spend the first few minutes of a talk saying unimportant things in order for their listeners to adjust to their voice. At other times the distraction may be overly emotional feelings about the topic or the apparent lack of organization. As a listener you must constantly stay flexible and strive to hear the main points of the speaker's message.

This section focused on the type of listening that is used in everyday conversations, in large groups, and in situations where we need to remember what has been said. At every level in an organization people are required to use this kind of listening daily. You may wish to turn now to listening exercise 9 on page 175 and follow the above six steps for improving your listening skill. Listening to speeches introduces some additional factors for consideration.

How to Listen to a Speech

Sometimes the interaction between speaking and listening is most apparent in a public speech setting. One of the best training experiences for improving your listening skills is to apply your new skills to each speech you hear. Listed below are the three steps that you should follow when listening to a speech and several suggestions that will help you continue to grow in this area.

1. *Before you hear the speech*

a. *Learn as much as you can about the speaker and his or her subject.* This will help you mentally and physically prepare for the occasion.

b. *Analyze the setting and the scene of where the speech will occur* and position yourself in the most appropriate spot, where you can best see, hear, and possibly interact with the speaker.

c. *Establish a set of standards for the speech and speaker.* What is the speaker's purpose? What is your purpose in listening? How will you evaluate what the speaker is saying and how he or she is saying it? Select objective criteria that conform to quality artistic and intellectual standards. Avoid a subjective bias that filters out important content.

d. *Make decisions regarding potential listening problems.* If there are physical, personal, mechanical, or other types of potential problems that can hinder your hearing and understanding, decide how to overcome them.

2. *While you are listening to the speech*

a. *Start constructing your mental outline as soon as possible.* If the speaker gives you his or her purpose and main points at the beginning of the speech, list them in your mental outline; if not, construct the outline as you listen to the speech.

b. *Immediately relate the purpose to your life* and make some decisions on how the purpose relates to you, what you can possibly learn, how this knowledge can help you, and what you must know to be persuaded.

c. *Become a partner in the speaker's dialogue.* Pretend he or she is talking only to you and you can respond only nonverbally. Send the speaker feedback he or she can use.

d. *Analyze and test the speaker's evidence* as the data and facts are presented. Test their validity and whether the information is consistent with other facts you have. Attempt to discern between the speaker's facts and inferences.

e. *Watch the speaker's gestures, facial expressions, and physical movement.* Draw meaning from these nonverbals that either augments or contradicts what he or she says verbally.

f. *Continue your mental outlining* by frequently summarizing the speaker's main points.

g. *Reinforce your mental outline by writing* any key points, numbers, and so forth.

3. *After the speech is over*

a. *Momentarily review your mental outline and notes.* Recheck in your mind the speaker's thesis and main points. If you are taking written notes, finalize them.

b. *Ask the speaker questions for clarification* if you are puzzled over information or facts.

c. *Review your thoughts with others in the audience.* This step occasionally allows you to also obtain differing ideas, information, or facts that others in the audience might have. It also reinforces what you heard.

d. *Broaden the information through additional research.* If what the speaker had to say was of interest to you, look for books and articles that will provide more information about the subject.

Steps for Improving Interpersonal Listening Behavior

Listening with accuracy and understanding in group meetings and speeches is an important skill, but another area that is just as important is interpersonal listening behavior. This type of listening occurs in one-to-one conversations and requires more than hearing and remembering information. It requires that one person attempt to take on a mental and physical understanding of the other—an involvement that is usually missing from large group settings. It goes beyond hearing words to the development of feelings and empathy. The remainder of this chapter explores ways that you can become a better interpersonal listener. Two dimensions, physical and personal, help us go beyond words and achieve greater understanding with others.

Physical Dimensions

Conversations always take place in settings that have limits and usually follow patterns. If you can control these factors, you can drastically improve the listening that occurs between people.

1. *Pick a time and a place that are conducive to listening.* The day is full of minutes and hours when we can listen. Wise listeners examine the required communication situation and the dynamics of the time and place and make decisions based on the desired outcome.

Some people do their best work early in the mornings. They set up breakfast meetings because their minds work well at 7:00 A.M.; others don't start functioning well until 10:00 A.M. For some, the worst time of the day is immediately following lunch (it is hard to listen on a full stomach) or immediately before closing time (people then are fearful they will have to work late).

The place of the conversation is also important. You may gain power by holding the meeting in your office, but goodwill could be established by going to someone else's office. Some supervisors find it necessary to leave their offices for important counseling sessions because they have no way to transfer telephone calls or their offices are not completely private. Others walk outside the plant doors for meetings, to avoid the roar of plant machinery.

2. *Avoid time restraints.* If you have only a few free minutes, but you know a conversation will take longer, schedule it for another time or date. The other person will probably agree to the rescheduling when you explain that you want enough time to discuss all issues in depth.

3. *Attempt to shut out all distractions.* Tell your secretary to hold your calls, take your telephone off the hook, close your office door, or hang a "Do not disturb" sign outside your door to get the privacy you need.

4. *Arrange your office furniture.* Position the furniture for the best interaction. Chairs should be arranged so that you can look the other person in the eye, convey your attention, and understand his or her non-verbal messages.

Personal Dimensions

After making the necessary physical arrangements, focus your attention on the personal dimensions.

1. *Stop talking.* If you know you listen poorly because you talk too much, stop talking. If your intent is to listen, you can display it best by being completely silent—even if you must bite your tongue. Listening starts *only* when your talking stops.

2. *Prepare yourself for listening.* Realize that true dialogue involves two people. Try to understand your own emotions and feelings so that they will not influence the other person. Try to perceive the other person as he sees himself, and picture yourself as you think he sees you. This will help you create an empathic attitude.

3. *Look at the other person.* Sometimes, especially in embarrassing conversations, it is hard to look into the other person's eyes. But a sensitive and caring listener communicates best by looking at the person, instead of out the window, up at the ceiling, or over the person's shoulder. If looking at the eyes is difficult, look at the hairline, neckline, mouth, or forehead directly above the nose.

4. *Listen to what is said and what is not said.* Words are important, for they tell us what others are thinking. But counselors and psychotherapists have proven that we sometimes glean more meaning from an encounter from what is not being said. If particular issues are overly repeated, while others are ignored, the wise listener will focus on and ask questions about the area least discussed.

5. *Listen to how something is said.* The nonverbal behavior of a person tells much about the true meaning of his or her message. Wise listeners try to understand any nonverbal behavior that contradicts what is said verbally.

6. *Overcome prejudices.* If you enter a listening situation with an existing prejudice toward the speaker or topic, you will never hear what the other person is saying or trying to say. Listen before you judge. If you still disagree when finished, call in a third person as a negotiator.

7. *Realize that listening is not the same as problem solving.* Some managers don't like to listen because they fear that they will be put on the spot and have to answer questions and solve problems. Listeners do not have to solve other people's problems for them. They can, however, help others as they sort out and make decisions for themselves. A good listener will listen for what the talker is repeating and for what she is ignoring. The listener will mentally put these together and will ask questions aimed at helping the talker arrive at new answers that she can use to solve her own problems.

8. *Actively listen and establish clarity checks.* Active listening restates or paraphrases the speaker's message. It clarifies and obtains accurate facts and gives feedback to the speaker. In "active listening," a clarity check designed by Carl Rogers, a listener responds to a speaker with, "What I heard you say was . . . ," and then gives comments.

For example, a supervisor tells an employee to check on the Blair account, get an update on the production schedule along with cost factors, and order a new machine. Before following the instructions the employee gets a "clarity check": "What you want me to do is check the status and cost of the Blair account and then order the new machine, right?" Wrong! The supervisor really wants her to check the status of the Blair account. The update and the order of the new machine were separate tasks.

Clarity checks are vital when critical decisions must be made, important issues are being examined, or face-to-face communication is not available, as in telephone conversations. One excellent method of obtaining clarity is to send a written memo so that everyone concerned will get the same information.

9. *Ask questions.* Your primary job as a listener is to understand what the other person is saying. Just hearing another's words often does not lead to understanding. But asking questions regarding what is heard does

produce better understanding for both participants. Practice asking questions often, but ask them in a way that produces understanding, not critical defensiveness. Ask questions that focus on who, what, where, when, and how. Here are some examples:

- "Joe, *who* worked with you on the Morris account?"
- "*What* was the status of the account when you took it over?"
- "*Where* do you perceive the present policy is taking us?"
- "*When* do you plan to make the new proposal?"
- "*How* have you been able to complete the project in such a short time period?"

Each of the above questions asks for basic information and is stated in a nonthreatening manner. This type of question will provide clarification, improve understanding, and is even helpful for dealing with shy, nervous, and disorganized speakers.

Did you notice that the question "Why?" was omitted? That one word has stopped more conversations than any other. When asked "Why?" we have to immediately stop our train of thought, respond to the question (sometimes in order to defend our actions or beliefs), and then try to work our way back to the original place in the topic. Often the momentary stop causes us to deviate from the original issues and never return. Sensitive listeners use words other than *why* to ask questions and get information from the speaker. If *why* is the only word that will work, try a creative method of asking for the same information. Instead of asking, "Why did you do that?" try, "That's interesting, tell me more about it," or, "I'm interested in hearing the reason for your action."

Robert L. Montgomery, in his book *Listening Made Easy*, illustrates the power of questioning. He tells the story of the late Fred Herman and his unique ability to ask the listener questions:

Herman was introduced on the Mike Douglas television show one day as "the greatest salesman in the world." What happened next was purely spontaneous; Herman vowed he had no idea what Mike Douglas would ask him.

Douglas began by saying, "Fred, since you're hailed as the No. 1 salesman in the world, sell me something!" Without any hesitation, Fred Herman responded instantly and instinctively with a question: "Mike, what would you want me to sell you?"

Mike Douglas, who is paid a couple of million dollars a year for asking questions, was now on the defensive. Surprised, Douglas paused, looked around and finally answered, "Well, sell me this ash tray."

Fred Herman again spoke instantly, "Why would you want to buy that?" And again, Mike Douglas, surprised and scratching his head, finally answered, "Well, it's new and shapely. Also, it's colorful. And besides, we are in a new studio and don't want it to burn down. And, of course, we want to accommodate guests who smoke."

At this point, Mike Douglas sat back in his chair, but not for long. Instantly Fred Herman responded, "How much would you pay for the ash tray, Mike?"

Douglas stammered and said, "Well, I haven't bought an ash tray lately, but this one is attractive and large, so I guess I'd pay $18 or $20." And Fred Herman, after asking just three questions, closed the sale by saying, "Well, Mike, I'll let you have the ash tray for $18."[5]

Excerpted, by permission of the publisher, from *Listening Made Easy*, by Robert L. Montgomery, pp. 70–71. © 1981 by AMACOM, a division of American Management Associations, New York. All rights reserved.

10. *Retain the confidentiality of what you hear.* Occasionally our conversations with peers and subordinates include some disclosing and sharing. This information can be personal and private and is usually discussed under the assumption of confidentiality. While such disclosures are hard to utter, the end result for the listener can be released tensions and frustrations, lowered feelings of pressure, and even warm feelings of established friendship. But such sharing can also make us vulnerable, for the person that we shared the information with possesses, in a very real sense, a part of us. If the conversation session and the shared information are handled wisely, relationships are strengthened, conflicts resolved, and potential trouble often avoided. But if the same information is leaked or gossiped to others, reputations can be ruined and credibility destroyed. A wise listener will try to discern before the conversation whether he or she should listen to, and probe, such topics. If a decision is made to listen, the information should be maintained in strict confidentiality.

11. *Follow up.* All of us have had conversations where personal information was shared but the next time we saw the other person, the previous conversation was never mentioned. In fact, a strange, nonverbal feeling clouded the second meeting. Usually, neither person wants to reopen and examine what was previously said. Yet to ignore the time and feelings that were shared is tantamount to saying you are embarrassed about what was said. To avoid this situation, and to keep the lines of communication open, a sensitive listener will follow up with a brief and simple statement. It could sound something like this:

Say, Fran, I appreciate your sharing your feelings about your work situation last week. I trust everything is OK? We don't have to talk about it, but I just wanted to tell you that if you want to talk again, I'd be happy to listen.

A simple acknowledgement tells Fran that she was not stupid for revealing her problem and that a good listener is available if she should need to talk again.

As these eleven ways to improve interpersonal listening behavior have shown, listening is not an end in itself. Listeners have responsibility to help complete the communication process, which occurs when feedback is shared between two people. The last section of this chapter discusses the use of interpersonal feedback.

Giving and Receiving Interpersonal Feedback

Speakers contribute to better listening on the part of their audience by responding to feedback that they receive and then making immediate adjustments. In an interpersonal setting, listening is enhanced by giving, receiving, and responding to feedback. Wise managers establish written and oral feedback systems that monitor how well employees understand their messages (see Chapter 2). Such systems keep managers from being isolated and bypassed.

In communication, feedback is the reception and consequent response to what a person sees, hears, reads, or feels. We receive feedback through our different senses: seeing, hearing, smelling, touching, and tasting. During communication, we normally respond to what we see and hear.

The study of feedback became popular in the late 1940s during the scientific studies of communication engineering. *Cybernetics* was the term that people like Norbert Wiener used to refer to their feedback research. Early studies examined how systems, like guided missiles, are corrected for accuracy by receiving feedback on how far off course a missile missed its intended target. Such knowledge is vital in technical fields.

In interpersonal communication the knowledge gained by feedback is essential: Feedback tells us when our instructions are misunderstood, how our comments lack necessary relevancy, and how our nonverbal behavior contradicts what we say verbally. For feedback to be helpful to the person receiving it, information must be given clearly, be understood, be accepted, and be usable in making changes to both verbal and nonverbal messages.

Feedback Must Be Given Clearly

As listeners we give both verbal and nonverbal feedback to the speaker. *Nonverbal messages* are communicated through body movement, gestures, and facial expressions. As the chart on pages 138–139 indicates, messages are sent when we stand, sit, smile, frown, or even look questioningly.

Verbal messages take the form of clarity checks, questions, or sharing of feelings or reactions. Larger and often repeated behavioral patterns can be discussed. When listeners share give this type of feedback, speakers can use listeners' reactions as a mirror for observing the consequences of their own behavior: They become aware of what they say and do and how they say and do it. This awareness, if used correctly, can become a behavior modifier.

Feedback Needs to Be Understood

Before individuals can make verbal and behavioral changes based on feedback, they have to understand specifically what they are saying and doing, how they are saying and doing it, and how others feel about what they hear and see. Listeners have this information, but they must be careful not to "dump" it unreservedly on the other person.

Describe behavior. Feedback should describe another's behavior only in terms of what the listener sees and hears and not in relation to what the listener believes the other person is like. Sandra, a manager, was holding a performance appraisal with Ed, a supervisor. Sandra listened to Ed describe his job and then responded, "Ed, I've observed you in staff meetings. You are a motormouth and don't give your people a chance to talk." Ed, of course, was dumbstruck and defensively argued his case. Sandra could have better phrased her comments around Ed's behavior instead of his person: "Ed, I observed your staff meeting today, and you talked a lot and didn't allow comments from the others." Personality traits are difficult or impossible to change; changing behavioral habits is much easier.

Feedback Must Be Accepted

Focus on observations, not inferences. Chapter 4 discussed the danger of acting on inferences rather than observations. Making that distinction is critical for listeners: Describing behavior that we have viewed gives us credibility, but developing inferences based on second-hand knowledge or guesses destroys that credibility, fogs perception of the other person, and can cause inappropriate filtering of what we hear and see.

Cover the "now" instead of the "then." The best time for providing feedback is immediately following an observation or discussion, when the feedback carries more meaning and impact. Focusing on yesterday or some time in the past, instead of now, is unfair and also subjectively distorts the message we want to convey. One of the worst types of poor listeners is the "closet stuffer." This person observes the action and hears the words but builds up ammunition from several episodes before she responds. When she finally shares her feedback, there is too much for the other to hear, much less to utilize.

Feedback Must Be Usable in Making Changes

Sharing instead of giving advice. Too often feedback is given because the "release" feels good; this type of feedback usually takes the form of advice. Instead of giving advice, focus on sharing ideas so that others are free to use the information when and if they like.

Give what the other person can use, not what you are capable of giving. We are all capable of continually critiquing others. But the best feedback comes after selectively deciding what will really help the other person to make behavioral changes. Maybe it is a simple word of encouragement, or a point of clarification, or a comment regarding what someone said or how they said it. Thoughtful listeners ask themselves, "If I were that person, what would I need to hear and how would I need to hear it?" Once this question is answered, feedback can then be formulated and communicated.

Summary

Listening is the most used but least taught communication skill. Most people are poor listeners because perception and semantics problems interfere with their accurately hearing what another person says. Add to this physical gap time and passive behavior, and we have a poor listener who costs his company a large amount of money. We can even typecast poor listeners into categories like "the faker" or "the critic." But there are ways to improve listening.

The skill of listening can be improved by the proper construction of mental outlines. This is accomplished through (1) creating an interest in the topic, (2) constructing your mental outline, (3) continually reviewing your mental outline, (4) using key words in your mental outline, (5) judging between important and unimportant information, and (6) tackling distractions head-on. Listening to speeches can be improved by following certain suggestions before, during, and after the speech. In addition, several interpersonal physical and personal dimensions can enhance the ability to listen.

A listener can most effectively communicate through dialogue with others by giving and receiving interpersonal feedback. While the "right way" to exchange feedback may become instinctive after much practice, it will do so only if sensitive behaviors and attitudes are the basis for that practice.

Answers to Chapter Tests
Profile Analysis of the Sperry Listening Test

This is how other people have responded to the same questions that you answered in Table 7.2 on pages 152–153.

Quiz #1

A. Eighty-five percent of all listeners questioned rate themselves as *Average* or less. Fewer than 5 percent rate themselves as Superior or Excellent.

B. On the 0–100 scale, the extreme range is 10–90; the general range is 35–85; and the *average rating* is 55.

Quiz #2

When comparing the listening *self-ratings* and projected ratings of others, most respondents believe that their best friend would rate them highest as a listener. And that rating would be higher than the one they gave themselves in Quiz #1 . . . where the average was a 55.

How come? We can only guess that best friend status is such an intimate, special kind of relationship that you can't imagine it ever happening unless you *were* a good listener. If you were not, you and he or she wouldn't be best friends to begin with.

Going down the list, people who take this test usually think their bosses would rate them higher than they rated themselves. Now part of that is probably wishful thinking. And part of it is true. We *do* tend to listen to our bosses better . . . whether it's out of respect or fear or whatever doesn't matter.

The grades for colleague and job subordinate work out to be just about the same as the listener rated himself or herself . . . that 55 figure again.

But when you get to spouse . . . husband or wife . . . something really dramatic happens. The score here is significantly lower than the 55 average that previous profile-takers gave themselves. And what's interesting is that the figure goes steadily downhill. While newlyweds tend to rate their spouse at the same high level as their best friend, as the marriage goes on . . . and on . . . the rating falls. So in a household where the couple has been married 50 years, there could be a lot of talk. But maybe nobody is *really* listening.

Quiz #3

The average score is a 62 . . . 7 points higher than the 55 that the average test-taker gave himself or herself in Quiz #1. Which suggests that when listening is broken down into specific areas of competence, we rate ourselves better than we do when listening is considered only as a generality.

Of course, the best way to discover how well you listen is to ask the people to whom you listen most frequently—your spouse, boss, best friend, etc. They'll give you an earful.[6]

Review Questions

1. Name and describe each of the four stages of listening.
2. How does listening compare with how the skills of reading, writing, and speaking are taught and used?
3. This chapter gives six reasons for why we listen poorly. What are they? Which ones do you feel that you can apply to yourself?
4. Name five reasons for improving listening skills. Describe the ones that apply to your own skills.
5. Name the nine types of poor listeners, and give an example of how listening is affected by each type of listener.
6. The skill of listening can be improved. List the six steps for bringing about improvement, and describe what a listener must do, in each step, to be successful.
7. Describe the four ways in which we can arrange the physical dimensions of our interpersonal listening.
8. Eleven methods are available for improving our personal behavior as a listener. Name and describe the methods.
9. Define feedback as a part of the listening process.
10. Explain the seven ways to give and receive interpersonal feedback.

Exercises

1. Become aware of the world of sounds that you live in. Find a place where you can listen undisturbed, and for fifteen minutes list the different sounds that you hear.

2. Find an article in your daily paper that describes a well-known person. Read the article to a friend, but delete the famous person's name. See if your friend, by listening to the description, can guess the name of the person.

3. For a few minutes consider one or two lectures, speeches, or staff meetings that you have attended recently. Outline the major theme and the supporting points of each. What types of arguments and examples do you remember hearing? How much of that event do you remember? How do your answers compare with the information presented in this chapter?

4. With a friend watch a local or national newscast tonight. Your friend should take notes during the program, but you should not. As soon as the newscast ends, write down an outline of the stories and characters that were covered. Compare this with what your friend recorded. How accurate is your list? Now turn to another station, and exchange the roles of note taker and listener. After the exercise discuss why certain news items and characters were easy to remember while others were difficult.

5. Spend a few minutes reflecting on listening situations you have encountered. Make a list of the words or phrases and the nonverbal behavior that speakers have used that have caused you or others to tune out of the conversation or turn off the speaker. How has such behavior affected how you listen and how you speak and talk to others? Discuss your findings in class or with friends.

6. The three sections of this exercise will demonstrate how the poor listening habits of another affect you.
   a. Divide the class into groups of four or five.
   b. In the following exercises each person in each group should have a turn at talking.
   c. In the first exercise each person should share with the other members the "most exciting" thing that has happened in his or her life. During this short sharing, each of the other small group members should be playing the role of "the faker." They should pretend to be listening but obviously be mentally involved in their own thoughts. They should be polite and should nonverbally behave as if listening.
   d. After all members have finished the exercise take a few minutes to share the "feelings" the participants had because of the behavior.
   e. Next, go around the room and let each person describe his or her best vacation. Each new respondent should start the discussion with an attitude of "I've done one better."
   f. Again, take time for the group to discuss the feelings regarding the displayed behavior.
   g. Finally, each group member should focus on a problem that he or she has

and a way in which he or she would like to change. Each person should be in this discussion. While each hears others describe their problems, he or she should mentally be concentrating on his or her own problems and the possible change.

   h. After this segment, discuss the behavior of group members, the feelings of the participants, and any real-life situations where this same behavior has occurred.

   i. Now bring the entire class together for a few minutes to talk about what has been learned in this series of exercises.

7. Find a picture that has a variety of detail, such as one of buildings, active people, or cars. (A sample picture is in the instructor's guide for this book.)

   a. Five participants should be selected and brought to the front of the room.

   b. Four are immediately sent outside the room, and the door is closed.

   c. Show the picture to the fifth, and give him or her two or three minutes to study it in detail. Tell this person that he or she will be responsible for describing the picture, in detail, to someone else who in turn will describe it to another.

   d. If extra copies of the picture were made, they can be circulated to all other classmates. This will give people in the audience a chance to determine when descriptive changes are made between the real picture and what someone heard and perceived.

   e. After two or three minutes take the picture away, and bring in the first person so that the observer can describe what he or she saw.

   f. The listener then repeats the description to the second outside person, and this process continues until each of the four has heard the description.

   g. After the fourth receives the instructions, he or she should then describe the scene to the entire audience.

   h. The class should take several minutes to analyze where mistakes and listening errors occurred, when major additions or deletions were made in the description, and how close the end product resembled the original.

   i. Spend a few minutes describing real-life situations where similar results have occurred.

8. Divide the class into groups of three. In this exercise two people will discuss an issue, and the third person will observe the discussion (speaking-listening process). Designate in each group which person will be A, which one B, and which one C.

   a. Start the exercise with A and B picking an issue about which each has a different viewpoint. The issue can be one of economic, political, or social importance or one where personal preference is involved.

   b. A and B should then proceed to discuss the issue for five or ten minutes. During the discussion C will observe how well listening occurs.

   c. In their conversational interaction, A and B should use active listening and clarity checks. Both individuals should also practice giving and receiving feedback. The goal is to understand and clarify the message and not to judge, analyze, or question the person.

   d. C's job is to listen and indicate whether clarity checks are observed, see if a more accurate speaking and listening process results, and determine whether better understanding occurred between A and B.

Each small group should rotate roles so that every individual receives a turn at being the observer.

9. This exercise tests your skills of hearing and remembering.
   a. Ask a friend or classmate to read the following story aloud.
   b. Ask the person to read the story once at a normal rate of speech.
   c. Even though you may be tempted to read it to yourself, please don't. By having someone else read it, you'll have a lot more fun, and you'll learn more from the exercise.
   d. After the story is read, take the test that follows.

The Long-Awaited Day

Harvey Wolff got home at 3:20 P.M., over two hours earlier than usual. The reason? This was July 14, the day when the family would start its annual two-week vacation. Harvey and his wife Carol had mapped out a terrific plan for their twelve-day, 7,500-mile trip.

They would leave their home in Atlanta and drive through to Colorado, where some fishing was in store. From there they would head up to Yellowstone Park, after stopping in Jackson Hole, Wyoming. A drive down the west side of the Teton Mountains would take them through Utah and into California. The kids would love Disneyland. Harvey was looking forward to first seeing San Francisco.

After several days on the West Coast the family would head straight east, back to their home in Georgia.

Carol had things packed in their station wagon. Their two children, Allen, age 10, and Dedra, age 7, were very excited. The children were so eager they even volunteered to help Carol mow the yard, take out the trash, and water the plants that morning while Harvey was at work. That was unusual because they seldom volunteered to help with chores.

When Harvey got home, he changed clothes and gulped down a hamburger and Coke. Carol and the kids had eaten. Harvey wanted to leave soon so that they could drive 240 miles to Shreveport before dark. He quickly drank another Coke.

At 4:40 P.M. they pulled out of their driveway but only got two blocks before the girl cried, "I forgot my doll." Harvey turned around and went back. When they left the second time, the kids exclaimed "Oh boy" as they headed down the highway.

Forty miles and one hour and ten minutes later Harvey was about to pull his hair. The kids were starving and "just had to eat." Carol explained that she had fed them only minutes before Harvey got home, but she persuaded him to stop at a roadside café for snacks, just to keep the peace. The name of the place was "The Hungry Man." The children had hamburgers and lemonade. Harvey and Carol had hot dogs, french fries, and coffee. Snack time took forty minutes.

When they piled into the wagon, Carol pulled out comic books for the kids to read. After reading his book Allen pulled out his electronic watch and started playing the tunes. All was peaceful until that happened. His sister complained that she couldn't read with all that noise. Carol didn't like the sound either.

Seventy-five miles from Shreveport, as darkness fell, Harvey thought, "Ah, the same old vacation problems."

Write down the number for the correct answers.

1. The last name of the family was: (a) Harrison (b) Huff (c) Wolff (d) Anderson
2. Harvey got home at: (a) 3:10 (b) 3:20 (c) 3:30 (d) 3:40
3. The vacation started on: (a) July 4 (b) July 14 (c) July 10 (d) July 17
4. The length of the trip would be: (a) 10 days (b) 12 days (c) 14 days (d) 15 days
5. On the trip they would drive: (a) 4,000 miles (b) 5,500 miles (c) 6,000 miles (d) 7,500 miles
6. The family lived in: (a) Atlanta (b) Dallas (c) Montgomery (d) Shreveport
7. The boy's name was: (a) Allen (b) Alvin (c) William (d) Bill
8. The boy's age was: (a) 7 (b) 9 (c) 10 (d) 12
9. The girl's name was: (a) Debby (b) Dedra (c) Patty (d) Sharon
10. The girl's age was: (a) 7 (b) 9 (c) 10 (d) 11
11. What was the first major sight-seeing event scheduled on the trip? (a) Yellowstone Park (b) Jackson Hole (c) Disneyland (d) Colorado
12. The family was driving a: (a) car (b) station wagon (c) Bronco (d) Wagonneer
13. The kids did not help Carol: (a) cut the lawn (b) take out the trash (c) water the lawn (d) water the plants
14. Before leaving Harvey had (a) a hamburger and two Cokes (b) a hotdog and two Cokes (c) two hamburgers and a Coke (d) two hamburgers and two Cokes
15. How far did Harvey want to drive before dark? (a) 140 miles (b) 180 miles (c) 220 miles (d) 240 miles
16. They first pulled out of their driveway at: (a) 4:30 P.M. (b) 4:40 P.M. (c) 4:50 P.M. (d) 5:00 P.M.
17. Before stopping they drove: (a) 1 hour (b) 1 hour 10 minutes (c) 1½ hours (d) 1 hour and 40 minutes
18. The distance they drove before stopping was: (a) 30 miles (b) 40 miles (c) 50 miles (d) 60 miles
19. They arrived at the eating place at: (a) 5:30 P.M. (b) 5:50 P.M. (c) 6:00 P.M. (d) 6:15 P.M.
20. They stopped at a: (a) café (b) truck stop (c) roadside park (d) cafeteria
21. The name of the place was: (a) Country Kitchen (b) Roadside Café (c) Frank's Grill (d) The Hungry Man

22. The children ate: (a) hamburgers (b) hot dogs (c) french fries (d) ice cream
23. The stop took: (a) 30 minutes (b) 40 minutes (c) 45 minutes (d) 50 minutes
24. The children started arguing over: (a) a comic book (b) a game they were playing (c) the boy's watch (d) something to eat
25. How far were they from Shreveport when it got dark? (a) 50 miles (b) 75 miles (c) 85 miles (d) 100 miles

Answers: 1(c), 2(b), 3(b), 4(b), 5(d), 6(a), 7(a), 8(c), 9(b), 10(a), 11(d), 12(b), 13(c), 14(a), 15(d), 16(b), 17(b), 18(b), 19(b), 20(a), 21(d), 22(a), 23(b), 24(c), 25(b).

Key Words

listening	coping	interpersonal listening
gap time	remembering	
passive listening	emotions	active listening
understanding	mental outlining	interpersonal feedback
accuracy		

References

1. Dr. Lyman K. Steil, President of Communication Development, Inc., St. Paul, Minnesota, "Your Personal Listening Profile," a brochure prepared for the Sperry Corporation, New York. Reprinted by permission of Dr. Steil and the Sperry Corporation.
2. John Lewis DiGaetani, "The Sperry Corporation and Listening: An Interview," *Business Horizons* (March/April 1982), p. 36.
3. *Ibid.*, p. 39.
4. Ralph G. Nichols, "Listening Is a 10-Part Skill," *Nation's Business* (July 1957), pp. 56–57.
5. Robert L. Montgomery, "Are You a Good Listener?" *Nation's Business* (Oct. 1981), pp. 70–71. This article contains excerpts from Montgomery's book, *Listening Made Easy* (AMACOM, a division of American Management Associations, New York, 1981).
6. Steil.

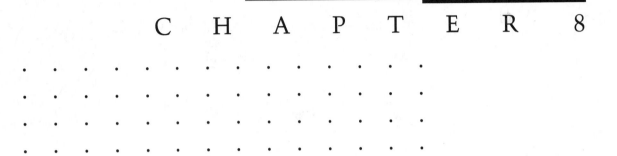

C H A P T E R 8

Presentational Speaking
in Business:
A Four-Part Process

Introduction

Speakers communicate both verbally and nonverbally with listeners, and their professional presentations of information are vital to any business. Although the amount of actual time that a speaker spends in front of an audience is relatively short, he or she spends innumerable hours on research, writing, artwork, and oral rehearsals. Contracts, jobs, bonuses, and individual reputations often ride on presentations. With so much at stake, a manager should strive to make each presentation perfect.

Unfortunately, things go wrong. Maybe it's because the manager has a fear of speaking. Wallechinsky and Wallace, in *The Book of Lists*, tell us that their survey of 3,000 Americans revealed that giving a speech is the greatest fear people possess; they fear it even more than dying.[1]

Fear of making presentations is more often than not linked to ineffective presentations. For a presentation to accomplish its goal and be effective, several things must happen: The speaker must have a purpose; the material must be organized in such a way that the listener can understand and follow it; and the event must be enjoyable for all involved. If those things happen, fear is usually displaced. If they do not, then the chaos of giving a talk can cause more than fear: It can bring disaster.

This chapter presents a simple, four-step process for ensuring the success of presentations. Ask yourself certain questions as you organize the presentation; construct the presentation solidly and clearly; spend time in practice and rehearsal prior to the final performance; take certain steps as you give that final performance. This four-step process can help you maximize the effect of all your presentations.

Organizing an Oral Presentation

Since we orally present information to others in a variety of ways, all these situations can be referred to as "presentations." By asking the questions Who?, Where?, When?, Why?, What?, and How? in sequence during the opening stages of preparation, you will obtain information necessary for the successful completion of the talk and will then be able to construct an effective presentation.

To Whom Are You Speaking?

The composition of every group is different, and your speech must be designed for the unique needs of a specific audience. Consider these questions when reviewing your audience:

- What do the listeners know about my topic and the information I can present?
- What is the age level of my audience? You can say and explain things to adults that you might not want to share with children.
- What is the educational level of my listeners? This information can give you insight into their knowledge, attitudes, and value.
- Will the listeners be men or women or both? (Ideally, factors of this nature should not make a difference.)
- What position do the listeners occupy in business or society? Position reveals information about attitudes, values, types of jobs, and social involvement such as club membership and community concerns.

You should aim for the lowest common denominator of your audience when you prepare your presentation.

Where Will Your Presentation Be Given?

Location is important in planning presentations, as is the occasion for the speech.

Place. Big differences exist among office conference rooms, hotel seminar rooms, large auditoriums, and boardrooms. The setting will affect what you will say, how your listeners will hear you, and the outcome of your talk. The differences include factors like seating arrangements, lighting conditions, air control, acoustics, and freedom of movement. Knowing these conditions in advance can help you take steps to overcome many problems and obstacles.

Occasion. Will your talk be a part of a weekly staff meeting, learning session, banquet speeches, product promotion meeting, or monthly PTA meeting? Each occasion is different and can determine the level of audience enthusiasm, the tone of the remarks prepared, and especially what you should say to the group about their purpose for being there.

When Will Your Presentation Be Given?

Find out both the date and time of day for your talk. This will help you plan your practice sessions. Several practice presentations should be delivered at the same time of day the speech will be delivered, even if it is 7:00 A.M. or 8:00 P.M.

Why Give Your Talk?

Every presentation has a purpose. The two most common purposes for business presentations are to inform and to persuade other people.

To inform. Presentations to inform present either new information on a topic or old information presented in a new way.

To persuade. A persuasive presentation can also present information, but in addition the speaker will seek to have listeners *accept, believe in,* and *act on* the information.

What Do You Want to Communicate?—Patterns of Organization

Information can come in different sizes and shapes, and the speaker can organize it to maximize the effect he or she wants to make. The facts gleaned about the audience and the occasion, the content of the talk, and the speaker's personality help determine these patterns of organization. As you consider the information you want to relate, make decisions about how you can arrange it for ease of listening and accomplishment of the desired results. Examples of outlines that follow various organizational patterns discussed below are located at the end of this book in Appendix A.

Chronological. In this pattern, events are organized according to the time and order of occurrence. This works best for historical information or for describing how something can be accomplished.

Spatial. Sometimes information can be described according to physical location. For instance, a truckers' strike could be described as it starts on the East Coast and gradually moves, through regions, toward the West Coast. Or a company's hierarchy can be explained by "The president is at the top and her three vice presidents are below."

Topical. Some subjects can be naturally divided into subgroups. For example, a manager at Sears could describe his market position in terms of monthly sales compared to those of K-Mart and J. C. Penney.

Sequential. Information described in terms of a series of steps, processes, or procedures requires the sequential method. For instance, you may release the gas pressure by turning the valve two turns; then you wait five minutes until the pressure is gone.

Classification. Data can be divided into different categories. For instance, a speech on the top housing markets in the United States could divide its information into major cities and number of housing starts.

Comparative. Use this method when two or more things can be compared. If a manager is viewing several potential training programs for her employees, she may compare them according to cost of travel, cost of tuition, depth of the program, and amount of preparation.

Problem/solution. With this method the problem is usually described, and then one or several solutions are offered. Here is how one speaker used the pattern to describe the critical impact of the nation's social security problem on personal savings:

---

1. Social Security's Effect on Savings
   a. Described by budget line and indifference curve
   b. Described by the effect on savings
   c. Net reduction of savings rate because of pay-as-you-go pension plan
2. Effect of Reduced Savings on the Economy
   a. Savings directly or indirectly finances investment in productive capital
   b. Less is invested, thus slower rate of economic growth, reduced future "real" income

3. Other Effects
   a. Expenditures of the system grow at 18 percent a year
   b. Instead of several workers supporting one retiree, one worker will
      support several retirees

The speaker then went on to describe several possible solutions as he said, "I now want to introduce you to three proposed reform methods that could solve this horrendous problem."

Advantage/disadvantage. A pattern that closely resembles the problem/solution is that of advantage/disadvantage. It is used to show that one or several factors outweigh others. For example, an employer could offer employees the opportunity to tax-shelter some of their earnings. When the personnel representative explains the possibilities at a special meeting, she gives the advantages and disadvantages of a tax shelter over an IRA:

Advantages of a Tax Shelter over an IRA

1. You may be able to shelter more money.
2. Employers often match your contributions.
3. Sometimes you can withdraw your contribution at any time.
4. You get better tax treatment when you leave the company.

Disadvantages of a Tax Shelter over an IRA

1. You get less investment freedom in the company plan.
2. Your contribution is not tax deductible, and you can't keep your company's matching contributions unless you are in the plan five to ten years.
3. Salary reductions lock in your money unless you show a hardship.

Cause/effect. In this pattern, a problem can be examined from its causes and effects. Usually the causes are examined first, but in some instances the order is reversed. For example, one manager who proposed that his company use the management by objectives (MBO) process used the following cause/effect pattern:

    I. The MBO Process
      A. Goals and objectives are discussed by the superior and subordinate.
      B. Worker responsibilities are enumerated.
      C. Worker performance is evaluated.
      D. Methods for evaluating progress are determined.
      E. Methods for measuring performance are decided.
      F. Workers and supervisor meet to discuss performance.
    II. Effects of the Process
      A. The process encourages worker involvement.
      B. It evaluates true performance.
      C. It improves morale because workers take part in planning, implementing, and evaluating.

How Can You Best Present Your Information?

Decide the best way to communicate information in your presentation by examining all the above organizational patterns and your personal knowledge of the topic. Structure your information into units called verbal supporting material; you may decide to use audio-visual aids that support and present the information with the help of tools like overhead projectors, flipcharts, slides, and manuals.

Verbal Supporting Material

The verbal support used in presentations is important because it helps listeners picture ideas. Verbal support also helps the speaker verify, clarify, and amplify points. As you select supporting material, ask yourself several questions:

- Do the particular items really support or explain your contention? Your selection should be relevant, complete, and concise in development and explanation.
- Will each support be accepted by your listeners and help you accomplish the result you are seeking?
- Will the information be interesting?

• Is it motivational?
• Is it too confusing?
• Will the listeners immediately understand it?
• Is it believable?
• Will the audience identify with it?
• Is it factual and reliable?
• Is it really needed?

If you can answer yes to each of these questions, the support that you selected is probably a good one. Some of the most common types of verbal support are comparison, definition, example, illustration, statistic, story, and testimony.

Comparison. A comparison examines the features of one thing in relation to something else. In a business presentation a speaker often takes ideas, events, or products that the listener knows and uses and through comparison presents information that is unknown in hopes of developing both knowledge and acceptance of a new item. In marketing, for example, one product is often compared to another in terms of quality, usage, durability, and price.

Robert C. Rosenberg, senior vice-president of the Starrett Housing Corporation, used a comparison of the past and present American family in a speech on the future of residential housing delivered to a New York City Rotary Club (see Exhibit 8.1).

The American family has undergone a remarkable transformation which has drastically changed the size and features of new and remodeled housing. The traditional family concept of working father, stay-at-home mother, two or three children, and the yard dog is vanishing . . . and being replaced by a household with two family incomes. We can expect this trend to continue, as the second income becomes more and more a matter of survival and maintenance of the family's standard of living. . . . Two-worker families have less time and desire for yard and home care and fewer children; consequently, less area to maintain and closeness to places of employment will become more important than trees and grass. This is why we see such a revival of remodeling taking place in Victorian mansions in Brooklyn and brownstones on the West Side. In fact, the once unmarketable row house has already become one of the hottest items in the marketplace.

Exhibit 8.1

Source: Robert C. Rosenberg, "Future of Residential Housing: A Decent Home—The American Dream," a speech delivered to the New York Rotary Club, New York, on April 9, 1981, in *Vital Speeches* (June 15, 1981), p. 524. Reprinted by permission.

Definition. Using the definition as a support allows you to give the precise meaning of a word or concept and avoid the possibility of listener misunderstanding. This is especially important if a word has a double meaning or interpretation or if the talk encompasses technical concepts. Avoid an often repeated, "According to Webster . . ." phrase, and think about the possibility of giving your own definition.

Robert H. Edmonds, an economist, decided to use a series of definitions as he explained the difficult concept of inflation. The first two are widely accepted, the third less so. But Edmonds molded that definition into one that he refered to throughout the remainder of his speech (see Exhibit 8.2).

Example. Examples are used to give listeners specific information about a general idea. Sometimes they are used to stimulate the mind or the emotions. More often they simply allow listeners to use their imagi-

---

The most common definition for inflation is too much money chasing too few goods. This is a perfectly good, all-purpose definition. It has the advantage that it emphasizes both money and goods. If money is increased too much, inflation will result. If goods are increased more than money, inflation will lessen. Its major drawback is that it is not particularly useful in trying to limit or control inflation. . . .

A second definition is that inflation is a continuing increase in prices. This refers to prices in general, as expressed by an index of the prices of many commodities, not of any special goods. A rise in the price of oil, for example, does not constitute inflation, nor does an increase in the price of automobiles. Inflation refers to the rise of enough prices so that money clearly has less buying power in general. . . .

A third definition is that inflation is a continuing decrease in the value of money. Although this definition is not as widely recognized as the other two, it is the one I will adopt. My definition is this: Inflation is a continuing decrease in the purchasing power of money, MEASURED by a rising index of prices in general, and CAUSED by an excessive supply of money.

Why is this definition to be preferred?

The answer is simple. BY FOCUSING ON MONEY, WE CAN SOLVE THE PROBLEM. BY FOCUSING ON PRICES, WE CAN'T. Actually, money is the CAUSE and prices are the EFFECT. Understanding money is the only workable approach for ending inflation because money is the central part of the problem.

Exhibit 8.2

Source: Robert H. Edmonds, "Appropriate Economics: The Goals of Zero Inflation and Full Employment," a speech delivered at Monterey Peninsula College, Monterey, California, May 17, 1981, in *Vital Speeches* (July 1, 1981), pp. 560–61. Reprinted by permission.

nation while trying to understand the speaker's thoughts. Examples can take the form of a specific instance, a real example, or a hypothetical example. Illustrations are commonly thought of as synonymous to examples, but they are employed as a separate type of support.

Illustration. This form of support is really a detailed form of an example. It is used to give impact and clarity to a specific idea. Illustrations serve as a verbal visualization for listeners. They capture the interest and attention of listeners and help clarify information that is often difficult to understand. Illustrations differ from examples because they include a large number of details.

Joseph C. Kennedy, director of international development of Africare, Inc., delivered an emotional speech on world hunger at the World Hunger Hearings before the United States House of Representatives. In his presentation he explained the critical problem of hunger in the Third World, described how the problem affects the continent of Africa, defined his Africare organization, and then used an illustration to explain a specific project in Africare's food production program (see Exhibit 8.3).

At Ramsa, on a five hectare plot, two wide-diameter hand-dug wells were placed at each end of the plot. Small hand-dug canals were put in. Around the plot, eucalyptus trees were planted to serve as wind breaks, to prevent soil erosion, and later to be used as firewood. Africare provided the funding, masons were paid to do the cement lining of the well, and the villagers contributed all of the rest of the labor free—the digging of the wells, the canals, and the preparing of the land. By the end of the second year, the people were growing tomatoes, cabbages, lettuce, onions, carrots, potatoes. Each of the farmers engaged in this project—about 100—not only grew enough to eat, but recognized a revenue of $225 from sale of their produce. This in a country where the per capita income is less than $150 per month.

Exhibit 8.3

Source: Joseph C. Kennedy, "World Hunger: The Opportunity to Feed Themselves," a speech delivered to the United States House of Representatives Committee on World Hunger, World Hunger Hearings, Washington, D.C., July 21, 1981, in *Vital Speeches* (September 15, 1981), p. 719. Reprinted by permission.

Statistics. Numerical data in presentations are statistics. Statistics are one of the strongest types of support, for they help organize the collection and interpretation of information. They also can be misleading. For this reason ensure that your material is from reliable and well-known sources, proves exactly what you want it to prove, and is organized in the most easily understood way. This example comes from Mr. Kennedy's

Mr. Chairman, Members of the Committee, I know we are all aware of the statistics of hunger. There are four billion people in the world today. One billion have per capita incomes of over $5,000 per year, and by and large are the well fed and the well off. Three billion live in what has become known as the Third World. Their per capita income is generally under $500. They are the poor and the hungry. In the world one billion people go to bed hungry each night and 85 percent of the children born the rest of this century will grow up in poor countries.

In Africa—a continent richly endowed with 95 percent of the world's diamonds, 87 percent of the cobalt, and 65 percent of the world's gold—the overall per capita income is about $450 per year, and in many countries such as Upper Volta, Mali, Chad, Somalia, Ethiopia, per capita income is less than $150 per year. We know full well the relationship between poverty and hunger.

Exhibit 8.4

Source: Kennedy, "World Hunger," p. 717.

speech on world hunger. He uses a variety of easy-to-remember classifications for his statistics (see Exhibit 8.4).

Story. A speaker who wishes to narrate an event or series of events can use the story form of support. A story can be true or fictitious and can be drawn from readings, other speakers, or real-life incidents the speaker has encountered. A story can be expertly used in the introduction of a talk and is best employed in a quick, lively manner. A problem many speakers have in using stories is overdetailed, rambling narrative.

Testimony. The testimony uses the views, opinions, or experiences of someone other than the speaker. Often the material is delivered in the form of a quotation and in most instances the source is acknowledged. In fact, the strength of this type of support is a result of the status, importance, and authority of the person making the original statement. In Exhibit 8.5, Joel Chaseman, president of Post-Newsweek Stations, Inc., uses a quotation from a recognized historical figure.

Audio-Visual Aids

We commonly refer to items like facts and figures used in presentations as verbal support. Often, however, the same material can be made more exciting, presented more clearly, and received by the audience more persuasively if audio-visual aids are used. Such aids can help the speaker explain complicated concepts in moments, where words would take

What a week this has been for America! Most of us have spent many extra hours watching television just to keep up with it—the inauguration, the hostages, the Super Bowl. This week's events helped me understand how much we take for granted, most of all, that we can react to events together, as a people. Today I'd like to examine that assumption and the challenges to it—present and future, so that the probability of our sharing experience as a nation is preserved without damage to the media which have become so crucial to our viability as a people.

Alexis de Tocqueville said this in 1835:

Only a newspaper can put the same thought at the same time before a thousand readers. . . . [I]n democratic countries it often happens that a great many men who both want and need to get together cannot do so, for all being very small and lost in the crowd they do not see one another at all and do not know where to find one another. Then a newspaper gives publicity to the feeling or idea that had occurred to them all simultaneously but separately. They all at once aim toward that light, and these wandering spirits, long seeking each other in the dark, at last meet and unite.

Exhibit 8.5

Source: Joel Chaseman, "The Media Revolution in America: Television News," a speech delivered at the Town Hall of California in Los Angeles on January 27, 1981, in *Vital Speeches* (April 1, 1981), p. 374. Reprinted by permission.

many minutes. As you consider the possibility of using audio-visual aids, ask yourself these questions:

- Will this aid add to or distract from my presentation?
- Can the aid be used simply?
- Will the aid bring balance and unity to my presentation?
- Is the cost of this aid reasonable and does it fit my budget?
- Can the aid be read? Can it be heard?
- Is it clear?
- Is the quality of the aid good?
- Is the aid appropriate?

Constructing the Presentation

After the organizational stage comes the job of constructing the speech. The construction of a speech can be considered analogous to the construction of a house. An unconstructed house has many independent boards; when the boards are properly constructed, you have a strong and sturdy house. Likewise, an unconstructed speech has many single words and independent ideas; when ideas are properly constructed, you have a solid informative or persuasive presentation. Both the speech and house in Figure 8.1 represent a rough structure. Before the house is suitable for living, a lot of finishing-out is required; before the speech can be delivered, it also needs to be finished-out. Figure 8.2 represents the finished version.

The Parts of the Presentation

Organized speeches have three main parts, each with a specific function: an introduction, a body, and a conclusion.

The Introduction

First, the introduction of a presentation helps the speaker gain the audience's attention. After the opening attention-getting lines, you clearly

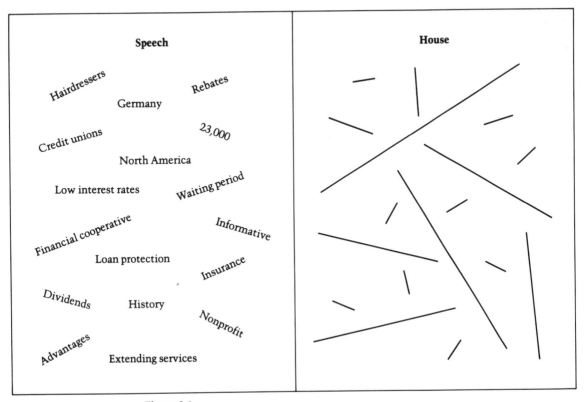

Figure 8.1

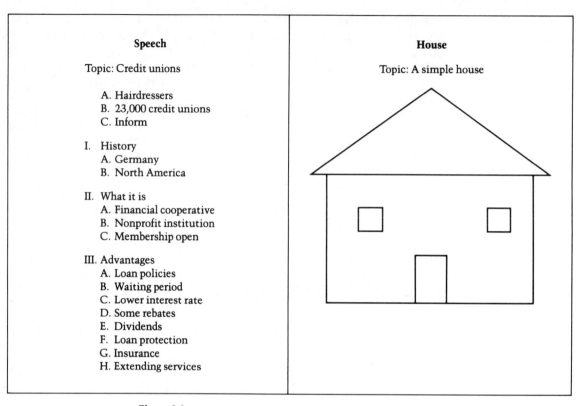

Figure 8.2

and specifically connect the topic to your audience. In some way you must assure them that their time and attention will be rewarded. You then develop for your listeners, in some simple form, the main points of your organization. This development serves as the verbal road map that helps your audience listen well and retain the information.

The Body

The body of your presentation contains all the information and arguments that you will give the audience. In a presentation to inform, the body consists of the different parts of the topic that together create the whole of that topic. A speech can be divided into any number of parts. The value, however, of the speech ingredients is in the *balanced integration* of each part. A talk sounds unbalanced when one part is larger than the others. The best method for balancing the presentation is to pick an organizational pattern that corresponds to the topic, information, and results that you want to accomplish.

The Conclusion

The conclusion of your talk has three functions. First, you briefly recap the main ideas; this aids the listener in finalizing the mental organizational ladder. Second, you reiterate the importance of the talk to your audience. Third, you end with a cordial, polite statement of goodwill.

The Outline of the Presentation

The organization of a presentation starts with abstract parts that are expanded. When the three main parts are connected, they take the form of the skeleton outline in Exhibit 8.6 on page 192. As you add unique illustrations, examples, and facts, the presentation grows in its strength and beauty. But weak main ideas and insufficient evidence and support can keep you from accomplishing your desired results.

The necessary balance starts with a strong *specific purpose statement*. This statement is a simple declarative sentence that describes what a speaker intends to cover and defines the parameters of the presentation. Using the analogy of a tree, the specific purpose would be the tap root, the main root of a tree that securely connects the trunk to the earth. Your presentation should be firmly rooted both in what your audience wants and needs and in what you wish to accomplish—as well as in how your ideas will be presented, the words used, the nonverbal means used to convey the message, and any audio-visual aids that will clarify your message.

As you research and write your speech, continually re-check this purpose statement to ensure that each main idea reflects the topic adequately and is a clear division of the balanced topic. If a main idea or a subpoint does not fit the outline, either that idea must be deleted or changed or the topic must be revised. Exhibit 8.7 on page 194 shows the finished outline of the credit union speech that was roughly presented in Figure 8.2 on page 190. Look back for a moment at that page and compare the two outlines.

In Table 8.1 (page 193) we see how the motivated sequence steps of attention, need, satisfaction, visualization, and action are placed within the traditional divisions of a speech. These steps, along with the various patterns of organization (pages 180 to 183) and the types of verbal supporting material (183 to 188), are displayed in the eight sample speeches found in Appendix A, at the end of the book, on pages 435 to 446).

Topic: _____

Purpose: _____

Specific purpose: _____

Introduction

A. (Attention getter) _____

B. (Topic/audience relationship) _____

C. (Main point outline) _____

Body

I. Main idea _____

  A. (Subpoint) _____

  B. (Subpoint) _____

    1. (Support) _____

    2. (Support) _____

II. Main idea _____

  A. (Subpoint) _____

  B. (Subpoint) _____

III. Main idea _____

  A. (Subpoint) _____

    1. (Support) _____

    2. (Support) _____

  B. (Subpoint) _____

  C. (Subpoint) _____

IV. Main idea _____

  A. (Subpoint) _____

  B. (Subpoint) _____

Conclusion

A. (Recap) _____

B. (Topic/audience relationship) _____

C. (Goodwill) _____

Exhibit 8.6 • Skeleton Outline

Table 8.1 • The Relationship Between the Steps of the Motivated Sequence and the Traditional Divisions of a Speech

General Ends	Introduction		Body or Discussion		Conclusion
To inform	Attention step Provoke curiosity in subject.	Need step Show its relation to the listeners: why they need to know.	Satisfaction step 1. Initial summary, outlining points to be covered to satisfy this need.	2. Detailed discussion of points in order.	Satisfaction step (concluded) 3. Final summary: a recapitulation of the main points and of important conclusions.
To convince	Attention step Direct attention to basic elements of the proposition.		Need step Demonstrate that a need for decision exists and lay down criteria for judgment.	Satisfaction step State the proposition and evidence to induce belief in it and its benefits.	Visualization step Briefly make its desirability vivid through imagery. / Action step Restate the proposition and recapitulate the reasons for belief.
To stimulate	Attention step Stimulate attention and direct it to —		Need step Present the conditions, objects, subject, which demand an emotional reaction from audience.	Satisfaction step Briefly state attitude desired.	Visualization step Bring about climax of emotional stimulus by picturing desired attitude. / Action step Restate the attitude desired or challenge to audience.
To actuate	Attention step Direct attention to —		Need step Present conditions showing a need for action.	Satisfaction step State proposed action and prove its workability and benefits.	Visualization step Picture future conditions as a result of the action taken. / Action step Appeal for or demand the specified action.

Note: Not everything listed above is always included. The chart is used merely to show the relationship between the two methods of organization.

Source: Alan H. Monroe and Douglas Ehninger, *Principles and Types of Speech*, 6th ed. (Chicago: Scott, Foresman and Company, 1967), p. 286. Reprinted by permission.

Introduction
   A. Hairdressers in Connecticut do it; Barbers in Vermont do it; even Arabian-horse owners in the United States do it.
   B. At some point in your lives you will probably be eligible to join a credit union. One out of every 7 Americans today belongs to one of the 23,000 credit unions in the U.S. today.
   C. Today, I'm going to talk to you about credit unions, where and how they began, what they are, and the advantages of joining one.

Body
I. History
   A. Started in Germany in 1849, by Friedrich Raiffeisen to help his people.
   B. At time of his death he had started 425 CUs.
   C. 1900—first credit union in North America in Quebec.
   D. 1909—first credit union in the U.S., New Hampshire.
II. What is it?
   A. A financial cooperative organized under state or federal law, by and for people who already have a common bond.
   B. Democratic nonprofit institution with members electing the credit union directors and voting on credit union policies at annual meeting.
   C. Membership is open to everyone in the group.
   D. Every member has an equal vote.
III. Primary advantages of joining
   A. Because loan policies set by directors elected by members, it is easier to get a loan.
   B. Waiting period for a loan is usually less.
   C. Lower interest rate on loans. Maximum is 15 percent by law.
   D. Some of the larger CUs rebate to loan customers at the end of the year. In effect you end up paying 1 to 2 points less interest.
   E. Dividends by law as high as 7 percent on regular savings.
IV. Secondary advantages of joining
   A. CUs provide loan protection insurance.
   B. CUs offer life savings insurance.
   C. Credit unions are extending financial services.
      1. Financial counseling
      2. Consumer education
      3. Group travel discounts
      4. Auto purchase discounts
      5. Home mortgage loans
      6. Real estate loans
      7. Master Charge—12 percent
      8. Share draft—similar to checking
      9. Electronic transfer of funds
      10. Travel checks and money orders
   D. Deposits are insured up to $40,000

Conclusion
With all the advantages in joining a credit union, you should consider joining when you become eligible. Someday you will need a loan. As the old American saying goes, "In God we trust—all others must pay cash."

Exhibit 8.7 • The Inside Story of Credit Unions
Source: A speech outline prepared by Theresa Canales-Jud for BA 6114, "Effective Communication," in the Edwin L. Cox School of Business, Southern Methodist University, Dallas, Texas, June 16, 1977. Reprinted by permission.

The Final Outline

Once the construction phases of speech preparation have been passed through, the finishing-out of an outline can be done by three methods: simple word, key phrase, and manuscript.

Simple word. The outline in Figure 8.1, on page 189, contained a list of simple words. When you read those words, they did not convey complete meanings. To the person who prepared the outline, however, they carried meaning and triggered ideas that were stored in the mind. During brainstorming sessions start the outlining process by listing simple words. You may continue the practice throughout the writing and delivery of the presentation, but usually the process quickly changes to writing out key phrases.

Key phrases. While the phrase often looks like a complete sentence, it is usually a set of words or pictorial nouns and verbs that are concrete and suggestive. When examined and used in several practice sessions, they imprint an easily remembered and recalled image on your mind. The completed outline in Exhibit 8.7, page 194, combines both key phrases and complete sentences.

Complete sentence. In this type of outline, all the main ideas and subpoints are written as complete sentences. The value of this approach is that complete ideas can be expressed as complete units of thought. Also, the complete sentence represents a method that the speaker would use to communicate those specific ideas.

There is a danger, however, in using this approach. The written sentence is recorded in the way that you normally write. Consequently, when you speak, the words may be hard to pronounce, destroying the smoothness of your talk and failing to convey your original message.

Manuscript speeches are valuable if you want to read your message and cannot deviate from the text. Heads of state, politicians, and other leaders use this approach so that a slip of the tongue is next to impossible. But the average speaker is better off avoiding a complete sentence outline and attempting to use simple words with much practice.

Incidentally, please do not attempt to memorize your speech. Practicing until you know major portions by heart is fine, but the time and energy required in memorizing a talk cannot be justified in a productive business environment. Avoiding the temptation to memorize the speech lets you avoid the potential for forgetting a portion and destroying your concentration and credibility. If you rely on key words and forget a point, you can always go on to the next point or make up a new idea out of the many available thoughts in your mind.

Preparing Your Notes

As soon as you have finalized your presentation by organizing and writing it, you should convert your ideas to notes that you will use during the talk. The sooner you start practicing with your notes, the smoother and more complete your final delivery.

Never be afraid to use notes. No audience, whether in a large auditorium or a small boardroom, expects you to remember the organization and main ideas for more than a couple of minutes. Just remember not to signal "distractions" to your listeners.

The key to effective use of notes is in their neatness and unobtrusiveness. Many speakers scribble ideas on large sheets of paper that have been folded and crumpled. Others carry large clipboards that remind the audience of a military drill sergeant. The neater the notes, the easier they are for the speaker to follow and the less distracting for the audience.

In transferring your ideas from the outline to your notes try using the key word approach. If you practice by actually talking through your entire thought, you will find that key words are sufficient. When your eyes see the word, the word will trigger your mind to remember the full ideas you have researched and practiced. In a short talk you should be able to list most of the key words on one or two small cards that can be cupped in the palm of the hand and used undistractingly in front of the audience. Here are some additional hints for effectively using the notes.

1. *Use as few notes as possible.* By listing only key words you can put even a long speech on two or three cards. Many cards or sheets of paper probably mean that you have filled the cards with complete sentences.

2. *Number your notes.* As soon as you have placed your note cards in proper sequence, number them in case they are dropped or misshuffled before your talk.

3. *List your words lengthwise.* Writing across the narrow portion of the card or paper will facilitate easy viewing and will more closely approximate your original outline.

4. *Avoid dividing lists and complete units of thought onto two different cards.* It is very distracting when a speaker is listing several ideas for his audience and gets to the last one, only to have to shuffle the cards to find it.

5. *Write your key words in outline form.* The visual likeness of your notes and the original outline will psychologically help you remember your ideas.

6. *Use symbols to indicate where audio-visual aids are used. Never make new notes immediately prior to your talk.* Occasionally speakers want to replace their worn practice notes with clean new ones prior to their talk. Many have regretted this because the mind remembers the original pattern of words and symbols. The new arrangement is mentally distracting and can cause you to make long pauses and to mispronounce words.

Finalizing Your Audio-Visual Aids

The last construction task, prior to practice sessions, is for you to put the finishing touches on any audio-visual aids you plan to use. Be sure to eliminate any items that are not completely necessary for clarity and understanding. Have these aids available for practice. Practicing with them will help you eliminate rough edges and ensure that your final performance is smooth and professional.

Practicing the Presentation

For professional speakers, "practice makes perfect." If you work under a time limit that doesn't allow you to perfect a particular task, the end result will probably be less than satisfactory. Some tasks don't have much reward riding on the finish; but sometimes a reputation, a commission, a grade, or a job may rest on the result of a presentation. Future presentations can even be clouded by the negative feedback and response that a speaker receives if he or she fails to live up to personal expectations and those of the audience. The practice and rehearsal are just as important as the organization and construction phases of preparing a presentation.

Athletes, musicians, and professionals in all fields spend countless hours working out routines, smoothing the fine points, and perfecting their skill. The same is true for professional speakers. Excellent speakers are not born; they develop through continual hard work. Speaking is a skill, like any musical or athletic skill, that can be learned and perfected.

Don't Read Your Presentation—Talk It

After you have written your notes, start talking through them as if you were telling a friend or colleague what you have developed. Don't fall into the trap of reading the speech. If you do, you'll never trust yourself to leave the written word, and the result will be less than perfect.

Source: By permission of Johnny Hart and Field Enterprises, Inc.

The story is told of a young minister who preached her first sermon in a little country church. When her grandmother, who happened to be present, approached her after the sermon, she asked, "How did I do?" "Well," the grandmother said, "I only saw three things wrong with it. First, you read it. Secondly, you read it poorly. And third, it wasn't worth reading anyhow."

Written material is designed for the eyes to see and easily read. Presentations, when written, sound like other types of written prose. Only after the words have been spoken several times does the content take on a form of its own and sound good to the ear.

Talking your presentation establishes the main ideas firmly in your mind. As you practice, work on clarifying the ideas, not the words. When ideas are understood clearly, the words will usually be there to explain them. By having established the ideas firmly in your mind, you will be able to give attention to other factors that will be present during your final talk.

As you practice, talk the entire speech through from start to finish. Don't leave portions out. If you do, they are liable to be the parts you understand least and need to work on the most. Talk through the speech at least five to ten times. Three is a must for being able to pronounce the words easily. By six or seven times the smoothness and continuity are established, and by the ninth or tenth time you have major parts firmly remembered. When you are tempted to say you don't have time to practice, remember that a ten-minute speech can be practiced six times in one hour.

Time Your Speech

When you are given a time limit, be courteous and abide by it. As you practice, time yourself and add to or take away information as time allows. A good rule of thumb is to work on missing the allowed time by only 10 percent. For a five-minute speech, that is thirty seconds; for a one-hour speech, six minutes. Also try to strike a good balance between the introduction, body, and conclusion. The introduction should take about 10 percent of the time, the body 80 or 85 percent, and the conclusion between 5 and 10 percent.

Maintain Good Posture

When you practice, stand straight and tall, just as you will when you deliver the formal talk. Don't sit at your desk or in an easy chair to talk through your material. Practice away from a podium. The proper feel of how you should stand, move, and gesture are best learned by actually standing and having the freedom to move. A tennis player would never practice a serve seated at the end of the tennis court. For a speaker the analogy is just as true because speaking to others involves the whole person: body, mind, and emotions.

As you practice, correct any offensive and distracting mannerisms like leaning on the podium, standing with one leg casually in front of the other, or slouching. A straight stance facilitates breath control, and proper breath control helps you minimize nervousness.

Move—Don't Just Stand There

Polished speakers move with freedom and ease: They look as graceful in front of the audience as an NFL fullback side-stepping tacklers or an actor walking from one side of the stage to another. These speakers know that nervousness produces adrenaline, adrenaline is available for energy, and energy is provided for movement. The last thing a speaker should do is lock herself behind a podium and stand in one place until the speech is over. Also avoid the "fig-leaf" and "parade-rest" positions, where your legs are stiff and your arms are extended downward in front or in back. Lift the hands up above the waist to a "gesture ready" position. This minimized movement forces the body to contain the nervous energy instead of channeling it into complementary actions. By practicing movement in your rehearsal phase, it will feel natural and will be a habit to follow in the formal presentation.

Gesture Freely

Another physical thing that good speakers do is to gesture naturally. Gestures are made with the arms, hands, and fingers. They add impact to words and turn a "blah" delivery into one that is exciting.

As you rehearse, practice gesturing descriptively to indicate size, shape, design, and other information that can be visually depicted. Make your gestures natural. Avoid using the same ones, in the same way, in the same parts of your speech. At times it is appropriate to build a gesture into a certain part of the speech as long as it appears natural and spontaneous. As you gain experience as a speaker, attempt to spontaneously feel the hand movement as it complements your words.

Practice Communicating Enthusiasm with Your Face

A speaker's face can show interest, excitement, and enthusiasm, or it can show depression, fear, and nervousness. Practice smiling and delivering nonverbal facial messages to your imaginary audience. Let your face show your listeners that you want them to listen and that you are drawing feedback from them. When you form the habit of wearing a warm, friendly, confident smile during practice, you will automatically wear the same look during the actual performance. If you don't practice that way, it becomes almost impossible for you to automatically look confident and happy as a speaker.

Eye contact is an extremely important part of your facial expression. As you practice, look at every imaginary person in the audience. When you are in front of the actual group, continue the practice and look at the eyes of each person at least once during the speech. Make each member of the audience feel that you are delivering that speech to him or her.

Develop a Pleasing Vocal Sound

The voice enhances the words we say. It also indicates things about us that we might not want revealed. Through our voice people know when we are tense or relaxed, tired or sleepy, excited or depressed, happy or sad, angry or pleased. The speakers we know and respect for their delivery qualities have many things in common, but their voices are unique. Each sounds different and varies according to several characteristics: pitch, rate, volume, quality, flexibility.

Pitch is the highness or lowness of the vocal tone. Mechanically it is produced by the thickness of the vocal cords and the speed at which they vibrate. Pitch is changed by either tightening or relaxing the vocal cords. As you practice using your normal pitch, you will hear your natural sound and know the sound you should have during the actual delivery. If that sound varies during your performance, you can control it to a great extent by breathing deeper, slowing down your rate of speech, and projecting your voice either higher or lower.

Rate. Speech rate is the speed at which you speak. It is a combination of the duration of each word and the pause between words. As we stated in the listening chapter, an average speaker talks at around 150 words per minute. In a formal presentation, however, there is a tendency to talk faster. This is another reason for timing your talk during practice. By establishing a smooth, controlled rate during practice, you are more likely to repeat it during the final performance or at least shift it to a faster or slower rate if needed.

Volume. The loudness of the speaking voice is a combination of force and energy. Most people talk at a normal and pleasing degree of loudness. Occasionally speakers are too soft or too loud. By taping your voice once or twice during rehearsal you will discover if you need to change. Even when nervous, speakers generally use the same amount of loudness during formal talks as in informal conversations. But speakers must occasionally adapt to new requirements, such as when the microphone goes out just before the talk and the auditorium is full of people. Even if you have not practiced with that situation in mind, you can meet the challenge by breathing deeper, slowing your speech down a bit, and directing your words to the back row with added force and clarity of pronunciation.

Enunciation. To enunciate means to clearly and distinctly articulate the words we speak. Again, by listening to an occasional tape of your practice you will hear if you slur certain consonants or syllables or drop letters at the ends of words like saying *comin* or *goin* instead of *coming* and *going.* You can improve your enunciation by speaking those words sharply and distinctly. In the early stages of your rehearsal you may find that certain words are very difficult for you to pronounce. After working on those words, if they still give you problems, look for synonyms you can substitute. Sometimes words that look good to the eye and seem good to the mind are difficult for the tongue to pronounce. Give yourself time to find and practice new words. In the case of proper nouns, foreign words, and other difficult words that you cannot substitute, work on these a hundred times if necessary and then write your own pronunciation shorthand on your notes.

Quality. As you practice, think about the total vocal quality that you want to develop. This is the fullness of your vocal sound and can be enhanced by practicing new vocal techniques like speaking with a foreign accent, using regional dialects, and even reading aloud from books of poetry and prose.

Flexibility. The best thing you can do for your voice is to work on maintaining flexibility. This is the ability to change as needed the rate, pitch, loudness, and quality of your voice. Flexibility to the voice is like spontaneity to the physical presence. It allows you to adapt to whatever conditions exist and to always come out victorious.

Nonwords. A final vocal comment is required. During the past few years Americans have developed a tendency for using vocal nonwords. Some call the utterances "speech tics." They are sayings like *ah, so, and uh, ya know, well,* and *OK!* If you know you have this problem, actively think about what you are saying by picking and choosing each word. Don't worry if the habit is hard to overcome at first. Habits that have been consistently used for years cannot be overcome in mere minutes. But if you keep working at organizing your thoughts, you will gradually overcome the habit. Say only the information that relates to your thoughts, and pause silently between sentences and paragraphs instead of substituting nonsense words while you decide what to say next. A pause is appropriate when looking at your notes and deciding what you want to say next. That is proven to us each time we hear a professional news commentator, politician, or business executive on television or in person. Professional, polished speakers have long ago omitted junky phrasing. You can too.

The Actual Performance

If you have moved successfully through the organization, construction, and practice phases of your presentation, the final performance will also be successful. This section gives some hints for helping you to make that final performance a smashing success.

Warm Up at Home or Backstage

Anxiety, stress, and nervousness are things that all members of the business world experience at different times. While many good books deal with stress reduction, some simple relaxation exercises will help most speakers displace their prespeech nervousness with controlled energy. Practice the following relaxation sequence regularly so that it will work automatically for you when you make your next presentation. Allow yourself a few extra minutes before you have to talk to stop by the rest room, sit quietly in your car or office, or find a solitary place backstage to run through these exercises.

Deep breathing. Babies breathe the right way. As adults we get the process turned around because we are taught to pull our stomach in and push our chest out. Consequently we use the top third of our lung capacity. Sometimes when we are very nervous we even "forget" to breathe.

Shallow breathing tenses up the solar plexus and signals our involuntary nervous system to prepare to fight. This starts the heart beating faster, the blood rushing to our heads, and the horrible feelings we don't want as speakers. Deep breathing, on the other hand, tranquilizes the involuntary system and shuts down the desire to fight or flee. Here's how speakers should practice breathing:

Deep Breathing

1. Push all the air out of your lungs, and clamp your nostrils with your thumb and forefinger.
2. Hold for three or four counts.
3. Release the hold, and without breathing let your lungs fill automatically and deeply with air through your nostrils. You should feel an expansion from the top part of your chest to the upper portion of your groin area.
4. Exhale completely, and try to touch your spine with your abdomen.
5. Inhale again through your nostrils. Stick your abdomen out and fill it first, next your rib cage, and then your chest.
6. Alternate exhaling and inhaling for two or three more times. Be careful to do it slowly and deliberately to avoid hyperventilation.

After doing these exercises, you should feel a calming sensation that is deeply relaxing. Try this sequence the next time you get nervous and especially before a big presentation. It works. When you are talking before the audience and you feel the tightness of the chest that indicates shallow breathing, force your stomach out and the air deeper until you breathe more deeply.

Physical relaxation. While breath control is the starting point for total relaxation, several exercises can help you stay relaxed during your speech. Practice these exercises on a regular basis and run through them prior to your speech:

Physical Relaxation

1. Sit comfortably in a straight-back chair.
2. Tell yourself that it is time to relax, to shut out distractions, and to loosen various tension spots.
3. Start with your head. Alternate between tensing and relaxing the muscles in your scalp, forehead, face, and jaws. Now let the muscles in each of these areas go limp.

4. Move to your neck and shoulder muscles. Focus on those muscles, and force out all the pressure. Let them go limp also.
5. Let the relaxation spread down your arms to your elbows, forearms, wrists, hands, and finally fingers. Tense and relax these muscles, and then let your arms and hands dangle freely beside your body and chair.
6. Focus now on the chest, and do your breathing exercises once or twice until any tightness is gone and your breathing is normal and relaxed.
7. Focus on your spine. As you move down from your shoulders, relax your back muscles, waist, buttocks, thighs, and even knees.
8. Continue on to relax the calves, shins, ankles, feet, and toes.
9. When your entire body has relaxed, you should feel very limp. Continue to sit in your chair for three or four minutes with your mind free of thought and your body completely relaxed.
10. When you return to the rest of the world, maintain the tranquil feeling, and shut out any attempts by other people or events to interfere with your relaxed state.

Make a Positive Entrance

Arrive early enough at your destination to find out where you will sit, the arrangement of the room, and any unknown obstacles you will have to deal with. When your name is called, walk professionally to the place where you will talk. By avoiding the following "bad entrance" behavior you can add to your credibility as a speaker.

- *The carpet sampler.* This speaker closely checks his path to make sure he doesn't trip over any obstacles. He should have checked earlier so that he could walk boldly to his place.
- *The condemned.* This person's walk nonverbally signals to others that she fears she will be executed as soon as she reaches her speaking place.
- *The ceiling gazer.* This person seems to be looking toward heaven for the words that he will soon give his listeners.
- *The groomer.* This person did not get completely dressed at home and is busy buttoning her jacket, pulling up her skirt, straightening her earrings, or brushing back her hair. An earlier stop by the rest room could have eliminated this display of grooming.
- *The early starter.* This speaker often starts talking as soon as he leaves his seat instead of waiting until he is firmly positioned in his place, fully aware of his listeners, and ready to start.

- *The dizzy dreamer.* As this person gets ready to start talking, her every nonverbal action and movement shouts "total disorganization." All her hard preparation work quickly can be lost if she doesn't regain credibility soon.
- *The steam kettle.* You don't have to ask if this speaker is nervous; you hear it. A slow "Whew" is emitted from his mouth before he catches his breath and starts his opening. By breathing deeply while he is walking toward his place and by slowly taking a deep breath before he starts talking, he could avoid displaying this nervousness to his listeners.

Establish Eye Contact

The sooner you maintain eye contact with your listeners, the sooner you start communicating your credibility and delivering your message.

Work on Warmth and Spontaneity

No one wants to listen to a dull and boring speaker who doesn't seem to enjoy talking to his audience. From the early moments, throughout the talk, and into the final period maintain a warmth that conveys, "I'm really happy and excited to be here with you." Work on spontaneously responding to your listeners' eye contact, their puzzled looks, their nods of agreement, and any unexpected happenings that so often come up in real-life situations. By avoiding the following speaker styles you can convey needed warmth and excitement:

- *The apologizer.* This person minimizes her credibility by telling listeners she is unprepared, didn't have much time to organize her thoughts, is nervous, won't take too much of their time, doesn't know why she was chosen for the talk, or will not try to bore them with facts and figures.
- *"Today I'm going to talk to you about. . . ."* Never let this line be the first one out of your mouth. It is important to establish rapport with your audience before you tell them the topics that you will cover.
- *The shy guy.* This speaker looks scared throughout his talk. He never smiles, plays off his audience's responses, or even pretends to be happy. His eyes usually are downcast, as is his countenance.

- *The dilly bopper.* Quite the opposite from the shy guy is the speaker who has so much nervous energy that she can't stand still or move smoothly in front of her audience. While some movement is needed and necessary in a speech, undefined and out-of-control movement is a real turn-off to an audience.
- *The magnetic pocket.* Occasionally inserting one hand into the pocket can contribute to a casual and controlled look, but often the "pocket magnet" takes control and doesn't let the hand out of the pocket. A good rule is to try to keep the hands out of the pockets and use them for proper gesturing.
- *The coin jingler.* One reason to keep the hands out of the pockets is to avoid jingling loose change and keys stored there. A good trick is to remove all potentially distracting items from the pockets prior to the talk.
- *The prayer.* Sometimes a speaker takes a stance and holds it throughout the talk. If the stance is one where the hands are folded reverently in front, it can convey an image of praying for help.
- *The walker.* This person absentmindedly walks from side to side, back and forth, or across the room as he talks. There is nothing wrong with walking and moving while talking to your listeners. But do it in a dynamic way where every step and movement looks orchestrated for the hearer.
- *The mumbler.* This speaker has trouble articulating and speaking out. Sometimes she sounds as if she has a mouthful of marbles. If you have this problem, work on clear pronunciation and sharp articulation when you practice.
- *The fumbler.* This speaker seems totally uncoordinated, but he probably has failed to adequately practice. He busily shifts through his notes, occasionally drops items, misplaces transparencies, looks absently at charts that have already been explained, and generally seems to be out of control.

Close Definitively and Cordially

If you have worked hard to create and maintain credibility throughout the talk, you don't want to destroy it at the end. Avoid false endings that send the listeners mentally packing. Maintain to the end a high energy level and also the cordiality that sends to your audience the message "I really enjoyed myself." To ensure that your closing is successful, avoid several pitfalls:

- *Don't hurry home.* Some speakers are so eager to finish and sit down that they either drop their final words or end their talk while walking to their seat. As you put the period on the last word of your talk, continue standing a few seconds to nonverbally acknowledge the ending and wait for applause and possible questions.

- *Avoid the "thank God it's over" look.* Some speakers think that the audience observes them only while they are up front speaking. They consequently sigh, give all sorts of "I'm glad that's over" looks, and immediately destroy the positive image that they worked so hard to create with words and deeds during the presentation. Maintain your professionalism throughout until you reach your seat and even until you are completely out of the presence of anyone in your audience.
- *Don't be an approval seeker.* Closely akin to the last speaker is the one who verbally and nonverbally seeks approval by saying, "Did I really do well?" If you have done your homework and have practiced hard, you will automatically know whether you were excellent, just OK, or terrible. Don't ask for feedback. Wait and let others give it to you.

Before you forget specific events and your subjective recall takes over, find a quiet, secluded place, and review your presentation with the help of the following checklist:

Did the INTRODUCTION of your presentation:

    get the audience's attention at the start? _____

    make a connection between your audience and the topic? _____

    describe your specific purpose? _____

Did the ORGANIZATION of your presentation:

    contain several main ideas? _____

    arrange your ideas and information in a "logical pattern"? _____

    contain "supporting material" that was clear? _____

    contain "supporting material" that was convincing? _____

    use smooth transitions? _____

Did the CONCLUSION of your presentation:

    briefly summarize the main ideas? _____

    briefly restate your specific purpose? _____

    move your audience toward desired action? _____

Did you in the DELIVERY:

    approach your listeners with confidence? _____

    get set before speaking? _____

    establish eye contact before speaking? _____

maintain that eye contact throughout the talk? _____

refer only occasionally to your notes? _____

maintain the right degree of excitement and enthusiasm? _____

speak in a spontaneous, relaxed manner and not from memory? _____

avoid speech tics like *ah, you know*, etc.? _____

maintain good posture? _____

use your vocal qualities of pitch, volume, rate, etc., effectively? _____

gesture appropriately? _____

move freely? _____

enunciate clearly? _____

pronounce words correctly? _____

finish speaking before walking away? _____

finish on time? _____

Make a list of things included in this evaluation that you did not do in your speech or prefer to do differently in your next one. Decide to take some self-prescribed steps to ensure that you don't make the same mistakes in your next presentation.

Summary

Every oral presentation can be effectively delivered if the speaker follows certain preparatory steps. The talk can most easily be constructed if the speaker uses the questions Who?, Where?, When?, Why?, What?, and How? to help shape the presentation. When properly constructed, each presentation has an introduction, a body, and a conclusion that form a skeleton outline. A final outline combines key words with complete sentences and incorporates audio-visual aids.

Practicing the presentation is the next critical step in oral presentation. Specific techniques have been proven successful aids in helping to coordinate memory, physical posture, and clear enunciation.

The actual performance of an oral presentation includes such critical elements as making a positive entrance, establishing strong eye contact, projecting warmth and spontaneity, and focusing on a definite and cordial close.

Oral presentations can communicate plans, set the tone of a new organizational direction, or even sell a group on a different approach to goal accomplishment. Whether they are directed at superiors or at a manager's staff, they are a critical component in determining career success.

Key Words

informative presentation	cause/effect	key phrase outline
persuasive presentation	verbal supporting material	complete sentence outline
motivated sequence	comparison	gestures
patterns of organization	definition	facial expression
chronological	example	pitch
spatial	illustration	rate
topical	statistics	volume
sequential	story	enunciation
classification	testimony	quality
comparative	audio-visual aids	flexibility
problem/solution	introduction	deep breathing
advantage/disadvantage	body	physical relaxation
	conclusion	positive entrance
	simple word outline	eye contact

Review Questions

1. One of your first tasks as a speaker is to identify the types of people to whom you will be speaking. Name and describe the five questions you should ask to determine this information.

2. What are two important things to know about the "where" of the presentation?

3. Name the two major purposes for the business presentation, and describe the results of each.

4. As a speaker you can organize your information into nine different patterns. Name and describe each pattern.

5. Speakers use verbal supporting material to verify, clarify, and amplify their contention. Name and describe the seven types of support that were presented in this chapter.

6. Name and describe the purpose of each of the three parts of all presentations.

7. In this chapter three types of outlines were discussed. Name and describe each type, and tell which one is recommended for general use.

8. Preparation of the final note cards is an important task for the speaker. Explain this chapter's seven hints for effective note usage.

9. You can relieve anxiety before you speak by doing warm-up exercises. Describe the exercises given in this chapter.

10. Describe some of the ways that speakers ineffectually enter their talks.

11. Discuss some of the ineffective styles that speakers use that destroy the warmth and spontaneity of their delivery.

Exercises

1. Take a sheet of paper and draw a line from top to bottom down the center of the page. At the top of one side of the page place the word *good,* and on the other side the words *needs work.* Now recall the last presentation that you made and list in the appropriate column each phase of the organization, construction, and practice of the speech. On the back side of the page make a list of ways in which you could improve the items on the *needs work* list. Refer to the list before starting on your next presentation.

2. Attend a special guest presentation on your campus. During and after the presentation, record the following information about the event. Share your findings with other members of your class.
   a. Were the time and the place of the presentation conducive to listening to the speaker?
   b. Did the speaker do her homework in learning who she was speaking to? If not, what changes could she have made?
   c. Were you able to clearly determine the purpose of the presentation?
   d. Which pattern of organization did the speaker use?
   e. Describe at least three different types of verbal supporting material that the speaker used. Were they effective? Were they sufficient? Were they adequately clarifying?
   f. If the speaker used audio-visual aids, were they appropriate and helpful and did they complement the words? If not, tell why.
   g. Describe the speaker's delivery style. Did it add to or distract from her credibility? What about the vocal quality?
   h. In what overall ways was the presentation effective?
   i. In what ways could the presentation have been improved?

3. This chapter has undoubtedly discussed things that you want to change in your presentation making. On a separate sheet of paper, write out a contract with yourself to improve specific things in the way you speak. Write down the items, list the steps you must take to improve them, and indicate a date by which time you expect to complete the task.

4. Interview a presentor; he or she could be a salesperson, a teacher, a minister, or someone else who regularly talks to large groups of people. Ask that person questions about how he or she organizes, constructs, practices, and actually delivers his or her presentations. Share your findings with your class.

Reference

1. David Wallechinsky and Irving Wallace, *The Book of Lists* (New York: William Morrow, 1977).

C H A P T E R 9

. . . .
. . . .
. . . .
. . . .

Managing Small Groups

Introduction

Group meetings are such an inescapable part of business that they are often the butt of organizational jokes: "A meeting is a meeting to decide when the next meeting will be held"; "A meeting comprises a group of the unfit, appointed by the unwilling, to do the unnecessary." Still, the wheels of modern organizations and industry are turned by group meetings.

As one author stated, "The problem is not so much committees in management as it is the management of committees."[1] Members of management and staff of an organization attend meetings daily and weekly. In fact, when we add up the groups to which we belong (academic, professional, religious, civic, and athletic), we sometimes feel that there are more groups than people in the world. Professional businesspeople attend an average of one meeting a day. The average executive spends nearly 3½ hours a week in committee meetings, serves on three committees, finds an average of seven fellow executives sitting with her on each committee and wishes there were only four others, and meets with each of the committees about every two weeks. In addition to the formal meetings, she spends the equivalent of one working day a week in informal conferences and consultation with fellow executives.

Meetings are one of the most effective communication devices used in business. They allow one person or several to give information and ideas to many others in a short period of time. They can be labor and cost effective when used in the right ways.

This chapter examines purposes, types, and weaknesses of small business groups and the common characteristics of group meetings. It concludes with suggestions for what managers should do before, during, and after meetings.

Importance and Weaknesses of Groups

Importance of Groups

Although social interaction remains essential within organizations, recent improvements in technology have decreased face-to-face human contact in businesses. Future technological changes will in some instances further decrease this contact.[2] Instead of walking to a colleague's office we simply call him on the telephone or send a message to his electronic message center. We call neighbors instead of walking to their houses. But a problem develops because this type of communication replaces the human elements of contact, nonverbal information, and listening, with a voice projected by one medium. Electronic devices such as radio, television, video games, and computers have helped replace human interaction.

Without face-to-face interaction, communication is enormously impeded. High-level managers recognize this and are reluctant to give up small group meetings for the colder mode of sending electronic messages. According to Rosenfield there are four primary reasons why groups are important:

1. They encourage meaningful human interaction and participation that can take place only in face-to-face contact.
2. They provide individuals an opportunity to expand world views, improve problem-solving methods, and discover alternatives they would never know outside the group.
3. They facilitate an individual's ability to make commitments to others.

4. They provide a backdrop for understanding the depth and impact of communication: our nonverbal behavior, listening, speaking, and interacting together.[3]

Groups in general are important, but in business and industry the small group has become a regular place for communication to occur. Zelko and Dance outline five trends that have contributed to this:

1. The work climate and environment are socially interacting. We have become so specialized in our vocations that we are interdependent; consultations and conferences are an essential part of just doing our jobs.
2. Employees have participative opportunities to express themselves and be heard and to have a voice in matters that concern them. The conference is in a dominant position as a major forum for such opportunities.
3. "Consultative management"—managers consulting with subordinates—relies heavily on the conference setting for drawing out opinions and judgments of members of a work group.
4. A supervisor's reliance on group decision-making directly affects the supervisor's use of the conference method.
5. The objectives of democratic management strongly emphasize the group/leader relationship.[4]

A Group Meeting Defined

A group meeting is two or more people who interact in an organized face-to-face manner over a period of time and who share a common purpose. They meet because of shared goals. While the group survives, individual roles and leadership patterns emerge, and communication patterns become established. Because of the nature of business groups the duration of some groups is long while that of others is very short.

Advantages of Group Meetings

Group meetings have become a regular part of business life for definite reasons.

More involvement. Employees who work in groups are committed to a decision-making process.[5] Such involvement ensures that group members are familiar with the problem, the need for change, possible solutions to the problem, and why a particular solution is adopted. They also feel personally involved in the decisions.

Better decisions. There is wisdom in numbers: The decision reached by several people should be better than the decision an individual reaches alone. When responsibilities are passed out and completed by several people, more ideas are available during discussion. Also, the presence of several members helps individual members escape the biases that often interfere with decision making.

Quicker completion. When many minds and hands work on a project, the job can be completed more quickly than it could have been with one person.

Disadvantages of Group Meetings

Although there are definite advantages to having people work in groups, their major limitations must be confronted and resolved.

Time consuming. As Chapter 2 showed, face-to-face communication and interaction is more desirable than one-way communication. It takes longer, however, for two people to talk, work through issues, and make resolutions when the two-way process is used. When several members are added and the two-way process observed, the time requirements are even greater. According to Rosenblatt, Cheatham, and Watt, the time issue would not be such a problem if so much time were not wasted:

> Groups waste time in a number of ways: (1) too much time is spent pursuing a single train of thought, with the result that the agenda cannot be completed; (2) members insist on discussing irrelevant points; (3) members spend so much time maintaining group morale and other human relations matters that time does not permit solving the problem assigned to the committee.[6]

Answerable to management. Groups are only as effective as the decisions they reach and the action steps that they send to management or other groups to implement. If management has endowed the group with the freedom to make decisions that will be carried out, the group's work accomplishes the purpose for its existence. If management rediscusses each issue that the group spent time on and arrives at its own decisions, the effectiveness of the group is minimized. Such a group will "spin its wheels" only a few times before management's behavior reduces morale and incentive to the point of crippling the group.

The wrong people attend. Unless the meeting is attended by the people who have the needed information and the power to make the right decisions, the effectiveness of the group is limited. A survey by management of the attendees should give a clear picture of the roles represented in the group, who should be replaced, and the types of new members who should be invited.

Expensive. You may have never considered it, but a typical group meeting is a very expensive activity. It can cost hundreds of thousands of dollars. For example, if we take the average executive described earlier, we can calculate how much of the company's money is spent weekly on her participation in meetings. On a salary of $25,000 per year, each work hour costs $12.50. Multiplying this by the 3½ hours in committee meetings, plus one complete eight-hour day of informal conferences, the cost to the company for this executive attending those meetings is $143.75 per week. If we multiply that times the number of people whom she met with, and the number of other groups that met on a weekly basis, we see the cost is staggering for the company.

The longer the meeting and the greater the number of participants, the more expensive the gathering. For this reason meetings should be held only when the results justify the expense. Before calling a meeting a manager should consider if there is a more time- and cost-saving way of communicating the same information. If a decision is made to go ahead with the meeting, the leader should concentrate on having it highly organized and running it efficiently.

Slow and poorly run. This problem affects the cost problem. It arises when the leader and members lack the skills necessary for successful information presentation and discussion.

Functions of a Group

The objective of all group business meetings is to accomplish the goal as quickly and effectively as possible. The two primary functions of the meeting that must be completed for success to occur are called *task* and *maintenance.* Before we discuss these functions, take a few minutes to complete the questionnaire that appears in Exhibit 9.1. Your answers should relate to a group meeting in which you recently participated. When you finish the questionnaire add the scores in both columns. The T score is for the task function. The R score is for the maintenance function. The highest possible score for the T is 70; the high score for R is 50.

Task

A group's task function is to achieve the goal toward which it is working. In most business interactions all members focus their attention on the task. The group format is selected in terms of its task, and many of the group characteristics (roles, leadership styles, and so forth) are designed to enhance task accomplishment. A high score in the T area indicates that the group is highly task motivated.

How to Assess Business Meetings

All managers spend considerable periods of time in business meetings. Rarely do they evaluate in a systematic manner how effective they feel these meetings are. Are they effective or ineffective? The Task/Relationship Index gives you the opportunity to consider one way in which meetings can be assessed. Consider either a specific meeting or a normal work meeting, and allocate a score on the scale below to each of the statements:

1	2	3	4	5
Not at all	Occasionally	A fair amount	A considerable amount	A great deal

	Score T	Score R
a. The meeting helped me understand the job we are doing more clearly.	———	———
b. I learned a lot about people's attitudes during the meeting.		———
c. It was a useful meeting insofar as people got to know each other.		———
d. It was a meeting in which I had to use my knowledge and skills.	———	
e. People built on each other's ideas.		———
f. Ideas were expressed freely.		———
g. The technical content of the discussion was of a high level.	———	
h. People kept to the point and did not waste time.	———	
i. The decision-making process was fair.	———	
j. Each item on the agenda received sufficient time.	———	
k. There was a high degree of honesty and openness in the conversation.		———
l. The acceptability of decisions was high.		———
m. Problems were carefully diagnosed.	———	
n. Creative solutions to problems were developed.	———	
o. Solutions to problems were carefully assessed.	———	
p. Differences of opinion were thoroughly discussed.		———
q. The meeting was well organized.	———	
r. The decision taken was of a high quality.	———	
s. Everyone in the meeting received a fair hearing.		———
t. The purpose of the meeting was clear.	———	

(continued)

u. Objectives were clearly established during the
    meeting.   ———

v. I felt satisfied that I had an opportunity to
    influence the decision taken.   ———

w. Time was used to the best advantage.   ———

    Totals   ———   ———

Exhibit 9.1

Excerpted, by permission of the publisher, from *How to Assess Your Managerial Style*, by Charles Margerison, pp. 72–74. © 1979 MCB Human Resources Ltd., England. Published in U.S. in 1980 by AMACOM, a division of American Management Associations, New York. All rights reserved.

Maintenance

At the same time that the group works on its task it must fulfill another function. The maintenance function involves meeting the interpersonal needs of the group members. When people interact, certain dynamics must be dealt with, such as morale, feelings, conflict, cooperation, and communication. The higher the R, or relationship factor, score on the questionnaire in Exhibit 9.1, the more your group was focusing on internal needs of the members.

The longer the group meets, the more attention it requires for its maintenance needs. Some committees and other task-oriented groups that have been meeting for long periods of time suddenly find themselves in a meeting where all communication revolves around the participants' social needs and little input is focused on the task. The members, without realizing it, are reaching out for interaction with others. At that time some form of social endeavor probably is in order for the group.

The rest of the chapter shows how groups are classified according to whether their purpose is primarily task or maintenance and how the characteristics of a group indicate whether the basic orientation is successful.

Types of Groups

The purposes of groups in the business world can be best understood by examining the different categories of groups. Groups are divided into personal, work, organizational, and public groups, and several types are found under each division.

Personal

Personal groups are usually informally constructed and sometimes have no real purpose for meeting. Often the main function is maintaining relationships and interaction among members.

The happening. Occasionally people find themselves in the midst of others. It can occur at a bus stop, standing in line at the office building snack bar, interacting at cocktail parties, or seated at the same lunch table. There does not have to be a purpose for the meeting, conversation can be shared or unshared, and the individuals can feel either high or low degrees of comfort and involvement.

The conversation group. After an initial happening people may seek out the other individuals and develop friendships or working relationships. If they meet regularly, the conversations can extend from social, non–work-related talk to grapevine gossip and even to some hypothetical ways to solve the organization's problems.

The study group. Participants in a classroom learning situation can develop an informal personal group into a study group. The emphasis is on learning and sharing knowledge with one another and clarifying original thought.

Work

Work groups are highly task oriented and can consume a large amount of time if they are not structured and run efficiently. The proper conduct of work meetings will be described later in the chapter, after the following introduction to the various types of work groups.

Staff Meeting

One of the most common work groups is the staff meeting, which consists of the supervisor and staff of a particular area or division. Since an organization is made up of numerous staff-level groupings, this type of group is often the most visible within a company. The purpose of the meetings, which are usually held weekly, is to make assignments, give instructions to subgroups, disseminate organizational information and policies, examine staff problems, and decide on solutions for these problems. The staff meeting is sometimes the only opportunity for the entire staff to assemble and talk; a tight agenda and effective facilitator are necessary if the group is to progress successfully and not turn into a free-for-all. If a manager uses an open and honest communication process, this meeting can facilitate upward, downward, and horizontal communication within the organization.

Production Meeting

When different departments are involved in work on a common project or in some way contribute to the work being done by others in the organization, they participate in production meetings. Either department heads or designated employees attend. The focus of the meeting can be on generating new information that will be sent to other divisions of the company, discussing procedures or instructions, or, more likely, solving budget, production, or work-flow problems.

Advisory Meeting

When a manager or supervisor wants to discuss information, disseminate news, or generate ideas, he or she calls an advisory meeting. For example, the IRS may have issued a new reporting procedure that takes effect immediately; the manager of the accounting department calls a special advisory meeting to discuss the proper handling of the procedure within the department. If a manager has received a "rush order," he or she might call together certain key people and lead off the discussion with "I need some input from you on . . . " or "Can you tell me what would happen if . . . ?" or "How can we . . . ?"

Committee Meeting

A committee is formed when major decisions must be made but a superior does not want to waste the time of the regular meeting group or he or she knows that the input from several groups is important. Committees consequently consist of members who represent others. The people usually come from different parts of the organization with different information, different views, and different needs. But a group is heterogeneous in nature, develops a mutual interest in the topic, and can be a "standing," a long-lasting, or a short-lived group.

The very nature of a committee means that it is task oriented and involved in information generation, problem solving, fact finding, or strategic policy-making. Committees are designed as democratic decision-making groups and consequently often use parliamentary procedure.

Quality Circle

The influence of Japanese management techniques on American business in the last few years has led to the growth of quality circles. A quality circle is a meeting of five to ten employees who either work together or do work that affects others in the group. The homogeneous group meets regularly to identify, analyze, and solve work-related problems. These can be both task and maintenance related. Membership is always voluntary, and the groups receive training in time usage and problem-solving techniques before they meet to actually discuss and solve work-related problems.

While problem solving and decision making occur in each of the types of work groups just discussed, this group is designed so that employees can discuss and make job-related decisions on their own without management's input and can then, with management approval, implement their solutions. This has been found to improve morale and generate the most accurate solutions to problems. The groups meet regularly, and solutions can take between three months and a year to accomplish.

Professional Sharing Meeting

Rapid technological changes have led more and more businesses to send their technical and professional employees to seminars and professional association meetings. When these employees return, they update others in the organization at a professional sharing meeting. Usually the participants are colleagues, have a similar status, or have similar knowledge and skills.

Sales Meeting

For those involved in product sales and marketing, meetings are held to announce or explain new products, analyze customer acceptance, describe sales aids, and motivate employees. The meeting can focus on the design and production of the product but more often examines aspects of marketing and sales. The meeting is conducted with a series of individual presentations and the use of multimedia devices.

Organizational

Two types of task-oriented groups pertain exclusively to the organization and generally reflect on communication activities external to the business.

The Annual Meeting

In public corporations an annual meeting is required; most take place in the spring and are attended by the company's officers, the board of directors, and the stockholders. During this meeting stockholders have a rare opportunity to question the officers and directors on matters pertaining to the company. Usually the agendas consist of re-electing the directors, ratifying the appointment of outside accounting firms, approving changes in the company's pension or profit-sharing plans, and authorizing an increase in shares to smooth out stock splits or acquisitions.

Board of Directors' Meeting

The directors of a company are picked because of their knowledge, skills, backgrounds, affiliations, and desires to help run a particular organization. They also have varying tenures and display managerial ability and social consciousness. They are usually generalists, not specialists in the business focus. While the board does not directly manage internal (management and staff) affairs, it is legally and ethically responsible for the total enterprise. A board will usually meet between two and four times a year and more often if necessary to make decisions. Meetings can be held in the company boardroom or at different sites. The meeting facilities are usually more attractive than those used for in-company groups.

Board meetings are usually closed to the public, although some members of management and staff are usually present to observe and answer questions. The president of the organization usually chairs the meetings. As chairperson he or she offers no opinions but guides the group according to procedure. Since this group consists of individuals who closely guard their time, it is imperative that those meetings start and end on schedule and are tightly organized around an agenda.

Public

Public meetings differ from those held within the business because they are presented to an audience that often has no specific affiliation with the organization. The meeting focuses on a specific topic, usually informally discussed by a group and projected to the observers, such as a city council zoning hearing. Because of their often large size and their potential for disarray, public meetings require forceful leadership and control of time, items to be discussed, and speakers.

Panel Discussion

When groups are too large to accommodate participation from each individual, panels of three to five members can be selected to discuss the topic in front of the general audience. Panel members should be well informed on the topic, an agenda should be developed and made known to the panel, and a moderator should control the ebb and flow of the conversation.

The format of each panel discussion will be different. Members can all present short prepared statements; they can question and discuss among themselves the issues; and they can answer questions asked by audience members. If time is available, the panel may wish to talk through parts of the discussion in private before speaking to the public.

Symposium

This meeting is more structured and involves little interaction among the participants. Three to five persons are again picked because of their expertise, and each presents a short prepared speech or report to the audience. A moderator introduces the program, acknowledges each speaker, and makes transitions between each speech. There is little interaction among the speakers, but the formal presentations can be followed by audience comments or questions directed to individual speakers.

Forum

This is not a meeting in and of itself. It is instead a part of a panel, symposium, or other public presentation where the audience has a chance to interact. Here the audience members participate in the question and answer session and provide feedback to the speakers.

Characteristics of Groups

As was noted earlier, each group has two distinct functions: to accomplish the established task or goals and to maintain internal relationships. These two key functions are at the heart of each of the groups just discussed. As we evaluate groups more closely, we find there are characteristics that tell us how well the group is functioning and meeting its objectives.

Goals

In the business world groups meet for a reason. All groups have one thing in common: a goal or task to work toward and accomplish. To save time and energy, the goal should be well defined, the group should have the means to see the goal accomplished, and each member should be willing to commit time to that accomplishment.

In some groups, members have personal reasons for being a part of the group. If these personal reasons are controlled and channeled toward the common goal, no problems develop. If, however, members try to fulfill their own needs at the cost of group time and energy, opposition erupts, and the rest of the members move to pull them back to a position of uniformity.

Communication Lines

In order for ideas to be fully evaluated, decisions made, and problems solved, they must be communicated. An open, two-way flow of information between all members takes more time than the one-way process, but its results are more fulfilling for all members, and the quality and quantity of the information is more useful.

Leadership

Groups are moved toward their goals by output from the members and by leadership that organizes the output into a workable form. In *personal* type groups no leadership is needed. But in *work, organizational,* and *public* groups, the leader is usually designated because of position, knowledge, or power.

Group leaders normally do seven things: (1) start the meeting, (2) keep the meeting on target with the agenda and prevent the participants from wandering, (3) help the members develop the essential problems and solutions, (4) make sure all members have an opportunity to participate, (5) keep the peace and help control and resolve conflict, (6) help the group accomplish the goal, and (7) summarize agreements.

Roles

The leader is not the only participant in the group. In fact, the best leaders withdraw at the most opportune time so that other members can participate fully. To participants it seems at first that only a few roles are played in group meetings; while one or two people talk, the rest of the group listens. A closer examination reveals a variety of roles played by group members.

Cohesion

Effective participation by members produces another important characteristic—cohesion. When this element exists, members feel commitment to other members and the goals of the group and establish good, strong communication lines. The more cohesive the group, the more the group communicates, desires social interaction, finds additional goals to pursue, exerts influence over members, adheres to normative behavior, and projects a high degree of member satisfaction.

Norms

Norms are expectations or rules that are agreed on by the group and that govern behavior of group members. While norms are not standardized for every form of behavior, they develop as a group spends time together, and the consequences for violating norms become apparent to all members.

Research shows that norms are established to reduce uncertainty in groups and to encourage conformity by members. Both of these factors lead to increased participation and interaction. A positive side-effect also becomes apparent. When norms are in place, even very rigid ones, members are more free with their communication and are more likely to disagree openly than do groups with less cohesion and fewer norms.

According to the findings of Litterer, there is a four-stage process whereby groups bring members into compliance. In the *education* stage the group introduces important norms. From there the group is involved in *surveillance* to see if the behavior is conforming or deviant. If deviation is observed, a *warning* message is communicated either through verbal or nonverbal means. Finally, *disciplinary or rewarding actions* are administered.[7]

In a staff meeting format the sequence might work this way. One member, Ed, had a tendency to always go to meetings unprepared. He not only did not do the necessary research, he brought no handouts (which was the norm) and consistently sent the prior week's work to his colleagues two or three weeks late. Ed's colleagues at first stated their displeasure about this behavior in joking ways. When the behavior did not change, they started keeping track of the number of weeks that the behavior persisted. Finally Ed's supervisor read him the riot act, but to no avail. Ten weeks later the group met without Ed and agreed that he should be replaced.

Problem Solving

Effective groups are characterized by their ability to solve problems quickly, efficiently, and accurately. Group leaders develop an almost sixth sense for when problems are developing, what measures need to be taken to deal with the problems, and the appropriate way to make the best decisions. This process is enhanced by strong communication lines and appropriate role behavior. Problem solving and decision making from a managerial position will be discussed in depth in Chapter 16.

With a foundation on the types of group meetings and their characteristics, we now move to an examination of a manager's small group skill before, during, and after a meeting.

Before the Meeting

Must You Have a Meeting?

All of us have taken time out of a busy schedule to attend a meeting, only to find that our attendance wasn't needed, there was no purpose for the group to meet, the leader wasn't prepared, or the group was meeting because its meetings had become a habit. Before you schedule a meeting as a manager, ask yourself whether the meeting is the best use of everyone's time.

Aronoff, Baskin, Hays, and Davis list several factors that indicate when meetings should and should not be held:[8]

Meetings should be held
1. When issues require that several people be involved;
2. When interaction is needed to spur creativity or critical analysis;
3. When there is time to prepare for and to complete meetings;
4. When participants must act on the decision;
5. When a mutual exchange (feedback) is needed to assure that participants understand.

Meetings should not be held
1. When time pressures prevent adequate preparation;
2. When communication is to be one-way and no participant response is wanted;
3. When the problem is simple and can be handled by one person;
4. When commitment and input from participants are not required;
5. When participants cannot handle the conflict that is usually found in the problem-solving process.

What Is the Meeting's Objective?

Every meeting should have a clear purpose or goal toward which the group is advancing. Determining whether the purpose is to define a problem, seek a solution, share information, or exchange feelings about an issue will help you determine the type of meeting to hold, who should participate, and other important factors.

Every Monday at 7:00 A.M. salespeople at the Wilson Insurance Agency meet for coffee and donuts with agency owner Harold Wilson. The purpose of the meeting is to motivate personnel to achieve higher sales during the week that follows. Employees, however, will tell you that Mr. Wilson uses the same worn-out "positive mental attitude" stories and that they personally would rather sleep in for the extra hour each Monday. Contrast that nonproductive meeting with the one held by the Dana Corporation each Friday at 3:00 P.M. The purpose of that social meeting is to relax and share socially, and it has increased productivity.

Who Should Attend the Meeting?

The only participants who should be invited are those whose attendance is really necessary and who can contribute to achieving the goal. Consider the following factors:

1. What resource will each person bring to the group?
2. What is each potential member's knowledge, attitude, and working relationship to the topic and the other members?
3. Is there anything about the future member that will cause him or her to help or hinder goal accomplishment?
4. Will the person's organizational position, title, or status interfere with or help the group as it moves toward accomplishing its goal?
5. Are there political factions, hidden agendas, previous hurt feelings, and so forth that should influence the selection of new members?

How Large Should the Group Be?

Determining who should attend the meeting can help you decide how large the group should be. What is the complexity of the problem? How many people can the meeting facility hold? How much participation do you want from the members? Answers to these questions will help you make a decision about group size.

Research has shown that most committee meetings have an average of eight members, although the preference of most members is for a group size of only five members. One classic study by Slater reinforced the preference for five-member groups:

> Size five emerged clearly . . . as the size group which from the subjects' viewpoint was most effective in dealing with an intellectual task involving the collection and exchange of information about a situation, the coordination, analysis, and evaluation of this information, and a group decision regarding the appropriate administrative action to be taken in the situation.[9]

For each additional member there is less participatory time for all, more possible conflicts, the need for additional interaction, and more people to listen to and speak with.

At What Time Should the Meeting Be Held?

The time you pick for the meeting can have dynamic impact on the outcome. Berko offers some insight into this problem:

> When and where the group meets may have an effect on the decision-making process. Meetings held extremely early or extremely late in the day can cause problems. If people feel inconvenienced, they may react negatively, make quick and unfounded decisions, or not participate. The length of a meeting can also have an effect. As time drags on people get irritated, distracted, and bored. It may be better to have several short meetings than one very long one. It is often wise to have a coffee break during what has become a long session. A simple physical action, such as standing up, can have a positive end result in relieving anxiety and indifference. A leader of a group should watch for such verbal or nonverbal signs as temper flares and fidgeting as possible signs of "it's been too long."[10]

Establishing time limits for the meeting is just as important as determining the right time for the meeting. The meeting should start and end on time, and a limit should be set for the minimum amount of time needed for the meeting.

Where Should the Meeting Be Held?

The place of the meeting can support or hinder the working of the group, and for this reason many companies hold meetings away from the workplace whenever possible. The new location and surroundings contribute to a sense of the importance of the work task, and members benefit from the absence of telephone calls and other interruptions. Likewise, the room itself should be well lighted, a comfortable temperature, without physical distractions, and have seating to accommodate all those involved.

Because seating arrangements either facilitate or hinder the flow of communication between people, rooms should always be arranged for the type of group using them (see Figure 9.1). Personal groups sit around a table, pull several chairs together in a circle, or find other seating arrangements that work best for study or discussion. Work groups usually use a conference table approach, sometimes with the designated leader at one end. Quality circles usually operate in a large circle of chairs, and sales meetings use a modified auditorium style with the speaker in front of the other members.

At the organizational type of meeting the directors normally sit around a large, rectangular boardroom table, while annual meetings are best housed in an auditorium setting. Most public meetings also use the auditorium style.

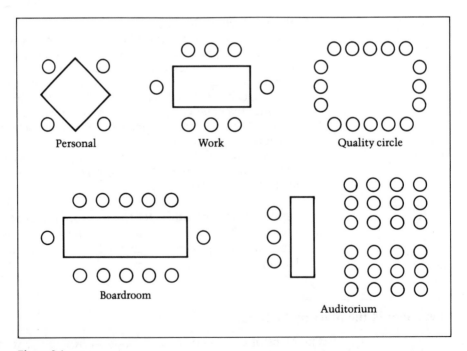

Figure 9.1

Develop an Agenda

The agenda is an outline or master plan for the meeting. It includes the topics to be covered, the order in which they will be covered, additional ideas and suggestions from members, and a designation of who is responsible for what during the meeting. The agenda merely presents factual information to be covered during the meeting. It does not advocate or evaluate any of the ideas or factual material.

Whenever possible an agenda should be prepared before the meeting. If this is not possible, take a few minutes at the start of the meeting to set the agenda before proceeding. Circulating an agenda prior to the meeting will cut down on comments like, "I would be prepared if I had known we were going to discuss this issue." During the actual meeting the agenda helps the leader cut off undesirable ramblings and smoothly bring the group back to the agenda items.

The agenda in Exhibit 9.2 was used by the personnel director of the Ferguson Company at an advisory meeting to investigate the feasibility of a presupervisor training program.

The Pre-meeting Checklist

When you are in charge of a meeting, it is best to develop a checklist to make sure each item is covered. Although you should develop your own, Exhibit 9.3 is an example.

During the Meeting

The successful completion of a meeting requires much advance work, continued efforts throughout the meeting, and a final follow-up and review. The following ideas focus on how to conduct a meeting.

The Start

It is important that the members arrive a few minutes early to mingle informally and take care of some social-emotional, or maintenance, needs. This friendliness shows a readiness to cooperate and to work together.

An early arrival will allow the person who is in charge of the meeting

The Ferguson Company

To: Al Richards, Plant Manager
    Jim Williams, Night Supervisor
    Ed Bradley, Maintenance Supervisor
    Carl Richey, Production Manager
    Janet Simmons, Line Foreman
    Leon Hughes, Assistant Personnel Director

From: Boyd Nixon, Personnel Director

Date: March 13, 1986

Subject: Advisory meeting to examine the feasibility of establishing a presupervisory training program. Monday, March 20, 1986, 2:00–4:00 P.M., Conference Room C.

Background

As you know, we have had a large turnover the past three years of first-time, first-line supervisors. We have a sizable pool of people to select new supervisors from, although we spend lots of hours training the ones selected to be a quality supervisors.

After discussing the problems with each of you individually I have decided to form an advisory board to study the feasibility of establishing a presupervisory training program. This program would be for those key employees that we feel have supervisory potential, would allow us to examine them early and make a decision on whether they should remain on the supervisory path, and would equip those chosen with the tools they could use to step into the role of supervisor when the time comes.

Agenda Items

1. Feasibility of a presupervisory training program.
   a. Pros
   b. Cons

2. Goals of a presupervisory training program.
   a. Identification of potential leaders
   b. Development of leadership skills
   c. Retention of employees at supervisory level

3. Can the goals be accomplished?
   a. Goals achievable in such a program?
   b. Can the goals be transferred to the job?

4. Structure of the program.
   a. Objectives
   b. Topics to be covered
   c. Instructors
   d. Amount of time

5. Are the goals worth pursuing?
   a. Will they produce high levels of skill development?
   b. Is program justified in terms of supervisor/worker productivity?
   c. Is program justified in terms of cost benefits?

Exhibit 9.2 • Meeting Agenda

```
                        Pre-meeting Checklist

Type of meeting _____        Location _____
Date _____                Time _____

Initial Preparations

_____  Is the meeting necessary?
_____  Have you narrowed the purpose of the meeting?
_____  Have you contacted everyone who should attend?
_____  Have you scheduled a room?
_____  Have you written an agenda?
_____  Have agendas been mailed?
_____  Have you mailed announcements to others such as the public?
_____  Have you made arrangements for refreshments?
_____  Does the caterer know the exact time and location?

The Meeting Room

_____  Is the room large enough?
_____  Is it well ventilated? Is it air conditioned?
_____  Is the room free of distracting noise, visuals, etc.?
_____  If equipment like audio-visual aids will be used, are electrical
         outlets convenient, and is there enough space to use the equip-
         ment?
_____  Are there enough chairs and tables?
_____  Is a podium needed?
_____  Are all audio-visuals secured? _____ charts
         _____ projectors _____ recorders _____ mikes
         _____ Have they been checked?
_____  Are all miscellaneous items in place?
         _____ pencils _____ writing pads _____ ash trays
         _____ water glasses and pitchers of water
         _____ name cards _____ reference materials
```

Exhibit 9.3 • Pre-Meeting Checklist

to make sure that the arrangements are in order, enough chairs and miscellaneous items are available, and the chairs and tables are arranged appropriately.

It is vital that the meeting start on time, thus discouraging rewards for those who arrive late. A short, leader-conducted or self-introductory session at the outset is appropriate, especially when some members do not know others in the group. Explain why any outside visitors are there.

Following the introduction the leader should briefly give any preliminary remarks such as items or announcements not related to the topic, a description of other groups examining the same problem, or a summary of any subgroups working on the current topics under discussion. This short preliminary talk can help the present group stay on target during the discussion. Finally, individual roles, such as note-taker, can be designated by the leader.

All time spent on preparation now gives way to the meeting itself; this is the important activity. While the interaction and functional role behavior of each member is vital, the leader at this point must direct the flow of the meeting, solicit involvement from all participants, keep the group on the track of following the agenda, and reach the final goal.

The Leader's Responsibility

The leader not only starts the meeting but is responsible for several other actions.

State the Purpose of the Meeting

The leader should state explicitly the purpose of the meeting and explain the agenda that the group will follow. These remarks should describe the group's task, the impact of the problem on the organization, a review of the problem and its frequency or relation to the group, and any procedures the leader will use at the meeting, such as parliamentary procedure.

Encourage Member Participation

Running a meeting and encouraging member participation is not easy. A leader's style at the start, both verbally and nonverbally, tells the members whether their ideas and input are welcome and respected. As a leader, try to build an atmosphere that is open to honest and frank discussion, but beware also of the controls you place on the group. If you run the meeting too tightly, it might dampen output, group morale, and creative ideas. To let the meeting run too loosely might allow it to flow completely out of control and to accomplish nothing. Some of the ideas of Jack Gibb are pertinent:

- If you appear to be a judge and always evaluate others, they will not talk or participate.
- If you attempt to control the meeting instead of letting it flow in a natural yet productive way, you will receive resistance.

• If the members see you as spontaneous, instead of manipulative, they will trust you and give you more response.
• If you attempt to project yourself into the other person's position, instead of remaining neutral and passive to the other's expressed feeling, you will strengthen your leadership position.
• If you maintain a "superior" attitude, others will be closed and unresponsive.
• If you will "keep an open mind" to the different sides of the issues, and leave room for member differences, both you and the group will receive less resistance.[11]

Direct the Flow of Communication

One of the best ways to encourage member participation is to actively direct the flow of communication. A leader who helps all members to have vocal input builds a climate of trust, acceptance, and encouragement, as opposed to a climate of intimidation, manipulation, oppression, and resentment. One of the best devices for keeping communication flowing is for the leader to ask questions. Loban offers suggestions for effective use of questioning:

1. Phrase questions to avoid "yes" or "no" answers.
2. Keep questions brief.
3. Use only the most simple words.
4. Use questions with a direct relation to the topic.
5. Use questions that cover a single point.[12]

Use the Agenda and Problem-Solving Mode to Guide the Group

A leader must be open to the flow of ideas presented to the group and realize how those ideas help the group accomplish its goal. Thus, a group leader must constantly practice effective listening. A leader must be able to hear and understand what is said, what is not said, and how something is said. She must be able to note when the discussion wanders and help the group get back on course. She must ensure that all key points are considered and dealt with and that this takes place in the allotted time frame.

Present the Final Comments

The leader should guide the group to close at the proper time. As this time draws near, she may wish to call for a vote or consensus on key issues, make assignments for additional out of group action, and finally summarize the key areas discussed and the decisions that were reached.

Rules of Procedure

While most informal personal groups, and some small work groups, run on informal procedures, most formal organizational meetings employ parliamentary procedure. Probably the most recognized set of procedures are found in *Robert's Rules of Order*, which describes how groups should conduct their official meetings and actions.

All members of a group, especially those in leadership positions, should know and be able to apply these rules. Their purpose is to help the group accomplish its goals, implement the will of the majority ("more than half"), protect the rights of the minority members, and expedite business.

This section capsulizes rules of procedure and provides you with a working knowledge of the rules. Also, there are a variety of books on the subject that should be available at your library or bookstore.

Chairperson

The president or designated leader of a group automatically becomes the presiding officer. If no officer has been designated, the first order of business is to elect a chairperson, from the group, by majority vote.

Order of Business

Most organizations have a prescribed and regular order of business that they follow at each meeting. The order follows this sequence:

1. Call to order
2. Reading, correcting, and approving of minutes
3. Reports from treasurer, standing committees, and boards
4. Reports from special committees
5. Consideration of unfinished business from the previous meeting
6. Consideration of new business
7. Announcements, setting of time and place for next meeting
8. Adjournment

Voting Procedures

Each organization must decide how decisions will be made. Usually motions are made, information is presented, and a vote is taken. The four most common methods for reaching agreement are majority vote, plurality, part-of-the-whole, and consensus:

1. *Majority vote* is the most common form and takes a vote of one more than half of the voting members.

2. *Plurality* means "most," so the item receiving the most votes is the winner. A plurality can be less than a majority.

3. *Part-of-the-whole* is used when a part or percentage of those voting is agreed on as a minimum needed for taking action. Usually 66⅔ percent is the amount selected when groups want more than a majority, but any percentage can be selected as the minimum needed for approval.

4. *Consensus* means "all." For an action to be accepted with this vote, everyone must agree to the proposal. Since the likelihood of everyone agreeing is not great, this method is used only in very important matters.

Motions

1. *Main motions.* Any member can introduce new business by making a motion. This is generally done by saying, "Mr. Chairman, I move that. . . ." For this business to then be considered, another person must second, or support, the proposal. A second is expressed, "I second the motion." Once a main motion has been introduced, no additional main motion can be considered until the pending motion is processed.

2. *Subsidiary motions* usually help the group dispose of main motions. "The intent may be to remove a motion from consideration by postponing it indefinitely; it may be to refine a motion by amendment or by referring it to committee where it can receive more detailed attention; it may be to postpone a motion definitely or temporarily or to speed a vote by limiting debate or calling for immediate vote."[13]

3. *Incidental motions* arise because of a question on the floor, and thus they take precedent and must be settled before other discussion or votes on pending questions.

4. *Privileged motions* do not relate to the pending question and can interrupt any question on the floor.

The chart in Table 9.1 shows the most frequent motions and the action that can be taken on them.

Following the Meeting

While the main emphasis of a meeting is placed on the preparation and actual meeting itself, the post-meeting period is just as important. During the meeting, decisions were made and now must be carried out. New problems probably also became apparent and new issues were voiced. All of this requires analysis by the leader and the assigned committees.

Table 9.1 • Frequently Used Parliamentary Motions

Motions	Purpose	Needs Second?	Amend- able?	Debat- able?	Vote Required?	Reconsidered at Same Meeting?	May Interrupt Speaker?
I. Principal motion							
1. A main motion	Introduce business	Y	Y	Y	Majority	N	N
II. Subsidiary motions							
2. Postpone indefinitely	Suppress action	Y	N	Y	Majority	N	N
3. Amend/substitute	Modify a motion	Y	Y	Y	Majority	Y	N
4. Refer to committee	Modify a motion	Y	Y	Y	Majority	Y	N
5. Postpone definitely	Defer action	Y	Y	Y	Majority	Y	N
6. Limit/extend debate	Modify freedom of debate	Y	Y	N	Two-thirds	Y	N
7. Call for the previous question	Force immediate vote	Y	N	N	Two-thirds	Y	N
8. Lay on the table	Defer action	Y	N	N	Majority	Y	N
9. Take from table	Consider again	Y	N	N	Majority	Y	N
III. Incidental motions							
10. Suspend the rules	Take action contrary to stand- ing rule	Y	N	N	Two-thirds	N	N
11. Modify/withdraw mo- tion	Modify motion	Y	N	N	Majority or unanimous consent	Y	N
12. Divide motion	Modify motion	Y	Y	N	Majority	N	N
13. Object to consideration	Suppress action	N	N	N	Two-thirds	N	Y
14. Raise point of order	Correct parliamentary error	N	N	N	Decision of chair	N	Y
15. Call for division of house	Correct/reverse chair	N	N	N	Majority if chair desires	N	Y
IV. Privileged motions							
16. Call for orders of the day	Force consideration of pro- posed motion	N	N	N	Less than two- thirds negative	N	Y
17. Make matter a special order	Force consideration at speci- fied time	Y	Y	Y	Two-thirds	Y	N
18. Raise question of privi- lege	Make request during debate	N	N	N	Decision of chair	Y	Y
19. Take a recess	Dismiss meeting for specified length of time	Y	Y	N	Majority	Y	N
20. Adjourn	Dismiss the meeting	Y	N	N	Majority	Y	N

Y = yes   N = no

The Ferguson Company

Minutes of the Advisory Meeting

Date: March 21, 1986

Present: Richards, Bradley, Richey, Simmons, Hughes, Nixon

Absent: Williams

Discussion summary

Boyd Nixon opened the meeting with a brief background of the current supervisory selection process and the high turnover rate.

A general discussion followed on:

1. Feasibility of presupervisory training program
2. Goals of such a program
3. The accomplishment of the goals
4. How the program would be structured
5. Whether such a program should be pursued

Ed Bradley reported on his understanding of the success of such a program with our competitor, Allied.

Janet Simmons stated she thought it would improve morale drastically.

Al Richards said he would check into whether such a program has been packaged commercially and is presently available. Everyone agreed such a program would save development time and would probably be better, although certain changes undoubtedly would have to be made.

Agreements reached

1. Such a program is feasible
2. The goals would be:
   a. To identify future supervisors
   b. To let several individuals see if they really want to be supervisors, before they are selected
   c. To provide a higher level of supervisory skill on entering that job level
   d. To retain more of our supervisors who seem to quit out of frustration over problems they didn't realize they would face

(continued)

Action to be taken	Due Date
1. Al Richards will check on prepackaged programs.	April 10
2. Boyd Nixon will discuss with management possible incentive bonuses for those completing such training.	April 1
3. Ed Bradley will call several former employees who now work for Allied, to find out what their program is like.	April 10
4. The entire group will meet again on April 13.	

Exhibit 9.4

Within twenty-four hours of the meeting a complete set of minutes should be given to each group member. Sigband and Bateman have identified three advantages of preparing and distributing the set of minutes.[14]

1. Everyone present will have an identical summary. This should avoid comments like, "I don't remember our discussing that issue."
2. The minutes should clearly list the items demanding action and the name of the person responsible for completing the action. This will eliminate comments like, "I didn't know I was responsible for following up on that."
3. Since the minutes become record, they can be reviewed by those who attended the meeting, those absent, and others who may have need of the information discussed.

An example of a set of minutes is found in Exhibit 9.4.

Summary

Managers spend considerable time participating in and running group meetings. Groups are important because they encourage individuals to interact with each other and to participate together to achieve mutual goals. Within groups individuals can express their views, expand on ideas, present solutions to problems, and facilitate goal commitments. Understanding the types of groups and their characteristics can help managers plan strategies for working in and leading many different types of groups.

An awareness of group dynamics also helps the manager determine when to use a group as part of the management process. Some goals may be best accomplished in a group meeting, but for other goals a group meeting is definitely *not* the context for achieving results. Once a decision to hold a group meeting is made, the success of that meeting is affected by the group size, the time at which the meeting is scheduled, the location chosen for the meeting, and the agenda.

By assessing group goals and dynamics prior to, during, and after each meeting, managers can conduct successful meetings. Their skills as meeting leaders will also constantly improve.

Key Words

group meeting	quality circle	forum
task function	professional sharing	goals
maintenance function	meeting	communication lines
personal group	sales meeting	leadership
the happening	organizational	roles
conversation group	meeting	cohesion
study group	annual meeting	norms
work group	board of directors'	problem solving
staff meeting	meeting	agenda
production meeting	public meeting	rules of procedure
advisory meeting	panel discussion	minutes
committee meeting	symposium	

Review Questions

1. What is the definition of a group?
2. Why are groups important in the business environment? List several of the reasons mentioned in the chapter.
3. What are some of the disadvantages of groups? Again, list several reasons cited in the chapter.
4. Describe the difference between task and maintenance group functions. Give an example of how both of these functions have been important in groups you have been a part of.
5. Describe four different types of business groups, and list several types of groups found in those categories.
6. Each group has several characteristics that tell us how well the group is functioning and meeting its objectives. List the seven different characteristics.
7. In order for meetings to run smoothly several questions must be answered prior to the meeting. What are these questions, and why are the answers to them important?
8. Describe what happens during the meeting, especially the rules of procedure.
9. Even when the meeting ends, a manager's communication tasks are not complete. Describe what needs to be done following the meeting.

Exercises

1. In your educational, social, or work experience you have been involved in a variety of groups. Recall some of those groups, their purposes, characteristics, functions, and successes. Have the class divide into small groups of three or four to describe those groups.

2. When you attend another group meeting, think about the dynamics and characteristics that have been described in this chapter. After the meeting analyze the process by speculating on what questions the leader asked before the meetings, critiquing what could have been done more productively during the meeting, and also contemplating what the leader will do following the meeting. If you are not an active member of a group, seek out groups that will allow you to sit in on their meetings, such as student or faculty senate or community forum.

References

1. Rollie Tillman, Jr., "Problems in Review: Committees on Trial," *Harvard Business Review*, 38 (May/June 1960), p. 168.
2. Daniel Goleman, "The Electronic Rorschach," *Psychology Today* (Feb. 1983), pp. 36–43.
3. Lawrence B. Rosenfield, *Human Interaction in the Small-Group Setting* (Columbus, Ohio: Charles E. Merrill, 1973), p. 7.
4. Harold P. Zelko and Frank E. X. Dance, *Business and Professional Speech Communication* (New York: Holt, Rinehart & Winston, 1965), p. 161.
5. Howard H. Martin, "Communication Setting," in *Speech Communication: Analysis and Readings*, Howard Martin and Kenneth Anderson, eds. (Boston: Allyn & Bacon, 1968), pp. 70–71.
6. S. Bernard Rosenblatt, T. Richard Cheatham, and James T. Watt, *Communication in Business* (Englewood Cliffs, N.J.: Prentice-Hall, 1977), pp. 225–26.
7. Joseph Litterer, *The Analysis of Organizations* (New York: John Wiley & Sons, 1967).
8. Craig E. Aronoff, Otis W. Baskin, Robert W. Hays, and Harold E. Davis, *A Practical Guide to Business and Communication* (St. Paul, Minn.: West, 1981), p. 293.
9. P. E. Slater, "Contrasting Correlates of Group Size," *Sociometry*, 21 (1958), pp. 137–38.
10. Roy M. Berko, Andrew D. Wolvin, and Ray Curtis, *This Business of Communicating* (Dubuque, Iowa: William C. Brown, 1980), p. 146.
11. J. R. Gibb, *T-Group Theory and Laboratory Methods* (New York: John Wiley & Sons, 1964).
12. Lawrence N. Loban, "Questions: The Answer to Meeting Participation," *Supervision* (Jan. 1972), pp. 11–13.
13. Joseph A. Wagner, *Successful Leadership: In Groups and Organizations* (San Francisco: Chandler, 1959), p. 11.
14. Norman B. Sigband and David N. Bateman, *Communicating in Business* (Glenview, Ill.: Scott, Foresman, 1981), p. 382.

C H A P T E R 10

Writing:
A Skill of Lifetime
Career Importance

Introduction

Writing is a communication skill that people learn early in life. From grade school to high school and college, writing is an important way that students communicate to teachers what they have learned. College graduation may free students from writing term papers, book reports, and essay examinations, but writing is a basic ingredient in the life of all professional people.

Those just beginning their business careers may hear comments like, "Look into this and send me a memo by Wednesday." "Here is a letter from a disgruntled customer, answer it for me." "We have a loan application from the XYZ Company. Examine it and write me a review telling me whether or not to grant it." "Your employment review needs to be completed this month. Write me a description of what you have accomplished during this past year."

Management consultant Bill Sears put it this way:

You'll be writing reports on why your work is late or early . . . overspent or underspent . . . letters to outraged customers or upper levels of management . . . memos recapping an understanding . . . summaries of conversations held at off-site meetings . . . [and] overviews of five-year plans and programs. . . . Ability to write good, clear business prose is one of the measures by which a growing number of companies are watching people for advancement. Simple reason: it's a vital part of the job.[1]

The importance of learning to write well relates to the "bottom line" of business because bad writing costs money. An engineer may know his profession well, yet top management will never agree to drill the oil well he is recommending unless he can explain to them his ideas and reasons. Managers do not have time to waste in trying to figure out what others want. Since companies today are built around reports, letters, and memos, poor writing is a significant factor in the decline of productivity. This chapter focuses on three important aspects of business writing. The first section discusses report writing; the second section examines letters and memoranda; and the third section looks at editing.

Report Writing

Reports are factual documents written to a specific audience for the purpose of informing or persuading. The report may present past events, new information, or recommendations for the future. The writer's purpose is accomplished when the reader reacts as the writer desires.

Directional Movement

Reports written within an organization move in three directions: vertical, horizontal, and radial.

- *Vertical reports.* These can be upward or downward reports. The downward flow includes policy statements, procedural plans, and managerial decisions that employees need to know about. The upward flow is directed at management and includes progress summaries, status reports, anticipated problems or successes, figures for financial documents, and general requests.
- *Horizontal reports.* Reports on this plane move from individual to individual and department to department. Often they carry data that others need to perform their work adequately.

- *Radial reports.* An organization also sends reports outward. These might include proposals for future work, professional research conducted internally, or general public relations brochures and annual reports.

Report Objectives

Organizations generally use two kinds of reports: informational and analytical.

- *Informational.* This report presents information but carefully avoids making any recommendations. The material is designed and presented so that the reader is better able to make a decision based on the newly acquired information. No action is usually required on the part of the informational report reader other than to read the document. While some people feel the chronological sequence is the best way to present information, we feel that the inverted approach, which is described below, serves a better purpose. Typical examples of the informational report are progress summaries, status reports, employee procedural manuals, policy statements, and annual reports.
- *Analytical.* Within this report form, facts are presented and analyzed, interpretations and conclusions are drawn, and recommendations are offered. The report is organized and written to motivate the reader toward action. Examples of this type report are marketing and personnel services, budgets, system analyses, cost analyses, and sales proposals.

Report Formality

Since reports are prepared in different sizes, shapes, and levels of formality, it is good to determine what level your report requires before you write.

- *Informal.* An informal report covers less important information, such as routine status and progress reports, trip and expense reports, and minor requests (see Exhibit 10.1). These reports take the form of a letter or memorandum and are usually typed (although they can be hand-written), written on pre-printed forms, or sent electronically. The writing style is informal and may address the reader as "you." If copies are needed, they can be made and reproduced inexpensively. The length is usually one or two pages, and the pages are stapled together. The informal report seldom goes outside the organization and usually travels no more than two vertical levels.

LONE STAR BANK

To: Sam Lewis, Head, Training Department

From: Mary M. Rydesky, Director
          Customer Service Department

Date: April 5, 1986

Subject: Development of Programmed Instruction on Punctuation Skills

---

I would like to work with one of your instructional developers to create a review of punctuation skills for my staff. All sixty-four of my employees must maintain good writing skills because they all prepare memos, reports, and letters to clients. Recently, I've noticed that the correspondence has become difficult to read due to punctuation errors.

Other banks have used letter-writing improvement programs, and I considered importing one. However, they are costly to implement and do not reflect the Lone Star philosophy. My next idea was to develop a program that would accomplish four goals:

1. Allow employees to work at a self-determined pace;
2. Allow employees to study at home rather than in a scheduled class;
3. Reinforce our style of correspondence;
4. Minimize costs and time loss.

Programmed instruction seems to meet these goals, but I am not familiar enough with it to develop my own materials. Is there a member of your staff who might assist me?

I will call you on Friday so that we can discuss a timetable for the project. I would like to begin just as soon as you can assign an instructional developer!

mmr:td

Exhibit 10.1 · Informal Memo Report
Source: Mary M. Rydesky, "Lone Star Bank Memo," prepared for this book.

• *Semiformal.* This report is longer, typically between two and ten pages, and is typed and reproduced inexpensively (see Exhibit 10.2). The semiformal report usually stays within the organization but is occasionally distributed outward. It travels both horizontally and vertically and reaches several readers at several levels. Although the report is written in a formal style, it is not as detailed or broad as the formal report. The added length often requires several internal headings.

IMPROVING WRITTEN COMMUNICATION SKILLS
PROPOSAL

PRESENTED BY:
MARY M. RYDESKY, DIRECTOR
CUSTOMER SERVICE DEPARTMENT

SUBMITTED TO:
THE COMMITTEE OF EXECUTIVES
APRIL 15, 1986

   Spelling, dictation, punctuation: All are skills that our Customer Service Staff must have for effective communication through writing. Yet these skills easily become rusty and in need of upgrading. At present, the letters, memos, and reports being prepared by my staff have more errors in punctuation than I think allowable. As a result, these materials are difficult to read.

   Improving the writing skills of the sixty-four employees in Customer Service is possible to achieve without spending great sums of money and without taking time away from the job. By developing programmed instruction materials that can be studied at home, we can accomplish the goal of improved written communications at the least cost.

   Programmed instruction refers to an educational style in which a sequence for learning is frequently stopped for a test of student understanding. For example, I could insert a question asking you to complete this sentence: ''Programmed instruction is an _____ style.'' By writing in the word ''educational,'' you would reinforce your memory of the definition. By continuing the sequence, you would learn more about the concept.

   Programmed instruction is usually developed in a workbook so that each employee may have a copy. It can be studied at one's own pace and is thus more individualized than a classroom presentation that requires all students to absorb material at the same rate. It can be studied alone rather than in the presence of an instructor because it provides the answers immediately following the questions. Later, the workbook

---

(continued)

can be used as a reference when the employee wants to recall a particular point.

Ann Ford, an instructional developer in our Training Department, has had college coursework in programmed instruction. With her help, I would like to create a workbook to improve the punctuation skills of my staff. If errors decrease, the same technique could be used to upgrade other writing skills. Once the project is approved, Ann will need two weeks to draft the punctuation program. We would then set up conditions for its trial and would submit a timetable for reporting on its effectiveness. Estimated costs for this development and evaluation of materials total $170.00, or approximately $2.00 per employee. In comparison with other banks, our costs would be low.

Other Banks' Programs	Costs	Methods
Fidelity National	$11.00 per employee	Consultant hired to conduct three-day seminar
Capital Hill	$ 7.90 per employee	Purchased videocassette/workbook course from Kent Publishing
Exchange State	$ 4.25 per employee	Purchased paperback reference texts for each work station
Allied Republic	$ 4.00 per employee	Presented four one-hour classes to supervisors who were to hold seminars for their employees; used films from the public library

Exhibit 10.2 · Semiformal Report

Source: Mary M. Rydesky, "Improving Written Communication Skills Proposal," prepared for this book.

Formal. This is the traditional report that is several pages in length, printed on quality paper, often bound, and implies an official source (see Exhibit 10.3). It presents important information, and thus its readership goes beyond one or two levels. These reports often go to readers outside the organization and are filed or placed on bookshelves for future reference. A long, traditional, formal report may be divided into several parts; not all are found in every report, but Exhibit 10.3 shows their preferred sequence.

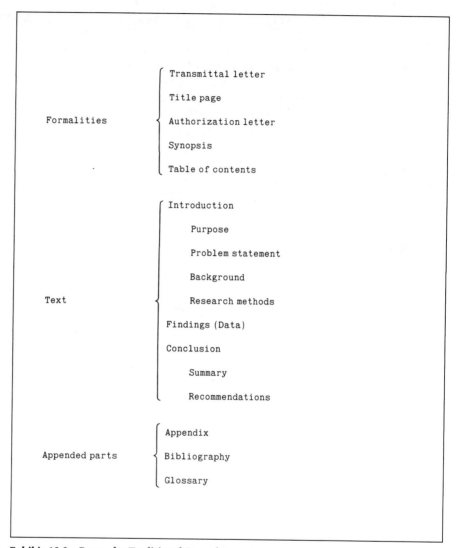

Exhibit 10.3 • Parts of a Traditional Formal Report

Parts of a Traditional Formal Report

Formalities
In the opening pages of the formal report the writer places all the information that will help a reader move quickly and clearly to the main text.

Each of the opening elements serves a distinct purpose:

- The *transmittal letter* is a cover letter that sends the report to the reader. Any information that might help the reader as he prepares to read and understand the report is included.
- The *title page* contains the report title, names of the author(s), for whom it was prepared, the date of issuance, and any additional source material that might be helpful to the reader.
- The *authorization letter* is a copy of any correspondence sent to the writer that requested or contracted the report.
- The *synopsis* is a short summary or abstract of the report. It succinctly capsulizes the text content, problem, research procedures, findings, and recommendations.
- The *table of contents* is an outline of the entire report, from cover to cover, with corresponding page numbers.

Text

Three main parts of the text are normally used:

- The *introduction* presents the background, problem, and research procedure followed in the report.

  1. The *purpose* describes why the study was undertaken, its importance, and the significance and impact of the findings.
  2. The *problem statement* serves the same purpose as the thesis statement of a speech. Here the writer succinctly states in a few short sentences or paragraphs the precise problem under research.
  3. The *background* brings the reader up to date with information needed to understand what was researched, investigated, and consequently found.
  4. The *research methods* describe how the data was collected, any statistical procedures, and the significance of the findings.

- The *findings (data)* section contains the body of the information discovered or proposed.
- The *conclusion* wraps up the heart of the report:

  1. The *summary* brings everything together and briefly highlights the report's most important points. Some reports also contain a conclusion section that shows a logical progression from research, to data, to recognizable facts.
  2. The *recommendations* section is the place where the writer makes his request for action.

Appended Parts

Information that appears in tables, charts, or pictures but is not easily placed in the body of the report can go here.

- The *appendix* is for supplementary materials.
- The *bibliography* is where references can be categorized and listed in alphabetical order.
- The *glossary* is where frequently used but often unknown or misunderstood words are listed along with definitions.

Sample pages from a traditional formal report are illustrated in Appendix B.

Inverted Report Writing

Word processors and dictation equipment are available to help writers commit their ideas to paper, but few aids are available to help readers understand what they're reading. This is especially true when the reader is searching for the hidden meaning of a report that is poorly organized and wordy.

One aid for report readers is the report that is written in an inverted manner.[2] The inverted approach begins with the important points of a report instead of concluding with them. Melba Murray calls it the "engineered report writing" style.[3] Only 20 percent of readers reach the most important part of a traditional report, as Figure 10.1 shows; the inverted style captures 100 percent readership at the start. Four questions to ask before beginning the report are (1) What is the news? (2) Why? (3) How? (4) Now what? When this approach is employed, 100 percent of the readers start with the real facts, or "news," in the report. Because this approach automatically deletes unimportant information, the report is shorter, and most of your readers stay with you to the end.

The Initial Research

Murray lists five steps to properly research and prepare for writing:[4]

- Step 1: Make decisions concerning people.
- Step 2: Make decisions concerning the report.
- Step 3: Construct a topic outline using the pattern of conversation.
- Step 4: Expand the topic outline with summarizing topic sentences.
- Step 5: Hold a pre-report conference.

When the research is finished you are ready to construct your message.

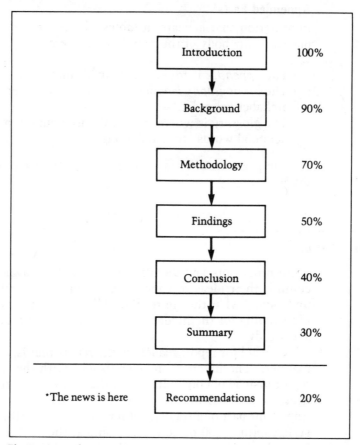

Introduction	100%
Background	90%
Methodology	70%
Findings	50%
Conclusion	40%
Summary	30%
*The news is here Recommendations	20%

Figure 10.1 · The Progression and Readership of a Traditional Report

What Is the News?

The first part of the report tells the reader the primary thing you want him to know: "Your answer might be that you've built something, developed it, surveyed it, tested it, analyzed it, read it, proved or disproved it, started or completed it. Perhaps the news is something you've succeeded in doing, failed to do, or think should be done. It may be a method, a piece of equipment, an idea, a concept, an opinion, or a recommendation for action."[5] Whatever you have to convey, say it quickly, clearly, and briefly.

Why?

If supporting facts or background information is needed, this is the section where it should go. If there is something to be gained from a recommendation that you are making, present it here. But present no more than is absolutely necessary for the reader to know.

How?

The "how" takes your reader a step further and describes the way you propose to carry out the "what." In this section you may need to support your position or further develop the major premise.

Now What?

Often by the time you respond to the first three sections you won't need this one. But if you want to reinforce a point, once again propose a particular thing, focus on the urgency of action, or cite specifics, this is the appropriate place.

Exhibit 10.4 displays an internal report for Honeycutt's Honey Corporation. The report is written in the traditional formal report style. Exhibit 10.5 shows the same information in the inverted report mode. Note how the vital information is presented and how succinctly it is covered.

HONEYCUTT'S HONEY, INC.
REPORT

TO: William S. Honeycutt, President

FROM: Martin J. Spears, Vice-President, Sales

DATE: May 12, 1983

SUBJECT: Safety Packaging

Introduction

Purpose. At your request I undertook a comprehensive study of the feasibility and need for devising tamper-resistant packaging for our products. This report describes that study, the conclusions it led to, and
my recommendations.

Method. The primary method of research was a bibliographical study of
current issues. Business Week and Advertising Age magazines and the
Wall Street Journal and New York Times were especially helpful in providing information. Also, at my request our advertising agency, Morris

---

(continued)

Associates, conducted a marketing survey concerning our product. The
methodology and results of that survey are presented in the ''Findings'' section of this report. Financial data in this report were obtained from records of our Production Department.

<u>Background</u>. Tamper-resistant packaging has been an issue of some con-
cern to the food and drug industry for several years. This issue was
briefly brought to the attention of the public a few years ago when a man
was poisoned (not fatally) from a jar of pickles that had been tampered
with. When it became evident the incident was an isolated occurrence,
public concern dwindled, and no regulatory or industry-induced action
was taken. In August 1982 two people in California were injured by using
Murine and Visine A.C. eyedrops spiked with acid. Packaging was not
considered a real problem in this incident; because the seals of the
products were broken before purchase, it was evident they had been tampered with.
       The Tylenol scare, however, was a different matter. When seven
people in the Chicago area died from cyanide-laced Extra-Strength Tylenol, national media attention focused on the packaging problem, and
Johnson & Johnson was forced to take drastic action. The company eventually withdrew all Tylenol from store shelves and announced a national
recall of all Tylenol capsules. Johnson & Johnson watched helplessly as
its Tylenol share in the pain-killer market dropped precipitously from
35% to 6.5%.
       In November 1982 a national survey revealed 94% of Americans knew
of the Tylenol tragedy, and even though 90% of those people placed no
blame on Johnson & Johnson, it was evident the public desired more
stringent packaging rules. The government agreed. The Food and Drug
Administration established a regulation requiring at least one type of
tamper-resistant or tamper-evident seal on all drug packaging.
       Even before the ruling, Johnson & Johnson had ordered several
$11,000 machines that seal mouths of bottles with an aluminum or plastic
wrap. In December Tylenol returned to store shelves with triple seals: a
glued box flap, a tight neck seal, and an inner foil wrap. The seals were
estimated to cost 2.4 cents per package.

Findings

<u>Implications</u>. The first obvious result of the Tylenol tragedy is that
improper packaging cost Johnson & Johnson a lot of money. It's not that
the packaging was unsafe; it's just that the packaging was not tamper-
resistant or at least tamper-perceptible. In other words, the fact that
Tylenol bottles were susceptible to hidden tampering allowed the tragedy to occur. Johnson & Johnson was not negligent; it was simply not
prepared for the eventuality of concealed tampering, and it cost the
company dearly.
       Recall, replacement, and repackaging of the Tylenol product cost
Johnson & Johnson an estimated $100 million. The company's 1982 after-

(continued)

tax income fell by $50 million as a result of the crisis. Perhaps even more revealing, a survey of people who have never used Tylenol indicated 80% of them now would never even try the brand. It may take Tylenol a long time to recover the marketing momentum it enjoyed.

Other food and drug manufacturers sat up and took notice of Johnson & Johnson's problems. Even though the FDA has established no tamper-resistant guidelines for food product packaging, Kraft, Borden, and Procter & Gamble are evaluating various sealing options. Alternatives include plastic ''blister'' packs, foil wrapping over bottle openings, and plastic bands that shrink tightly to seal lids.

<u>Marketing Survey</u>. The purpose of Morris Associates' survey was to determine what effect consumers' new safety packaging awareness has on their purchase decision and, in particular, if safety seals would make a difference in selling our product. A random telephone survey was taken of the greater metropolitan area. Sample size was 500. Accuracy of these responses as compared to the population as a whole is estimated to be within 3%. Results of some of the more important survey questions are listed below:

	Yes	No	Uncertain
1. Are tamper-resistant seals something you look for when purchasing pain killers and other pharmaceuticals?	77%	17%	6%
2. Are tamper-resistant seals something you look for when purchasing food products?	56%	32%	12%
3. Do you purchase honey at least once every four months?	33%	62%	5%
4. If yes, do you regularly purchase Honeycutt's honey products?	39%	57%	4%
5. Whether or not you use Honeycutt's honey, would you be willing to pay a few cents extra for honey if it had a safety seal around its lid?	55%	32%	13%

The results of this survey are important for two reasons. First, as question 4 indicates, we have a 39% share of the local market. This compares favorably to the 32% share recorded in last year's survey. Second, as question 5 indicates, safety sealing our product could enhance sales.

<u>Financial Aspects</u>. Our Production Department agrees with me that plastic bands around our jar lids is the most cost-effective method to

(continued)

safety seal our product. Sealing machinery is available in the local area for $9,800, or it can be leased for $1,300 per month for each machine. This machinery could be incorporated at the end of our production line to serve as the final stage of the production process. Three machines would be required, one for each size of jar we pack. The machines are fully automatic and require no additional labor. Production Department estimates that after installation, seals would cost an average of 0.8 cents per jar.

Additional advertising is necessary to inform the public of our new, responsible packaging. A three-month campaign of newspaper ads, coupons, and store displays would cost $8,400. At the end of this period the effectiveness of the seals could be assessed. Morris Associates recommends retaining our present honey prices during the campaign, evaluating the increase in sales, and then raising prices three or four cents if we decide to go with the program.

Total costs for the three-month campaign with leased machinery would be $20,260. If we buy the machinery immediately, the cost of the campaign without considering depreciation would be $37,960.

Conclusion

Summary. Due to the Tylenol tragedy, the vast majority of the public know what tamper-resistant packaging is and would prefer to have it on all the edible products they buy. A local survey indicates most people would be willing to pay a few cents extra for sealed honey. Because of this opinion, sealing our honey products can provide two distinct advantages. First, there is a good possibility of increased sales. The exact nature of the increase would not be known until after a trial program. Second, sealing our product provides some insurance against the increasing number of lunatics our society seems to be producing. The seals we have in mind would not prevent tampering, but they would make tampering evident to the consumer. This is an intangible benefit, to be sure, but I bet Johnson & Johnson would have been glad to pay for it to avoid the events of the past several months. Enhancing our image as a responsible, caring food manufacturer can only augment the value of our goodwill and provide positive publicity.

Recommendations. I recommend we proceed with the three-month sealing program as soon as possible and begin by renting three sealing machines. Depending on the results, at the end of the three months we can either make a national announcement of our new policy and extend the program to our other regional plants, or if sales drop, we can quietly phase out the program. It is my opinion that the program will succeed, and I recommend we begin allocating funds for the nationwide purchase of sealing machinery.

Exhibit 10.4
Source: Timothy Riggins, "Honeycutt's Honey Report," prepared for this book.

HONEYCUTT'S HONEY, INC.
REPORT

TO: William S. Honeycutt, President

FROM: Martin J. Spears, Vice-President, Sales

DATE: May 12, 1983

SUBJECT: Safety Packaging

I recommend we initiate a three-month trial program of safety sealing our honey products in the local metropolitan area. With leased machinery, total costs for the project will be $20,260.

Due to the Tylenol tragedy, most Americans prefer tamper-resistant packaging on all the edible products they buy. A local survey we conducted indicates our market share of 39% could improve if we safety seal our products, because most people would be willing to pay a few cents extra for sealed honey. This survey and my bibliographical research indicate safety packaging can provide two distinct advantages for us: increased sales and improved goodwill.

It is almost impossible to prevent tampering, but it is fairly simple to seal our products so that tampering is made obvious to the consumer. The most cost-effective method to safety seal our jars is to install plastic bands around the lids. The three-month program would involve placing sealing machines on each of our packing lines, a local advertising campaign, and a final evaluation. If the program is as successful as I envision, we can then proceed with a national program, including the purchase of sealing machines for each assembly line and a national advertising campaign. If the local program is determined not to be cost effective and if public approval is not as high as expected, we can quietly phase out the program.

Because this plan has been discussed and developed with the Marketing, Production, and Finance Departments, it is ready to begin immediately. Please call me if you have any questions about marketing or finance details.

Exhibit 10.5

Source: Timothy Riggins, "Honeycutt's Honey Inverted Report," prepared for this book.

Letters and Memoranda

Writing an effective business letter ranks among the top communication abilities of people in business. Letters and memoranda are planned and written each day to summarize agreements between several parties, initiate contracts for prospective clients, and communicate the time and place of meetings. Letter writing can be an effective way to get a job done.

When to Use Letters and Memoranda

The inexperienced often go to one of two extremes when it comes to written communication: They communicate almost totally in writing or avoid written communication altogether. We know from communication research that the receiver will remember a message longer if it is received both orally and in writing. This should be a key principle in deciding when to use letters and memoranda. Because written communication is most effective when it is used in conjunction with oral communication, a letter can initiate contact for a face-to-face meeting or act as reinforcement by summarizing a discussion. Before writing, analyze both the situation and the receiver.

The Situation

Ask yourself what you want to accomplish. If your outcome requires a complex explanation, a letter is the wrong communication channel unless you intend to also provide a demonstration of the task or use the letter to set up a meeting (or series of meetings) to explain the process. There are four typical uses of the letter or memorandum:

1. *Daily routine.* Daily routine correspondence includes requesting information, providing information, approving requests, or denying requests. The routine purposes of letters are discussed later in the chapter.

2. *For emphasis.* Sometimes a memo can be a very effective way to give emphasis. For example, if employees have begun to ignore an organizational policy and are extending the normal coffee break beyond sensible limits, a manager may send a memo to the group members that reminds them of the policy and notes displeasure. While the memo itself provides emphasis, the amount of space devoted to the issue will also communicate how important it is for the manager.

3. *For the record.* As a manager, you may participate in activities such as meetings that need to be recorded for future reference. These formal minutes are only one form of memoranda for the record. Others include summaries of discussions that result in recorded agreements and written reprimands.

4. *As a follow-up.* A final purpose for correspondence is to follow up a discussion. Opportunities may be lost because no one acted to follow up a decision to implement an idea. A consultant may lose business because he or she waited to be called and did not send a letter summarizing the plan, fees, and anticipated time frame for the proposed activity. Letters keep the momentum of a situation going toward the goal by indicating interest, commitment, and action.

The Receiver

Adapt your message to your receiver. What does the reader know about the subject? Consider vocabulary level, educational background, and technical knowledge. This information will help you determine the words and examples that will be most effective in communicating your message.

How well you know your reader will affect the formality of your letter. You probably would not want to address someone you had never met by that person's first name, yet it would sound stilted to address a friend and fellow worker as "Dear Mr. Smith." The less familiar you are with the other person, the more space you will have to devote to creating common ground in the opening of your letter.

When you communicate face to face, you can observe the nonverbal reactions to your message as well as reinforce the meaning of your words through your own nonverbal actions. In letters, the words alone must convey your meaning. The words you select are critical and must be aimed at the reader's realm of experience to be effective, especially if it is your only channel of communication.

The Style of a Letter

You may have received a letter beginning with the phrase, "This is to inform you that. . . . " The language did not convey warmth or a personal style and delivered an impersonal message, at best. Good letter writing requires a conversational style that avoids stilted conventional jargon. Use correct language, but choose words that convey the friendly tone of spoken language. Avoid "rubber stamp" expressions that take away from the personalization of the letter.

Select Words Carefully

Take care in word choice in order to set the appropriate tone. Anger and sarcasm expressed in writing will not accomplish most objectives, nor will they create goodwill. Your choice of words should convey sincerity. Contrast the following approaches to expressing employee disagreement to a company policy change:

1. "I am concerned about the impact our policy will have on employee turnover."
2. "This policy will be a disaster. People will quit rather than work under these conditions."

Identify with Your Reader

Write at a level your reader can easily understand. Do not use technical words unless your reader is well versed in the technical area. Identify with your reader, and select words that are part of his or her everyday experience. Attempt to see things from the reader's point of view, and then write your letter to accomplish your purpose with this in mind.

Use a Positive Tone

Always use a positive tone, even when you must say no. Provide an explanation that logically presents your position before refusing a request. Let the reader know that you understand the problem and provide an alternative solution.

Use the Correct Emphasis

The amount of space you devote to an issue suggests its importance to you. Be sure to put things in their proper perspective by using the correct emphasis. Taking two paragraphs to explain why an applicant did not get the job will leave the recipient wondering whether there is more to the message than meets the eye.

Direct Letters: The Good News

When you receive a letter with good news, you don't want to wade through details and explanations: You want the good news first. For example, if you have been selected for a job, the reasons are secondary to the fact that you have the job. Direct letters are written to save time and get to the point and include little explanation or background. The basic format of the direct letter is:

1. State the good news;
2. Present explanation and details;
3. Maintain goodwill.

Types of letters typically requiring directness are routine inquiries, responses, and acknowledgments.

Inquiries

The inquiry seeks information; it is one of the most frequently used letter writing approaches. The letter should get to the point quickly and place the key question in the first line of the letter. If the information you seek is more complex, analyze your objective, and prepare a series of questions that will elicit the specific response you desire. Then, start with a general question, and place more specific questions later in the letter.

To encourage a response that will meet your expectations, tailor the message by determining what would motivate the reader to help you. Place general explanatory material following the direct opening sentence, and include questions where needed. Ask the minimum number of questions to get the necessary information.

Be sure to structure your questions carefully. Ask directly for information—don't hint. Itemizing questions adds clarity, as is illustrated in Exhibit 10.6. End your letter with goodwill by expressing your appreciation for the reader's time and assistance, but avoid trite expressions such as "thanking you in advance." Unless you have an unlimited time schedule, include a reasonable time frame for the response. A statement that presents a reason and gives a date is most effective, for example:

> Since I will need this information for a report that must be completed by September 1, may I have your reply by August 29?

Positive Responses

If you are replying favorably to a request, say so in the beginning of your letter. You may want to use a subject line in your letter that identifies the inquiry or refer to the request in the opening statement of your letter. Answer the question as completely as it requires. If you are providing a series of answers, you will want to place them in a logical order in the body of the letter.

Sometimes bad news must accompany the good. If so, begin with the good news to emphasize it. Put the bad news in a secondary position in the middle of the letter. Remember also that the amount of space you devote to a topic adds emphasis. You will want to deemphasize the bad news by stating it briefly.

Everyone appreciates a little extra effort on his or her behalf. If you can provide additional information, assistance, or provide another reference, it will benefit your public relations. Exhibit 10.7 is an example of a favorable response to a job reference.

Acknowledgments

An acknowledgment lets someone know you have received his or her letter and apprises that person of the status of an order or request. Many

```
Ms. Cathy Johnston
Salter Chemical Company
2353 Bankston Ave.
Baton Rouge, LA 70810

July 29, 1986

Sales Department
National Communication Institute
1258 Dexter N.
Seattle, WA 98109

Dear Mr. Hurston:

Will you please send me some information concerning the film "The Im-
portance of Effective Written Business Communications"? Our company
has a small collection of films, a few of which apply to communication,
and we would like to update our collection. I would specifically like
responses to the following questions:

1. Will you please provide a summary of the film's contents?
2. What is the rental fee and the cost of purchase?
3. What is the copyright date?
4. What is the length of the film in minutes?
5. We plan to use it to train and instruct supervisory staff. Will it be
   appropriate for this level audience?

Since my training program proposals for purchasing must be submitted by
the end of next month, may I have your reply within two weeks? I appreci-
ate your assistance and look forward to doing business with you and your
company.

Sincerely,

Cathy Johnston
Director of Training
```

Exhibit 10.6 • An Inquiry

BAKER AND COMPANY
1321 Benton St.
Rockford, IL 61107

April 21, 1986

Mr. Kenneth Cochran
Personnel Director
Welford and Company
320 Napoleon
New Orleans, LA 76143

Dear Mr. Cochran:

Your request for a performance evaluation of John Richardson arrived last Friday. John has worked for us for four years during which time he has demonstrated outstanding qualities of skill, knowledge, and leadership.

His skill and imagination made him our top customer service employee. His helpful, sincere attitude toward customer inquiries has earned only praise from them.

John's superiors commend him for his loyalty and dedication. He rarely leaves the office until he completes his work. In addition he is fast and efficient, evidence of his efforts to maintain good public relations within our company.

As his employer, I could not ask for a better customer relations worker. Though I am disappointed he is leaving, John has my highest praise and recommendation. His skills and hard work will definitely meet your company's needs. If you need any additional help in evaluating him, please write me again.

Sincerely,

Judy Smythe
Office Manager

Exhibit 10.7 • Positive Response

organizations use a form letter or postcard as an acknowledgment. Individually written, an acknowledgment can convey goodwill and reinforce the relationship between the client and the organization. It should begin with the acknowledgment of the request or order, proceed to establish goodwill, and close with a friendly statement that encourages future business, as in Exhibit 10.8. A checklist of the things to include in a "direct" letter is found on page 459 in Appendix B.

ORDER DEPARTMENT
SELECT GIFT COMPANY
1650 E. 46th St.
Portland, OR 97213

October 30, 1986

Ms. Susan McDaniel
6678 Carroll Lane
Columbus, OH 43204

Dear Ms. McDaniel:

Your Christmas order is on its way to your home and should arrive early next week. United Post Carriers will deliver between 8:00 a.m. and 5:00 p.m., Monday through Friday. If you give them a call at 766-5343, you can specify the delivery time. You will be billed as soon as we have received confirmation that you received the order from the carrier.

We want to welcome you as a new customer of our product line. You will find the convenience, quality merchandise, and variety an advantage to you in gift selection.

We sincerely appreciate your order and look forward to serving your future select gift needs.

Sincerely,

Michael Conrad, Manager
Sales Department

Exhibit 10.8 · An Acknowledgment

Indirect Letters: The Bad News

Sometimes it is necessary to send letters that contain bad news. Perhaps a very good job candidate was not selected during intense competition for a job, yet you must present the bad news and maintain goodwill. Such letters require an indirect approach with a buffer statement that delays the bad news and seeks to gain understanding. You might begin your letter with the statement, "We have just completed the review of several outstanding candidates for our vacant position in the accounting department." The buffer should be followed by the details and reasons behind your decision that supports the bad news:

> We have ranked each candidate according to his or her strengths for the job, and selected the top candidate.

Your third step is to announce the bad news as briefly as possible. If you can present an alternative, do so. For example, you may know of another position for which the candidate might apply. Finally, you should try to maintain goodwill by closing in a friendly manner such as, "We appreciate your interest in our firm."

Indirect letters should convince the receiver that you not only gave his or her request or inquiry your attention and an objective review, but that your decision is also unavoidable. The order of items within the indirect letter is:

1. Begin with a buffer statement.
2. Present reasons or details.
3. Present the bad news.
4. Give an alternative if possible.
5. Close in a friendly manner.

Letters that need an indirect approach include letters refusing credit, claims, or requests and should generally follow the outline presented above. The sample letter in Exhibit 10.9 expresses concern and states the refusal in positive language.

Persuasive Letters: Overcoming Resistance

You will find that there are many occasions in which you will have to overcome the resistance of the reader to your objective. In such instances the persuasive letter establishes an argument for your position by pre-

---

OFFICE OF STUDENT AFFAIRS
THE NORTHEASTERN UNIVERSITY
250 Boyd Hall
Bethesda, MD 20016

May 18, 1986

Mr. George Stevens, President
Student Government Association
P.O. Box 11145
Bethesda, MD 20016

Dear Mr. Stevens:

Your interest in the current parking situation on campus indicates a genuine concern over an increasingly complex problem. Certainly, this problem is one that deserves considerable deliberation in attempting to come to a reasonable solution.

A suitable parking system centers on fairness and equality for the student body, faculty, and staff. Faculty and staff must have parking to meet the needs of the school itself. Handicapped students present an obvious priority. After careful reexamination of the current parking situation, the members of the review committee feel that equality and fairness may best be preserved by retaining the current system.

Your continuing concern over campus problems will certainly aid in making our campus a better one.

Sincerely yours,

Jeffrey Travers

Jeffrey Travers, Chairman
Campus Traffic Committee

Exhibit 10.9 · A Refused Request

senting information that will allow your reader to understand and accept your point of view.

The first step, therefore, is to determine your objective. What outcome do you want from your correspondence? Understanding? Support? Action? Once you have specified the objective, analyze your reader's reaction to it. What objections would she have? Put yourself in her place and try to see it from her point of view. It will probably help to list these objections using education, background, experience, attitudes, biases, and so on as broad categories.

Because you are trying to overcome resistance, an indirect approach that begins with your specific information and supports it with sound reasoning will probably be most effective. You are establishing a case for your argument and thus should direct each piece of evidence at dispelling an objection of your reader. The persuasive letter should have three parts: (1) an attention-getting opening, (2) the argument, which presents the facts and reasoning, and (3) an action-getting close.

An Attention-Getting Opening

The first paragraph in a persuasive letter must get the receiver's attention and convince her to continue reading. If the first sentence has a negative tone or creates a negative reaction, the reader's perception of the following information will be affected by it. In other words, a negative filter will block or color the remaining information no matter how well it is presented. How would you like to receive a letter with the following opening line?

> I was extremely disappointed to be informed that you violated our guidelines for implementing the personnel policies.

While the remainder of this letter may present a reasonable and acceptable explanation of the problem and action to be taken, the reader will probably be too disconcerted by the opening remarks to process it.

The opening should present a buffer statement that establishes common ground and gains attention so that the reader will want to read the rest of the letter. For example:

> We have previously discussed our mutual concern for the effective implementation of the new personnel policies. One area apparently is still not clear and is creating problems for our staff.

This opening establishes mutual objectives and focuses on a specific area for analysis and mutual problem-solving. Neither blame nor a defensive tone has been established.

The Argument

The word *argument* often conjures up thoughts of two parties who fail to agree with each other. Here, however, we will define it to mean a case or the presentation of persuasive appeals that are logical, ethical, or emotional.

The body of the letter should establish your case though a logical presentation of reasoning. Since you are trying to persuade the reader to commit to your objective, choice of words and arrangement of sentences are important. Avoid leading statements or loaded words. Begin with the arguments that will have the greatest effect or success. Use an indirect approach first, presenting evidence that leads to a logical conclusion.

An Action-Getting Close

The argument should bring the reader to a logical close. It is here that you present to the reader the action you desire her to take. State it in the form of a question, emphasizing the positive aspects of the action:

> Since we need to handle personnel grievances at the lowest level possible, will you grant an interview to Ms. James concerning this problem by March 30?

In addition, the close of the persuasive letter should convey goodwill to the reader by emphasizing his or her importance to the effective handling of the situation. The sample letter in Exhibit 10.10 emphasizes the benefits to be gained by following through with a personal interview.

Employment Letters and Resumes

One of the most important persuasive letters you will write is the letter of application for a job. Your letter of application and data sheet are reflections of you. In a highly competitive job situation, two equally qualified applicants may very likely be evaluated according to who has submitted the more persuasive letter and set of credentials. Your ability to present yourself will be perceived as a key to your effectiveness in the job.

Before you apply for a position, take a thorough inventory of your assets and abilities, including interests, education, experience, and aptitudes. It may be helpful to write an autobiography recounting the significant things you have done in your lifetime. You should include awards, degrees, extracurricular activities, leadership positions, technical knowledge, interesting courses, part- or full-time jobs, hobbies, training, military service, and so on in chronological order. By preparing an autobiography, you will become aware of your own skills, knowledge, and achievements and can evaluate them in terms of which you enjoyed most and how they relate to the job for which you are applying.

Most employers will request that you submit a resume and a letter of application with references. This information should provide the em-

QUICK COMMUNICATIONS, INC.
CONSULTING DIVISION
125543 Clearview Parkway
Conway, AR 72032

March 18, 1986

Dr. Jacob Kirschman
Route 3
16 Silver Creek Rd.
Huntsville, AR 35802

Dear Dr. Kirschman:

As your clinic continues to grow, so will its need for effective accounting services and personnel systems. We think you will find that our
reputation for quality hardware, proven software, support services,
and state-of-the-art counseling will provide the computing resources
to meet this need.

Your QUICK COMPUTER is designed to operate with the greatest versatil-
ity available in the field. Our consulting team will provide all the
information you need to check out, hook up, and operate your system
within seventy-two hours at a maximum quoted installation cost of
$300.00.

Our system has proven its effectiveness in medical clinics all over the
country—as a matter of fact, it is the single most widely used system,
providing a variety of peripherals for enhancement of filing systems,
graphic and letter quality printing, and state-of-the-art software.

Our consulting services are readily available in Oakhaven—you won't
have to shut down your system waiting for assistance. Experienced program personnel will trouble-shoot your problems when you need them.

May we stop by your office at your convenience this week to give you a
complimentary consultation and needs analysis? You cannot help but to
gain from the few minutes we will spend together.

Sincerely,

Horace Weatherford
Consultant

Exhibit 10.10 · A Persuasive Letter

ployer with everything necessary to evaluate your qualifications for the job.

The Resume

Exhibit 10.11 is a sample resume. While there are many acceptable formats, we recommend one that is simple and allows the recipient to locate information easily. Numerous other styles may be found in your local library's business correspondence section.

The resume should summarize your background, education, and experience as they relate to your professional goals. It should be brief and concise with easily read headings to help the reader locate pertinent information. Use phrases rather than complete sentences, but keep them parallel in form. Note that our sample has plenty of white space to set off headings, provide readability, and avoid a crowded look. You may need to use two pages, but avoid wordiness. Target your strengths, and make them stand out.

Our sample includes education, experience, honors and memberships, activities, and references. Depending on the type of job for which you are applying, there may be other major headings you will want to include. Organize these sections in terms of their relevance to the job. If experience is of paramount importance, put it first. It is a good idea to list your credentials in reverse chronological order, beginning with the most current job, as shown in our sample.

Your references do not need to be listed on the resume. Often references will differ depending on the position for which you apply. You may want to keep a separate sheet with complete addresses and telephone numbers readily available. Be sure to get permission from the reference to use his or her name.

Remember that your resume is a reflection of your standards and performance expectations. If it is not carefully prepared, negative conclusions will be made about your capabilities. Cheap paper, poor typewriter ribbon, and a sloppy format have been the downfall of many job candidates. Give the resume a professional look by having it professionally prepared on a word processor or by typing and photocopying multiple copies. A final caution: Keep your resume updated to reflect your current experience and education. It will have numerous uses (introductions, consulting, recognition, and so forth) and should be easily accessible.

Letters of Application

While the resume summarizes your achievements and interests, the letter of application requests consideration for a specific job. Since you are

SAMUEL J. CARSON
6687 Wilmington Dr.
San Antonio, TX 78293

EDUCATION

B.A. Business Administration, graduated with honors, Texas State University, 1984

Graduated from Sterling High School, Baytown, TX, upper 10% of class, 1980

EXPERIENCE

1982–1984: Student worker in Records Division at Texas State responsible for filing and preparing student records, servicing counter requests, and answering the telephone.

1980–1981: Student worker in Student Aid Division at Texas State responsible for sorting, organizing, and filing student aid requests, and handling inquiries over the counter.

1977–1983: Held summer jobs at the following establishments to save money that paid one-half of college expenses:

    1979 Chuck's Steak House, Baytown, TX (busboy)
    1980 Baytown Construction (laborer)
    1981 Baytown Construction (office clerk)
    1982 Gleacon Oil Refinery (welder's helper)
    1983 Henderson Construction (laborer)

HONORS AND MEMBERSHIPS

Pi Beta Kappa Honorary, Omicron Delta Kappa, football scholarship, team captain senior year, Honorary Engineering Society, Union Governing Board, Who's Who Among Students at Texas State.

ACTIVITIES

Weightlifting and conditioning, football, ham radio, downhill skiing, amateur dramatics.

REFERENCES

Furnished on request.

Exhibit 10.11 • A Sample Employment Resume

Thomas L. Vinton
9876 St. James St.
Columbus, OH 42304

February 16, 1986

Mr. Charles Durban
1615 No. Boynton St.
Columbus, OH 43216

Dear Mr. Durban:

Now that you have opened the new Fitness Center, won't you need a full-time supervisor who has years of experience with weightlifting and has trained under the most modern of programs?

As a football player at State University, I have weightlifted for two years under the supervision of three highly trained strength coaches. The programs involved work with the most modern and up-to-date equipment. I have also trained six years with barbells and Universal weight sets, beginning with my first year of high school.

With today's rapidly growing interest in physical fitness, you need an instructor who can apply specific weightlifting programs to specific sports. As an accomplished athlete in football, baseball, basketball, and tennis who also has working knowledge of track events and several other sports, I have the qualifications to apply such programs to the needs of the athlete.

As you know, a physical fitness instructor should be able to work well with people and be interested in fitness in order to encourage others. Athletics has been a major focus of my life, and I will be able to share this feeling with the members of the Center.

In order to tell you more about my qualifications for the full-time supervisor you need, may I have an interview this week? You will discover, I am certain, that I will be an asset to your new establishment.

Sincerely,

Thomas L. Vinton

Thomas L. Vinton

Exhibit 10.12 · A Letter of Application

trying to convince the reader to hire you, use the persuasive format. Note that the sample letter in Exhibit 10.12 has emphasized the applicant's strengths as they relate to the specific position of a physical fitness instructor—knowledge of the latest equipment, accomplishments in a variety of sports, the ability to get along with people, and a proven record in fitness. It begins with an attention-getting opening and ends with a request for an interview during a specific time-frame.

It is also neatly typed on quality bond paper. While a resume may be printed and used for many positions, the letter of application should be an original, prepared specifically for the position.

Memoranda

Memoranda are informal messages that can be used to request information, reinforce agreements, clarify previous messages, or deliver short reports about daily problems. While letters are directed to people outside the organization, memoranda are internal correspondence and directed to people inside the organization—boss to boss, boss to subordinate, office to office, and so forth. Typically, the memorandum uses a standardized form with the words *To, From, Subject,* and *Date* at the top of the page, as in Exhibit 10.13. The sender usually places initials beside his or her name rather than using a signature line.

November 1, 1985

TO: Charles Rountree, Director
         Personnel Services

FROM: Dorothy Jameson, Head   D.J.
         Accounting Department

SUBJECT: Vacant Position

One of our employees has decided to accept a vacant position in another department beginning June 1. Will you please send me a pool of applicants that would be qualified for the accounting clerk III position?

Since we are in the process of preparing the audit for this year's expenditures, the vacancy will pose a problem regarding workload. Can we begin interviewing as soon as possible in order to fill the position on June 1?

I will sincerely appreciate your assistance with this problem. If you need any further information, please give me a call.

Exhibit 10.13 • A Sample Memorandum

The content of the memorandum may be organized in direct or indirect order, similar to the formats for letters and formal reports. Long explanations are rarely necessary because both parties usually have some background about the situation and need only to clarify the specific point of the memo.

Because of the memo's brevity, direct order is commonly used. A summary statement and recommendation are followed by a paragraph that describes the problem and its implications and then presents the facts and analysis. Headings may be used to separate its parts, similar to the formal report. The memorandum rarely should be more than four pages in length.

Memoranda are a valuable tool for the manager because they provide a means of recording events for later review, act as documentation, and convey information at the convenience of the receiver. Nevertheless, because of their informality and brevity, memoranda do not require a lengthly preparation by the sender. While more informality is permissible than in a letter, memos should be complete and courteous.

Standard Parts of a Letter

Business letters make an impression on the receiver. If the message is neatly presented on quality paper, the receiver will conclude that the sender takes pride in his or her work. Use quality white bond paper, and type with a clean, dark ribbon using a standard typeface such as pica or elite—or have someone type the letter for you. Letters usually have six standard parts: heading; receiver's name and address; salutation; body; complimentary close; typed name, title, and signature of the sender.

- *Heading.* The heading tells the reader the address of the sender and when the letter was written. Depending on the format you select, you may place this information at the center of the letter, lined up with the right margin, or typed at the left margin. If you use letterhead, you need only center the date two lines below the address.
- *Receiver's name and address.* The address of the receiver should provide the name, identification, and location of the receiver. Use *Mr., Mrs., Ms.,* or *Miss* unless another title is required. Use double titles only if they indicate different accomplishments, for example: Dr. John Thomas, M.D. Be exact in using the name of a position or company, and use standard, two-letter postal abbreviations or spell out the name of a state. Type the zip code on the same line as the state.
- *Salutation.* The salutation is a courteous greeting that should include the reader's title. Avoid using impersonal greetings such as *To Whom*

It May Concern or *Gentlemen*. Whenever possible, use the title and name of a specific person.

- *Body*. The body of the letter contains the message and answers for the receiver the questions *what*, *why*, and *who*. It begins two spaces below the salutation and is single-spaced with two spaces between paragraphs.
- *Complimentary close*. The complimentary close brings a letter to a courteous ending. There are a variety of accepted conventional closings, and one should be selected according to the mood you are trying to create. *Sincerely yours* and *Cordially yours* are appropriate for most business situations.
- *Typed name and title and written signature*. The name and title are typed four spaces below the complimentary close, thus allowing space for the written signature.

Basic Letter Formats

Whatever you select for a letter format, it should have a symmetrical arrangement and be framed by white space or a margin—like a picture within a frame. Appendix B includes examples of the three following standard formats:

- *Modified block style*. The modified block style is the most widely used because it gives the letter a balanced appearance. The beginning of each paragraph is indented, and the date and complimentary close are centered.
- *Block style*. The block style is becoming the preferred style of many organizations because it can be easily and quickly prepared. All lines begin at the left margin, which circumvents the need for setting tabs and indenting paragraphs.
- *AMS style*. The AMS (Administrative Management Society) style uses the basic block format without the salutation and complimentary close. A subject line is often substituted in caps for the salutation.

Editing Your Writing: The Polish That Accomplishes Your Purpose

Reports and letters are your personal representatives. Your writing presents an image of you to each person it comes into contact with. To ensure that the image is favorable, make your written messages clear, concise, and correct in every detail.

Clarity assumes that the writing has sound logical development, a well-developed outline, solid sentences, good transitions between the major parts, smooth pace, unity, and cohesion; *conciseness* means that all unnecessary words have been removed; *correctness* means your writing is free of errors in spelling, punctuation, grammar, sexism, and typing. To achieve these, you will need to read and re-read your written copy.

Turning Poor Writing Into Professional Writing

The Convention Travel Report
Beth Williams graduated from college in May and found a job in the following month. In the first month George Harris, her boss, sent her to a convention so that she could gain some insights into her new profession. When Beth returned, Harris requested a memo from her describing what she had learned.

Beth's grades on her college papers had been high; the content was always good, and that, she thought, was the most important consideration. She drafted her thoughts onto paper and gave them to her secretary, who had also just started working, to type.

Read Beth's report (Exhibit 10.14). Circle any errors in grammar, word usage, spelling, and punctuation, and add the number of those errors that you found. Check yourself with the following listing:

- 0–20 errors: You need to refresh your understanding of the rules of grammar, word usage, spelling, and punctuation. Read this chapter very carefully.
- 20–30 errors: You are good at picking out most of the common errors. This chapter will show you how to avoid even more mistakes.
- 30–40 errors: You are very sensitive to the tricky errors that people sometimes overlook. This chapter should serve as a reinforcement for what you already know.
- 40–50 errors: Excellent. You have a superb ability to distinguish between what is right and wrong. Use this chapter as a review to help you polish your writing.

A complete list of the errors Beth made in her writing can be found in Appendix B, on pages 463–466, followed by the memo reproduced with correct English usage on page 467. Take a few minutes now to review the many errors.

Few professional writers submit for publication the first draft of their work. They realize that rewriting is as important as writing. Some au-

To: George Harris,
          Vice President in Charge of Policy

From: Beth Williams,
          Government Relations Division

Subject: Convention Report

Sir,

In compliance with your directive to report on the ''Government Regulations in the Aerospace Industry'' colloquium which I have attended,
this memorandum is submitted for your perusal.

The convention discussed three main topics – the DIA's interferance in
companies internal security programs, OSHA's noise exposure standards,
and the fact that the U.S. Government must inspect the new teflon rivet-
ting technique for quality control purposes and to make sure it meets
their requirements. First off, the Fed's position on internal security
is full of baloney. They say one hundred and fifty million dollars of
microprocessing equipment were stolen last year by spies. And even more
was destroyed by espionage! I know our company doesn't have any problems
like that, never.

OSHA's decision to impose more strict noise exposure standards could
deleteriously impact on our production plans. Their talking about requiring 90 dBh exposure limits, which has me worried; but I don't think
we need concern ourselves about it to much at this point in time.

The new rivets is another matter, though. The principle problem with the
rivets is that they shear off at high altitudes, so the Govern–ment
wants to inspect everyone in the Aeorospace Industry to make sure we're
doing it right. Federal stress engineers think our men and girls should
reinforce their rivets with a steel backing, during air–frame assembly.
Otherwise, the affects on high–altitude test flights could be disastrous.

Well, after rivets the discussion was completely finished. For the
purpose of quantifying goals and objectives and developing viable alternatives, the convention was a resounding success.

Respectively,

_____ number of errors

Exhibit 10.14

Source: Timothy Riggins, "Convention Reports," prepared for this book.

thors rewrite their novels up to ten times and spend as much time rewriting as writing the original draft.

The editing process allows the writer to correct mechanical changes and add professionalism. For example, Franklin D. Roosevelt announced the entry of the United States into World War II by declaring, "Yesterday, December 7, 1941, a date that will live in infamy. . . . " While those words remain in the memories of millions, Roosevelt's original words, before editing, were less memorable: "Yesterday, December 7, 1941, a date that will live in world history. . . . "[6]

The author of "Teaching the Boss to Write" emphasizes that while the biggest problem in writing is hiding the conclusions, other major errors follow: "The most common complaint of managers about the reports they receive is that the conclusions of the writer are either buried or missing altogether. . . . But there is a whole catalog of other sins . . . excessive wordiness, poor grammar and sentence structure, atrocious spelling, and general confusion."[7] Most of these errors can be avoided if the writer takes the time to properly edit.

Three Reasons to Edit

1. *The writer is lazy* and produces vague, unclear, and incorrect copy, and often believes good writing is something that must be excessively pompous and stilted. Consequently this person writes on and on, never getting to the point.

2. *The writer has basic problems in distinguishing between what is right and wrong in writing.* Editing will be harder for this individual. This writer should seek help and feedback from others and have other people check his or her work. This individual should always edit with the help of a dictionary, word speller, and reference manual.

3. *The writer is working under a tight deadline and runs out of time.* This sometimes happens to everyone, but better planning and time management will give the time necessary for thorough editing.

Seven Methods for Reaching Clarity and Conciseness

"Plain English" is becoming a fact in today's business world. A writing consultant recently worked on a major airline's printed materials, rewriting the copy with fewer words and making it easier to read and understand. According to his estimates, the company could have saved over $150,000 a year in paper and printing costs if the material had been written concisely in the first place.

Never let the first draft of your writing leave your office without being edited. Your reputation, your future promotions, and your company's money are at stake.

> Another revealing example is the case of a publisher who produced a book for a group of professionals. He planned to sell the book by direct mail advertising. Although his sales manager wrote a good sales letter, the publisher called in an editorial consultant. This resulted in a second letter.
>
> The publisher then printed a "split run": half of his mailing was the sales manager's letter; the other half was the consultant's letter. Twenty thousand copies of each were mailed. The result? The edited letter produced *230 percent more* orders than the nonedited letter—at exactly the same cost for the mailing list, the printing, and the mailing.[8]

Work on making your final copy clear, concise, and correct. Remember, it is less expensive to write a good letter or report than a poor one. Vague or ambiguous writing requires further correspondence to clarify the situation. Wordy, meaningless phrases require your reader to spend excess time and energy deciphering your thoughts. It is therefore good business and good public relations practice to edit your work by eliminating all useless phrases and unneeded words, using short words and action verbs, and making your writing correct. Edit to help your reader understand your message.

Many organizations have learned the value of editing, and sometimes completely rewriting, messages directed to their customers. A major bank, for example, decided to rewrite its consumer loan note, which contained over 360 words and used such cumbersome phrases as "shall become subject to distraint proceedings or any order or process of any court" and "the remedies of the Bank hereunder are cumulative and may be exercised concurrently or separately." The new version of fewer than 100 words comes directly to the point.[9]

> I'll be in default:
> 1. If I don't pay an installment on time; or
> 2. If any other creditor tries by legal process to take any money of mine in your possession.
>
> You can then demand immediate payment of the balance of this note, minus the part of the finance charge which hasn't been earned figured by the rule of 78. You will also have other legal rights, for instance, the right to repossess, sell, and apply security to the payments under this note and any other debts I may then owe you.

As you read your reports and letters looking for errors and shortcomings, look for only one problem at a time. This will make your editing more specific.

1. Eliminate Unneeded Words

The quickest way to achieve clarity and conciseness is to cut the average length of sentences. As a reader you don't like to read long sentences, so don't write them. Readers lose the point of long, drawn-out thoughts. They also tire easily when they have to stop and punctuate a long sentence; they lose interest and mentally tune out. Good writing deserves sufficient headings, short paragraphs, and adequate white space on a page. But a piece of writing with all sentences in the fifteen-word range would be terribly dull; a good balance of long, short, and in-between sentences is best.

Years ago, two writers were assigned the task of writing an advertisement for Ivory brand soap. The first wrote:

> The alkaline elements and fats in this product are blended in such a way as to secure the highest quality of suponification, along with the specific gravity that keeps it on top of the water, relieving the bather of the trouble and annoyance of fishing around for it at the bottom of the tub during his ablutions.

The second writer got the contract when he wrote, "It floats!"[10]

Writing frequently does not convey its intended message. The following statements, for instance, were taken from a business memo: "This facility has production capability in the area of a magnitude of 2,000 units per day"; "The project will affect a savings in the neighborhood of $40,000 on an annual basis." Regardless of what you think the statements said, the author really meant to say, "The plant can produce 2,000 units a day," and "The project will save about $40,000 a year."

Examine the following groups of words taken from business reports and letters. Those that are "too wordy" can often be changed to simpler alternatives.

Too Wordy	Alternatives
At the present	Now
At your earliest convenience	Soon
Be in a position to	Can
Take action	Act
Hold a meeting	Meet
Study in depth	Study
Consensus of opinion	Consensus
In accordance with	As
Due to the fact that	Because
Until such time as	Until
Basically unaware of	Did not know
The overall plan	The plan
In the amount of	For

Too Wordy	Alternatives
In the event that	If
In reference to	About
In order that	So
For the purpose of	To
Despite the fact that	Although

2. Explain Abbreviations and Acronyms

In some professional and highly technical fields, the use of abbreviations and acronyms (pronounceable abbreviations) is widely accepted. Yet be careful to use abbreviations only when they save time and will be understood by the reader. Their use is frequently excessive and confusing. For example, M is code for a thousand in the United States but for a million in England. In the United States 9/12/81 means September 12, 1981, but it means December 9, 1981, in England. If you must use abbreviations like M and MM, be sure to define them the first time they appear in your paper.

An article in the *Dallas Morning News* (see also Exhibit 10.15) describes how abbreviations and acronyms have flourished in the military service. The U.S. Army alone has over 10,000 abbreviations ranging from AA for arrival angle to ZTO for zone transportation. A few of the more simple are MICOM (U.S. Army Missile Command), USAREUR (U.S. Army Europe), MACOM (Major Army Command), and SCAMPERS (Standard Corps Army). Some of the more complex, like REPSTACOMBRE, are harder to decipher and show an excessive and confusing tendency. (Incidentally, it stands for "Report EM [enlisted men] on gaining unit morning report in FSA Code 7. The first day of the seventh month for E7–E9 personnel, or the first day of the fifth month for personnel in Grades E6 and below, preceding the expiration of a year's stabilization, EM will be reported in the appropriate FSA code.")

3. Eliminate Jargon

Every profession has established jargon. In some instances it takes the form of abbreviations and acronyms; often, the terms are technical and apply only to a specific field. The following examples were used by corporate PR representatives at the Three Mile Island nuclear facility following the near-disaster several years ago.

Explosion became *energetic disassembly*.
Fire became *rapid oxidation*.
Plutonium didn't contaminate things; it became a friendly little substance that *took up residence*.

Read this 4 a LARC; it'll just take U a SEC

MIAMI (AP) — The space agency has just published a list of about 3,000 acronyms and abbreviations used in the space shuttle program. So, on a LARC, we thought we'd take a SEC to SCAN and ASSESS the booklet. We hope no one gets MAD.

Many of the abbreviations and acronyms have more than one definition, some as many as 10. For instance, AC can mean Associate Contractor or Aircraft, and CDT means Countdown Time, Central Daylight Time and Command Descriptor Table.

That policy would seem to invite trouble. If someone says, "We have to go ASAP," it could mean "Let's leave As Soon As Possible," or "We should visit the Aerospace Safety Advisory Panel."

If the FAR (Final Acceptance Review) is faulty, a FAR (Failure Analysis Report) might be needed to comply with a FAR (Federal Aviation Regulation).

Other entries might be confused with more everyday affairs. Autoland is not an auto parts store; it stands for Automatic Landing. BARS are not the places to which perplexed aerospace technicians might retreat; it stands for Baseline Accounting and Reporting System.

MAIDS is the Management Automated Information Display System.

If we're not careful, we'll end up in HAL (High Order Assembly Language, or Houston Aerospace Language).

NASA, you know, the National Aeronautics and Space Administration, also sent a glossary to help us understand some fancy space terms.

Like an "Attaching Part" which, we are told, is "an item used to attach assemblies or parts to the equipment or to each other." Or "Multiple Payloads," which are "more than one separate payload carried in the cargo bay."

We admit, though, that we were glad to have some help with "Repair Parts." According to NASA, "Repair Parts" are those "support items that are coded as 'not repairable.'"

LARC, incidentally, stands for the Langley Research Center in Hampton, Va.; SEC for Secondary, Second or Sequential Events Controller; SCAN for Selected Current Space Notice; and ASSESS for Airborne Science Shuttle Experimental System Simulation. MAD can be either Maintenance Analysis Data or Madrid, Spain.

Exhibit 10.15

Source: *Dallas Morning News*, Feb. 11, 1977, p. 1. Reprinted by permission of the Associated Press.

When asked why the simple became the complex, the PR representatives commented, "We wanted to keep our jobs."

The medical world has a language all its own. *Cephalalgia*, means headache to a doctor. *Pruritus* is itching, and *deglutition* is swallowing. Many professionals believe the use of such words in their trade aids precise speech, but this technical jargon does little to inform readers, alienates them, and masks fuzzy thinking. As you edit, look for the simple, down-to-earth words that will better explain your meaning than the vague abstractions:

Jargon	**Down-to-Earth English**
Bottom line	Final result
Implement	Carry out
Input	Results
Interface	Discuss, meet, work with
Judgmentally	I think
Meaningful	Real, actual, tangible
Net	Conclusion
Optimum	Best
Proactive	Active
Resultful	Effective, achieve results
Suboptimal	Less than ideal
To impact	To affect, to do to
Viable	Practical, workable

4. Eliminate Unnatural Phrases

The fourth way to attain clarity and conciseness is to find and change unnatural phrases. These often will be eliminated when unneeded words are excised, but sometimes overused and trite expressions tend to linger. The careful editor will cut those words.

Some Phrases to Avoid	**Alternatives**
As provided by the provisions of your policy	Your policy provides
Attached please find	Here is
In compliance with your request	As requested
The company's present practice is	Our practice is
We do not appear to have received	We haven't received
You will find enclosed herewith	Enclosed is

The above examples represent sloppy thinking and uncritical editing. Business letters and reports, however, are often filled with meaningless clichés and trite or outdated expressions that should be avoided.

Trite Expressions	Alternatives
As per your order	According to your order
At some point in time	At some time
Attached herewith please find	Attached is
At the present writing	Now
Avail yourself of this opportunity	(outdated)
Beg to acknowledge	(never beg)
In conclusion I would state	(say it)
In lieu of	In place of
In other words	(say it the first time)
In view of the fact that	In view of
Regarding said order	(outdated)
Take stock of	(outdated)
Thanking you in advance	(never thank people in advance)
Very	(overused)

5. Use Small Words

Lack of clarity and conciseness is often caused by the use of large, stiff, polysyllabic words when small words would sound better. Consider using small words if appropriate. They will help your reader to understand your message sooner and will make for concise letters and reports. If a large word expresses it best, use it; variety makes for understanding and more pleasurable reading.

Letters

Large Words	Possible Smaller Words
Accomplished	Done
Approximately	About
Currently	Now
Demonstrate	Show
Forwarded	Mailed or sent
Initial	First
Initiate	Start
Investigate	Check
Purchase	Buy
Remunerate	Pay

Reports

Large Words	Possible Smaller Words
Accelerate	Quicken
Accurate	Correct or exact
Alternative	Choice or option
Analyze	Study or understand
Bilateral	Two-sided
Circumspect	Prudent
Corroborate	Support or confirm

Large Words	**Possible Smaller Words**
Demonstrate	Show
Eliminate	Cut out
Establish	Begin or found
Exterior	Outer or outside
Incorporated	Included
Methodology	Procedure or practice
Modification	Change
Participate	Join or share
Proficiency	Ability
Proximity	Nearness
Quantitative	Numerical or mathematical
Significant	Important
Subjective	Personal or intuitive
Utilize	Use
Voluminous	Large or prolific

6. Use Active Instead of Passive Verbs

Your readers will more likely respond if you treat them like people instead of objects. Do this by writing in the same style as you would talk. In conversations with clients you don't say, "It is recommended"; you say, "I recommend." Here is another example of a passive, impersonal statement that you'll never overhear in a conversation: "Personal endeavors are being made, although the magnitude of their participation is not absolutely identifiable." You may, however, overhear this personal explanation: "People are trying, but we don't know for sure how many or how much."

You may be balking at the first example, especially if the voice of your high school English teacher is alive in your mind with the instruction, "Never start a sentence with *I*." If that bothers you, there are alternatives for substituting active for passive verbs.

```
We all hope you are feeling better.
Someone representing your division could contribute a lot.
You can see how much a representative from your office would con-
    tribute.
```

Verbs are the strongest parts of speech, and they are strongest when used in the active voice. Active voice verbs show that their subject is "doing the action." When dull, passive verbs are employed, they act on their subjects.

Passive	**Active**
The books were inspected by the accountant.	The accountant inspected the books.

The second example is clearly stronger. In the active sentence the one doing the action (accountant) acts, and the verb (inspected) is short and clear. In the passive sentence the word *were* does not help but instead dulls the verb. Thus, the doer of the action takes a role in a prepositional phrase. Look at the difference in strength and clarity when the following active voice sentences are used:

Passive	Active
The policy will be enforced by Mr. Jones.	Mr. Jones will enforce the policy.
An improvement in quality has been made.	Quality improved.
Increases in sales of 15 percent were obtained in July.	In July, sales increased 15 percent.
An executive leadership program was conducted by the Cleveland Chamber of Commerce, and hundreds of people attended.	The Cleveland Chamber of Commerce conducted an executive leadership program attended by hundreds.
Enrollment for the seminar was seventy people.	Seventy people enrolled for the seminar.

Although the unnecessary use of passive verbs produces weak sentences, there are times when the passive voice has its place. When the *performer's identity is unimportant*, the passive voice can give a sentence its proper emphasis:

Oil is refined in Louisiana.
Productivity is often criticized for its effect on prices.

If the *performer of the action is unknown*, the passive voice may be preferable:

Anonymous calls have been received.
During the last fiscal year, arson has been committed five times.

There are four specific ways you can strengthen the verbs in your sentences:

a. *Eliminate impersonal constructions* like *it is, there is, there are,* or *there were.*

Weak:	Stronger:
There were repeated delays caused by a malfunctioning machine.	The malfunctioning machine caused repeated delays.

b. *Change verb killers* because they often diminish the strength of your writing, and they take the form of *is, was, to be, have, could,* or *should.*

c. *Pick active verbs instead of nouns or adjectives* when you need a word to express action. When events and activities consistently appear as nouns instead of verbs, writing becomes stiff and colorless.

d. *Use forceful action verbs.* Static verbs like *occur, take place, exist,* or *prevail* should be changed to more forceful ones.

Static:	Improved:
Throughout the committee's deliberations an atmosphere of increasing distrust existed.	As the committee deliberated, distrust increased.

While you are concentrating on verbs, consider also the *adjectives* and *adverbs* in your writing. Learn to spot lazy adjectives and adverbs, and replace them with vigorous ones. These six lazy adjectives and adverbs are clichés today because of their overuse:

Very good	Great success
Awfully nice	Richly deserved
Basically accurate	Vitally important

But vigorous adjectives and adverbs, like the following, more sharply define your ideas:

Instantly accepted	Moist handshake
Short meeting	Black coffee
Baffling instruction	Lucid recommendation

7. Use the Readability Index

As a final check of your editing, calculate the readability of your edited copy. Readability indexes have been developed by several contemporary writing authorities. The late Robert Gunning developed the "fog index" (see Table 10.1). Gunning's research focused on such questions as, How long can sentences be, on the average, before they discourage readers? How many long, complex, or abstract words will readers tolerate? The fog index is based on long word and sentence length count and approximates the number of years of education the reader should have to understand the copy easily. Many companies, such as BankAmerica, use a fog index based on several experts' readability measures. Written work is analyzed by a computer program for the years of schooling readers would need to understand the message.

Table 10.1 · Fog Index

	Readability Index	Reading Level	Typical Reading Material
Extremely difficult range	25		Professional journals
	20	Postcollege graduate	No popular magazines
Difficult range	19	College graduate	
	13	College freshman	*Fortune*
Ideal range	12	High school senior	*Time, Newsweek,*
	9		*The Wall Street Journal*
Easy Range	8	Eighth grade	*Readers Digest*
	6	Sixth grade	

Indexes of this type should not be used as a guide during initial writing; use them instead as a yardstick after you have written. You can find your own readability index by following these steps:

Count 100 words. If you reach 100 in the middle of a sentence, continue counting to the end of the sentence.

Count the number of sentences in the 100-word block of copy. Divide the number of words by the number of sentences to get an average sentence length.

Circle all the words which have three or more syllables. Do not include proper nouns, such as people's names, cities, company names, etc., which people will probably understand easily. And do not include simple compound words, even though they're three or more syllables—words such as *bookkeeper, however,* etc. Words that are very common to your industry and which have no easy substitutes, e.g., *underwriting, medicine, computer,* might be included in the simple compound words category.

Not counting those exceptions, add the "high-calorie" words—those with three or more syllables.

Divide the total number of words into the total of high-calorie words and multiply by 100. Add that figure and the average sentence length. Multiply the total by .4.[11]

The following example shows the calculated index for a *Wall Street Journal* article:[12]

John A. Newton had a piece of machinery that didn't produce anything. Now, thanks to government bureaucracy, he has two.

One machine is a $1,200 pollution-control pump that hums away at Mr. Newton's iron foundry. The other is an identical pump that is a backup required by the Ohio Environmental Protection Agency. "Normally, you wouldn't have a spare, $1,200 pump on hand. But they insisted on it,'' Mr. Newton says.

The spare pump symbolizes for Mr. Newton the endless rules, red tape and regulations that confront his company, Meech Foundry, every day. They consume his time, drain his capital and, he says, drive him crazy with local, state and federal rules about noise, dirty air, pensions, operating permits, labor negotiations, and hiring and firing.

High-calorie words

Machinery	Symbolizes	Bureaucracy	Federal
Government	Regulations	Identical	Operating
Negotiations	Pollution-control		

- 125 words
- 8 sentences
- Average 15.6 words per sentence
- 8 percent high-calorie words

$$15.6 + 8 = 23.6 \times .4 = 9.44 \text{ fog index}$$

Tests of this nature should not be taken as gospel. Plain English sometimes cannot be measured by formulas. While tests do show how many words are in an average sentence in a piece of writing and how many sentences are in an average paragraph, they do not show whether a consumer contract is grammatical, sensible, or logically organized. It is possible for a piece of the writing to test as easy to read but be unintelligible to the reader. As someone once said, "Words often have to be weighed instead of counted."

By taking each of the seven steps to editing, you will produce written work that is clear, concise, and conveys your desired message. Remember to eliminate unneeded words, explain abbreviations and acronyms, eliminate jargon, eliminate unnatural phrases, use small words, use active instead of passive verbs, and use the readability index.

GOOSEMYER   **by parker and wilder**

Source: Parker and Wilder, "Goosemyer", August 28, 1980. © by permission of News America Syndicate.

Final Check for Correctness

The final editing procedure is to check your work for misuse of words, punctuation or grammar errors, and sexist remarks. Mistakes such as these signal the reader that you have either writing problems or low standards of performance. Correctness is important. The mechanics of writing are the foundation on which creativity rests, and they should be learned early in life. Space in this book does not permit us to cover all the basics; however, an awareness of three common problems will help you avoid them.

Use the Right Word

The editing process should uncover any words that you misused. Writers know the precise meaning of every word they use. When unsure of which word to use, turn to a dictionary or a style manual. Readers do not respect illiteracy.

Correct Spelling and Grammatical Errors

An important part of editing is to proofread your copy for misspellings and grammatical errors. It is embarrassing when a letter or report contains a misspelled word, but costly credibility can be lost when important words or names are not spelled correctly. If errors remain in the final version, the reader, who may be an excellent speller, may question the amount of care and effort you put into your writing. Errors can also drastically change the meaning of your message. A premed student wrote the following instructions for handling a shock patient, but we feel sure he didn't mean what he wrote: "Bleed the wound and rape the victim in a blanket for shock." If you know you are a bad speller, have someone else check your work. Better still, check your words with a dictionary or word speller.

Writing experts have found certain words are more frequently misspelled than others in the business world. Appendix B, on page 473, lists over 100 of the most frequently misspelled words.

Correct Sexist Errors

The word *sexism* originally referred to prejudicial activities against females but now indicates "any arbitrary stereotyping of males and females on the basis of their gender." Today, changing public attitudes toward words such as *man* and *mankind* have led to more widespread use of sex-neutral terms such as *people* and *humankind*. Business and government now encourage the avoidance of sexist language—especially in writing.

Appendix B, pages 473–475, lists six areas that effective business writers should be aware of as they edit, in order to avoid traditional sexist terms and attitudes. Your company may not require that its employees follow these guidelines completely. The changes in language, however, are becoming an accepted part of business speech and should be incorporated into all business writing.

Summary

Effective letters, memoranda, and reports accomplish specific purposes while maintaining goodwill. Written communication can be most effective in conveying meaning, however, when used in conjunction with oral communication. The writer should carefully evaluate his or her audience to avoid misunderstandings. Words should be selected carefully, and technical words and jargon avoided. A positive tone and correct emphasis will add to the effectiveness of the writing.

Reports may be written for different purposes, and it is important to identify the intended goal. This is best accomplished, and the goal best achieved, through an inverted style of report writing that presents conclusions first, before the reader's attention lags.

Letters can convey good news or bad news and require different approaches. Little explanation or background is needed for good news: Use a direct approach and get to the point quickly. For letters with bad news use the indirect approach, and provide reasons or details that will convince the reader your decision was unavoidable. Persuasive letters should overcome resistance by establishing a case through a logical presentation of reasoning and an action-getting close.

Your written communications are reflections of you. They should be neat, well-organized, and easily readable, and should follow an acceptable format. When properly edited, they can be effective tools for achieving power and completed action.

Key Words

vertical report	informal report	emphasis
horizontal report	semiformal report	direct approach
radial report	formal report	letter
informational report	traditional report	indirect approach
analytical report	inverted report	letter

persuasive approach   AMS style   plain English
    letter   edit   jargon
resume   clarity   active verbs
letter of application   conciseness   readability index
memoranda   correct   grammar
block style   gobbledygook   sexism
modified block style

Review Questions

1. Describe the three directions that reports can move, and name some of the different reports that are represented by each direction.
2. Reports normally follow one of two objectives. What are they?
3. Three levels of formality exist in reports. Compare and contrast the different types.
4. Three main areas are found in the traditional formal report. Name the three areas and the different parts that are found in each area.
5. What is the inverted report style?
6. Name and describe the four parts of the inverted report style.
7. Compare the difference between the inverted and traditional report styles.
8. The essence of well-edited writing is found in the requirements for clarity, conciseness, and correctness. Describe each and its importance to writing.
9. This chapter listed methods by which clarity and conciseness can be achieved in writing. Describe these methods.
10. Explain fully the difference between active and passive verbs.
11. What does the readability index describe, and how is it calculated?
12. There are three steps in the final check for correctness. What are they?
13. Describe how sexism appears in writing, and list three ways that it can be eliminated.
14. Discuss the statement, "Written communication is most effective when it is used in conjunction with oral communication." In your discussion, include a specific example.
15. List and give examples of some routine purposes for letters.
16. What is meant by the *personal style* of a letter? Why is it important?
17. In what order is a letter presenting good news formatted? Why?
18. In what order is a letter presenting bad news formatted? Why?
19. What is the objective of persuasive letters, and what are the steps involved in writing one?
20. How do letters of application and resumés differ? Why are both important?
21. When are memoranda used? Write five guidelines for preparing memoranda.

Exercises

1. Find a report that has been prepared for a business. You can find one either at the library, by asking friends, or by calling business colleagues and asking for a sample. When you receive it, look for its major parts. Are they in the order that this chapter outlined? If not, is there a particular reason for the difference?

2. Read the report that you obtained for exercise 1. As you read it, try to determine in which parts your interest either wanes or increases. What could the writer have done to better capture your interest?

   Now make some notes on how the report could be rewritten in an inverted style. Use the four questions for the inverted report: *what, why, how,* and *now what?* Would the report topic be better represented by using the inverted style? How many pages do you think could be cut? How much reading time could be saved?

3. Select an advertisement from a magazine, and write a letter to the company advertised requesting more information about its product or service. Submit a copy of the advertisement with your letter for evaluation by the instructor. Use the block format.

4. Request information from a local company about an area that you are researching for a course. The topic may range from biomedical research to nutrition, depending on your interests. Gather as much information as you can—brochures, names of films, videotapes, references, cost estimates, and so forth. Before mailing your letter, have it evaluated by your instructor. Use the modified block format.

5. Review the local classified advertisements for jobs for which you feel you may qualify. Select one, and write the company requesting more information about the position and the company. For example, you may ask for information on the company size, job travel requirements, opportunities for career advancement, working conditions, required skills, and promotional materials. Use the AMS format.

6. Exchange one of the above letters with a classmate, and write a letter of acknowledgment.

7. Write a letter trying to persuade one of your classmates to take on a responsibility, make a contribution to a nonprofit organization, or support a cause. When the class breaks into groups of three to four, exchange letters. Evaluate the letters' effectiveness. Were you persuaded to act? Why or why not? What kind of persuasive appeals were in the letter—logical, emotional, ethical? Which were most effective?

8. Look through some magazines or journals for a sales message in letter form that you feel is effective. Analyze the style, tone, organization, and appeals. Display a copy of the advertisement and present your analysis before the class.

9. Write a sales letter that you feel would convince a white-collar worker to

contract a weekly cleaning service. The service provides floor care, cleans windows, and so forth. You may want to check with a local firm for the typical services and fees.

10. Write an autobiography that relates your accomplishments, activities, interests, education, and job history in chronological order. Which experiences were most meaningful? Which did you enjoy the most? What would you like to be doing ten years from now? twenty years from now? Now prepare a resume.

11. Review the job announcements at your school or the job listings in a newspaper or trade journal, and select a job for which you feel you qualify. Prepare a letter of application that points out your strengths. Attach your resume, and submit it to your instructor for an evaluation.

12. You have received a job inquiry from an outstanding young woman whom you would like to have on your staff. Because of recent economic difficulties, however, your company has cut down on hiring, and all vacant positions have been temporarily frozen. You are not certain but feel that the position may open up again in three or four months. You would like to hire her then, if it is feasible. Write a response to Jane Jorgenson, 12789 Corby Drive, Baton Rouge, LA 70810, telling her that the accounting division at the National Business Office Supply Company, 43552 Florida Blvd., Baton Rouge, LA 70821, does not have any job openings.

13. You have been asked to accept the chair of the travel committee on the Student Union Activities Council. You are very interested in this committee and, in fact, were chairperson last year. Unfortunately, you are currently involved in a number of other activities and are beginning to have problems keeping up with your classwork. The president of the council is a good friend of yours who is doing a great job but needs help. She has personally asked you to accept the position for another year as a favor to her. Write a letter to her (Sharon Fitzmorris, P.O. Box 1135, College Station, Your University, State, Zip) refusing the position.

14. You are the supervisor of a group of counselors in the Department of Human Resources in your state. Your counselors carry heavy caseloads and work with handicapped teenagers who have difficulty making the transition between adolescence and adulthood. While most of the handicaps are not physically severe and the young people can learn to support themselves, many of these teenagers have severe emotional problems related to their handicaps. Lately, you have had an opening on your staff. Because of a tight job market, the number of responses to your advertisement was quite large—sixty-eight applicants. After a very tough screening and interviewing process, you have selected Jason Templeton, who has a M.A. in counseling and five years' experience counseling in a similar position at another agency. You were particularly impressed with his references. Write him a letter stating that he has been selected for the position. His address is 1538 W. Idaho Ave., St. Paul, MN 55108.

15. Put your learning into practice by rewriting the following "too wordy" statements with only half as many words. Be careful not to change or discard the main thought. Sample answers are in Appendix B on page 468.

a. In order to keep you informed of the results of the sales meeting held on August 13 to consider ways and means of reducing the cost of the proposed spring sales campaign, we are submitting herewith a brief resume and the procedure outlined for the cost reduction plans.

b. Memoranda intended for internal distribution should be written just as carefully as those to be distributed outside of the division, and, actually, they serve as an excellent opportunity for developing an individual's proficiency in writing.

16. Rewrite the following passive sentences into the active voice. Answers are in Appendix B on page 468.

a. A sharp decrease in sales was noted.

b. The department is dependent on our aid for its success.

c. It is desired by the president that this problem be brought before the board of directors.

17. Correct the misused words in the following sentences. Answers are in Appendix B on page 469.

a. We shall be seriously affected by the new corporate policy.

b. The amount of conventioners who come to New York City varies with the season.

c. We shall appreciate your advising us of your decision.

d. The estate was divided between the millionaire's three sons.

e. Can we have your permission to proceed with the instructions outlined in this letter?

18. Correct the grammatical problems in these sentences. The answers are in Appendix B on page 469.

a. Divided into two sections, the accountant balances the accounts more readily.

b. Depreciation accounting is not a system of valuation but of allocation.

c. To form an opinion as to the collectibility of the accounts, they were reviewed with the credit manager.

d. This problem can only be alleviated by a change in policy.

e. Bob Smith's interest and devotion to his work are not to be questioned.

19. Find the misspelled words in the following list. Several of the words qualify. The correct answers are in Appendix B on page 470.

	Correct	Incorrect	Correct Spelling
a. semi-annual			
b. occurrance			
c. facimile			
d. supercede			
e. government			
f. disasterous			
g. proceedure			
h. deficit			
i. permissable			
j. prevalant			

	Correct	Incorrect	Correct Spelling

k. irrelevant
l. questionaire
m. promissary
n. preferance
o. maintainence

References

1. William R. Sears, "An Open Letter to College Students, Their Teachers and Parents" (San Mateo, CA: Sears & Co., 1976), pp. 6–7.

2. Melba W. Murray, *Engineered Report Writing* (Tulsa: Petroleum Publishing, 1969).

3. *Ibid.*, pp. 26–28.

4. *Ibid.*, p. 17.

5. *Ibid.*, p. 26.

6. M. C. Kirkland, "Effective Writing," *Future* (March/April 1977), p. 50.

7. "Teaching the Boss to Write," *Business Week* (Oct. 25, 1976), pp. 56, 58.

8. Kirkland, "Effective Writing," p. 18.

9. Alan Siegel, "How to Say It in Plain English," *Management Review* (Nov. 1979), p. 15.

10. Kirkland, "Effective Writing," p. 18.

11. Buff Silveria, "How Fogbound Is Your Copy?" *Journal of Organizational Communication*, 7:2 (1978), p. 5.

12. *Ibid.*, p. 6.

P A R T 4

Putting Effective
Communication into Action

The preceding three parts of this book explained what communication is and how it occurs in the business world (Chapters 1–2); three major hurdles to effective communication in the business world: perception, language, and the organizational structure (Chapters 3–5); and specifics on improving five communication skill areas: nonverbal, listening, oral presentations, group meetings, and writing (Chapters 6–10).

This final part describes how knowledge of communication theory, understanding of potential communication barriers, and the development of specific communication skills can be applied to several managerial areas. Chapter 11 explains how a manager uses communication in the *interviewing process*. Chapter 12 describes how a manager communicates *leadership* to others through motivation. Chapter 13 describes the manager as a *decision-making problem solver*. Chapter 14 describes how managers communicate to help *resolve conflicts*. Finally, Chapter 15 examines how managers use communication to overcome resistance and *promote change*.

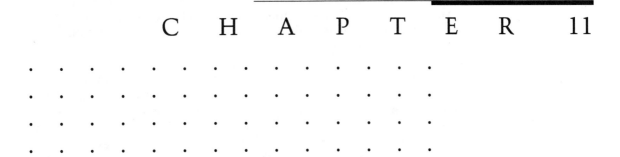

C H A P T E R   11

The Communicating Manager as an Interviewer

Introduction

The increasing complexity of business operations has made the managerial functions of planning, organizing, directing, controlling, leading, and communicating more demanding. The resulting pressures can impair even the best manager's ability to apply the techniques that lead to being an effective interviewer. Nevertheless, failure to apply good communication skills because you "don't have time" rarely impresses higher administration. You are expected to know communication techniques and to apply them well.

During the workday a manager talks one-on-one to a number of employees. In one instance it may be necessary to discuss the reasons an employee is leaving the organization, while in another, an employee may be frustrated and need coaching. A third instance may involve reprimanding a problem employee for failing to meet the expectations set by a superior. In addition, the manager may need information to solve a complex problem and thus meet with an expert in order to get essential facts.

297

Finally, the manager may need to conduct a job interview to maintain a fully staffed and effective organization.

This chapter examines each of these interview situations—their contexts and requirements. It examines the role of the manager as an interviewer and provides guidelines for interview preparation and analysis. Several interview approaches using key questioning techniques are presented.

Definition. Interviewing is a critical managerial skill and communication activity. Interviews yield information needed to solve problems and make decisions that are essential to an organization's welfare. A manager unskilled in applying interviewing techniques wastes organizational resources. For the purposes of this chapter, an interview is defined as interaction between two parties to gain information to accomplish a predetermined purpose. We have selected the word *party* because more than one person may act as the person gathering information or supplying information.[1]

The Manager's Responsibility as an Interviewer

The responsibilities and purposes of an interviewer are fairly clear. First, you must communicate your purpose to the interviewee in understandable terms. Never combine two purposes in one sitting or interview, since your interviewee will be required to spend critical thought-time determining what you want rather than listening to your questions.

Your second responsibility as an interviewer is to prepare for the interview. How will you structure it? Where will you conduct it? Who should be present? What problems should you avoid? Preparation will contribute to the effective completion of your goal by (1) avoiding the necessity to reconvene with the other parties, (2) steering clear of questions that are unethical or illegal, and (3) creating the climate most conducive to a positive experience.

Finally, you will want to record the information gathered during the interview. This may require a special form for ranking job candidates, notes that summarize the basic content of the interview, or a memorandum for the record that stipulates the action that will be followed.

Each of these responsibilities needs to be viewed in the context of the primary interview purpose: to conduct a job interview, to orient, to coach, to counsel, to hear a grievance, to appraise performance, to reprimand, or to discover why an employee is leaving the organization. For all of these purposes, however, there are key steps for preparing and conducting the interview.

Preparing for the Interview

Preparing for the interview includes four steps common to all interviewing situations: (1) defining the purpose, (2) deciding who should be involved, (3) analyzing the other party, and (4) planning the interview format or structure.

Defining the Purpose

A clearly defined purpose sets the tone of the interview and helps determine your plan of action. Once you have clarified your purpose, write it down in terms of a goal-directed outcome. For example, "The purpose of this interview is to determine the cause of the production slowdown and agree on a solution that will meet our quota in a specified period of time." Once you have determined your purpose, you will need to decide who can best assist you in reaching your goal.

Determining Who Should Be Involved

While this may seem a rather obvious step, it is one that is often neglected by the most experienced managers. Failure to include the necessary participants in the interviewing process can lead to wasted time and resources. For example, a job applicant may need to interview with several people before the process is complete. To do this, a carefully planned schedule taking into account possible conflicts will need to be prepared. Overlooking a key administrator may create a poor impression and may mean that the applicant will need to return for a second round of interviews.

In order to determine who should be involved in the interview, ask yourself the following questions:

- Who has the knowledge or information needed?
- Who knows the history of the organization that may affect this decision?
- Who will be involved in the implementation of the solution (supervise the employee, meet performance expectations, and so forth)?

Analyzing the Other Party

Each participant in the interview has a point of view based on beliefs, attitudes, experiences, traits, capacities, needs, and aspirations. Your approach will vary depending on the other party's characteristics, awareness of the problem, and willingness to discuss it. For example, if a manager discovered a productivity problem that involved two of her subordinates, she may wish to interview them in order to gain insight. Beth, who is outgoing, competent, secure, and friendly, would probably be easy to approach about the problem. On the other hand, Bob, while competent, has been in his current supervisory position for only three weeks and appears somewhat insecure in the manager's presence. Obviously, the manager's approach with him would be different than it would be with Beth. While she may follow the same basic format, she would spend more time trying to put Bob at ease.

Planning the Interview Structure or Format

Whether you are conducting an informational or a problem-solving interview, you will follow a basic structure that includes an opening, a body, and a close.

The opening. The opening should accomplish several important steps. First, a greeting establishes contact and sets the tone. Second, common ground should be established by sharing concerns about the need to solve the problem or gain the necessary information. Finally, the purpose should be clearly stated and agreed on.

The body. The body of the interview attempts to accomplish the goal through questioning, explaining, verifying, and summarizing. A problem-solving interview usually follows the problem-solving sequence amplified in the chapter on decision making. The informational interview focuses on drawing out information using both general and specific questions. The problem-solving and informational formats can be compared in Table 11.1.

The close. The interview close should include a summary of the information and agreements that took place during the body of the interview. The intended use of information and any action that needs to be taken should be restated and summarized at this point. Finally, the manager should signal the completion of the process and express appreciation to the participants.

Key Questioning Techniques

An effective exchange of information is often the result of a sequence of carefully structured questions. Questions serve three important functions: to gain information, to encourage participation of the interviewee, and to gain insight about the interviewee's motives, needs, and attitudes.[2] This section discusses several types of questions and the circumstances in which they are used.

Table 11.1

	Problem Solving		Informative
Opening	Greet interviewee Establish common ground State purpose	*Opening*	Greet interviewee Establish common ground State purpose
Body *(in sequence)*	Define problem Analyze problem Propose solutions Select solution Agree on action	*Body* *(as appropriate)*	Seek information Question Reflect Verify Summarize
Close	Provide summary Summarize action to take Make acknowledgments	*Close*	Provide summary Summarize action to take Make acknowledgments

Use Closed Questions to Limit Response

Almost every interview encounter will require the use of closed questions. Closed questions request specific information and limit the interviewee's freedom of response. Often the question implies the answer or provides a list of options such as, "Did you receive a B.A. or a B.S. degree?" An extreme form of question acts as a problem-solving guide without directing the employee to a solution. The manager may say, "Joe, what do you think is causing the leakage in the main valve?" Thus, the manager encourages Joe to consider the causes and state them in his own terms. We have listed some situations that may call for open versus closed questions in Table 11.2.[3]

Table 11.2

Use closed questions if:

- The interviewer seeks measurable facts.
- There is a secure relationship between parties.
- The interviewee is informed and knowledgeable.
- The interviewer has limited time to obtain specific information.
- The interviewee's attitudes are not important.
- The interviewee either cannot or is not willing to discuss answers.

Use open questions if:

- The interviewer seeks to establish supportive climate.
- The interviewee's feelings and attitudes are important.
- The interviewer seeks to clarify the interviewee's point of view.
- The interviewee has an undetermined amount of information on the topic.
- Time is not essential.
- The interviewee is conversant and knowledgeable.

Use Probing Questions to Explore

Often the interviewee must be encouraged to discuss a specific topic or encouraged simply to communicate. Probing questions direct the interviewee to expand on a response and allow exploration of attitudes and beliefs. While the probe may simply be a verbal response such as "Please continue," it may also be a nonverbal response such as the nod of the head to indicate attentiveness. A thoughtful answer may take as much as six seconds to formulate.[4] Do not try to jump in and fill the silences because it will put you in a controlling mode and set a precedence for future discussion.

Mirror a Response to Encourage Further Discussion

The mirror question is a form of probe that encourages the interviewee to expand on a response by reflecting back what was just said. For example, a job applicant might say, "I had some difficulty with my last job because my boss was overly concerned with reaching quotas and goals at the expense of the organizational climate." A mirror question that would encourage further discussion might be, "You say you feel your boss was overly concerned with quotas and goals?"

Avoid Leading Questions

You have probably heard the phrase "Don't you think so?" numerous times and may have recognized it for what it was—a leading question. The person asking it assumes agreement or at the very least presumes to lead you to the correct response. Leading questions influence the respondent to give a desired response. Frequently used by salespeople to influence clients, leading questions can result in invalid responses. An example might be the manager who attempts to influence opinion at a meeting by stating, "You do agree that this is the right solution to the problem, don't you, John?" Whether or not John agrees, he will probably acquiesce under these circumstances. Vocal emphasis may be all that is needed to state a leading question. Consider the question above phrased as follows, but with heavy emphasis placed on the word "disagree": "Do you *disagree* with this solution, John?"

Sequencing Questions

You will find there are three general approaches to sequencing your questions for an interview. Each of these approaches should be considered depending on the type of interview, the person(s) involved in the interview, and the information you need to gain from the interview.[5]

The Funnel

The funnel approach begins with a general question followed by increasingly specific questions. It is the most widely used approach and works best with an interviewee who is well informed about the subject under discussion. An example of the funnel approach might be:

- Question 1: How do you feel about the salary structure at the new plant?
- Question 2: What kind of structure would you recommend?
- Question 3: Why do you feel that this approach is the most effective?
- Question 4: When do you feel it should be implemented?

The Inverted Funnel

The inverted funnel sequence begins with a specific question and each question that follows becomes more general in nature. This approach is particularly suited for counseling situations because specific questions encourage discussion at the outset of the interview. As interaction continues, probes and mirror questions motivate the respondent to participate more freely. The following questions exemplify the inverted funnel sequence:

- Question 1: How is the recruitment program proceeding?
- Question 2: Can you pinpoint any specific problems we may be able to solve?
- Question 3: Of these problems, which one will have the greatest effect on our ability to reach our goals?
- Question 4: Can you tell me more about the problem and what you feel needs to be done about it?

The Tunnel

If there is a compressed period of time in which an interview needs to be conducted and the information needed is fairly specific, the tunnel sequence is most appropriate. It consists of specific questions requesting specific information and is most frequently used by interviewers to obtain vital information—such as for a loan application or for screening purposes in the emergency room of a hospital. An example of the latter might be:

- Question 1: What is your full name?
- Question 2: Do you have insurance?
- Question 3: Are you employed?
- Question 4: Do you have your own physician?
- Question 5: Are you allergic to any medications?
- Question 6: How are you injured?

Planning your question sequence will save you time in the long run by keeping you on the appropriate path toward your goal. In addition you will avoid confusing the interviewee about his or her role and your purpose. An individual who expected to participate in an informational interview but suddenly finds you exploring feelings will question your motives.

Types of Interviews

The Employment Interview

Millions of people participate in employment interviews each year hoping to find suitable jobs. The decision-making process for the manager in selecting a suitable employee is critical, since placing the wrong person in a position can lead to complex organizational problems in the long run. The astronomical costs of orienting and training new employees in technical positions emphasize the importance of hiring decisions that put the right person in the job. To be effective, the interviewing process must begin with a thorough understanding of (1) the organizational policies and practices and (2) the job requirements.

Preparing for the Employee Interview

Usually, a manager will find the interview only one of a series of decision-making steps that culminate in the selection of the job candidate. First, there should be an examination of the nature of the job that has been vacated. Second, a job description should be prepared and publicized in the appropriate media. Third, a screening process should be agreed upon. Fourth, applications should be reviewed to determine which candidates meet the job requirements. Fifth, interviews should be set up with those candidates who meet the screening requirements. The final selection completes the process.

What Is the Nature of the Job?

Can you imagine hiring a chemist to do office filing? How long do you think such an employee would be motivated and interested in the work?

You may feel this is a ridiculous example, but similar errors in judgment occur frequently in employee selection. As a manager, you must identify the personal characteristics associated with effective performance of a job. One method that may help you determine whether the current requirements are realistic is to evaluate the reasons why the previous employee left the position. Was he or she bored and unproductive? If so, why? Perhaps the job itself needs to be redesigned.

Among the things you will be identifying are education, experience, knowledge, skills, interpersonal relations, trustworthiness, and unusual working conditions. Under the law, these are referred to as bona fide occupational qualifications (BFOQ) that are necessary to perform the work. Anything of a discriminatory nature—such as sex, age, race, religion, ethnic origin, and veteran status—cannot be part of an employment decision unless the qualification is inherent to the nature of the work. For example a bartender must be of legal age; however, age cannot be a consideration for employing a professor as long as he or she meets the qualifications for the position.

Prepare a Job Description

Once you have evaluated the job, prepare a job description that clearly outlines the duties, authority, and responsibilities of the position. Be sure to include organizational lines of authority, both upward and downward. To whom does this person report? Who reports to the person in this position? Does he or she have functional authority? If so, over whom? What are the major job functions, and what percentage of effort should be spent on each? For example, a trainer may need to spend 50 percent of his

---

Table 11.3 • Employment Interviews: What You Can't Ask

A question is unlawful if it does any of the following:[6]

1. Requests information on date of birth or birthplace
2. Asks information about age, sex, religion, ethnic origin, race, or veteran status unless it is a BFOQ
3. Requests marital status, number or list of dependents by name or age, or the names of relatives other than immediate family
4. Asks about membership in any clubs or organizations
5. Asks if applicant is a naturalized citizen
6. Requests previous name unless requesting a woman's maiden name
7. Requests a photograph or color of hair or eyes
8. Asks if applicant owns home
9. Asks if spouse works
10. Requires personal questions

effort in the classroom, 30 percent preparing and researching materials, and 20 percent coordinating programs.

The job description will be a valuable tool for advertising the position and clarifying the job requirements during the interview session. Before preparing the position description to advertise the job, check with the personnel representative to ascertain appropriate communication channels. Most organizations must advertise a position internally as well as in the local newspaper to allow equal opportunity for employment. In addition it may be necessary to advertise on a larger scope depending on the pool of applicants. For example, if you are trying to hire a college dean, you will probably have to place an advertisement in *The Chronicle of Higher Education* since the applicant pool would include deans from other colleges outside your immediate geographic area. In addition you may need to consider professional journals, trade association newsletters, and local and regional newspapers.

Establish a Procedure for Screening Applicants

To fairly evaluate applicants, an effective screening process should be established. A system whereby applicants' qualifications can be quantitatively measured against job requirements is most effective. A search committee may have to review credentials and select the top three or five candidates in the pool. These candidates may then be interviewed before making the final decision.

Review Credentials and Screen Applicants

Typically, the candidate's resume and references provide information about educational background, job experience, and work history. These credentials should be reviewed to identify qualifications of each applicant and then ranked according to agreed-on criteria. The process should follow the Equal Employment Opportunity Commission (EEOC) requirements. Familiarize yourself with *The Supervisor's EEO Handbook: A Guide to Federal Antidiscrimination Laws and Regulations.*[7]

Conducting the Job Interview

The job interview provides an opportunity to obtain information, explore attitudes, and make observations. The setting should be comfortable and project a positive impression of the organization. One job candidate drove sixty miles to an interview only to be asked to wait in an empty classroom for thirty minutes while a secretary located the department chairman. Her interview lasted fifteen minutes, during which time the chairman received two telephone calls and dismissed her so that he could attend a luncheon appointment. Even though she accepted the job, her negative impression of the chairman affected her interactions with him for many months thereafter.

During the opening moments you should make the interviewee comfortable and create a relaxed atmosphere. Asking the applicant to discuss former work experience is a good place to start, since it is an easy question to answer. As the applicant talks, listen for cues that might provide insight into her background and attitudes. Questions that ask the applicant to discuss successes and frustrations are especially meaningful. You will also find it helpful to describe the job and explain how it fits into the organization, including salary. The kind of questions the applicant asks you should tell you something about his or her concerns. Problem-solving questions related to the job allow you to evaluate spontaneous reactions and judgment. Finally, when you close the interview, be sure to let the applicant know when he or she can expect to hear from you.

You may wish to use the questions in Table 11.4 as a resource. Those questions are meant simply as a guide and can be used with the employment interview checklist (Table 11.5) to plan an effective strategy. Be sure to allow the interviewee to ask questions as well. Remember that the more you are able to learn about an applicant's background, interests,

Table 11.4 • Employment Interview Questions

1. What is your past work experience?
2. What is your present job?
3. How do you spend most of your time in your present job?
4. Of what successes do you feel particularly proud in your former jobs?
5. What are some of the tasks you find difficult to do? Why?
6. What were some of the things in your past jobs that you particularly disliked?
7. Did your job require you to work frequently with people? Were any of your co-workers difficult to work with?
8. Why are you leaving your present job?
9. What are your personal goals in terms of a career path?
10. How do you measure whether you have been successful in your job?
11. What was your supervisor like?
12. Did you agree with your supervisor's approach to managing the organization?
13. How did you feel your supervisor evaluated your performance?
14. How important is education to your life?
15. In what subjects did you perform best/worst?
16. Did you help finance your education? To what extent?
17. Do you prefer to work on your own or with others?
18. How do you see yourself fitting in with this organization?
19. What contributions can you make to this job?
20. What aspects of your background would you like to strengthen? Why?

Table 11.5 · Employment Interview Checklist

Opening
- Greet and make introductions.
- Establish common ground.
- State purpose: to interview prospective employee.
- Provide overview of interview structure.

Body
- Begin with topics that are easy to discuss such as previous experience and interests.
- Review the job description.
- Explain the organizational structure.
- Listen for cues that might provide insight into employee background and attitudes.
- Use probes to explore specific areas of interest that relate to the job, particularly weaknesses.
- Ask problem-solving type questions that allow the applicant to respond to situations that may occur on the job.
- Avoid questions that refer to age, race, religion, ethnic origin, sex, or veteran status.

Close
- Have applicant summarize his or her understanding of the job.
- Clarify any misunderstandings.
- Inform applicant when you will notify him or her of your decision.
- Express your appreciation for his or her interest in the position.

and interpersonal skills, the better chance you have of finding possible problems that may prevent effective performance on the job. The checklist given in Table 11.5 is meant to aid you in preparing for an employment interview.

The Orientation Interview

The first day on the job leaves a lasting impression on the new employee. He has come to work motivated to succeed on the job but lacks the specific information to effectively perform. The overriding question in his mind is, "Can I meet the expectations of my boss?" Too often the manager fails to take the time to clearly outline these expectations and provide needed training and resources.

The objective of the orientation interview is to acquaint the new employee with the organization, provide information and resources needed to perform the job, establish a positive attitude between the employer and the employee, and create an atmosphere conducive to productive performance. Obviously, this is a complex task requiring several interviews and much of the organization's staff. Poor or ineffective orientations often result in unmotivated employees and high turnover.

Planning the Orientation

The effective orientation of employees relies on effective planning. You will find the following checklist helpful in preparing for an employee orientation interview:

- Have a copy of the job description available to give to the employee.
- Make arrangements for essentials such as parking, insurance, and office space during the first few days.
- Have information on company policy, organizational structure, and procedures available for reference and discussion.
- Prepare any materials needed for the performance of the job including telephone equipment, desk, paper, or machinery.
- Arrange for the new employee to meet with key people to assist in training and orientation.
- Have a series of meaningful tasks set up that increase in difficulty and aid in the training process.
- Prepare organizational members for the employee's arrival: A new group member can be threatening. Emphasize that the employee will be a benefit to the organization and in turn to each of them.
- Recognize the importance of social contact in today's high-tech world. Arrange for the employee to meet and eat with others.

Conducting the Orientation Interview

The impression you make as the manager is critical in establishing a climate that will encourage the employee to discuss future problems with you. Do not let a handbook of rules and procedures substitute for a personal orientation. Use this opportunity to clearly express your expectations, but allow personal questions and follow up to see if things are proceeding according to plans.

New employees are wonderful resources for information about the organization. Try to find out what makes them comfortable or uncomfortable about their new work situation. Did the employees have to search for anything? Ask for a comparison of their new experience with experiences at other firms. Have the employees identify major job-related problems in the work area.

A properly oriented employee feels good about his or her job and has the resources and information necessary to meet performance expectations. Just as important, the manager has established a positive impression of an organizational climate that encourages interaction and recognizes the importance of the individual.

Table 11.6 · Orientation Interview Checklist

Opening
- Greet new employee.
- Establish common ground.
- State purpose: to orient new employee.
- Provide overview of interview structure.

Body
- Review the job description.
- Explain the organizational structure, particularly in relationship to the employee's position.
- Explain your performance expectations.
- Give the employee materials necessary to the performance of the job (policies, procedures, machinery, supplies, and so forth).
- Assign specific tasks.
- Introduce the employee to key people.

Close
- Have employee summarize his or her understanding of the job.
- Clarify any misunderstandings.
- Agree on follow-up actions.
- Acknowledge employee as an important part of the organization.

The Counseling Interview

At one time or another all managers become involved in giving or receiving help. Different words may be used to describe this process such as counseling, teaching, guiding, training, or coaching; nevertheless, the ultimate goal is to help someone solve problems and face crises. This is a critical role for the manager for three reasons: (1) It develops employees, (2) it provides insight and understanding, and (3) it promotes a trusting relationship through mutual sharing and problem solving.

Counseling Develops Employees

Problem-sensitive managers who help employees learn the skills to solve their problems will gain by developing a mature, competent work force. As a helper or counselor, the manager can also coach the subordinate in the skills to identify and solve problems. As the subordinate masters these skills, he or she becomes more mature and increasingly independent of managers, direct supervision, and feedback.

Counseling Provides Insight and Understanding

Many problems can be resolved in their initial stages—before they become crises—if the manager is aware of the causes. The counseling interview can be a revealing communication experience during which the manager gains as well as gives insight and information. Learning about a problem early on can lead to less costly solutions and save time and resources.

Counseling Promotes a Trusting Relationship

Finally, the counseling interview provides a means to strengthen the trusting relationship between manager and subordinate by helping the receiver understand the problem, receive support, learn new skills, or modify behavior. Counseling involves a dynamic, transactional relationship through face-to-face verbal and nonverbal interaction. Both parties have unique biological and psychological feelings, values, needs, as well as unique perceptions of each other, the situation, their expectations, and their roles. The effective counseling interviewer recognizes that the situation requires the helper to listen, encourage exploration, and establish a trusting relationship.

Preparing for the Counseling Interview

Because of the nature of the counseling interview, you often cannot prepare for a particular situation. Your subordinate may appear in your doorway and request a few minutes of your time for an urgent matter. While it is fairly easy for most of us to give advice based on past experience, most employees will see their problem as unique and your advice as both inappropriate and an attempt to circumvent their problem. Even if the employee seeks your opinion, providing advice will not encourage the development of exploration and problem-solving skills.

Conducting the Counseling Interview

In the role of helper or counselor, your task will be to clarify roles, identify the problem, and determine a course of action.[8]

Clarify roles. You will need to begin the interview by clarifying both your role and that of your subordinate. The first step will be to create an atmosphere that is relaxed, warm, receptive, and sincere in order to get the employee to talk openly. Once you can identify the nature of the problem, you will be able to determine your role. To do this, you will need to answer the following questions:

1. *Can I meet the interviewee's expectations?* Suppose that George has come to you with a complex personal problem that is placing stress on him and affecting his job performance. Can you help him? If the problem requires a professionally trained counselor, the answer to this question may be no, but you can act as a link in getting the employee help, perhaps through the employee assistance pro-

gram. If the problem does not require professional expertise, however, you may be able to help George gain insight into the problem.

2. *Can I work with the interviewee?* It may be that George needs some information or direction that you can provide, in which case you will want to assist him in solving his problem. If you have time constraints or a personality conflict, you may need to postpone the interview or get assistance.

3. *Do I want to work with the interviewee?* Sometimes employees take advantage of opportunities to be with the boss and actually are capable of handling their problem. Other times you may not want to become involved because of conflicting demands or needs. It is better to be honest with the interviewee than send crossed messages that may be perceived as lack of interest or concern.

4. *What structure do we need?* The nature of the problem will help you establish the structure or format of the interview. If the problem is complex and requires additional information or the opportunity to practice new skills, you will need to agree on a format that includes several meetings. If, however, all of the information is readily available and both of you have the time, it may be possible to follow the problem-solving steps and select a solution within a limited time frame in one sitting. Before proceeding, you will need to agree on the format.

5. *What do I expect from the interviewee?* A counseling interview is goal-directed, whether it is to give empathy or resolve conflict. You as an interviewer have expectations of the interviewee. These expectations may include a change in behavior, such as improved job performance or a better attitude.

Once you have answered these questions, you will have your roles clarified so that both parties will be better able to contribute to a positive outcome.

Identify the problem. During the first phase of the counseling interview, both the interviewer and interviewee engage in problem exploration. The interviewer should be listening for content and feelings and encouraging the interviewee to be concrete—identifying actual events and specific problems. Both parties should agree on the problem and follow the problem-solving steps. The interviewee should describe the symptoms, analyze the facts, and determine the causes. Finally, he or she should explore possible alternative actions and the probable consequences of each. The interviewer should act as a guide in the process and avoid a directive approach.

Determine a course of action. The close of the interview is vital and should not be rushed. The interviewer should summarize the interview by concluding with a statement of the action that is to be taken to eliminate the problem. The interviewee should leave the interview feeling that it has been time well spent and that there is genuine concern about his or her welfare. Nonverbal communication is crucial in conveying sincerity and warmth. This is the time for a warm handshake or caring pat on the back.

Table 11.7 · Counseling Interview Checklist

Opening
- Greet subordinate.
- Establish common ground.
- State purpose: to help subordinate solve problems or face crises.
- Clarify roles, expectations, and format.

Body
- Explore the problem and its seriousness.
- Use nondirective approach.
- Listen for content and feelings.
- Encourage interviewee to be concrete.
- Describe the symptoms of the problem.
- Analyze the facts.
- Determine the causes.
- Explore possible alternatives.

Close
- Summarize the problem and its seriousness.
- Agree on the action that is to be taken.
- Convey sincerity and warmth through nonverbal feedback.
- Acknowledge value of employee to organization.

The Performance Appraisal Interview

To achieve output goals, people must both cooperate and coordinate their efforts. They must know what to do, when to do it, and how to do it. It is the job of the manager to determine whether subordinates are performing to meet the goals of the organization. The performance appraisal interview is an essential activity in gauging and improving employee productivity.

Performance appraisal is a test based on the best judgment and opinions of evaluators using definite identifiable criteria that measure the quantity or quality of work or specific requirements. The primary purpose of performance appraisal is to improve performance. Secondary purposes are to review past performance, set goals for future performance, develop personnel to determine merit, and give recognition.

For its studies of performance, the General Electric Company compared the following approaches to performance appraisal: criticism, praise, and goal setting. Their findings indicated that criticism alone resulted in defensive behavior. If the employee received only praise during the appraisal interview, there was no change in performance. Only the third approach, goal setting, resulted in improved performance. As a result, G.E. developed guidelines for performance appraisal:

1. Emphasize strengths, not weaknesses.
2. Avoid discussing personal characteristics.
3. If you must discuss weaknesses, describe specific behavior and give examples of more acceptable behavior.
4. Concentrate on opportunities for growth.
5. Stress a few important items for growth.
6. Use a reasonable time frame.
7. Focus on an overall objective.[9]

By regularly giving feedback on employee performance, the manager maintains an open climate and avoids the anxiety and fear that precede the yearly evaluation, since the employee has a fairly clear understanding of her strengths and weaknesses.

Preparing for the Performance Appraisal

There are several steps you should take to prepare for the performance appraisal interview. The first of these preparatory steps is to be aware of the typical problems that might hinder your objectivity and effectiveness.

The halo/horns effect. If a person has performed well in one activity, there is a tendency for people to attribute other positive traits to that person, whether or not she actually has these traits. This "halo" then affects one's ability to objectively assess actual performance. For example, if Jenny, a secretary, has outstanding technical skills, her boss may assign an outstanding performance rating and overlook or ignore poor interpersonal skills and poor time management. Conversely, if Joe fails in an attempt to perform a task, there may be a tendency to place "horns" on him and assign other negative traits.

Central tendency bias. If a manager is not sure about an employee's performance, she may decide to classify the employee as average rather than give a rating that is too high or too low. This is a safe position that avoids the need to differentiate or distinguish performance levels. In lieu of central tendency, the manager may have a tendency to give lenient or very critical ratings. This should be avoided.

The recency effect. If performance appraisal occurs following an event during which the employee performed exceptionally well or made several critical mistakes, the timing of the event may affect the appraisal. An effective appraisal should be based on the overall performance of the employee during a specified period of time with emphasis placed on the achievement of goals.

The Appraisal Process

To fully prepare for the appraisal, you should review the requirements of the employee's job and the performance goals. Obtain written feedback from the employee concerning his or her perceptions of meeting these requirements and goals. By doing so, you will have an idea as to the employee's point of view prior to your interview. Finally, complete the appraisal form, keeping in mind that the interview should allow for employee input and mutual goal setting.

The performance appraisal process itself must be productive. The time and effort expended in the process must be justified by the results obtained. It should:

1. Allow both the supervisor and subordinate an opportunity to learn about each other's goals, aspirations, and expectations.
2. Give a clear indication of how these expectations are met in specific, measurable terms.
3. Assist in identifying obstacles to productivity that might result from inefficiency, competing goals, or misunderstandings.
4. Identify results, not just activity, and effectiveness rather than effort.
5. Assist in identifying career paths within the organization that allow for growth and development of employees.
6. Provide a clear outline of the performance expectations and how they will be measured.
7. Provide the information needed to effectively administer promotions, raises, and training.

Avoid pitfalls. There are some key pitfalls to guard against in common interview situations. Criticism typically produces defensive behavior and should be specifically related to a particular behavior. Even though you may emphasize employee strengths, praise will not take the sting out of the following criticism. Acceptance of criticism will depend on the employee's newness on the job, the competence of the superior, and the amount of trust and liking developed between the two of them. Minor faults should not be discussed during the annual appraisal. Whatever the deficiencies, the cause should be identified and a plan for improvement agreed on.

In addition, the employee's perception of the job may be different from the superior's, which might make it necessary to clarify job duties and responsibilities as well as the degree of delegated authority. Superior and subordinate may have differing opinions on the best method of performing a task, budgeting time, or setting priorities.

Participate in mutual goal-setting. Mutual goal-setting is a critical part of the appraisal interview in that it (1) capitalizes on employee strengths, (2) sets standards for improved performance, (3) allows for employee growth and development, (4) establishes priorities, and (5) clarifies organizational goals. Note that the process must be mutual: It must allow the subordinate the opportunity to participate in determining goals and priorities and the best means to accomplish them. It also must allow feedback from the superior that clarifies expectations and performance objectives.

Finally, the employee may be encountering obstacles to performance or problems on the job of which the superior is unaware. Time should be spent in the interview creating a climate that allows the subordinate to express any concerns or frustrations that may not surface in the normal interview process.

Emphasize strengths and capabilities. Appraisal interviews tend to concentrate on changing the employee rather than determining strengths and capabilities. There are a number of ways to improve performance that may prove more appropriate than changing the employee. Be alert for signals that indicate that (1) a change or alteration in duties may capitalize on strengths, (2) the employee may need to be transferred to a more suitable position, (3) the manager may need to alter his or her method of supervision and provide more feedback, training, or support.

Eliminate obstacles. Once the manager analyzes the work situation, changes should be initiated to eliminate obstructions. If the employee is not able to perform the job, she should be moved to a position in the organization in which she can perform adequately. Perhaps the employee has the capability but needs technical training or knowledge. It may simply be a matter of providing the necessary supplies or equipment to do the job.

A final note. Note that two factors are at work here: those things the worker can't do as opposed to those things the worker won't do. If the problem is a lack of knowledge, lack of skill, lack of feedback, difficult job requirements, or lack of resources, the worker can't do it. On the other hand, if there are no expectations of reward, the reward is not valued by the employee, or the obstacles to performance are too great, the worker won't do it. Some questions to consider are found in Table 11.8.

Table 11.8 · "Can't Do" versus "Won't Do"

1. Is the worker performing properly? If not, analyze the situation.
2. Does the worker understand what to do? If not, provide orientation.
3. Does the worker know how to do the job? If not, provide training.
4. Does the worker try to do the job? If not, evaluate the incentives.
5. Is the worker capable of doing the job? If not, consider job redesign or transfer.
6. Are there psychological problems? If so, can stress and conflict be reduced?
7. Are there health problems? If so, provide the employee assistance.
8. Is the employee's poor performance affecting others? If so, apply progressive discipline.

Table 11.9 • Performance Appraisal Checklist

Opening
- Greet employee.
- Establish common ground.
- State purpose: to appraise performance.
- Preview interview structure.

Body
- Review the job requirements and previous goals.
- Describe important elements of employee's performance.
- Allow employee to give observations of performance effectiveness, problems, or obstacles.
- Set goals and priorities for future performance expectations.
- Determine the type of support needed to reach these goals (training, altering of job duties, transfer, change in supervision).

Close
- Have employee summarize.
- Clarify any misunderstandings concerning performance.
- Agree on follow-up actions.
- Acknowledge value of employee to organization and the appraisal process.

Remember that the appraisal interview should be the confirmation of interaction and feedback that occurs frequently on the job rather than a yearly gathering of "do's and don'ts." Its primary emphasis should be to evaluate progress and set new goals that capitalize on employee strengths. Do not confuse the appraisal process by introducing a secondary purpose of disciplining employees. The latter is a separate type of interview that should be handled during a different encounter. The checklist above will provide a guide for planning a performance appraisal interview.

The Disciplinary Interview

Top management sets policies, rules, and regulations that must be observed and enforced by line supervisors. Organizations and the members therein are also subject to state, federal, and international law. As the importance and level of authority increase, the role of the first-line supervisor decreases. As managers, we can modify behavior through positive reinforcement. Occasionally, however, the manager must use force or outward control to correct, mold, or punish unacceptable behavior.

The disciplinary interview is probably the most critical interview you will conduct as a manager. Besides the personal stress that usually accompanies both parties, you must establish a tone and convey a message that is clear and purposeful. When preparing for a disciplinary interview, keep in mind that effective discipline should be appropriate, effective, consistent, immediate, and recorded.

The Disciplinary Action Should Be Appropriate

In most organizations guidelines establish the severity of the action to be taken so that it is appropriate to the offense. For example, it would be inappropriate to fire an employee for being five minutes late to work unless the employee has been consistently or excessively late over a specified period of time.

The Disciplinary Action Should Be Effective

Unless the interview is effective in meeting its objective, behavior is likely to continue and perhaps increase in its severity. You must act clearly in the supervisory role as manager to subordinate and explain the problem or describe the rule that has been violated. Once you have done this, tell the employee exactly what you expect of her in terms of improvement and what assistance you will provide as her supervisor. It is important to hear her side of the story in that you may discover obstacles to performance that you can remove. Next, you should explain what will happen if the employee does not meet expectations within a specified period of time. Finally, follow through with your commitment.

The Disciplinary Action Should Be Consistent

You cannot fire one person in your department for coming in late and slap another on the hand for a similar offense without jeopardizing the welfare of the organization. Most organizations use the personnel department as a resource to assist the manager in applying discipline. One of the primary concerns is consistency in the application of discipline.

Discipline Should Be Immediate and Private

Whether it is positive or negative, feedback must be immediate to be most effective. An employee may not be aware that she is not following the rules or accepted procedures, and so failure to give immediate feedback will more than likely result in repeated behavior. Feedback can also provide information about the reason for the employee's performance problem. Once the cause is identified, the manager has a number of corrective strategies available, such as training, orienting, counseling, transfer, demotion, suspension, or termination.

Since a corrective interview describes an incorrect or improper behavior of the employee, the manner in which it is conducted can affect the trust relationship between manager and subordinate. It should be conducted in the privacy of an office and out of the range of hearing of other employees.

The Disciplinary Interview Should Be Recorded

Normally, you will want to give an oral warning to an employee on the first offense. Nevertheless, you should document the interview. The employee should be told, however, that the purpose of the interview is an oral reprimand and your written notes are for reference; in contrast, a written reprimand will be permanently placed in her personnel file. Include the following information, and give a copy to the employee:

1. The problem or rule violated;
2. Expected performance;
3. The disciplinary action taken;
4. The time frame in which the behavior must be corrected;
5. The consequences of repeated actions.

Because of the severity of some disciplinary actions that affect pay—such as suspension, removal, or demotion—employees have the right to judicial due process. Familiarize yourself with the grievance and appeals procedures of the organization, keep accurate records, and meet with personnel and your Equal Employment Opportunity representative before notifying an employee of any adverse action.

Wohlking points out a number of factors that should be considered when disciplining employees:[10]

1. What is the seriousness of the offense?
2. How much time elapsed between offenses?
3. What is the nature and frequency of the offense?
4. What is the employee's work history?
5. Were there extenuating circumstances?
6. What degree of job orientation did the employee receive?
7. What is the history of discipline in the organization?
8. What are the implications for others?
9. Do you have management's backing?

The disciplinary interview is a critical managerial activity. It is important to set a tone that is firm but fair, friendly but instructive.

Table 11.10 · Disciplinary Interview Checklist

Opening
• Greet employee.
• Establish common ground.
• State purpose: to resolve a performance problem.
• Preview interview structure.

Body
• Review the problem and its seriousness.
• Allow the employee to give his or her side of the problem.
• Tell the employee what is expected.
• Set a time frame for improvement.
• State the consequences if behavior is repeated.
• Inform the employee of the nature of the action taken.

Close
• Have employee summarize of the performance expected and action taken.
• Clarify misunderstandings concerning performance.
• Agree on follow-up actions.
• Acknowledge value of employee to organization.

Summary

Interviewing is an important means of communication. The interview is the interaction that occurs between two parties who meet to accomplish a predetermined purpose essential to the welfare of the organization. It is the manager's responsibility to understand the interview's purpose, be prepared for it, and record the findings. Key steps include defining the purpose, determining who should be involved, analyzing the other party, and planning the interview structure or format.

Each interview situation follows a basic structure adapted to the specific purpose of the interaction. The opening establishes common ground, sets the tone, and clarifies the purpose. The body of the interview attempts to accomplish the goal through problem-solving or questioning techniques. Finally, the close includes a summary of the information and agreements and acknowledges the value of the encounter.

Effective interviews are often the result of effective questioning. Open and closed questions control the pace and direction of the interview. The nature and sequence of questions should be adapted to fit the situation and the people involved.

The manager's ability to handle the interview effectively—whether it is to counsel, discipline, or appraise performance—establishes his or her credibility with subordinates, develops trust, and encourages growth.

Since much of the manager's day is spent in face-to-face information-gathering and problem-solving interviews, interviewing may be the most important of the communication skills.

Key Words

interview	mirror questions	counseling interview
sequencing	leading questions	performance appraisal
closed questions	BFOQ	interview
open questions	employment interview	disciplinary interview
probing questions	orientation interview	

Review Questions

1. Why are interview skills important to the manager?

2. Describe a situation in which you were interviewed. What was the purpose of the interview? Did the interviewer dominate discussion or did you? What things did the interviewer do to get you to talk? to maintain control?

3. What are the purposes of performance appraisal? How often should it occur? Share your experiences with this form of interview.

4. What is the role of the manager as a counselor?

5. Why is it important to avoid giving advice?

6. As a manager, why is it important to prepare for the job interview?

7. Barbara is 65 years old and has applied for a job on the janitorial staff. The only position open includes as one of the tasks cleaning the men's rest room. Does she fit the bona fide occupational qualifications?

8. Why is it important to discipline employees? When is discipline effective? ineffective? Give an example of each.

9. Describe the elements of a disciplinary interview. Why are they important?

10. Try to recall the first day you went to work on a particular job (part time, full time, or volunteer work). What kind of orientation did you receive? Was it effective or ineffective? Why? If you could have designed an orientation to meet your needs, what would you have included?

Exercises

1. Interview someone you have not met before. Spend about twenty minutes finding out what makes the interviewee unique. Be sure to use each other's

names as frequently as possible. What techniques did you use, verbal and nonverbal, to get the interviewee to share with you?

2. Interview an expert on one of the communication topics that relate to this course. Follow the interview steps outlined in this chapter: Prepare an outline including sample questions, conduct your interview, and summarize your findings in writing. Present your findings to the class.

3. The way you say something can be more important than what you say. Select four or five words that describe your communication style (such as relaxed, honest, cautious). What styles get you in trouble? What styles do you find offensive?

4. Engage in a problem-solving discussion with someone in which you act as the helper or counselor. The problem can be real or hypothetical. Practice listening and reflecting skills. An observer should summarize the frequency and quality of your responses during the interview as well as the verbal or nonverbal behaviors that encouraged or discouraged the interviewee. Ask the observer to share this information with you at the completion of the interview.

5. Select a job for which you will be acting as an interviewer and prepare a job description. Write a job announcement and list the media in which you would advertise the position. Prepare an interview outline including a list of tentative questions that will help you in the selection process.

6. Prepare a resume and interview for one of the jobs described in question 5. Evaluate the interview.

7. Prepare a plan for orienting the person selected for the position you described.

8. Joe supervises an employee who formerly contributed 100 percent to her organization. She has been punctual, careful, considerate, and helpful to new employees. She is also pursuing a business degree at the nearby community college, is married, and is active in social activities. Her performance evaluations have been very satisfactory until two months ago when she was not interviewed for a new position. Lately, she has been late for work several times, negligent with accounts and records, sharp with her supervisor, and openly talking about co-workers to cause deliberate friction. Joe has noted the following specific incidents:

   a. The employee is supposed to be on the job at 8:00 A.M. Within the last month she has not reported to the office until 8:30 on six different occasions. Joe has overlooked this since she is an exceptional worker, but the employee is continuing to be late.

   b. The employee has always regarded her supervisors highly but has begun to talk back to them regularly.

   c. On three occasions she has conversed with other staff members communicating confidential or incorrect information, which led to unnecessary confrontations with other employees.

   d. On four occasions the employee has lost or misplaced important documents.

Determine Joe's plan of action and prepare an interview outline. Test your plan by role-playing the interview with another class member.

References

1. Allan D. Frank, *Communication on the Job* (Glenview, Ill.: Scott Foresman, 1982), p. 192.

2. *Ibid.*

3. Adapted from R. L. Kahn and C. F. Cannell, *The Dynamics of Interviewing* (New York: John Wiley), 1957, pp. 133–143.

4. Raymond Gorden, *Interviewing Strategy, Techniques and Tactics* (Homewood, Ill.: Dorsey, 1969).

5. William J. Seiler, E. Scott Baudhuin, and L. David Schuelke, *Communication in Business and Professional Organizations* (Reading, Mass.: Addison-Wesley, 1982), p. 222; and Allan D. Frank, *Communication on the Job*, pp. 205–206.

6. Patricia Hayes Bradley, *Communications for Business and the Professions*, 2nd ed. (Dubuque, Iowa: Wm. C. Brown, 1983), pp. 160–62.

7. "The Supervisor's EEO Handbook: A Guide to Federal Antidiscrimination Laws and Regulations" (New York: Executive Enterprises, 1981).

8. Lawrence M. Brammer, *The Helping Relationship* (Englewood Cliffs, N.J.: Prentice-Hall, 1979), pp. 45–46.

9. The film "Performance Appraisal: The Human Dynamic" by McGraw-Hill, released in 1978, vividly illustrates this research.

10. Wallace Wohlking, "Effective Discipline in Employee Relations," *Personnel Journal* (Sept. 1975), pp. 201–207.

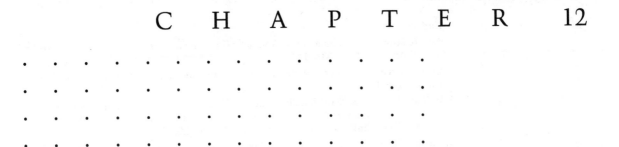

C H A P T E R   12

The Communicating Manager: Leading and Motivating

Introduction

As organizations have become more complex, so has the role of the leader. During the days of scientific management the manager made all decisions and communicated these decisions to the workers, who performed the tasks. Today the manager must consider government regulations, union contracts, and legal pressures before rendering a decision. In addition, more employees desire to participate in the decision-making process, and computer technology has increased the availability of and access to information analysis. Add to this fluctuations in the economy, global conflicts, and continually changing personal relationships, and the leader's task begins to resemble what Warren Bennis describes as "a set of conditions that seem to take shape suddenly, like an unscheduled express train looming out of the night."[1]

Earlier chapters defined a manager as someone who "gets things done through others." The manager's goal is to accomplish, bring about, conduct, or direct—and be effective. Bennis carefully distinguishes between the leader and the manager, since they are not necessarily embodied in the same role: "The difference may be summarized as activities of vision and judgment versus activities of efficiency. . . . The leader today is a multidirectional broker who must deal with four estates—his immediate management team, constituencies within his organization, forces outside his organization, and the media."[2] Each area requires effective communication.

Followers have certain expectations of their leaders: to provide resources, give directions, provide compensation, give information. Leaders also have expectations of their followers: to lend support; cooperate in offering their abilities toward achieving defined goals; communicate wants, needs, and desires in a constructive manner. In addition, a leader must be concerned with employee motivation; the individual who does not produce or is erratic affects the productivity of others.

How do managers become leaders? How do they create stimulating work climates? These questions plague every organization. This chapter is intended to help managers or prospective managers to better understand the concept and processes of leadership and motivation. The chapter reviews leadership traits, theories, styles, and postulates; defines motivation as it relates to leadership; and emphasizes the essential role of communication as a leadership skill.

Traits and Styles

On November 14, 1980, *The Wall Street Journal* published the results of a Gallup survey of 728 chief executives who identified the most important traits that people need to advance in business. Foremost among these traits were integrity, the ability to get along with others, and industriousness. These chief executives found that the major failings of subordinates were the inability to understand or work with others and limited points of view.

Leadership Traits

The trait theories of leadership can be traced back to the ancient Greeks, who concluded that leaders were born, not made. According to "the great man theory," leaders have natural abilities or talents that allow them to rise to specific situations. Examples of early leaders with the right traits were Pompey, Caesar, and Napoleon.

The influence of trait theory was minimized by the school of behavioral psychology, which contended that leadership skills could be taught and learned through experience. Research efforts concluded that intelligence, initiative, extroversion, humor, enthusiasm, fairness, sympathy, and self-confidence were universally possessed by leaders.[3] Davis summarized these behavioral traits:

1. *Intelligence:* The leader usually has higher intelligence than followers, yet not exceedingly so.

2. *Social maturity and breadth:* Leaders tend to be self-assured, have a healthy self-concept, be emotionally stable, and have a broad range of interests and activities.

3. *Inner motivation and achievement drives:* Leaders have intense achievement drives and seek intrinsic rather than extrinsic rewards.

4. *Human relations attitudes:* Leaders recognize the importance of human relations. They are considerate and are employee-centered rather than production-centered.[4]

Physical traits that were associated with leaders were also identified. Stogdill's research identified physical traits of energy, appearance, and height as being associated with leaders. Recent attempts at trait theory have focused on communication skills and decision making. Geier found that poor leaders are uninformed, fail to participate, and are rigid, authoritarian, and offensive in verbalization.[5] Russell found effective leaders to be more agreeable and less opinionated than less successful leaders.[6]

Generally, the study of traits has not been very successful in explaining leadership, since not all leaders possess these traits, while many nonleaders do. Researchers in trait theory have also failed to determine how much of each characteristic is necessary to be a successful leader. Most of the identified traits are expected of a person in a position of leadership, and they describe patterns of effective behavior. The more important studies of leadership have revolved around leadership styles.

Leadership Styles

You have probably had experience with numerous leadership styles during your educational, social, and work experiences. Below are three examples of the styles or approaches some leaders may have used in asking you to assist in reaching a group goal:

1. The due date on that activity is next Tuesday. Your job is to call all the group members and tell them we will meet to assign roles tomorrow.

2. Let's get together to formulate a plan for that project. Can you meet with me tomorrow at 2:00?

3. Don't forget we have that project due next Tuesday.

Each of these approaches represents a different leadership style. While the democratic style is favored by most researchers, studies have indicated that different styles are appropriate in different situations, depending on the people involved.

The authoritarian and democratic styles have been examined by Tannenbaum and Schmidt on their boss-centered to employee-centered continuum. As Figure 12.1 shows, the boss-centered leadership style emphasizes the authority of the manager.[7] For example, a manager may use authority to persuade or coerce employees, present ideas and invite questions, or present a tentative decision subject to change. On the other end of the continuum where subordinate-centered leadership occurs, an area of freedom and involvement in decision making leads to a more democratic approach. In it the manager permits subordinates to function within defined limits, asks the group to make the decision or present problems, or solicits suggestions and makes the decision based on these suggestions.

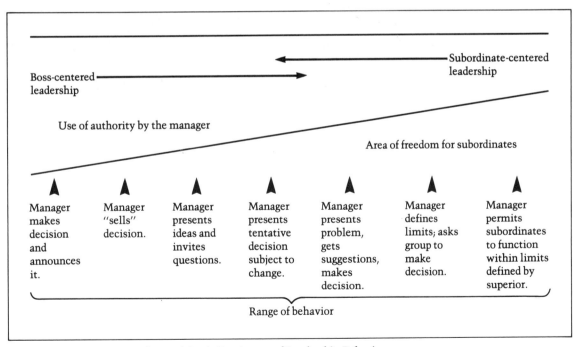

Figure 12.1 • A Continuum of Leadership Behavior

Source: Robert Tannenbaum and Warren H. Schmidt, "How to Choose a Leadership Pattern," *Harvard Business Review* (May-June 1973), p. 96. Copyright © 1973 by the President and Fellows of Harvard College; all rights reserved.

The following discussion describes the leadership styles identified by the Tannenbaum/Schmidt (TS) continuum. A number of well-known leadership theories, associated with each, will also be examined.

Authoritarian

Keenly interested in the way employees responded to their superior's actions, Douglas McGregor formulated his theory X, in which he identified the characteristics of the autocratic manager. He noted that some managers inspired employees to new levels of productivity and created a climate of support, while others demanded effort, asserted dominance, and alienated employees.[8]

McGregor saw that a very small number of managers act on the assumption that people enjoy being productive and want responsibility. More commonly managers act on the assumptions that McGregor labeled theory X. These were examined in Chapter 1, page 11. The climate of theory X management includes direct supervision; small, distinct tasks without an overall objective; "checking" on workers to ensure that they are following specific instructions; a preponderance of negative rewards and reprimands; communication based on fault-finding, criticism, blaming, and accusations; lack of employee input into decision making; and the use of authority or power to silence opposition.

The theory X manager basically demands results and rarely engages in group decision making unless forced to do so. He uses a direct communication style that emphasizes the superior/subordinate relationship, and he frequently reminds you of his position and authority: "I'm the boss, so we'll do it my way."

Democratic

The democratic manager is a positive Pygmalion, as we described in Chapter 3. This communicative style includes praising employees for a job well done, delegating projects, clearly outlining expectations, setting high performance standards, minimizing direct orders, using authority to minimize obstacles, and assisting in accomplishing goals. In McGregor's terms, a theory Y manager recognizes and adjusts to personal abilities and encourages growth. Employee ideas are solicited, particularly about matters concerning their working conditions. The democratic manager keeps employees informed of new developments through staff meetings and team-building techniques in the form of problem-solving conferences. Encouraging employees to advance and develop as well as improve their jobs is a characteristic of the democratic style of leadership.

Participative

According to several theories of leadership, the participative leadership style lies somewhere between the autocratic and democratic approach. The participative manager encourages participation in decision making but lacks complete confidence in subordinates to make decisions. While the leader invites ideas and usually tries to make constructive use of them, he maintains control. This leader would stylistically lie right of center in the subordinate-centered range on the TS continuum. A typical scenario might go:

> I have asked you to meet today to discuss a problem we must solve. We have been allotted $X to establish a career center that can be used by all students in the university. You are to determine how this money is to be spent within the following limitations. [Here the manager proceeds to describe these limitations.]

The participative style is more predominant than the democratic style because few managers have full confidence that employees can and will solve problems in the best interest of the organization, without their input and direction. If a theory Y manager goes into an autocratic situation, his staff will need guidelines to follow in learning how to think more freely.

Laissez-faire

Laissez-faire leadership means "leave it alone." Employees offer little input and receive little information from the manager. There is lack of clear performance expectations and minimal direction. Hence, the climate of the organization often becomes chaotic as informal group leaders vie for control and power. Confusion and cliques abound as employees create and follow their own personal goals.

If a manager is not careful, one of the above styles will dominate the work environment. An effective manager seeks to change styles depending on the people, task, or situation.

Other Leadership Approaches

The Functional Approach

Leadership is really the behavior of any group member that promotes the achievement of group goals. More than one person may actually lead a group toward the accomplishment of the objectives, in which case leadership varies by *function*. Each person is capable of leadership—whether through providing information, relieving tension, encouraging participation, or keeping the group on course.

The Situational Approach

When research indicated that no one leadership style is always effective, a number of researchers examined the dynamics of business situations to determine which variables determined the most effective styles. Fiedler believed that the work situation would be favorable for the leader if (1) the leader is generally accepted by followers, (2) the task is highly structured, and (3) the leader has position power through formal authority in the organization.[9] If these three dimensions are not positive or have low values, however, the situation will not be favorable. The favorableness of the situation combined with leadership style would determine effectiveness.

As a result of his research, Fiedler found that the task-directed or hard-nosed leader was most effective in very favorable and very unfavorable situations. If the situation was only moderately favorable or unfavorable, the more lenient or human relations style of manager was more effective. Figure 12.2 depicts the relationship between leadership style and situational favorableness using Fiedler's model.

Path-Goal Leadership Theory

Another widely recognized theoretical approach to leadership is the path-goal theory. Related to the expectancy theory of motivation and attributed to Martin Evans and Robert House, the path-goal theory relates leadership behavior to employee motivation, satisfaction, and performance.[10] It differs from Fiedler's contingency theory in that it is based on the premise that the same leader can use a variety of styles depending on the situation. Evans and House outline four major leadership styles and two situational factors. The four styles are:

1. *Directive leadership:* An authoritarian leader gives specific directions to subordinates with no participation by subordinates.
2. *Supportive leadership:* The leader supports the efforts of subordinates, is friendly and approachable, and has genuine concern for people.
3. *Participative leadership:* The leader solicits and implements subordinates' ideas yet maintains decision-making power.
4. *Achievement-oriented leadership:* The leader sets challenging goals, trusts subordinates, has confidence in their abilities, and expects employees to accomplish tasks.

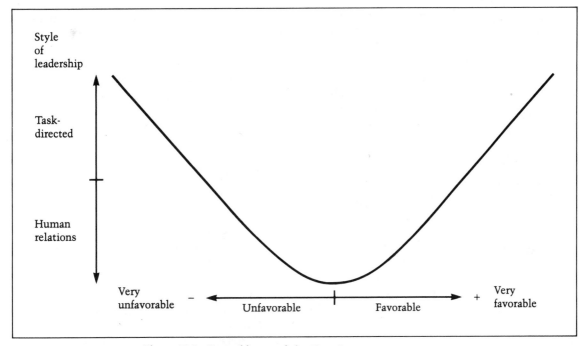

Figure 12.2 • Favorableness of the Situation

Source: Fred Luthans, *Organizational Behavior*, 3rd ed. (New York: McGraw-Hill, 1981), adapted from Fred E. Fiedler, *A Theory of Leadership Effectiveness* (New York: McGraw-Hill, 1967), pp. 142–48. Reprinted by permission.

The two situational variables are the personal characteristics of subordinates and the environmental demands:

    1. The leader's behavior will be acceptable if it is perceived as a source of immediate or future satisfaction.

    2. The leader's behavior will be motivational if effective performance will lead to satisfaction of subordinate needs and if it provides support and rewards formerly lacking.

    According to the path-goal theory, the manager should use one of the four leadership styles contingent on the two situational factors. The result should be to make the path to the subordinate's goals as smooth as possible. This may include:

    1. Eliminating barriers to performance;
    2. Providing rewards;
    3. Providing training, coaching, counseling, or direction;
    4. Clarifying expectations and roles;

5. Allowing subordinates direct access to information or experience that will help them recognize problems and arouse needs.

Research on path-goal theory supports the need to vary management styles to suit the situation. Employees experiencing frustration because of ambiguous tasks and vague roles prefer directive leadership, while employees with relatively clear tasks do not like directive leadership. Supportive leadership has a positive effect on subordinates performing in stressful situations.

A Model for Leader Effectiveness

According to Paul Hersey and Kenneth H. Blanchard, the manager must adapt to a dynamic environment, adjusting leadership style according to the people and the situation.[11] Their leader effectiveness and adaptability description (LEAD) assesses task and relationship behavior between the leader and the followers. The LEAD model is a relatively simple and effective means of helping you determine your leadership style.

Hersey and Blanchard are convinced that the relationship between the superior and subordinate is crucial. Through rigorous research they identify four leadership behavior quadrants based on the variables of task and relationship:

1. *High task, low relationship:* The leader clearly defines roles and communicates to group members specific directions concerning what tasks they are assigned, how to complete the tasks, and when the tasks must be completed. This style is most appropriate when employees are new to the job and low in both job and psychological maturity.

2. *High task, high relationship:* The leader remains directive but communicates encouragement through feedback and interaction. This style is used when an employee is low in psychological maturity and high in job maturity.

3. *High relationship, low task:* The leader and subordinate communicate or share decision-making and problem-solving tasks. The employee has the knowledge and the ability to do the task but needs emotional support, which the leader provides.

4. *Low relationship, low task:* The employee has the knowledge and the ability to do the task with minimal interaction with, and communication from, the leader.

These behavior categories are related to the maturity of the employee, both emotionally and in terms of job skills. Thus, the Hersey and Blanchard model differentiates among employees with varying levels of willingness or motivation to do the job as well as varying levels of competency to do it.

Motivation Defined

Motivation consists of three interrelated elements: needs, drives, and goals. A lack or imbalance that creates dissatisfaction or tension in the individual is a *need*. For example, a person deprived of rest for long periods of time will crave a means of restoring balance or homeostasis through sleep. Needs may vary in type and intensity among people and change from time to time within any one person, but they significantly influence behavior.

A *drive* is the state of the organism associated with the need, such as hunger or thirst. Someone deprived of rest will seek opportunities for rest, perhaps dozing or cat-napping whenever possible. The *goal* is the outcome that the person perceives will eliminate the need and restore balance: "A good night's sleep" may be perceived as a goal. While the drive arouses general activity, a *motive* is the learned state that affects behavior by moving an individual toward a perceived goal, hence the term *motivation*. Motivation is the reason behind the behavior or action. Consider the following situation.

Jim Hardcastle is a section head in a firm that is a major producer of microcomputers. He has been in this position for six years. Particularly skilled in his field, he has become frustrated with general management's current philosophy. Every change he recommends must be considered by the "higher ups" before he can act on it. Jim has lost his temper on several occasions when he believed a fair hearing had not been given to what he felt were excellent suggestions for change. As a result of his outbursts, his suggestions were denied. His current relationship with the higher administration is strained, and he avoids interaction with his supervisors. Instead of continuing to monitor and evaluate the production of the unit, he has begun to channel his efforts into personal endeavors. The morale and productivity of his unit have started to suffer.

Jim's behavior can be described in the following way: Jim experienced a stimulus that created an internal need. For example, an employee complains to Jim, acting as a stimulus. Jim recognizes the value of the complaint; perhaps there is a threat to physical safety of all employees. He becomes more and more aware that if a change is not implemented, the possibility of a costly, if not fatal, accident is imminent. This creates tension and a state of dissatisfaction until Jim presents the problem and suggested action to management with a goal of eliminating the problem.

As Figure 12.3 shows, Jim's goal-directed behavior reached a barrier

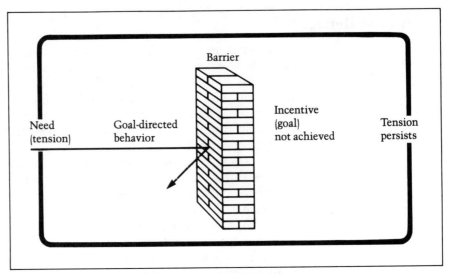

Figure 12.3 · Goal-Directed Behavior Prevented by Barrier

Source: Based on an idea from H. J. Leavitt, *Managerial Psychology*, 3rd ed. (Chicago: University of Chicago Press, 1972), p. 8. Redrawn from figure by Bruce Stevens. Used by permission of Southwestern Publishers.

when his changes were pigeon-holed or denied. As the tension built, he demonstrated his frustration through displays of temper. Finally, when he found no advantages to pursuing his goals, he redirected his behavior to satisfy personal needs. The results were nonproductive for the organization as well as for the individuals within it.

What is management's role in this situation? Jim is now a demotivated employee. Once management recognizes the signs—low morale and low productivity—it will have to determine how to regain former levels of performance.

Symptoms of Low Motivation

Individual symptoms of low motivation can be easily observed: Apathy, boredom, inattention, lack of concentration, intentional resistance, waste, sabotage, errors, time-wasting, and resistance to change are but a few. Others are tardiness, absenteeism, excessive sick leave, conflict, tendency to leave the work station, withholding resources, and lack of commitment to the organizational goals.

In addition to individual symptoms, organizational symptoms of low motivation can arise. Generally low morale, high waste costs, overall attendance problems, high health insurance costs, high turnover, high training costs, and adversarial management/labor relations are all indications of low motivation.

People are unique resources. They have different backgrounds and experiences, different needs and desires. Yet the manager must coordinate the efforts of all employees toward some goal. Before any person makes an effort to achieve the goal, she must *want* to cooperate. The manager, therefore, is faced with the dilemma of determining the factors that motivate employees to desire to behave in ways that will accomplish organizational goals.

Take a moment to consider what makes you want to act. What motivates you? Is it a challenging assignment? Recognition? A high performance evaluation? The possibility of improving your status? Compare your responses to these questions with those of your peers. Do they feel the same as you do? Probably not. Each of us has different values and needs. The manager's role is to determine what motivates and what "turns off" each employee. It is not unusual for a company to spend thousands of dollars to orient and train a new employee, but productivity losses due to high turnover add an additional burden. Losing good employees is costly. It is good business to maintain a motivated work force.

Theories of Motivation

A number of theories of motivation can help the manager determine ways to motivate individual workers. This section reviews three types of motivational theories: (1) content theories, (2) expectancy theories, and (3) equity theories. Each of the theories has strengths and limitations.

Maslow's Hierarchy of Needs[12]

Because of its ease of application, one of the most popular theories is Abraham Maslow's hierarchy of needs. Maslow based the hierarchy on his clinical observations of human behavior. In it he described two categories of needs. A model depicting the basic and secondary needs can be found in Figure 13.1 on page 359.

The Basic Needs

Maslow identified two levels of basic needs: physiological needs and security needs. The hierarchy implies that these needs must be satisfied before people can move to higher-level needs.

Physiological needs are those most essential to survival. They consist of hunger, thirst, clean air to breathe, rest, sexual fulfillment, and relief from pain. Based on his observations, Maslow concluded that tired, hungry, frustrated people concentrate their efforts on relieving their pain before they attempt to satisfy or even recognize higher-level needs.

Safety and security needs include stability and protection from danger and potential harm. An employee threatened by a lay-off or job termination will tend to channel personal efforts into finding a more secure work environment. Quality of work, productivity, and interpersonal relationships have little value under these circumstances.

The Secondary Needs

The next three levels of the pyramid identify secondary needs. These needs may directly affect individual productivity, but they will not be operational unless the basic needs are satisfied.

Belonging means that people depend on other people to help fulfill a need to identify with and belong to a group. People seek friendships, religious affiliations, and professional organizations for personal gratification. A manager must recognize his employees' desire to belong. New employees need to be reassured about their surroundings, instructed on the tasks they must accomplish, and become comfortable with co-workers. In his communication a manager must clarify his expectations, maintain a congenial work climate, and prevent bickering and isolation of employees. Attempts should be made to develop group cohesiveness, team atmosphere, peer recognition, and acceptance.

Ego or esteem needs relate to one's sense of value and worth. It is the feeling of being adequate, competent, and admired. Esteem can be internal or external. While the internal focuses on a self-respect for our own abilities and work-worth, the external sees appreciation and importance coming from superiors and peers. Esteem needs differ from social needs, since they are based on achievements. The manager needs to communicate to employees that their efforts are valued. A simple "thank-you" shows both recognition and appreciation. Recognizing an extra effort reinforces positive behavior and encourages employees to achieve.

Self-actualization is attaining mastery of a particular skill or profession and achieving life goals and self-control. Individuals who dedicate their lives to a particular goal and profession have strong needs for self-actualization. While self-actualization is the highest level of need according to Maslow's hierarchy, it is also the weakest. All of the other needs must be fairly well satisfied before the need to self-actualize emerges. It goes beyond recognition of achievements to the striving to realize full potential.

Postulates

The hierarchy visually reinforces the theory that people strive to satisfy the basic needs before secondary needs take root and motivate. In the United States about 85 percent of the basic needs are met and are therefore not powerful motivators in most organizations. In contrast only 50 percent of the social and 40 percent of the esteem needs are satisfied.[13]

Maslow recognized that each level of need was individually dependent. For example, some workers prefer to work alone with little supervision. Their need for social interaction is minimal. Others have maximum needs for acceptance and recognition and look for social interaction opportunities. Need levels are constantly in a state of change. Today your need for recognition and belonging may be minimal. Tomorrow or a week from now, you may feel the need to be rewarded for accomplishing a difficult and complex task that requires discipline and concentration of effort.

Need levels are permeable and not necessarily sequential. A professional may be absorbed in solving a theoretical problem (self-actualizing) and suddenly find herself suffering from hunger pains (physiological). Once she has eaten, she may need to meet with a co-worker with whom current relations have been tense (social). She may even satisfy two needs at once by eating lunch with the co-worker.

Herzberg's Motivation-Hygiene Model[14]

Drawing heavily from Maslow, Frederick Herzberg developed the motivation-hygiene theory. He emphasized that real motivation to do a better job depends on *growth* factors: those actions that result in a sense of achievement to the worker. According to Herzberg, true motivation is found in the challenge of the job itself or the internal experiences of the employee in completing the task. You probably have experienced pride when accomplishing a task that was particularly rewarding, whether it was playing an instrument or completing a challenging research assignment.

Herzberg also believed that factors surrounding the job—such as office accommodations, working conditions, and pay—result in unhappy or dissatisfied workers. If an employee works under conditions of poor lighting, extreme temperatures, dirty rest rooms, low pay, and no support, he or she may decide that the challenge of certain tasks isn't worth the aggravation. Areas to consider as hygiene factors are:

1. *Working conditions:* Employees may voice open concerns about lighting, temperature, space, lunchrooms, supplies, and so forth.

2. *Company policy and administration:* Rules, practices and policies may affect the work group, such as parking, work hours, lunch schedules, job rotation, and benefits.

3. *Interpersonal relationships:* The organizational climate is influenced by the quality and compatibility of its employee relationships.

Figure 12.4

Source: Redrawn from a cartoon in Jack Halloran, *Applied Human Relations: An Organizational Approach* (Englewood Cliffs, N.J.: Prentice-Hall, 1978), p. 96. Reprinted by permission of Prentice-Hall, Inc.

Good hygiene factors rarely motivate workers to perform better. A nice office, the name on the door, an excellent secretary, a high salary, and a key to the executive washroom can provide a pleasant environment, but they don't motivate. Good hygiene factors make the work environment more pleasant and prevent *dissatisfaction*. Herzberg made the analogy that garbage collection doesn't make people healthy; it just keeps them from being unhealthy. Motivators or satisfiers cause people to perform in a superior manner. Distinct from hygiene factors, motivators include the work itself, achievement, recognition, responsibility, growth, and advancement. In addition, motivators have a long-term impact on employee attitudes as opposed to the short-term impact of hygiene factors.

Motivation Factors (Motivators)	Hygiene Factors (Dissatisfiers)
(Job Content)	(Job Environment)
Work itself	Company policy
Achievement	Supervision
Recognition	Working conditions
Growth and advancement	Interpersonal relationships
	Salary

Herzberg advocates strategies to provide a "quick fix." Notice his emphasis on communication in each strategy.

1. Decide which concerns within working conditions can be eliminated and fix them. Their removal will advertise your concern.
2. If you aren't sure what concerns the group has, ask. Change for the sake of change can lead to confusion and larger problems.
3. Evaluate the climate of your organization and resolve serious personal conflicts. Express your concern and the negative effect of the conflict on the group. Insist that problems be resolved.
4. Rotate jobs between people who must interact with others so they can learn and appreciate the value of the others to the group.

In summary, motivation factors involve job content, while hygiene factors involve job environment. Excellent hygiene factors do not motivate people: They prevent unhappiness or dissatisfaction. Motivators unleash potential to perform in a superior manner but do not eliminate dissatisfaction.

McClelland's Needs Theory[15]

Considerable research has been conducted on David C. McClelland's needs theory of motivation. McClelland, of Harvard University, identified three basic motivating needs: power, achievement, and affiliation. All three must be recognized by management as essential to the effective operation of any organization.

Need for Power

The need for power is readily observable in U.S. society; the politician is an obvious example. Power is defined as the need to exert influence or control over people. It is the ability to manipulate or change others and can be found in many forms in the organization. The manager's ability to give promotions, merit increases, or other rewards is a form of power.

Power is not necessarily defined by a person's position in the organization. Some managers have very little power; they assume their role by name only. Power depends on the person, the situation, and the problem.

Studies have shown that expert power—the expertise and knowledge of the individual—had the strongest correlation with satisfaction and performance, and position power was the main reason for compliance with a supervisor's requests. Finally, coercive power, or the ability to administer a negative reward, was the least effective reason for compliance and had negative correlations with organizational effectiveness.

Need for Achievement

While the recognition of power needs is relatively recent, long-term interest has led to a preponderance of research on the need for achievement. Achievement is the need for mastery and the desire to succeed in competitive situations. More specific characteristics can be summarized as follows:[16]

1. *The willingness to take moderate risks:* In contrast low achievers take either a high or low risk.
2. *The desire for immediate feedback:* Persons with high achievement needs tend to select occupations that provide immediate and specific feedback on performance.
3. *The need for accomplishment:* Completion of a task is satisfying in itself. Rewards are not essential.
4. *Involvement in the task:* High achievers tend to become totally absorbed with a task and concentrate efforts on its completion.

Need for Affiliation

People who need affiliation desire love and acceptance from a social group. They enjoy friendly interaction, desire intimacy, and are strongly drawn to helping others.

Other Approaches: Expectancies and Equity

In contrast to the content theories of Maslow, Herzberg, and McClelland, expectancy theory is based on the idea that in addition to basic needs and drives, an individual *must* consider and decide how he or she will act. Consider the following situation.

Judy was an extremely competent employee with superior office skills. After working for an oil company for twelve years, she reached the top of her promotional ladder as a secretary. Her boss recognized her capabilities, expanded her job duties, and trained her in tasks that could be handled by employees with stiffer job requirements. Judy relished the opportunity and soon mastered her new tasks. It became apparent, however, that the organization would not reclassify her into a position in which she could make more money and have greater job opportunities. Several requests submitted by her boss were denied. Suddenly, Judy's boss noticed behavior changes. Judy would delay or disregard requests. She was frequently found in lengthy conversations that were not job-related. The quality of her daily work suffered.

Judy's boss took her aside and pointed out the problems she had noticed. In addition, she told Judy that any opportunities for future promotions would depend on how Judy handled her current job.

How will Judy react? Will she "shape-up" and improve her performance in expectation of a promotion in the near future? Maslow and Herzberg would say that we should evaluate the needs that are most important to Judy and use these as keys to motivation, but perhaps an approach that considers employee expectations would be more effective.

The content theories assume that all individuals are alike and that all situations are similar—with one right way to motivate individuals. Expectancy theories recognize that all situations differ and that because of these differences, the combination of individual experiences and expectations will affect how employees respond to the work environment.

Vroom's process recognizes that employees evaluate alternatives *before* performing. This decision is a result of their expectations. How much an individual "wants" something determines the "force" or "valence" of the drive.[17]

At this point let us clarify the difference between incentive and reward. *Rewards* are given on the completion of a desired behavior. Promotions, bonuses, titles, letters of recognition, and pats on the back are all forms of rewards. An incentive is something that has the potential to become a reward once the task is complete. It is an *identified* potential reward. Both incentives and rewards are identified and administered by someone other than the person receiving them.

A final word on Vroom's theory is essential. An individual may desire two different outcomes. First, *intrinsic* rewards relate to the nature of the work itself. Is it interesting? challenging? Second, *extrinsic* rewards relate to factors surrounding the work, such as salary increases and working conditions. The desire for extrinsic rewards usually occurs with work that has low levels of intrinsic motivational factors. Extrinsic rewards are an attempt to make up for the type of work. This is the reason that you hear about hazardous duty pay or piece workers who receive substantial hourly salaries. Research on the expectancy model confirms that intrinsic rewards are derived from the work itself and that extrinsic rewards are the result of performance.

Utilizing the basic premise of the Vroom theory, Porter and Lawler expand on the concept by recognizing the relationship between satisfaction and performance.[18] While Herzberg's model describes a theory of job satisfaction, it does not relate satisfaction to performance. Porter and Lawler deal directly with this relationship and present a model that is practical in its application.

Porter and Lawler point out that neither force nor effort leads to performance. The abilities and role perceptions of the person act as variables and mediate performance; it is the performance itself that leads to satisfaction. Their theory is expectancy-based because it examines the process that leads to need fulfillment. It includes the anticipation and choice/alternative aspect that is not considered by content theories.

Adams's equity theory expands on the variable of individual perception and decision making.[19] It asserts that one individual will compare work output and resulting rewards to that of another individual in a similar job situation and that people will strive to restore equity if they feel inequity exists. The following formula expresses this concept:

$$\frac{\text{Outcomes}}{\text{The individual's own inputs}} = \frac{\text{Outcomes}}{\text{A comparable individual's inputs}}$$

Individual inputs can include age, sex, education, experience, qualifications, organizational status, and effectiveness. The outcomes are primarily rewards such as pay status, promotion, or type of work. Keep in mind that the ratio is based on how the person *perceives* her or his inputs/outputs and others' inputs/outputs. If you perceive that you are working harder and receiving less pay for your efforts than an individual in a comparable job, equity will not exist. Unless you perceive a balance, you will attempt to restore equity. Such attempts may include working more or less efficiently, sabotaging another's work, attempting to manipulate perceptions of the other person's work, or placing pressure on the other person to minimize his efforts.

Failure to establish equity can create discord in the organization. If an engineer with ten years of experience discovers that a recent graduate has been hired at the same salary but lacks the knowledge and skill to perform the work, dissonance will occur. She or he might complain to management, refuse to help train or coach the new employee, or encourage other experienced engineers to file a grievance.

Laboratory research testifies to the validity of Adams's theory, and it receives some support from field studies.[20] In fact, employees who perceive that they are overpaid will *increase* their output in order to restore equity. Employees who are underpaid will decrease output until it is in balance with compensation.

Job Satisfaction
Work in the 1980s

Daniel Yankelovich conducted a study of job satisfaction and productivity and found evidence that the link between performance and rewards has been seriously overemphasized. Over 60 percent of the employees surveyed wanted jobs that resulted in payment commensurate with their performance, yet less than one-fourth of these employees saw this connection in their present jobs. Another conclusion was that while managers assume productivity and job satisfaction are positively linked, this is not necessarily true. Satisfaction more likely results in minimal improvement or no change in productivity.

Tables 12.1 and 12.2 identify the top ten motivators and satisfiers for managers and professionals, blue-collar workers, and clerical workers. Ambition tops the list along with the importance of the content of the job itself. The implications of these findings should be carefully considered by managers attempting to automate. Clerical workers must have opportunities for advancement, creativity, and challenge, but minute, repetitive tasks restrict these opportunities.

Intrinsic rewards appear to be the key motivators. This is given even more support by the survey of best-run companies in the book, *In Search*

Table 12.1 • Public Agenda Foundation Survey of Motivators: The Top Ten Motivators

Managers and Professionals		Blue-Collar Workers		Clerical Workers
Men	*Women*	*Men*	*Women*	*Women*
A good chance for advancement (48%/29%)*	A good chance for advancement (47%/22%)*	Good pay (50%/22%)*	Good pay (44%/28%)*	A good chance for advancement (56%/19%)*
A great deal of responsibility (45/28)	A job that enables me to develop my abilities (44/18)*	A good chance for advancement (47/23)*	A good chance for advancement (42/17)*	A job that enables me to develop my abilities (52/24)
Recognition for good work (44/32)*	Recognition for good work (43/30)*	Pay tied to performance (47/28)*	Pay tied to performance (41/30)*	A challenging job (47/23)
A job where I can think for myself (44/29)	A great deal of responsibility (40/22)	Recognition for good work (42/37)*	A challenging job (37/23)	A job where I can think for myself (45/21)
A job that enables me to develop my abilities (42/28)*	A job where I can think for myself (38/33)	Interesting work (38/34)*	A job where I can think for myself (35/29)	A job that allows me to be creative (45/25)
A challenging job (42/29)	Good pay (37/30)*	See end results of my efforts (38/32)	Interesting work (35/28)*	See the end results of my efforts (45/30)
A job that allows me to be creative (41/29)	Pay tied to performance (37/33)	A job that enables me to develop my abilities (36/29)	A job that enables me to develop my abilities (34/27)	Good pay (42/35)*
A job with pay tied to performance (40/39)*	A challenging job (35/25)	A challenging job (34/38)	See end results of my efforts (34/31)	A great deal of responsibility (42/37)
A say in important decisions (39/33)	A say in important decisions (32/33)	A job that allows me to be creative (34/34)	A job that allows me to be creative (33/33)	Recognition for good work (39/32)*
A place that does quality work (39/29)	A place that does quality work (32/32)	A job where I can think for myself (33/39)*	Recognition for good work (32/39)*	Interesting work (37/41)*

The first figure in parentheses is the percentage in the group that rated this factor a motivator; the second shows those who called it a satisfier.

* Items marked with an asterisk were on the list of the top-ten job features this group of workers most wanted more of.

Source: "Survey: Work in the 1980s and 1990s," *Working Woman,* July 1983, p. 16. Reprinted by permission.

Table 12.2 • Public Agenda Foundation Survey of Satisfiers: The Top Ten Satisfiers

Managers and Professionals		Blue-Collar Workers		Clerical Workers
Men	*Women*	*Men*	*Women*	*Women*
Job without too much rush and stress (71%/6%)	Job without too much rush and stress (57%/15%)	Job without too much rush and stress (57%/20%)	Job without too much rush and stress (55%/20%)	Convenient location (69%/13%)
Good working conditions (67/9)	People really care about me as a person (57/12)	Good working conditions (57/13)	Being informed about what goes on (55/10)	Working with people I like (69/8)
Convenient location (65/9)	Working with people I like (56/14)	Convenient location (53/10)	Getting along well with supervisor (51/17)	Job without too much rush and stress (66/12)
Being able to control work pace (61/9)	Convenient location (55/12)	Working with people I like (52/22)	Working with people I like (48/16)	Being able to control work pace (62/8)
Flexible working hours (61/15)	Getting along well with supervisor (54/17)	Getting along well with supervisor (52/20)	Flexible working hours (48/11)	Good working conditions (60/14)
Working with people I like (56/15)	Good fringe benefits (52/21)*	Being informed about what goes on (50/19)	Being able to control work pace (45/19)	Informal work environment (59/16)
Good fringe benefits (53/25)*	Job security, little chance of being laid off (52/27)	People who listen to your ideas (50/28)	People treat me with respect (45/17)*	All the tools I need to do my job (59/21)
Never asked to do anything improper or immoral (53/11)	Good working conditions (51/11)	Informal work environment (49/7)	Convenient location (44/14)	Efficient, effective managers (58/20)
Place I'm so proud of I want everyone to know I work there (53/20)	Never asked to do anything improper or immoral (50/15)	Being able to control work pace (47/29)	Good working conditions (44/14)	Fair treatment (54/15)*
Employer with good reputation (52/21)	Flexible working hours (48/19)	Fair treatment (46/26)	People who listen to your ideas (44/17)	Getting along well with supervisor (54/27)

The first figure in parentheses is the percentage of the group that rated this factor a satisfier; the second is the percentage that rated it a motivator.
* Items marked with an asterisk were on the list of the top-ten job features this group of workers most wanted more of.

Source: "Survey: Work in the 1980s and 1990s." Reprinted by permission.

of Excellence. Peters and Waterman found that excellent companies design reward systems that continually reinforce the concept that their employees are winners, not losers. Employees make and exceed targets and quotas that are set to allow and encourage that success. They cite an example:

> In the not-so-excellent companies, the reverse is true. While IBM explicitly manages to ensure that 70 to 80 percent of its salespeople meet quotas, another company (an IBM competitor in part of its product line) works it so that only 40 percent of the sales force meets its quotas during a typical year. With this approach, at least 60 percent of the salespeople think of themselves as losers. They resent it and that leads to dysfunctional, unpredictable, frenetic behavior.[21]

A review of the top ten satisfiers reinforces Herzberg's theory. When certain factors such as job benefits and job security reach unacceptable levels, this will have negative effects on productivity. Attention to these factors is important.

Research by William F. Whyte concluded that only 10 percent of the United States work force is most motivated by monetary incentives.[22] Three factors found to be more important motivators were:

1. Pitting oneself against a performance standard;
2. Escape from close supervision (working independently, participating in decisions, responsibility, and authority);
3. A regular fast pace (less fatiguing and more motivating than a slow or erratic pace).

Whyte found that power was the strongest motivator.

The most motivating work, then, addresses the highest level needs: self-esteem (satisfaction, recognition, meaning) and self-actualization (achievement and freedom). Its characteristics are *meaning* and *freedom.* On one hand the individual finds the work personally satisfying, important, or interesting; on the other hand the individual can work independently, without close supervision, has a voice in work-related decisions, and has responsibility and authority.

Communication as a Source of Job Satisfaction

Fundamental to the relationship between subordinate and supervisor or co-workers, communication satisfaction is a desirable end result in itself. Researchers have discovered that it is a major factor of job satisfaction.

Three dimensions of communication satisfaction have a high correlation with job satisfaction. *Communication climate* is one of the most important of these dimensions. Employees need to be part of a climate that stimulates, motivates, and encourages identification with the organization. Another important dimension is the *personal feedback* that tells them the performance standards and how well they are meeting the standards. The third dimension is the employee's *relationship with the superior.* In addition to the upward and downward flow of communication, this dimension includes the supervisor's openness to new ideas, willingness to listen, and assistance with problem solving.[23]

Robert C. Miljus determined steps to be taken to create and maintain a meaningful climate. According to Miljus, an effective manager must create a supportive environment in which employees can satisfy personal needs and contribute to organizational objectives at the same time. He outlined the following steps for the manager:[24]

1. Determine realistic resources;
2. Provide necessary resources;
3. Make expectations known;
4. Provide adequate reward structure;
5. Delegate authority and invite participation;
6. Remove barriers to effective performance;
7. Appraise performance and communicate results;
8. Show consideration for employees.

Fundamental Considerations

The manager should observe some fundamental considerations in any effort to increase motivation. First, take time to get to know personnel and let them get to know you. In order to understand individual needs and determine individual incentives, you must create an interpersonal relationship through which employees can express their feelings, wants, and needs.

Second, adjust the motivational approach used with each person or group. Recognize that people are different and want to be recognized and treated as such.

Third, give and receive prompt and regular feedback of results. Feedback should be specific. An employee needs a referent in order to understand how to improve performance. Tell him or her exactly what is wrong or right about an action.

Fourth, realize that people don't always react according to your expectations. Intervening circumstances, of which you may have no knowledge, will act as variables of behavior. In addition, reality may be perceived differently by each individual. As a result, they will behave in response to their perceptions of facts or situations.

Finally, managers should reward performance improvement with recognition and praise. One of the highest-ranked needs of personnel in Yankelovich's nationwide survey was full appreciation of work done. Behavior that is rewarded tends to be repeated.

Summary

The characteristics of effective leadership are leadership competence, a positive organizational climate, recognition of the worth and uniqueness of the individual, and an openness in communication.

Leadership Competence

A leader must be recognized as being competent to do the job and must have the intelligence and skill necessary for effective performance, a grasp of the importance of effective problem analysis, and the desire to gather information for intelligent decision making. Finally, the competent leader realizes that the knowledge of the group is greater than any one person within the group and uses the input and problem-solving skills of his or her subordinates.

Organizational Climate

The competent leader cultivates an organizational climate conducive to productivity, which includes fostering a sense of well-being and satisfaction. Opportunities for achievement and self-actualization are provided, and cooperation, collectivism, and teamwork are nourished. Each subordinate is recognized as an individual with unique needs. Trust, equality, and mutual respect are underlying principles in the superior/subordinate relationship. A democratic, theory Y approach to management predominates. Power is distributed through participation in decision making and delegation of authority.

Individual Worth

An effective leader realizes that each person has individual worth and can contribute to the organization's success. In some cases a star performer will assist in setting standards and goals. In other cases an employee with strong social needs may assist in attaining outlets for employee relationships and cohesiveness. Others may contribute to recognizing environmental needs or eliminating obstacles by bringing them to the manager's attention. Whatever his or her role, each employee has the potential to contribute to the organizational whole.

Open Communication

Effective leadership depends on having information necessary to effective decision making. An effective leader encourages open, direct, accurate communication. In addition he solicits negative feedback as well as positive feedback. Information exchange flows vertically, horizontally, and functionally. Finally, he listens to subordinates and by doing so gains information, confidence, support, and understanding of their needs, desires, fears, and obstacles to performance.

Key Words

leadership trait	contingency theory	Maslow's hierarchy
leadership style	LEAD	Herzberg's
authoritarian	competence	motivation-hygiene
leadership	Tannenbaum/Schmidt	model
democratic leadership	continuum	McClelland's needs
participative	motive	theory
leadership	need	communication
laissez-faire leadership	drive	satisfaction
functional leadership	goal	expectancy and equity
situational leadership	intrinsic rewards	theories
path-goal leadership	extrinsic rewards	

Review Questions

1. What is the trait theory of leadership? Identify the four universal traits as defined by Keith Davis. What are the limitations of the trait theory of leadership?
2. Hersey and Blanchard present two dimensions of leadership—task and relationship. What are some others?
3. Explain the difference between a leader and a manager. Can you be both? Explain your answer.
4. What are the predominant leadership styles of the following people?
   a. The President of the United States
   b. A member of the United States Senate or House of Representatives

c. The president of your company or university
d. Your immediate boss and one of equal status
e. Someone you greatly respect

5. What is the contingency approach to leadership? Explain Fiedler's model.

6. Define path-goal leadership theory. What are its four styles and two situational factors?

7. What are the basic leadership behavior styles described by Hersey and Blanchard? How do they relate to the maturity of the employee?

8. What keys to leadership effectiveness do the theories presented seem to have in common? How do they differ?

9. Discuss the importance of the following:
   a. Communication satisfaction
   b. Job satisfaction
   c. Motivators

10. What is the difference between an intrinsic and an extrinsic reward? Give examples of each. Which jobs have extrinsic rewards? Which jobs have intrinsic rewards?

11. Explain goal-directed behavior. What happens when a barrier intervenes? Give an example.

12. What are five fundamental considerations concerning motivation that are important to the manager? What considerations do you feel are important to the worker?

13. Which need is satisfied by money?

14. Give examples of incentives that are motivators for each of the following:
    a. salesman
    b. college professor
    c. legislator
    d. doctor
    e. high school senior
    f. secretary
    g. executive
    h. mechanic

15. Given Herzberg's theory, are the following hygiene factors or motivators?
    a. coffee breaks
    b. flextime
    c. merit raise
    d. promotion

Exercises

1. Take a few minutes and consider the material you have read in this chapter on leadership. Now think about the many leaders that you have come in contact with during your lifetime. Some are in the business world, some in the aca-

demic arena, and many in politics. What are some common characteristics about these leaders? Share your thoughts with some of your classmates. See if they have picked the same leaders and the same characteristics.

2. Spend some time observing a leader in action during a meeting. Does the person utilize task or maintenance behavior in working with the other members? How would the opposite type of behavior be interpreted and accepted by the group?

3. You accepted a job with a large accounting firm in 1982 as a junior member even though you had several years of experience with a small firm. Many of your peers earn several thousand dollars more even though they have less experience. You become acutely aware that you are just as competent, if not more so, than they are. As a matter of fact, you find you are carrying a heavier workload. Because of the promotion policies of the firm, it is not likely that you will ever "catch up" in salary earnings. How do you feel about this situation? What can you do about it?

4. Lately, you've noticed one of your clerks hanging around the coffee pot in your secretary's office, yet her unit is shorthanded and her supervisor, your subordinate, is coping with some personal hardships. Investigating the situation you find the clerk (1) has a college degree, (2) is earning several thousand dollars less than other employees in your organization with degrees, (3) does not get along with her supervisor, (4) has been involved in numerous interpersonal conflicts with clients and staff members, (5) openly criticizes the organization, and (6) is seeking employment elsewhere. Define the problem. What can you do about it?

References

1. Warren Bennis, "Leadership: A Beleaguered Species?" in *Intercom: Readings in Organizational Communication,* Stewart Ferguson and Sherry Devereaux Ferguson, eds. (Rochelle Park, N.J.: Hayden, 1980), p. 159.

2. Bennis, "Leadership," p. 159.

3. Fred Luthans, *Organizational Behavior,* 3rd ed. (New York: McGraw-Hill, 1981), p. 419.

4. Keith Davis, *Human Behavior at Work,* 4th ed. (New York: McGraw-Hill, 1972), pp. 103–104.

5. John G. Geier, "A Trait Approach to the Study of Leadership in Small Groups," *Journal of Communication,* 17 (1967), pp. 316–23.

6. Hugh C. Russell, "An Investigation of Leadership Maintenance Behavior." Ph.D. dissertation, Indiana University, 1970.

7. Robert Tannenbaum and Warren H. Schmidt, "How to Choose a Leadership Pattern," *Harvard Business Review* (March/April 1958), p. 96.

8. Douglas McGregor, *The Human Side of Enterprise* (New York: McGraw-Hill, 1960).

9. Fred E. Fiedler, *A Theory of Leadership Effectiveness* (New York: McGraw-Hill, 1967), pp. 142–48.

10. Robert J. House and Terence R. Mitchell, "Path-Goal Theory of Leadership," *Journal of Contemporary Business* (Autumn 1974), pp. 81–97.

11. Paul Hersey and Kenneth H. Blanchard, *Management of Organizational Behavior*, 2nd ed. (Englewood Cliffs, N.J.: Prentice-Hall, 1972), pp. 72–87.

12. A. H. Maslow, "A Theory of Human Motivation," *Psychological Review* (July 1943), pp. 370–96.

13. Theodore T. Herbert, *Dimensions of Organizational Behavior*, 2nd ed. (New York: MacMillan, 1981), pp. 225–27.

14. Frederick Herzberg, *Work and the Nature of Man* (Cleveland: World Publishers, 1966).

15. David C. McClelland, *The Achievement Motive* (New York: Appleton-Century-Crofts, 1955); *Studies in Motivation* (New York: Appleton-Century-Crofts, 1955); *The Achieving Society* (Princeton, N.J.: D. Van Nostrand, 1961).

16. Saul W. Gellerman, *Motivation and Productivity* (New York: American Management Association, 1963).

17. Victor H. Vroom, *Work and Motivation* (New York: John Wiley, 1964).

18. Lyman Porter, Edward E. Lawler III, and J. Richard Hackman, *Behavior in Organizations* (New York: McGraw-Hill, 1975).

19. Stacy Adams, "Inequity in Social Exchange," in L. Berkowitz, ed., *Advances in Experimental Social Psychology* (New York: Academic Press, 1965), pp. 267–99.

20. Fred Luthans, *Organizational Behavior*, pp. 197–99.

21. Thomas J. Peters and Robert H. Waterman, Jr., *In Search of Excellence* (New York: Harper & Row, 1982), p. 57.

22. William H. Whyte, *The Organization Man* (New York: Simon & Schuster, 1956).

23. Cal W. Downs, "The Relationship between Communication and Job Satisfaction," in Richard C. Huseman, Cal M. Logue, and Dwight L. Freshley, eds., *Readings in Interpersonal and Organizational Communication*, 3rd ed. (Boston: Holbrook Press, 1977), pp. 363–76.

24. R. C. Miljus, "Effective Leadership and Motivation of Human Resources," *Personnel Journal* (January 1970), pp. 36–40.

The Communicating Manager as a Decision-Making Problem Solver

Introduction

Most managers have faced the following problem more than once.

When Theresa Osmond is promoted to manage a group of ten employees, both her boss and the outgoing supervisor brief her on the group. The supervisor's closing remarks are, "In a nutshell, while the group is very capable, their productivity won't improve unless a way is found to get rid of John Eckland. We've tried every theory in the book with no success. His performance is poor and negatively affects the entire group."

After asking a few questions and reviewing the personnel files on Eckland, Osmond discovers that he has been given training, one-to-one supervision, and counseling. He showed some improvement after these but quickly went back to his old patterns.

Should Theresa act on the advice of her boss and the former supervisor to get rid of John? Perhaps her style of supervision will alter the situation. Maybe she needs to hear Eckland's side of it or observe his behavior before making a decision. Theresa faces a dilemma and needs to carefully weigh the alternatives before making a decision.

Every day you are faced with numerous decisions: What to wear? What to eat? Who to contact to get information or assistance? Many of these decisions are made instantly. Decision making is a critical element of planning, guiding, and problem solving. Managers are faced daily with activities that call for decisions of various complexities to be made. No matter what course of action the manager selects, it will directly or indirectly affect the organization.[1] For this reason, you need to understand the types of decision making and when to use them. This chapter reviews the three types of decision making and presents a model for generating ideas for problem solving.

Types of Decision Making

In the period of an hour, a manager may encounter problems ranging from a budget meeting involving the investment of millions of dollars to a discussion about who will be in charge of planning the Christmas party. Problems do not often easily identify themselves, but usually there are indicators to show that things are not as they should be. A *problem* is the difference between the existing situation and the desired situation, whether it means that something needs fixing or that there is an opportunity to improve current operations. In the opening case Theresa Osmond must decide how to improve the productivity of her group. To do this, she must first determine who should be involved in the decision-making process. She has three alternatives: (1) make the decision herself, (2) involve the group, or (3) hire a consultant.

Maximizing the effectiveness of both quality and acceptance of a decision is important. If the task is complex, the manager would be more likely to select the group decision-making process. However, if the knowledge needed to resolve the problem is not available from those in the group, the manager makes the decision or an outside resource is used.

Research indicates that creative or independent tasks are best performed by individuals. Tasks that involve integrative functions of the organization or goal setting are more appropriate for groups. A manager may be willing to make a decision that is unpopular when it is known that the decision requires the input of an expert. Any decision, therefore, needs to be weighed considering the following factors:

1. The nature of the task;
2. How important the acceptance of the decision is to its implementation;
3. The value placed on the quality of the decision;
4. The competency and investment of each person involved, and the role played in implementing the decision;
5. The anticipated operating effectiveness of the group, especially its leadership.[2]

Self Decision Making

Managers are paid to make decisions and solve problems. Sometimes they have the input of others to help them. Often they must make decisions alone. A manager who says, "Complete this report by March 15," is using a command. Often managers rely on personal experience and knowledge for decisions. Based on this experience and knowledge, the command allows the manager to act quickly and decisively.

Managers use the command when it is necessary to take immediate action. When an employee working on a very important project suddenly becomes ill, the manager must quickly decide who will substitute so that the project can be completed. The manager knows the capabilities of his or her staff, and the staff in turn understands that in a critical situation someone must help with the workload. Little time may be available for discussion or input from group members. The manager may issue a direct command, "Joe, you'll fill in for Sam this week." In this situation acceptance of the decision will probably be high, since the employees understand the constraints. Unless the manager has high credibility with subordinates, lack of understanding and an unwillingness to participate may hinder implementation of the decision. This is especially true if the decision requires complex procedures and strategies for implementation.

Group Decision Making

Group decision making is most effective when the need for acceptance is high or the task is complex. There are numerous advantages to this approach. For example, a group represents more knowledge than any one person in the group. Because the group works together to solve the problem, it promotes greater understanding and acceptance of ideas and solutions. The differing backgrounds, experiences, and education represented by the membership leads to a greater variety of ideas and solutions. There are fewer communication problems because the participants have actually thought through and worked together to evaluate, analyze, and implement the solutions. The solutions are usually solid because the group tests ideas from multiple viewpoints.

The manager may choose to delegate decision making to a committee, voluntary group, or group of specialists. When two or more people work together to reach a goal, they act as a group. In order to make a decision, several approaches may be used: consensus, compromise, or majority rule.

Consensus

Consensus decision making means that everyone in the group can live with the solution. There is no voting or compromise. Group members are encouraged not to compete internally, since no one wins or loses. Quick, early decisions and agreements are discouraged, and the group is encouraged to challenge and test the ideas of each of its members. The most important characteristics of the consensus group approach is that members listen and pay attention to what each has to say. The quiet members are encouraged to participate and offer their ideas. When the group gets to the point where each person can say, "Although this may not be everything I want, I can accept and support this decision," then the group has reached consensus.[3]

The consensus group should have a workable number of members. The ideal membership is about five,[4] which gives every member an opportunity to participate in a lively interchange of ideas. If groups get too large, it finds it difficult to reach agreement and may have to resort to other forms of decision making.

Compromise

Each party involved in the decision gives up something or gains something, as in union negotiating or in bartering. The compromise may result in side payments or become coercive in nature. For example, a manager may accept a new title such as assistant director in lieu of an increase in salary.[5]

Majority

When large groups are involved, it is often necessary to resort to majority rule. A vote is taken in which the majority wins and the minority loses. The disadvantages of this form of decision making are that the minority may be a substantial portion of the membership and may attempt to influence or sabotage the majority decision. Since the minority has no power, the majority may disregard the opinion of a fixed or small minority.

The outcome of any decision depends on the *quality* of the decision and the *acceptance* of the decision by the group members. All the forms of decision making discussed thus far hinge on these factors. If the quality of a decision is very poor, then it does not matter how great its acceptance is. Many groups can be very enthusiastic about a decision that has been challenged very little within the group, but this decision may in fact be very weak.

This is also true of the acceptance of a decision. We may have a high-quality decision made by a manager or consultant, as in the goal-setting example presented earlier. But if the acceptance by the organization is low, then again the task effectiveness will be poor.

Group decision making can be an exciting experience that leads to a sense of security and belonging resulting in pleasure and satisfaction to the participants. This satisfaction, if not handled well, may have harmful effects on group decision making. Irving Janis in his book *Victims of Group-Think* illustrated this point vividly. He described fiascos in governmental decisions where group pressure decreased the emphasis given to techniques that produce quality decisions. Group members emerged as "mindguards" that protected the cohesiveness of the group. The groups resisted contrary information and suppressed differing opinions. Several other studies have pointed out that groups may make riskier decisions than any one member might make individually. There is also a tendency to stereotype members in certain roles such as leaders, followers, or troublemakers.

The Consultation

When neither the manager of the organization nor the subordinates have sufficient knowledge to solve a problem, they must find another resource. That resource may be a consultant who specializes in troubleshooting technical problems by defining and analyzing the problem and then implementing the solution. The good consultant understands that acceptance of a solution by the group is critical in order to be effective. A high-quality solution could be proposed but then sabotaged if trust is not established with the group.

Consultants can help an organization clearly identify their problems from an objective viewpoint, help train employees to deal with these problems, and create a climate that contributes to effective decision making. This is particularly true in union negotiations when assistance is needed from a third party who is knowledgeable about the union and company policies and skilled in communication techniques. Consultants are used to help evaluate organizational structures and technical processes or provide expertise in any area in which the organization lacks knowledge and skill.

Creative versus Analytical Problem-Solving Phases

Right-Brain versus Left-Brain Activity

Popularly accepted views divide the brain into the logical/analytical and the sympathetic/intuitive hemispheres.[6] The left hemisphere is largely responsible for verbal, analytical, symbolic, sequential, and logical functions, while the right hemisphere is responsible for awareness, orientation, spatial relationships, emotions, and intuition. If we were to use both orientations to view the ladder of Maslow's hierarchy that was discussed in Chapter 12, it might look like the diagrams in Figure 13.1.

Dominance by left or right seems to be part of the human condition: We are right- or left-handed, -footed, -eyed, and so forth. Our dominance pattern also shows in occupational choice. An engineer, dominated by left brain functions, is likely to be logical and analytical. An artist, on the other hand, dominated by right brain functions, is usually space-, shape-, and color-oriented.

Problem Sensitivity

There is a saying that there are no new problems, just new solutions. Throughout a lifetime an individual learns many ways to do things and when a problem must be solved, applies learned responses, based on these experiences, to new ideas and solutions. Every time we turn the scope on this kaleidoscope of ideas, we view a new combination of colors that is complex and highly creative; all the colors and shapes existed previously, but the turning of the scope created the new arrangement.

To be a good problem-solver, you must first become "problem sensitive"—or aware that things are not as they should be. You must then be willing to take a new look at the world, rearranging experiences and resisting blocks to creativity. The following example is an illustration of problem sensitivity:

A student of creative problem-solving wanted to practice his creative abilities on a home problem so that his wife could appreciate creative problem solving. He noticed that his wife would remove about three inches from the small end of a ham before baking. His problem sensitivity alerted him to investigate why the end was cut off. His wife didn't know but said her mother taught her to bake ham that way. A subsequent visit disclosed that her mother did it that way because her mother had taught her to remove the end. The grandmother was then contacted to find if she knew why the end was cut off. "Sure," she said. "I didn't have a large enough roaster to take a whole ham."[7]

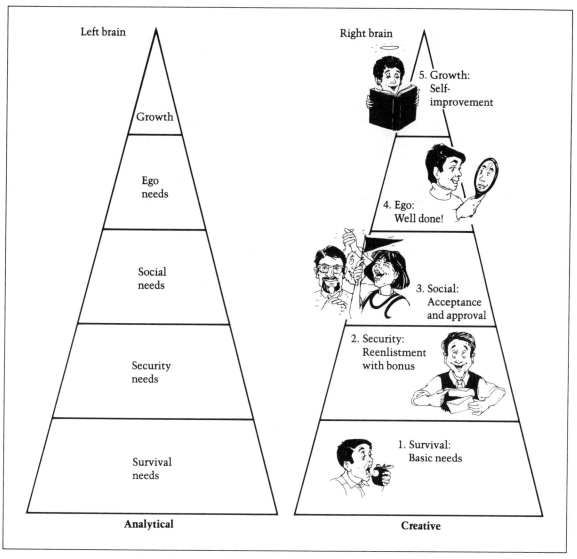

Figure 13.1

Blocks to Creativity

Before reading further, try the following exercise: "To some extent, we all consider ourselves birdwatchers. In one minute, list as many birds as you can think of." (Try to list at least thirty birds.)

Look at your list. Did you remember to list Big Bird or Woody Woodpecker? While Big Bird and Woody are indeed birds, the assumption you made was probably to list birds you would see in the outdoors. What type of bird appears at the beginning of your list? As your list lengthens, did the birds on your list become more unusual? This exercise often produces lists beginning with backyard birds and ending with exotic ones.

Language

Language is one of the primary inhibitors to problem sensitivity. It restricts and directs us with creativity-stifling comments such as "It won't work," "It costs too much," "It will never be accepted," "We tried it," or "Management won't like it." Did you wonder why birds in the backyard appeared on top of the lists? Probably because the word *birdwatchers* implied that you should respond with birds that you typically would see if you were birdwatching.

Culture

Culture is another block to creativity. Beliefs, viewpoints, experience, education, training, lifestyles, and roles all affect problem-solving behavior. Just reflect for a moment on the example of the ham and the roasting pan. Laws, rules, and procedures lay down the social do's and don'ts. From an early age we learn to conform to rules of behavior, whether we're

Source: Copyright, 1984 *USA Today*. Reprinted with permission.

eating at a table or attending a movie. Office decorum is quickly learned even though it consists of unwritten rules of behavior.

Emotions

Our problem-solving abilities are inhibited by emotions. When people are angry or fearful, they're not likely to be openminded and creative, and any attempts they make at problem solving may be futile. At a major hotel a reservation clerk handles irate customers with patience and understanding in attempts to diffuse their anger; the clerk realizes that no agreement can be reached until the customers calm down.

Creative Problem-Solving Traits

Flexibility

Flexibility is one requirement for creative problem solving. Eli Whitney utilized this trait when he was developing a mechanism to gin cotton. When a cat he was observing tried to catch a chicken through a fence, the cat's claw missed but came away with feathers. This episode led Whitney to conceive of the idea of pulling cotton through a comb.

Fluency

A second trait of creative problem solving is fluency, which refers to quantity and recall of ideas and associations. Language facility, not necessarily intelligence, is the most important characteristic of idea generation.

Originality

Originality is the ability to generate the uncommon, the remote, or the clever. It is a unique way of looking at life. Each person is unique and has the ability to provide an original experience or viewpoint. Putting feelings or ideas in one's own words can enlighten or clarify a problem.

Techniques for Generating Ideas

Brainstorming

A number of years ago Alex Osborn came up with a method to encourage the generation of ideas. He called this method brainstorming. In brainstorming, four to six group members meet to generate ideas or solutions by contributing on an equal basis. When this technique was evaluated by Dr. Sidney Parnes, it was found that groups that had more ideas had better ideas *after screening*. When deferred judgment was applied, groups generated 90 percent more good ideas. His studies also showed that the second half of the ideas generated by the group contained 78 percent more good ideas than the first half. Individuals who perform brainstorming use the principle of deferred judgment.[8]

While proposing ideas or solutions, the following rules should be observed:

1. *Criticism is ruled out.* Judgment should be suspended during this step of the process.

2. *Freewheeling is welcome.* The wilder the ideas, the better. It is easier to tame down than to think up.

3. *Quantity is desired.* The greater the number of ideas, the more likelihood of good ideas.

4. *Combination and improvement are sought.* In addition to contributing ideas of their own, group members should suggest ways others' ideas could be turned into better ideas. Two or more ideas may be combined into a still better idea. This method is called hitchhiking.

These rules, when enforced by the leader of the group, overcome many of the roadblocks to creative thinking. Ideas will flow much more freely when blocks to creativity are eliminated. The rules should be self-imposed when conducting individual brainstorming.

Synectics

Synectics is the process of bringing together previously unrelated elements or making the strange familiar. The process is attributed to W. J. J. Gordon.[9] Usually applied by a group of specifically trained people, it relies heavily on the idea of the metaphor.

The metaphor draws a direct analogy or relationship between two objects. Burns's verse, "Her lips are like a red, red rose," is an example of an analogy. The analogy helps us to link a behavior with something with which we are familiar. This eliminates our frustration and confusion in dealing with that behavior. The problem solver may attempt to *personally identify* with the problem being studied. You might imagine, for example, what it would be like to be hunted like an animal.

Another method is the *direct analogy*. In this approach, the problem might be compared with similar objects in nature. We might study the communication systems of whales or porpoises in order to get ideas for developing code systems.

Forcing Techniques

Methods designed to help ensure that all possibilities have been exhausted are called forcing techniques. They attempt to minimize chance and to recall by developing a structure to equalize consideration of all factors. The simplest form is the checklist.

Alex Osborn developed a *checklist* to be used in coordination with the brainstorming technique (see Table 13.1). The list encourages additional ideas by using key words that might trigger associations. For example, the words *adapt, minify, magnify, substitute, rearrange, combine, modify,* and *reverse* help stimulate the problem solver into looking at an idea from a new perspective.[10]

The matrix, which helps the problem solver consider ideas in combination, is the second form of the forcing technique. The structure should assist in creativity, not act to deter it. A maximum number of ideas should be stimulated by minimum structure. An example of a problem that might require this approach is, "How might Anderson Engineering

Table 13.1 • Idea-Stimulating Checklist

Put to other uses?	*Modify?*
New ways to use as is?	Change meaning, color, motion, sound, odor, taste, form, shape?
Other uses if modified?	Other changes?
Adapt?	*Magnify?*
What else is like this?	What to add?
What other ideas does this suggest?	Greater frequency?
Stronger?	
Larger?	*Substitute?*
Plus ingredient?	Who else instead?
Multiply?	What else instead?
	Other place?
Minify?	Other time?
What to subtract?	
Eliminate?	*Rearrange?*
Smaller?	Other layout?
Lighter?	Other sequence?
Slower?	Change pace?
Split up?	
Less frequent?	*Combine?*
	How about a blend, an assortment?
Reverse?	Combine purposes?
Opposites?	Combine ideas?
Turn it backward?	
Turn it upside down?	
Turn it inside out?	

Source: Alex F. Osborn, adapted from *Wake Up Your Mind.* Copyright © 1952, 1964 by Alex F. Osborn; copyright renewed © 1980 by Russell and Marion Osborn. Reprinted with the permission of Charles Scribner's Sons.

Company improve productivity in its various subsystems?" In order to exhaust all possibilities, a two-dimensional chart can be developed that lists departments on one of its axes and the *methods* for improving productivity on the other (see Table 13.2). In this example group members would brainstorm using the combination of departments and methods to stimulate ideas. Some solutions for "improving productivity in personnel, using communication" might be:

1. Have weekly meetings of staff to discuss current staffing needs;
2. Circulate copies of current applications to appropriate department heads;
3. Post job openings on centralized bulletin boards.

Each combination on the grid should stimulate several ideas.

Table 13.2 · Matrix Form

Departments \ Methods	Coordination	Communication	Goals	Rules and Policies	Procedures	Feedback	Resources	Equipment	Budget	Incentives	Structure	Etc.		
Personnel														
Engineering														
Marketing														
Design														
Accounting														
Purchasing														
Safety														
Etc.														

Depending on the complexity of the problem, this grid can be extended into a three-dimensional matrix. However, forcing techniques can become so detailed that the number of considerations becomes overwhelming.

Nominal Technique

This technique is often referred to as silent brainstorming. Its main focus is to combine idea generation with equalizing contributions of group members. Many times in group decision making, some members do not take part in active problem solving for a number of reasons. The group star may dominate discussion, preventing other, less dominant, members from participating. For various reasons, one member may be excluded completely by the rest of the group. Whatever the reason, the group outcome may not reflect everyone's opinion.

To circumvent this problem and yet incorporate the idea of brainstorming, Andrew Van de Ven developed the nominal technique.[11] The process combines idea generation and idea analysis in the following steps:

1. *Silent generation of ideas in writing:* During this phase, participants individually list all the possible solutions to a problem. This provides uninterrupted time for the participant to think. It also avoids conformity and group pressures, since the individual is working alone.

2. *Round-robin feedback:* After each group member has prepared a list of ideas, the lists are shared with the group. A recorder is selected to list the ideas on a piece of newsprint in front of the group. Each member then reads one of the ideas from his or her list, and it is placed on the group list. This process continues with each member reading one idea until all ideas are exhausted.

3. *Discussion of each idea for clarification:* Once all the ideas are on a common list, the group discusses them to ensure that they understand the meaning of each idea. The purpose of this phase is to clarify, elaborate, and evaluate. Ideas should be discussed in sequence, and no items should be eliminated from the list.

4. *Individual ranking of ideas:* At this point the group members again work individually. There is no interaction with other members. Each member selects and ranks the ten most important items on the total list. The rankings are then compared, and the group decision is made based on the individual rankings of the group members.

The nominal technique has many advantages. It incorporates brainstorming on an individualized basis, which assists in generating more ideas. It tends to equalize contributions by eliminating discussion in the early stages of idea generation and in the critical stage of idea selection. The input of dominant members is limited. Social pressure and conformity are minimized. Participant satisfaction is usually higher than it is in regular discussion groups; however, it can be dissatisfying to strong personalities.

A Six-Step Problem-Solving and Decision-Making Model

Depending on how simple or complex the task, the manager may be faced with decision making, choice making, or problem solving. All of these activities involve one or more of the following six steps:

1. Defining the problem
2. Analyzing the problem
3. Generating alternative solutions
4. Choosing a solution or course of actions
5. Implementing the solution
6. Evaluating the effectiveness of the solution.

Decision making includes steps one through four: problem identification, problem analysis, generation of alternatives or solutions, and evaluating and choosing among the alternatives or solutions. *Choice making* simply means choosing among the alternatives or solutions. *Problem solving* includes all six steps: problem identification, all phases of decision making, and the implementation and evaluation of the solution. The steps, as we imagine them to be divided, are seen in Figure 13.2.

Applying Creativity to the Six-Step Process

In an organizational setting, problem solving is often discouraged. Typical defensive behaviors are blaming, avoidance, or digression to other matters. Early and Rutledge outline three basic reasons why problem solving is frustrated in the organization:

1. The individuals assume the problem is bigger than their ability to handle it.
2. Many individuals are not aware of their problem-solving skill.
3. Groups tend to reject solutions before giving them a thorough hearing, reducing the desire of individuals to contribute more solutions.[12]

Creativity and problem-solving ability in an organization can be enhanced by specific techniques. For example, try solving the nine dot problem in Figure 13.3. Many people have struggled with this problem over the years. Inevitably, the problem solver will attempt to stay within

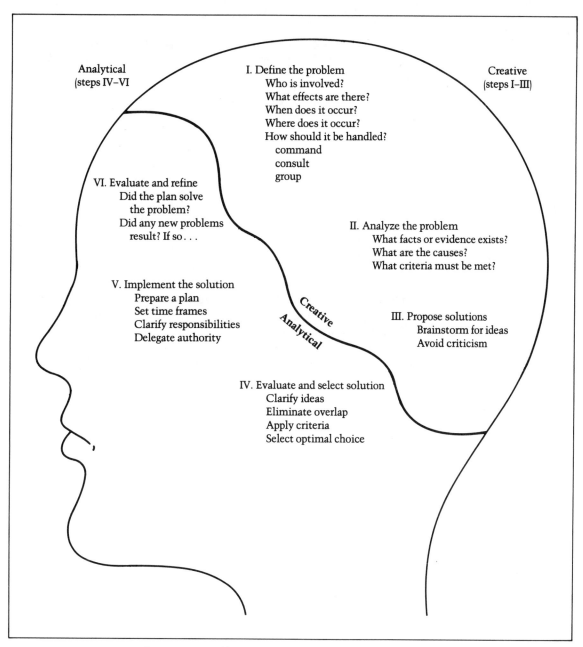

Analytical
(steps IV–VI

Creative
(steps I–III)

I. Define the problem
    Who is involved?
    What effects are there?
    When does it occur?
    Where does it occur?
    How should it be handled?
        command
        consult
        group

VI. Evaluate and refine
    Did the plan solve
        the problem?
    Did any new problems
        result? If so . . .

II. Analyze the problem
    What facts or evidence exists?
    What are the causes?
    What criteria must be met?

V. Implement the solution
    Prepare a plan
    Set time frames
    Clarify responsibilities
    Delegate authority

Creative
Analytical

III. Propose solutions
    Brainstorm for ideas
    Avoid criticism

IV. Evaluate and select solution
    Clarify ideas
    Eliminate overlap
    Apply criteria
    Select optimal choice

Figure 13.2 • Problem-Solving Model: The Creative and Analytical Process

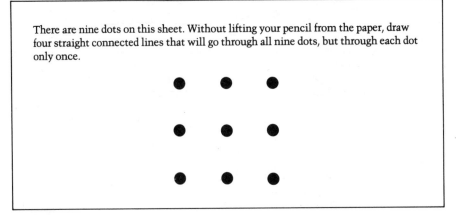

There are nine dots on this sheet. Without lifting your pencil from the paper, draw four straight connected lines that will go through all nine dots, but through each dot only once.

Figure 13.3

Note: The answer can be found on page 375.

the space implied by the nine dots. We have learned throughout our socialization process to follow steps, to stay within the lines, and to deal with problems as neat modules. This training, in fact, acts as a block to our creativity. Managers often face the same kinds of blocks within their organizational setting. The following steps can help the manager overcome these blocks.

Defining the Problem

The most difficult step in decision making is defining the problem. Unless a problem is clearly defined, the manager could end up with a solution that simply deals with an effect rather than the problem itself.

This can be likened to the individual who is not feeling well and takes an aspirin for a headache. The headache may be gone as long as the effects of the aspirin last. However, once the aspirin has worn off, the individual will again experience the headache. Here, symptoms are being treated rather than the cause. In order for a solution to be effective, it must eliminate the cause.

The example of taking an aspirin to deal with a symptom rather than a cause is an example of defining a problem in terms of lower, narrow goals. Another tendency that interferes with defining a problem effectively is defining the problem in terms of a solution. Take, for example, the manager who cannot meet deadlines for handling the workload and decides to hire more staff. She has defined her problem in terms of a solution, not in terms of the cause. There should have been many other considerations. For example, are the present procedures effective? Are positions clearly defined? Do the employees understand their roles? Have goals been clearly communicated to employees? All of these questions revolve around causes rather than solutions.

To effectively define a problem, take the following steps:

Write down the problem. Committing your problem to paper helps you to follow through. You can always go back and revise, adapt, and refine, but writing it down will lead to fuller commitment on your part to follow through.

Clarify any confusing words. Eliminate any jargon you might have used in stating the problem. If terminology needs to be defined, make sure you've clearly defined it. As you work through this process, you'll find that you also better understand the problem.

Discover the problems, effects, or symptoms. What evidence proves there is a problem? What have you observed that tells you things are not as they should be? Problem symptoms or effects are things that you can observe. Examples might be confusion, inability to meet deadlines, unresolved conflict, failure to meet work quotas, poor quality, or incomplete work. A complete analysis of the problem's symptoms will give you a better idea of what the causes might be.

Analyze and discover the size of the problem. How serious is it? Is it increasing or decreasing? What are the implications for the future?

Devise a concise statement that summarizes the nature and urgency of the problem. In this statement, indicate how soon a solution must be found. Writing down your problem helps clarify it. As you define it, consider the questions "who," "what," "when," and "why."

Analyzing the Problem

Once the problem has been clearly stated, gather pertinent facts, identify probable causes, and list criteria.

Gather the facts. Before facts can be gathered, you must determine what information is missing or needed to make a sound decision. Methods that may be used to obtain the information include surveys; face-to-face interviews; observation; library research of laws or decisions; and a review of rules, procedures, or historical files. Some excellent questions to pose in evaluating the usefulness of the information are:

- Is it first-, second-, or third-hand information?
- Is the source credible? an expert in his or her field? biased?
- Is the information recent? representative? documented?
- Is the information complete?

Discover the causes. The solution must be structured according to the problem's causes. You can observe effects or symptoms of a problem, but you cannot observe the causes. While effects are based on observations, causes are based on inference and probability. For this reason it is necessary to brainstorm all the possible causes of the problem and then evaluate them in terms of probability.

Set up criteria for the solution. Problem solving often is defeated because no criteria were established for evaluating a solution. Criteria set the parameters or boundaries for the solution. They are the basis on which implementation of the solution will be evaluated. For example, if you fantasize to the limits of your imagination, you may discover an ideal solution. However, if a manager has neither the funds nor the authority to implement the solution, it doesn't matter how effective it is.

Typical criteria involve budget limitations; time limitations; geographical limitations; level of authority; and laws, procedures, or rules that need to be observed. Consider the following questions:

- How urgent is the adoption of a solution?
- Which cause must be eliminated first?
- What rules, laws, or policies must be observed?
- How are the criteria weighed? (Not all criteria are equally important.)

Proposing Solutions

Once the problem has been clearly defined and analyzed, solutions or alternatives should be generated. Two methods we discussed are brainstorming and the nominal technique. It is important at this stage to generate as many ideas as possible, reject no ideas, and withhold evaluation. Many times a really good solution is overlooked because the manager did not spend enough time on this step. Groups sometimes come to an early agreement on a low-quality solution. The greater the number of ideas, the greater the possibility for a really good solution.

Evaluating Solutions against Criteria

Once solutions have been proposed, each solution should be evaluated according to the criteria that have been set. For consistent and objective evaluation, the same criteria need to be applied to all solutions. The solution that most effectively meets all or most of the criteria should be the solution selected.

A grid approach, like the one in Table 13.3, can be applied. On the

Table 13.3 • Problem-Solving Grid

Idea Comparison						
Idea	**Criteria and Weights** (l = lowest, 5 = highest)					
Solution	Cost = No More Than $1,000/mo	Less Than 50 Miles From Home	At Least 1,000 sq. ft.	At Least 150 sq. ft. of Storage	At Least 3 Offices	Total
Location A	5	4	3	5	2	19
Location B	3	5	2	1	5	16
Location C	5	5	1	1	1	13
Location D	3	3	4	4	3	17

Problem: Which location would provide the best site for a new suite of offices?
Solution: Location A meets the most criteria.

vertical axis, list your solutions. Horizontally, list your criteria and their weights. As you go through each solution, evaluate it against the criteria. As you discuss each solution, a number value may be entered in the block. For example, in the first solution above, you may rate location A as

5 on the first criterion, 4 on the second, 3 on the third, 5 on the fourth, and 2 on the fifth. Add these ratings, and compare the totals. Weak solutions are quickly eliminated.

Implementing the Solution

Many times subordinates participate in problem-solving sessions and committees only to find to their dismay that the solution agreed on by the group is never implemented. One of the primary reasons for this is the lack of a plan. Before problem solving is complete, the group should determine the steps needed to reach its goal. For each step, prepare a timetable, and select the person responsible for completing the step.

The group should also discuss what obstacles will be faced. For example, what groups or agencies might be hostile to the plan? The group may then determine the methods to implement the solution.

Evaluating the Plan

After implementation, the group should take time to evaluate the results on two levels. First, did the plan meet the goals and objectives set? Second, did the plan eliminate the problem? Once these two questions have been resolved, the group should determine what new problems have emerged as a result of the plan. At this point, the group can start through the six-step problem-solving model again.

Summary

As a decision maker and problem solver a manager is concerned with finding the right solutions. The effectiveness of a solution depends on its *quality* and *acceptance*. These two factors along with the *task* must be considered when the manager selects the type of decision making to use: *self, group,* or *consultation*. If the acceptance of the decision is of paramount importance, the group is usually the most effective method of decision making.

In all decision making and problem solving, two phases are important: *creative* and *analytical*. Creativity assists in idea generation and is most dependent on language facility. This phase is associated with the first three steps of problem solving and decision making. Idea analysis is deductive. All facts and information are given. In this phase, the participant clarifies, evaluates, and eliminates.

Several techniques have been developed to stimulate ideas. *Brainstorming* encourages participation without criticism. *Forcing techniques* help the group consider as many alternatives as possible. *Synectics* uses associations to trigger ideas. Finally, the *nominal technique* combines silent brainstorming with group sharing while minimizing group pressures.

Finally, managers need to determine whether they are involved in *decision making, choice making,* or *problem solving.* There are six steps associated with these activities in the problem-solving and decision-making model: defining the problem, analyzing the problem, proposing solutions, evaluating solutions, implementing solutions, and evaluating the success of the solution.

Key Words

decision making	blocks to creativity	synectics
consultation	problem sensitivity	forcing techniques
creativity	brainstorming	nominal techniques
analytical		

Review Questions

1. What factors are important to decision making? What methods can be utilized in decision making?
2. Explain when individuals and when groups can best be used in problem solving and decision making.
3. Describe several methods for generating ideas (brainstorming, nominal techniques, forcing techniques, synectics). What are the advantages of each?
4. List and describe the steps in the problem-solving process.

Exercises

1. In Better Jobs, Inc., there are five divisions, each of a different type and location. Each division is staffed by employees with different educational levels, ages, and number of years with the company, and also have different assistants.
   a. The employee with two years of college works in the Personnel Department.
   b. The employee with the Ph.D. has Gail for an assistant.
   c. The employee on the Board of Directors has been with the company thirteen years.
   d. The employee with the B.A. degree has been with the company four years.

    e. The employee on the Board of Directors is immediately to the right of Engineering.

    f. The forty-six-year-old employee has Dom for an assistant.

    g. The employee in the Accounting Division is thirty-five years old.

    h. The employee in the middle division has been with the company ten years.

    i. The employee with the B.S. degree works in the first division on the left.

    j. The employee who is twenty-seven years old works in the division next to the employee who has Sue for an assistant.

    k. The employee who is thirty-five years old works in the division next to the division where Jake works as an assistant.

    l. The thirty-two-year-old employee has been with the company five years.

    m. The employee with the M.B.A. degree is fifty-three years old.

    n. The employee with the B.S. degree works next to the Data Processing Division.

    o. The employee in the Accounting Division has been in the company for five years.

The Problem: Who has Lesley for an assistant? Who has been with the company the least number of years? Divide into groups of four to six students. You have twenty minutes to find the solution to the problem. Answers are on page 376.

    a. How did the time limit affect your solution? (How well do you work under pressure?)

    b. Whom would you rate as the most logically oriented person in your group?

    c. Who were the leaders? Who were the workers?

    d. Whom would you rate as the best communicator in your group?

2. Multiquip Corporation, an international manufacturer of multipurpose electronic equipment, received grant assistance for development of a relatively new area of electronics. A new director was hired whose job consisted of full responsibility for the staffing, training, development, and delivery of new electronic equipment. Reporting to him were two research technicians dealing directly with product design, a development lab of six electronic engineers, and one secretary with limited skills.

    After several months it became increasingly clear that things were not going well. Feedback about the new director from the other departments was negative, and one superior had strongly recommended firing him. Subordinates and peers were also complaining. Typical remarks were that he "doesn't listen," has "little contact with employees," "does not believe the program would last," and "spends too much time in other departments telling them how to run their business."

    Constant deadlines for submitting reports, budget requests, vouchers, purchase requests, personnel forms, and the subsequent red-tape seemed to eat up all of the new director's time. He was also trying to establish guidelines for measuring product effectiveness and proposals for future funding. The specific requirements for completing these items were complex, and everyone on the staff was relatively new. Consequently, much time was spent correcting deletions and serious oversights.

By the end of one year, turnover was high, with three of the six engineers and one technician leaving for other jobs in the company. The director's superior decided to have the director rated by a cross-section of people with whom there was regular contact. All evaluations rated him high on sincerity and initiative. The following is a general rating based on averaging the forms:

Table 13.4

Factor	−1	2	3	4	5+
Capability for job			X		
Leadership qualities		X			
Job performance			X		
Communication skills		X			
Supervisory skills		X			
Attitudes and work habits				X	
Professional development in field					X
Personal qualities					X

Prior to coming to Multiquip, the new director had supervised product development for a small, regionally oriented firm. His recommendations were very good. Shortly after he left, the firm declared bankruptcy. His educational background included a M.S. in computer engineering from a large state university.

After reading this case, answer the following questions.
a. What is the problem(s)?
b. What are the effects?
c. How soon must a solution be found?
d. What additional facts are needed? How would you get them?
e. What are the probable causes of the problem(s)?
f. Identify the criteria that must be met by the solution(s).

Answers to Exercises

Nine dots from page 368.

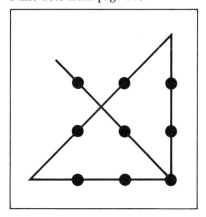

1. Exercise Answer

Accounting	Data Processing	Personnel	Engineering	Board
B.S.	B.A.	Two Years	Ph.D.	M.B.A.
Thirty-five	Twenty-seven	Forty-six	Thirty-two	Fifty-three
Five Years	Four Years	Ten Years	Five Years	Thirteen Years
Sue	Jake	Dom	Gail	Lesley

a. Lesley is the assistant to the Chairman of the Board.

b. The employee in the Data Processing Division has been in the company the least number of years.

References

1. Harold Koontz, Cyril O'Donnell, and Heinz Weirich, *Management*, 7th ed. (New York: McGraw-Hill, 1980), p. 238.

2. J. J. Sherwood and F. M. Hoilman, *Utilizing Human Resources: Individual vs. Group Approaches to Problem Solving and Decision Making*, Institute for Research in the Behavioral, Economic, and Management Sciences, paper No. 621, Purdue University.

3. Alan C. Filley, "Conflict Resolution: The Ethic of the Good Loser," in Richard C. Huseman, Cal M. Logue, and Dwight L. Freshley, eds., *Readings in Interpersonal Communication*, 3rd ed. (Boston: Holbrook Press), pp. 248–49.

4. While exact numbers differ, the ideal seems to be five to six members, but no more than eight.

5. Filley, "Conflict Resolution," p. 237.

6. Sally P. Springer and George Deutsch, *Left Brain, Right Brain* (San Francisco: W. H. Freeman, 1981), p. 185.

7. *Training Manual for Creative Problem Solving* (St. Louis: U.S. Civil Service Commission, St. Louis Regional Training Center, 1980), pp. 3–10.

8. Alex Osborn, *Applied Imagination: Principles and Procedures of Creative Thinking* (New York: Charles Scribner, 1953), p. 300–01.

9. William J. J. Gordon explains and comments on this theory in *Psychology of Problem Solving*, in Gary A. Davis, ed. (New York: Basic Books, 1973), pp. 96, 123–24.

10. Osborn, *Applied Imagination*.

11. Andrew Van de Ven, Andre L. Delbecq, and David H. Gustafson, *Group Techniques for Program Planning: A Guide to Nominal Group and Delphi Process* (Glenview, Ill.: Scott, Foresman, 1965), p. 8.

12. Leigh C. Earley and Pearl B. Rutledge, *The 1980 Annual Handbook for Group Facilitators*, in J. William Pfeiffer and John E. Jones, eds. (San Diego, Calif.: University Associates, 1980).

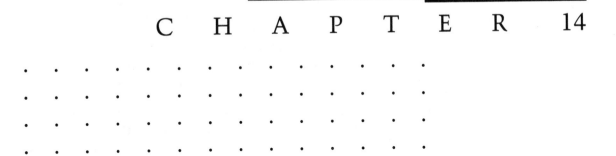

C H A P T E R   14

The Communicating Manager as a Conflict Resolver

Introduction

We often suppress conflict for a variety of reasons. Because conflict has been characterized as negative, people shy away from "arguing," "emotions," and "hostility." Conflict sometimes leads to constructive problem solving, however, and can be a positive force. In fact, it places ideas under scrutiny in order to determine their soundness and avoid superficial decisions.

Have you ever participated in a group where everyone came to quick agreement? Was the solution creative or challenging? Did members share common backgrounds and points of view? In other words, was there any testing of beliefs, knowledge, or experience? Be wary when you participate in a group that comes to quick agreement. Early agreement can result in implementation of an unsound idea and the need for further problem-solving activity. Conflict tests ideas. Peter Drucker believes that conflict alone encourages alternatives to a decision and the avoidance of faulty decision making.[1]

This point became vividly clear during a session in which a group of engineers engaged in a problem-solving activity. Joe, a section leader, came to the program director and complained about one of his group members. According to Joe, Betty just would not cooperate. Every time other group members came to some sort of agreement, Betty disagreed. She criticized everything, and nothing seemed to suit her. The problem, Joe said, was that everyone else was in agreement and Betty continued to belabor the problem. He concluded with a plea, "Please remove Betty from the group and assign her elsewhere."

The program director encouraged Joe to assign Betty a specific role. Perhaps Betty could strengthen the group by finding the flaws in each solution. Betty was quickly told that this was to be her role. She relished it, and a lively discussion ensued from her comments. In the end, the entire organization embraced a very sound solution because of Betty's role, and the success was attributed to "Betty's team."

Conflict can add to a greater understanding and identification of problems. It can increase alternatives and involvement. Conflict stimulates interest and interaction. Hoffman, Harburg, and Maier observed that conflict encourages creative thinking, commitment, and quality decision making.[2]

Conflict can also be destructive. When it presents a negative force, it must be managed. Group participants who are not aware of problem-solving skills can use conflict to compete with other members and subvert ideas, resulting in game playing, defense mechanisms, cliques, and hostility. Group participants need to be taught how to use conflict constructively.

This chapter focuses on the source of conflict and ways a manager skillfully handles it through communication. It examines the stages of conflict and the methods that research has identified to reduce conflict. Finally, it presents strategies and steps for resolving conflict.

Sources of Conflict

Huseman describes several sources of conflict.[3] Among these are organizational structure, performance measures, ambiguity, goal disagreement, and conflicting reality perceptions. During a series of training sessions on conflict at a chemical plant in Houston, approximately seventy-five first-line supervisors identified the sources of conflict in their particular work unit. Among the causes they listed were multiple direct bosses, unclear instructions, personality conflicts, poor attitude, lack of authority, lack of experience in superiors, lack of understanding of superiors, and differing standards of behavior among group members.

The organizational structure can cause problems by pitting depart-

"I've heard this group has had some trouble reaching agreement."

Source: Reprinted with the permission of George Kocar. Illustration originally appeared in *Industry Week*, March 20, 1978, p. 18.

ments within the organization against each other. This can be the result of unclear goals or perhaps power building within the unit. When two departments perceive their roles as overlapping or striving for similar outcomes, they may tend to compete with each other.

Performance measures can also be a source of conflict. If these have not been clearly explained to the employee in terms of expectations, the employee will fill in the gaps. Or if the manager bases rewards or punishments on behavior that seems unrelated to the job itself, the employee's behavior will pattern itself to receive the rewards. Consider the following situation.

My best employee has only one fault. He hangs around the coffee pot for twenty minutes each morning before he begins working. Some of this occurs before the start of business, but most of it is on the clock. The problem is that other employees who are not as productive as my "superstar" hang around the coffee pot, too.

My unit was the best in the division and received special recognition in a nationwide review of agency productivity. The superstar produced about 15 percent more than the average employee in my unit. I use him whenever time and high quality are important factors in the job. He troubleshoots major jobs and trains other employees in the technical aspects of the work. I can't remember his last mistake.

I distributed a memo to all employees reminding them that they are to be at their desks working at 8:00 A.M. Several of these employees are obviously upset, including my superstar. Production is slipping, and my unit is no longer the best in the division.

Penalizing the employees for "hanging around the coffee pot" changed the employees' perceptions of job expectations: Timeliness, not productivity, appeared a priority.

Unclear job roles can create conflict. Competition may result between members of the organization who have set the same reward as a goal. Conflict will continue until the job roles are clarified. The following incident is a good example.

The head of personnel and development at a leading manufacturing firm hired Sam and Jane to staff and develop a program for employee rehabilitation. Since this was a relatively new area of emphasis in the company, it was agreed that the two would cooperate by working out their roles and coordinating their activities. As the program grew, it soon became apparent that one of them would be chosen as director. Awareness of this coming opportunity resulted in duplication of effort as Sam and Jane competed for attention by performing roles that they perceived would be the key in deciding who would receive the promotion. Rather than discuss their conflicting behavior, they resorted to sabotage, game playing, and isolation. Jane described Sam to a friend as "manipulative, self-serving, and untrustworthy."

Sam and Jane never clearly understood their roles and how the roles meshed to accomplish organizational goals. At some point early in the conflict, their boss should have stepped in and clarified the relationships.

Conflict, then, can have many sources. To be resolved, it is important that you identify the source and act to eliminate or minimize its effect. It is also important to identify its stages. Conflict identified and managed early will lead to more positive resolution.

Stages of Conflict

One of the first steps in managing conflict is recognizing it in its early stages. The following situation includes all stages of a conflict episode.

Clara was an auditor. Formerly a college faculty member but unable to achieve tenure, she was the first auditor hired on what was to become a five-member auditing team. Accustomed as a teacher to keeping irregular hours, the new 8-to-5 job interfered with her personal schedule. Consequently, she volunteered for as much travel as she could get.

Clara's whereabouts soon became the daily mystery. Since she kept her office door closed, no one could tell if she was in or out. Soon the other auditors and support staff began to complain that Clara was getting privileges not extended to others in the organization. Co-workers' complaints included (1) she arranged trips to coincide with holidays, (2) she "conveniently" worked at home, (3) she exaggerated her travel allowance, and (4) she was never available for meetings or to act as an alternate for other auditors. In short, Clara did not have a workload comparable to others, yet because of her seniority was the highest-paid member of the staff.

The retirement of the department head resulted in promoting the assistant director and opened a coveted position. Because of her performance, Clara was not considered. This became a major frustration for her. Whenever she was "in," she visited with other staff members and critiqued the new director. These visits often gained her support in creating resistance to organizational changes.

The new director attempted to stop the meetings by rearranging the offices. Clara moved to a location that was fully visible to the main office and reception area, yet separate from all other auditors.

Clara considered this change in location a challenge. Again, she kept her office door closed. But she held her meetings in a variety of locations outside the office setting. These locations included the lunchroom, the lounge, and the offices of other departments. Thus, she foiled the director's plan to curb her visiting.

The director required weekly records from all employees. Each sheet recorded the hours an employee spent on specified activities during the workday. He also issued new regulations for travel, lunch, and work hours.

Rising to the occasion, Clara categorized as "other" all time for which she couldn't account and travel came within pennies of the maximum allowed. She arrived at work and left at the specified hours, but because she traveled so much, this became a clouded issue.

Fellow employees' frustration and protestations continued to grow. Finally, the director transferred her to a new position and location with a travel allowance and office 125 miles away.

Conflict-ridden situations similar to Clara's are not uncommon in the modern organization. Typically, the conflict episode, as Pondy describes it, begins with underlying conditions or *latent conflict*.[4] Clara's personal goals differed from those of the organization. Her drive for autonomy and competition with the other auditors for scarce resources (money, position) added to these conditions.

The second stage occurs when the parties realize that these conditions exist. Pondy calls this stage *perceived conflict.* Once the other auditors began to recognize that Clara received a greater portion of the resources (travel, compensation, free time), this stage was reached.

Felt conflict, the third stage, happens when parties become tense or irritated because of the conditions. This usually results in stage four, or *manifest conflict.* The auditors' complaints about Clara were overt means of expressing disagreement with her behavior. Auditors also made covert attempts such as keeping track of Clara's whereabouts and checking travel forms. In addition, her boss moved her office and finally relocated her as a means of releasing the tension and eliminating conflict.

The last stage Pondy identifies is *conflict aftermath.* This results from the conflict. If the consequences do not resolve the original conditions, they may again surface. The director's attempts to manage the impact of Clara's behavior on other employees did not eliminate the source of conflict. In fact, as we will discuss later, the use of force to

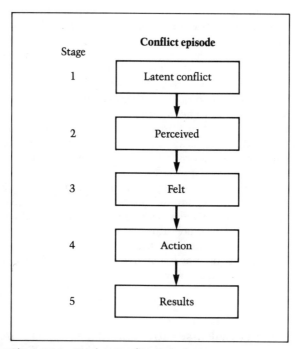

Figure 14.1 · Pondy's Conflict Episode

require weekly records and regulations for travel aggravated the conflict. The resulting *aftermath* renewed the conflict episode.

Strategies for Resolving Conflict

When two or more persons are in conflict, they often engage in strategies. Strategies can be either outcome directed (who gets what) or goal directed (what would benefit both). After studying conflicting groups, Filley describes three forms of conflict strategies: the win/lose, the lose/lose, and the win/win.[5] Both the win/lose and the lose/lose strategies are outcome directed. The atmosphere is one of victory or defeat. Each party centers on his or her own point of view. Hence, the parties want to achieve specific desired solutions rather than determine mutual goals, values, or motives. The conflict is personalized instead of objective.

Win/Lose

From the time we enter elementary school we learn to compete with our peers. Whether we participate in a spelling bee, a game of softball, or a video game, we strive to win. Rewards are given to the outstanding student, the top 7 percent, or the winning athlete. Winning enters every facet of life.

The drive to win spills over into the organizational environment. For example, in committee or group meetings members can compete with each other for attention and time. Instead of striving to accomplish the goals of the organization by selecting the best solution, participants often attempt to make points with the boss or win an argument. Even departments within an organization pit themselves against each other to gain prestige, power, or resources.

A number of problems result from the win/lose approach to problem solving. For example, much time may be spent discussing solutions that do not accomplish the goals of the organization. In addition, decisions may be delayed because of the implications of the decision to the winner or to the loser. If opposing forces are equal in power, a deadlock may result. Consequently, no solution will be implemented. People who are not aggressive may withdraw and refuse to participate. Focus of discussion on one or two solutions may prevent the analysis of more and better alternatives. Repeated involvement in win/lose confrontations may decrease or destroy the sensitivity of participants to the problem-solving process. Members may fail to participate in, let alone attend, the committee meeting. Anger itself may disrupt the meeting, interfere with the desire to understand problems from another point of view, and leave the losers resentful. Resulting solutions may be sabotaged by the losers. The resulting defensiveness of participants will prevent a positive team approach to problem solving.

The characteristics of the win/lose situation include dominance of power or authority.[6] This is often referred to as the boss syndrome. The boss asserts his role or position to get the job done. He implies, "You do it because I'm the boss."

A second example of the win/lose situation is ignoring attempts to influence or giving no support. For example, if someone poses a particularly controversial idea or one that does not suit your purposes, you give it no support.

Another approach to win/lose is majority rule or vote-taking. There is always a winner and a loser. The loser, or the minority, does not gain anything from the results and frequently undermines the solution.

A final form of win/lose approach is called railroading. This is the use of pressure and other tactics to enforce minority opinion. We may coerce a party, or we may apply pressure in some way concerning the person's future with the organization, so that he or she will go along with our point of view.

Lose/Lose

In theory, the lose/lose strategy is preferable to win/lose because it entails compromise. In other words, both parties get something, and there is no loser; or, conversely, both parties lose something, and no one side gets everything it wants. The solution may involve resorting to a third-party decision such as arbitration, or it may mean resorting to the rules. This latter approach frequently occurs with a manager who can't decide what to do or faces a situation in which neither solution is attractive.

Win/Win

This third form of conflict resolution is the most desirable. All parties agree on the solution, and the solution is not unacceptable to anyone. There are two kinds of win/win situations: consensus and integrative.

Consensus

In a consensus situation, the focus is on solving the problem rather than the solution itself. Voting, trading, or averaging do not occur. Conflict is accepted by the parties as healthful toward achieving a high-quality solution. Consensus centers on analyzing the alternatives. Parties do not become polarized because there are a variety of solutions from which to pick to satisfy everyone's needs.

Integrative

In an integrative situation, the focus is on a series of steps. The integrative approach stresses goals and values and deemphasizes solutions and win/lose tactics. As the result of extensive research, scholars have defined certain conditions necessary to this approach.[7] They are:

- Freedom from time pressures
- Free interaction of parties
- Shared information
- Limited number of participants
- Positive attitude toward goals
- Trust
- Positive feelings about self (parties are not defensive)
- Understanding of long-range costs
- Specifically stated issues
- Both parties agree on the problems
- Open and specific feedback
- Emphasis on goals and objectives
- Exhaustive search for alternatives
- Consideration of quality
- Involvement
- Questioning attitude
- Flexibility in leadership
- Acceptance of solutions

We all become embroiled in win/lose situations. The important thing is that we recognize the win/lose mode. If the outcome isn't win/lose, it's likely to be lose/lose, or everyone has to give up something. A manager's goals should be that everyone gains.

Recently, an angry student berated several faculty members because he could not schedule the courses he desired for the fall semester. Finally having lost his temper with the student, a faculty member approached one of the college deans and told her, "This is your job, you take care of it." By this time the student's face was red and the professor was seething. Both the professor and student were ready to come to physical blows. The administrative official immediately sought the assistance of a trained college counselor.

The first approach the counselor used was to remove the student to a quiet area and ask him to explain the problem. The counselor then stated calmly, "I understand why you're upset. I would be too. You have a scheduling problem, but we can work it out." As the student continued to display his temper, the counselor became even more low key. Recognizing the student needed a cooling off period, he said, "I can help you. We can either sit down now and work things out, or you can come back later. You have to make the decision." While it took a moment for the student to regain his composure, he realized that he was not making any progress by continuing his angry behavior. After working with the counselor for a few minutes, he resolved his problem.

It's difficult for one person to turn around a win/lose confrontation. To do so you must enlist the help of other participants. If you feel a discussion is becoming a win/lose confrontation, try to restate or clarify the group goal. Be sure the goals are clear and understandable. Try to look at things from the other person's point of view. This will provide insight and perhaps uncover problems you previously failed to recognize. Recognize that there is more than one way to solve a problem. Avoid categorical statements such as "there is only one real solution," or "I think that's the best way." Be sure everyone participates in the discussion, and if you detect hesitancy or lack of understanding from a group member, encourage questions and expression of point of view. Don't vote. Try to gain agreement by the whole group. Make sure compromises are not superficial agreements. Be alert to loaded language and persuasion. Try to encourage other group members not to use them. Statements such as "anyone can see that" or "an experienced person would know this" are off limits.

Strategies can be either outcome or goal directed. The win/win strategy is preferable because everyone agrees on the solution. In addition to strategies, however, scholars have also identified several methods for reducing conflict. Used in tandem with the win/win, win/lose, or lose/lose strategies, the method can reinforce either an outcome- or a goal-directed approach. The following section identifies and defines these methods.

Methods for Reducing Conflict

Pondy's stages of the conflict episode help us better understand how conflict occurs, and now we can identify the reactions to our attempts at resolution. With this knowledge, and an awareness of the source of conflict, you may apply several methods for reducing conflict that have been defined by Blake and Mouton. These methods include compromise, confrontation or problem solving, forcing, smoothing, and withdrawing.[8] They can be used separately or together.

Compromising

Compromising is solving a problem by mutual concession. Both parties get something out of the solution. An example of this might be accepting a new title rather than an increase in salary.

Confronting or Problem Solving

Confronting or problem solving means facing a problem rather than avoiding it. People who confront problems see and recognize the conflict; then they attempt to determine and eliminate the causes.

Forcing

Forcing is the exerting of pressure. It may include constraining or compelling action by physical, intellectual, ethical, or moral means. The manager in this case uses power and position to achieve the desired response.

Smoothing

Smoothing is minimizing what is harsh, crude, offending, or disagreeable. The manager who uses smoothing as a method attempts to explain or gain understanding of the problem.

Withdrawing

Withdrawing is retreating or retiring from areas of conflict: disengaging, abandoning, and eliminating them from consideration. The manager who withdraws avoids the problem.

Studies of these methods indicate that constructive handling of conflict-ridden situations occurs with confronting and smoothing. Withdrawing and forcing have adverse impacts. Compromising has little impact on conflict resolution.

Research findings show that the most effective supervisors used conflict-resolution methods in the following order: (1) confrontation, (2) smoothing, (3) compromise, (4) forcing, and (5) withdrawal. Less effective supervisors applied (1) confrontation, (2) forcing, (3) withdrawal, (4) smoothing, and (5) compromise. Forcing was the least effective means of resolving a conflict-ridden situation.[9]

Once you engage in a conflict-ridden situation, you must be able to determine the stage or intensity of the conflict, your strategy, whether it is win/win, lose/lose, or win/lose, and the methods that will help you achieve the desired outcome. Critical to each of these decisions is the form of intervention you will employ. You must ask yourself three questions: Are you directly intervening as a party of the dispute? Are you acting as a mediator between two disputing parties? Is it necessary to have an arbitrator decide the outcome? An affirmative answer to any one of these questions determines the role you will play. The next section explains each form of intervention and when it is appropriate.

Forms of Intervention

There are three kinds of intervention in a conflict situation: negotiation, mediation, and arbitration. The form of intervention affects the process, roles, and outcome.

Negotiation

Negotiation is the action or process of conferring with another to arrive at a settlement; the two parties work together to smooth out their differences. Negotiation can occur through discussion and can result in an agreement or a compromise. If this form of intervention fails to resolve the conflict, mediation may be necessary.

Mediation

Mediation is the intervention between conflicting parties to promote reconciliation or to interpret them to each other; it is the negotiation of a compromise between hostile or incompatible viewpoints, demands, or attitudes. A mediator is a third party who intervenes between the parties in dispute. Mediation, then, requires the two parties in conflict plus a third party who acts to gain agreement. For example, consumer protection agencies act as mediators between customers and retail establishments. If mediation fails to resolve the conflict, arbitration may be necessary.

Arbitration

Arbitration is the hearing and determination of a case in question by a person chosen by the conflicting parties or appointed under a statutory authority. The arbitrator acts as a judge and has power to decide. Small claims courts act as a form of arbitration when other forms of intervention fail.

While negotiation can occur at any time between two disputing parties, formal mediation and arbitration procedures are usually outlined by organizational policies. Grievance policies and union contracts formally identify the rules and procedures. An employee grievance may begin as a one-to-one problem-solving session between superior and subordinate. If the parties fail to resolve the problems, the subordinate may go to the next step and formally submit a written grievance to the next line of authority. As a mediator, the third party will attempt to resolve the grievance. If this step fails, a formal ruling may be necessary so that the employee can present the grievance to a grievance panel. After hearing the case, a decision will be made by the chosen authority.

Because of losses accrued in the form of time and productivity when mediation and arbitration are necessary, most organizations encourage conflict resolution through negotiation.

Steps in Conflict Management

The following steps in conflict management can lead to effective and efficient decision making.

Prepare for Conflict

Be aware that communication leads to conflict resolution. Know your participants. Study them meticulously to determine their opinions about the issue. Encourage them to share their point of view and the reasoning behind it. Remember that awareness of others' perceptions is an aid in leading to conflict resolution.

Defuse Emotions

Sometimes we add to conflict by dealing with a problem while participants are in an emotional state. People cannot be rational and act in a thinking mode when their emotions are overruling their logic. One of the most obvious examples of this is the child who throws tantrums. A parent cannot reason with such a child. Typical approaches are to send the child to his or her room or to walk away. When the tantrum is over, the parent can gain the child's attention. Sometimes employees also throw tantrums. If a problem-solving approach is tried while in this state of mind, very little will result. If participants become emotional in a group session, a break is essential. It's important to recognize that all of us become emotional at times and need an opportunity to cool off before proceeding to the business at hand.

In addition to cooling off periods, other approaches to defusing emotions are reassuring or smoothing and acceptance. Many of us need to be reassured about our worth and value to the group. Minor anxieties and fears may need some attention and understanding. Simply recognizing that we accept others' points of view and their right to express it is important to group participation. Communication spent in these modes can eliminate hidden agendas and problems during the discussion phase.

Focus on Questions That Ask Why, How, and What

What seem to be the fundamental difficulties? Are there indications that others are concerned? Conduct a problem analysis to determine the basic issues. State the problem as a goal or as an obstacle rather than as a solution. Identify obstacles to goal attainment. Depersonalize the problem.

Search Jointly for Solutions

Use creative approaches to problem solving, such as nominal techniques or brainstorming. Surveys and interviews can add information that may assist in decision making. Each participant should play a role and have an opportunity to express his or her point of view.

Evaluate Solutions in Terms of Both Quality and Acceptability

Parties should not be required to justify personal feelings or preferences. Specific criteria should be agreed on for evaluation and handled one at a time. Avoid expression of self-oriented needs. Avoid voting (unless the group is using a method of parliamentary procedure), averaging, coin flipping, or any form of win/lose agreement. Where necessary, divide the problem into parts that can be handled by subgroups. Resolve feelings of conflict before continuing the problem solving process.

Summary

Conflict is a natural phenomenon that can be managed. Since conflict encourages sounder decision making and stimulates interest, it can have a positive effect.

Differing attitudes and perceptions, struggles over power, prestige, or rewards, and unclear roles and expectations can all be causes of conflict. Communication between the differing parties increases cooperation and the likelihood of reaching agreement. To do this, you will need to minimize or eliminate the cause as well as recognize that conflict is a natural and manageable phenomenon. The absence of conflict is not necessarily good, since, as noted above, it can often have beneficial effects.

Effective management requires an understanding of the conflict episode. A set of underlying conditions creates the first or *latent* stage. The next stage occurs when the parties *perceive* these conditions exist. If they intensify in effect, the *felt* conflict stage begins. Left unresolved, the *manifest conflict* stage surfaces in overt or covert action releasing tension. Finally, *conflict aftermath* is the stage or condition that results from the action taken.

If you participate in a conflict episode, you will find several forms of intervention useful. These forms depend on the intensity of the conflict and the policies of the organization. *Negotiation* is direct intervention between two parties who attempt to arrive at a settlement. *Mediation* requires a third-party neutral who interprets the parties to each other and promotes reconciliation. Finally, *arbitration* is the intervention of an appointed authority given the power to decide after hearing the differing complaints. Of these forms of intervention, direct negotiation is least costly in terms of time spent and productivity.

Blake and Mouton identified five methods for reducing conflict: *compromising, confronting* or *problem solving, forcing, smoothing,* and *withdrawing.* Extensive research by Burke indicated the most effective way of handling conflict was *confronting* or *problem solving.* Forcing was ineffective.

An understanding of the methods is important, but an understanding of strategies is crucial. Parties engage in strategies that are *outcome di-*

rected (win/lose or lose/lose) or *goal directed* (win/win). The *win/lose* strategy sets an atmosphere of victory or defeat. Preferable to win/lose is the *lose/lose* strategy. Both sides lose something as well as gain something. Finally, the *win/win* strategy focuses on the problem rather than the solution. The solution is acceptable to everyone.

Several steps to conflict resolution can be used as guidelines to effective decision making. The following steps reinforce the win/win strategy:

1. Prepare for conflict.
2. Defuse emotions.
3. Focus on questions that ask why, how, and what.
4. Search jointly for solutions.
5. Evaluate solutions in terms of both quality and acceptability.

The key to managing conflict is an awareness that conflict is healthy and leads to better decision-making. If participants accept this principle and apply problem-solving skills, then greater commitment, more creative alternatives, and sounder decisions will more than likely be the results.

Key Words

sources of conflict	confronting	arbitration
latent conflict	forcing	win/lose
perceived conflict	smoothing	lose/lose
felt conflict	withdrawing	win/win
manifest conflict	mediation	consensus
compromising	negotiation	integrative

Review Questions

1. Explain how conflict can be both a constructive and destructive process.
2. Describe the different stages of conflict presented by Pondy.
3. The chapter presented three strategies for resolving conflict. Describe each of these strategies, and tell why one is the most desirable.
4. Five methods were listed for reducing conflict. What are the five, and how are they used?
5. Describe the three forms of intervention.
6. Five steps can be helpful in the overall managing of conflict. What are these steps?

Exercises

1. With your classmates, discuss the following problem and use Pondy's conflict episode as a guide. What is the source of conflict? Which stage of conflict does the employee describe? To manage the conflict, what should the employee do next?

> I get all the dirty jobs at the office because the foreman knows I won't complain or cause a fuss. I need his recommendation to get out of the division and into a better-paying job. Other people in the section don't have any ambition, so they don't work hard. They would stretch out a job all day if they could. But I want to get ahead.

2. Divide into groups consisting of six to eight participants. Each group should agree on a type of business they would like to represent as the board of directors.
   a. Your employees are listed below [see (d)]. Diagram a formal organization chart that includes eight positions, and assign each employee a position.
   b. Due to a financial squeeze, your organization must terminate an employee. Decide as a group which employee to terminate.
   c. Select one observer. The role of the observer is to evaluate the group's interaction using the following questions:
      (1) Which participants displayed emotional reactions?
      (2) Which participants asked questions to help clarify general statements?
      (3) What strategies did participants use?
      (4) What methods of reducing conflict did participants use?
      (5) Which participants kept open minds about the ideas of other members of the group?
   d. Your employees have the following backgrounds. Place the position they hold in your organization next to their names.

Position	Name	Education	Age	Years at Company	Current Job Rating[a]	Marital Status	Children
_____	Sam Jones	M.B.A.	52	5	4	D	2
_____	Sue Smith	B.S. (Accounting)	35	1	3	M	1
_____	Joe Barnes	2 years college	46	10	2	M	5
_____	Bill Goode	B.A. (Business)	32	4	3	M	2
_____	Gail Beck	High school	25	2	4	M	Pregnant
_____	Guy Great	3 years college	21	1	4	S	0
_____	Jane Grey	2 years college	37	7	3	D	2
_____	Sally Sweet	High school	26	3	3	M	Stepson

[a] Job ratings are based on a scale from 1 to 5 with 5 the highest rating.

3. With your classmates describe a recent conflict episode in which you participated. What strategies did participants use? What was the solution? Did it work?

References

1. Peter Drucker, *Management: Tasks, Responsibilities, Practices* (New York: Harper & Row, 1973).
2. L. R. Hoffman, E. Harburg, and N. R. F. Maier, "Differences and Disagreements as Factors in Creative Group Problem Solving," *Journal of Abnormal Psychology*, 64 (1962), pp. 206–214.
3. Richard C. Huseman, "Interpersonal Conflict in the Modern Organization," in Richard C. Huseman, Cal M. Logue, and Dwight L. Freshley, eds., *Readings in Interpersonal and Organizational Communication*, 3rd ed. (Boston: Holbrook Press, 1977).
4. Louis Pondy, "Organizational Conflict: Concepts and Models," *Administrative Science Quarterly*, 12 (Sept. 1967), pp. 299–306.
5. Alan C. Filley, "Conflict Resolution: The Ethic of the Good Loser," in Richard C. Huseman, Cal M. Logue, and Dwight L. Freshley, eds., *Readings in Interpersonal and Organizational Communication*, 3rd ed. (Boston: Holbrook Press, 1977).
6. *Ibid.*, p. 236.
7. *Ibid.*, p. 248–49.
8. R. R. Blake, H. A. Shepard, and J. S. Mouton, *Managing Intergroup Conflict in Industry* (Houston, Tex.: Gulf Publishing, 1964).
9. R. J. Burke, "Methods of Resolving Superior-Subordinate Conflict: The Constructive Use of Subordinate Difference and Disagreements," *Organizational Behavior and Human Performance*, 5 (1970), pp. 393–411.

C H A P T E R 15

. . . .
. . . .
. . . .
. . . .

The Communicating Manager as a Change Agent

Introduction

Organizations, like individuals, are constantly changing—through employee turnover, new leadership, economic disaster, regional growth and development, and environmental restrictions.

According to Ellingsworth, " . . . no complex organization can remain healthy and viable for long without the capacity to anticipate, execute, and adapt to change."[1] To change, an organization must have effective communication internally among its members as well as externally with its clients. A surgeon, for example, must be able to give clear instructions to the surgical team as well as be able to explain the purpose and expected outcome of an operation. Change involves communication on all organizational levels and in all forms: group discussion, one-on-one, formal briefings, written proposals, and memoranda.

The Change Process

Ellingsworth found that people follow a five-step process when changing their attitudes and behavior. The process is based on the research and theories of Everett Rogers and is composed of the following elements:

1. An innovation (an idea or practice that an individual perceives as new, regardless of how long it has been available);
2. Messages about the innovation, transmitted in some audible or visible form;
3. The passage of time from the first exposure until the innovation is no longer "new";
4. A group of people definable as a social system (by virtue of their common occupation, employment, proximity, formal membership, interest, or anything else that binds them together);
5. Some observable response to the innovation (as messages about it circulate in the social system over time).[2]

Each step in this process relies on *communication* as an integral part of implementing change in the organization. This chapter identifies the nature of the change process and the techniques for facilitating change. We focus on two questions: First, what are the constructive and destructive aspects of change? Second, how can change be effectively implemented? The chapter then explores these questions by examining the change cycle, approaches to change, and the techniques and strategies for facilitating change through communication.

Overcoming Resistance: Why People Fear Change

At every level and in all forms of organizations, people tend to resist change. The present means of operating, or the status quo, is safe and nonthreatening, but change creates inconvenience, uncertainty, and anxiety. The resulting resistance can be witnessed in typical responses such as "It's too much trouble," "We've tried it before," and "What's wrong with the way we do it now?" Some forms of resistance are reduction in output, increased sick leave, strikes, sabotage, political pressure, and fighting. Argyris, having reviewed the results of changes implemented in thirty-two major reorganizations of large companies, found resistant forces existing in all organizations up to three years after changes were announced. He explained why this occurred:

> I believe the reasons for this long delay are embedded in the change strategy typically used by management. . . . The basic strategy has been for

Source: Copyright © 1975 by NEA, Inc. Used by permission of Newspaper Enterprise Association, New York.

the top management to take the responsibility to overcome and outguess the resistance to change. This strategy does tend to succeed because management works very hard, applies pressure, and, if necessary, knocks a few heads together (or eliminates some). However, as we have seen, the strategy creates resisting forces that are costly to the organization's effectiveness, to its long run viability and flexibility, as well as to the people at all levels.[3]

Since management usually participates in both the decision-making and problem-solving processes, the rationale for change is usually clear. Management assumes that other members of the organization will accept its decision-making role and hence its solution without the need for discussion. There are a number of reasons why people resist alterations in their organizational role:

1. *Disruption of social relationships:* People become comfortable with predictable surroundings and adopt coping behaviors for problem areas. Since their interpersonal relationships fulfill social needs, change disrupts these relationships and causes anxiety.

2. *Threat to roles:* Change in the organizational structure and individual roles may threaten position and recognition. If an individual perceives that the change will result in loss of esteem or recognition, he or she will resist change. Conversely, increased responsibilities or promotion to higher levels may result in anxiety over the ability to perform new or more complex duties.

3. *Economic loss:* Many individuals fear change because they anticipate a loss of economic security. Since economic changes affect the basic physiological, security, and belonging needs, fear of economic loss creates strong resisting forces.

Uncertainty produces anxiety and results in resistance in 80 percent of the change efforts, yet rarely does change impede employee growth and development. In fact employees benefit as much or more than the organization, particularly in earning power. Only about 5 percent of those in the work force actually lose jobs as a result of change. Most reduction occurs through normal turnover and transfers.[4] If management communicates the changes in detail, much anxiety is alleviated and resistance lessened.

The Change Phase

To understand effective change management, you must first understand the steps involved in the change process. This is actually the implementation phase of problem solving. These steps can be depicted as occurring in a cycle. Chapter 13 described the problem-solving process and included both the creative and analytical phases. The first three steps of problem solving are *creative* because the manager relies heavily on thinking up ideas rather than the refining or eliminating of ideas. The second three steps are *analytical*, since the manager must select, implement, and analyze the effectiveness of the solution. It is in this second phase, the analytical, that the implementation of change takes place. We might say that the three beginning steps of problem solving are the *decision-making phase*, and the final three steps of problem solving are the *change phase*.

Often organizations find themselves in crisis situations because they have ignored over a long period of time the necessity for change. In the early 1980s automobile companies in the United States found themselves facing a dilemma. The great demand for energy-efficient vehicles suddenly resulted in the market's being overtaken by Japanese imports. Even with high import tariffs the Japanese imports thrived. The American public chose quality construction and energy efficiency over the luxurious comforts in a car. Because the industry resisted change, instead of anticipating and adapting to it, it suffered great losses.

Organizations and individuals must be problem sensitive. They must recognize that a problem exists. Perhaps a better way of stating this is that the organizational members must be able to *feel* anxiety, pressures, and tension and want to get better. Until individuals and organizations recognize that something is not as it should be, change will not effectively take root.

Once the problem is recognized, however, identification of causes can take place. As the last resort, this may require the assistance of a consultant, or any specially selected organization members familiar with the technical and administrative aspects of the problem. This person or group is often referred to as a *change agent*.

In Chapter 13 we restricted ourselves to emphasizing the processes involved with the first three steps of the change cycle (defining the problem, analyzing the problem, and proposing solutions). Many organizations complete these three steps and decide that they have "solved" their problem. In fact, the solution, if implemented at this stage, is inconsistent, and the cry may go out that "We already solved this problem, and nobody listened." What the group failed to do was recognize that the most critical phase of problem solving is the *change phase.* Here the actual plan or strategy unfolds, and the steps for implementation are defined. The steps of the change phase are (1) evaluate and select a solu-

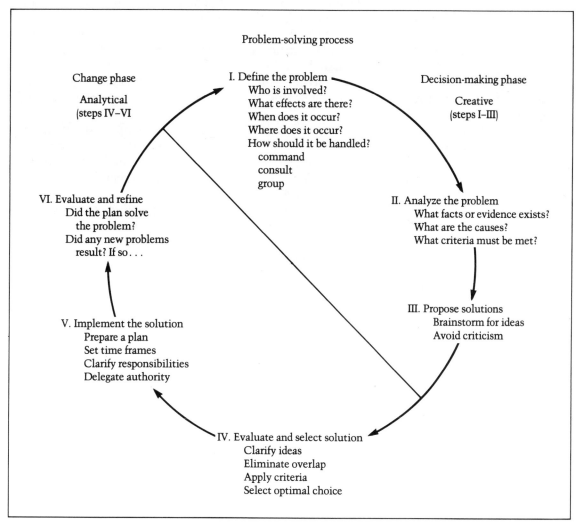

Problem-solving process

Change phase

Analytical
(steps IV–VI

Decision-making phase

Creative
(steps I–III)

I. Define the problem
Who is involved?
What effects are there?
When does it occur?
Where does it occur?
How should it be handled?
command
consult
group

II. Analyze the problem
What facts or evidence exists?
What are the causes?
What criteria must be met?

III. Propose solutions
Brainstorm for ideas
Avoid criticism

IV. Evaluate and select solution
Clarify ideas
Eliminate overlap
Apply criteria
Select optimal choice

V. Implement the solution
Prepare a plan
Set time frames
Clarify responsibilities
Delegate authority

VI. Evaluate and refine
Did the plan solve
the problem?
Did any new problems
result? If so . . .

Figure 15.1 • **The Problem-Solving Model Including the Decision-Making (I–III) and Change (IV–VI) Phases.**

tion, (2) implement the solution, and (3) evaluate and refine the solution (see Figure 15.1).

Evaluate and Select a Solution

It is extremely important that this step be included as part of the change phase. When individuals affected by the change participate in the actual selection of the solution, they have an opportunity to ask questions and clarify any misunderstandings about the solution.

If individuals involved in the implementation of the change do not have the opportunity to participate in the planning, someone must fully communicate to them both the solution and the reasons for its adoption. If any reasons that may influence that individual are left out, resistance to the change may develop. A recent problem-solving meeting exemplifies this situation.

Several university counselors stated that problems arose when students registered for courses without having passed the course prerequisites. Students preregistered prior to receiving their final grades for the prerequisite courses. The consequences were detrimental to both the students and the university.

The question at the meeting was, "How do we prevent students from enrolling in courses in which they failed the prerequisite?" Several solutions were proposed, and one was selected. The next day a counselor who was key to the implementation process notified her superior that she had not been in the meeting and preferred a different solution. All the counselors met again and reviewed the problem. The group discovered that some key information had not been passed to the counselor regarding problems of implementing her proposed solution. Her solution, while admirable in its purpose, was not practical, and once she heard the group's reasons for not adopting it, she was satisfied with the proposed solution. Because this counselor did not participate in the original meeting, more time was spent at the second meeting reexamining much of the same information that had been discussed at the first meeting. Those in the group knew the frustration that this key person had experienced following the first meeting, however, and that this would cause even greater problems during the implementation phase if further communication were not allowed.

Implement the Solution

Earlier we stated that many solutions fail because an action plan for implementation is never developed. Effective change management requires a plan. This is so critical that management techniques such as management by objectives (MBO) have been developed to assist managers in mapping out their strategies for change. Such a plan includes specific steps, time frames, assignment of duties, and clearly delegated levels of authority.

Specific Steps

The exact step-by-step plan for implementation should be prepared in sequence. The plan can involve briefings, mailings, formal presentations, designing complex programs for computers, selecting and purchasing new equipment, or constructing a facility. Each activity necessary for the implementation of the solution must be identified and arranged in order, from beginning to completion of the project.

Time Frames

A typical error by the manager is to tell an employee that a solution needs to be implemented "as soon as possible." As a matter of fact, the letters *ASAP* often appear on documents, but as we described in Chapter 4 the recipient often fails to recognize that different words have different meanings for different people. After the first two weeks on the job, a new worker was extremely frustrated by her manager's frequent use of *ASAP* to set a time frame. Finally she confronted her boss: "You have given me ten tasks and told me to complete them as soon as possible. My time at this point is precious. By "as soon as possible" do you mean 4:30 today or by the end of the week?" The manager's response was, "Oh, I don't need that for two weeks." Keep time frames specific. Many managers are caught empty-handed because they failed to communicate to their subordinates specific time frames for completing the task.

Assignment of Duties

Clarifying the responsibilities of each person involved in the implementation of the solution is essential. Competition and rivalry may result when two people see themselves as having similar responsibilities. On the other hand, if assignments are not clarified, employees may assume someone else will take care of it. This assumption leads to costly expenditures for the organization in terms of wasted time and effort. Be sure the employee knows it is his responsibility to complete the task.

Examples abound of what happens when individuals fail to understand their roles. A babysitter for five children ages 2 to 12 assumed that one week alone with the children while the parents were vacationing would present no problems, since the older children could look after the younger ones. Unfortunately, none of the older children took responsibility for watching the youngest. Finally, the babysitter assigned one of the older children the task of taking care of the two-year-old, and the job was well done. When the children's father heard about the assignment, his response was, "They are just like our ROTC cadets. They can do a heck of a job, if you assign them a specific task."

Duties should be clearly identified and authority delegated to assure the completion of all tasks associated with the implementation of the change. Role assignments should be reviewed with all team members present to allow questions and clarification, as well as to keep the lines of communication open.

Delegated Authority

Typically, implementing the solution also involves delegating authority. Authority is the right to give orders, set policies, or administer discipline. The ultimate authority in an organization distributes or delegates authority downward in the organizational structure. Usually, managers delegate authority by assigning a subordinate to speak or act as an agent of the organization and manager. Delegation typically occurs on one of five levels. The subordinate receiving delegated authority needs to know the delegation level in order to determine how to complete the task. The first three steps described below restrict the amount of delegated authority:

Level 1. *Don't do anything unless I say so.* The restraints at this level of delegation are most severe. The manager tells the employee exactly what to do.

Level 2. *Give me the information, I'll decide.* At this level the real message is, "Talk to whomever you need, and use your authority to get me the information, but don't express your point of view or act until I decide." This is a safe, low-risk level of delegation.

Level 3. *Do it, but keep me advised.* At this level the supervisor keeps tabs on what is happening, in case intervention may be needed. The message transmitted is, "You can handle it, but I'm still the boss. If someone asks me about the project, I want to have the information." Another version of this level is, "If problems arise, I may need to take over." The resulting thinking and behavior of the subordinate is somewhat of a mind-reading routine. Each action is considered in terms of, "Will the boss approve of this?"

Level 4. *Complete the job, then report to me.* The level of delegation allows the subordinate to use delegated authority to achieve the goal by whatever means are appropriate.

Level 5. *Do the job. The responsibility is yours.* This final level is where true delegation takes place. In all the other levels an assignment has been made. But here the subordinate is held responsible for the outcome.

Once the manager has prepared a plan, set time frames, clarified responsibilities, and determined the level of delegated authority, the next step in the change phase is to evaluate and refine the solution.

Evaluate and Refine the Solution

A manager must ask two key questions to determine the effectiveness of the change: First, does the plan solve the problem? Second, does it result in a new problem? The first question is crucial. If the problem still exists, the solution was probably aiming at symptoms rather than causes. The problem must be reviewed in order to attempt to identify the true cause, and the problem-solving cycle renewed.

Typically, however, when a cause is eliminated, new problems may arise. Depending on how monumental the problems are, the organization may need to act more or less quickly on a resolution. Again, problems need to be identified and the problem-solving process put into action. A *debriefing* is an organizational attempt to review an activity, process, or project to determine if it is effective. If it is not, new problems are identified. It is important that every member of the team involved in implementing the activity or process be involved in the debriefing. This ensures that most problems can be identified and can be evaluated as to their impact on the overall productivity of the organization.

Table 15.1 • The Change Phase of Problem Solving

Problem Understanding →	Action →	Review
Evaluate and select a solution	**Implement the solution**	**Evaluate and refine**
Clarify ideas	Prepare plan	Was the problem solved?
Eliminate overlap	Set time frames	Did any new problems result?
Apply criteria	Clarify responsibilities	
Select optimal choice	Delegate authority	

The change phase of the problem-solving process results in positive organizational development when effectively handled. It includes evaluating and selecting solutions, implementing solutions, and evaluating and refining the solution. Knowing the steps alone, however, does not necessarily ensure effective change. The skills and techniques needed to handle these steps are critical. For this reason, scholars and practitioners have developed various techniques and strategies for facilitating change.

The Force-Field Analysis

According to Kurt Lewin change involves opposing forces.[5] In other words, some aspects of a situation work to increase the chances of change while others work to decrease the chances for change. This is like a tug-of-war. By increasing the strength of positive change forces, change can overcome the resisting forces.

Change forces, which Lewin calls *driving forces*, include any aspects of the situation that increase the willingness to change. Examples include dissatisfaction with the present situation, external pressures, group pressures, anticipation of increased satisfaction, and the power or credibility of the change agent.

Resistance, or *restraining forces* include any aspect of the situation that reduces the willingness to change. They include such things as individual preference for the status quo, reluctance to admit a problem exists, fear, ignorance of trends in the environment, or investment in reputation or career. Fear itself is a primary resisting force. Individuals fear losing status because of a change. If a new boss does not regard an individual's capabilities as highly as the previous boss, the individual might become anxious and anticipate that the rewards and career paths may be curtailed. The following incident vividly illustrates the strength of resisting forces.

> At the Baltimore shipyards during World War II, management took action to slow the production of Liberty Ships and to start the production of invasion barges in response to changing military requirements. The novelty this change introduced into plant operations was not fully anticipated when the decision was made. Technological changes had been foreseen but the workers saw their most valuable personal assets, experience, and skill in building big ships suddenly devalued and liquidated. Workers who had identified with the product of their work on Liberty Ships took no pride in producing "row boats." Since the purposes of these barges was labeled classified information, workers could not be told they were turning out the craft to be used in the invasion of the European continent. In the absence of information about these technological and threatening changes, the shipyard became a rumor factory, morale and productivity declined, and a disastrous strike was narrowly averted.[6]

Lewin depicted the restraining and driving forces as shown in Figure 15.2. The line in the center represents equilibrium or the status quo. As long as the restraining forces are equal to the driving forces the organization will maintain the status quo. This state is termed *stationary equilibrium*.

The Three Alternatives

Lewin proposes several change alternatives: (1) Increase the strength of the driving forces, (2) decrease the strength of the restraining forces, and

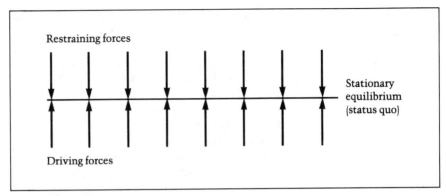

Figure 15.2 • Driving and Restraining Forces Establishing Equilibrium

Source: Based on model in Kurt Lewin, "Quasi-Stationary Social Equilibria and the Problem of Permanent Change," in W. G. Bemis, K. D. Benne, and R. Chin, eds., *The Planning of Change* (New York: Holt, Rinehart, and Winston, 1969, pp. 235–38).

(3) combine both 1 and 2 above. There are several risks involved with choosing alternatives 1 or 2. If driving forces are increased, there is risk that the old situation may return after pressure is removed. In addition, the use of authority to initiate change may result in counterpressure against change. Alternative 2, decreasing the strength of the restraining forces, may be accomplished by such strategies as increasing participation in problem solving or redistribution of power. The combination of increasing driving forces and decreasing restraining forces allows for the most effective alternative. Figure 15.3 illustrates movement away from the status quo resulting from using the third alternative.

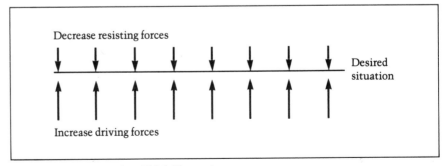

Figure 15.3 • Kurt Lewin's Third Alternative

Source: Based on model in Kurt Lewin.

The forces of change and corresponding strategies can be summarized as follows:

I. *Change forces:* any aspect of the situation that increases the willingness to change. These are also called *driving forces* by Lewin. Some examples are:
   A. Dissatisfaction with present situation
   B. External pressures
   C. Group pressure
   D. Anticipation of increased satisfaction
   E. Power or credibility of change agent

II. *Resistance forces:* any aspect of the situation that reduces the willingness to change. These are also called *restraining forces* by Lewin. Some examples are:
   A. Preference for status quo
   B. Reluctance to admit problem
   C. Ignorance of trends in environment
   D. Reputation or career invested in
   E. Status quo
   F. Fear:
      1. Of losing status
      2. That change would devalue current skill or knowledge
      3. That one hasn't skill or ability to change
      4. Of cost of change
      5. Of stress

III. *Change alternatives:* altering the strength of driving and resisting forces:
   A. *Increase* strength of *driving* forces
      1. Risk of old situation returning after pressure removed
      2. Using authority to initiate change may result in counterpressure

B. *Decrease* strength of *restraining* forces
   1. May be done by increased participation in problem solving by those affected
   2. Successful change requires redistribution of power
C. Combine *A* and *B*.

The Three Phases

The three phases for change, according to Lewin, are the *unfreezing phase,* the *moving phase,* and the *refreezing phase.* Each phase has several strategies (see Table 15.2).

The unfreezing phase involves making present behavior open to

Table 15.2 • Kurt Lewin's Change Model

Unfreezing	→ Moving	→ Refreezing
Recognition of the need for change	Action plan implemented	Change stabilized
	Resistance forces removed	Desired behavior reinforced
Change agent initiates action	Resources provided	Progress monitored
		Revisions made

Source: Based on model in Kurt Lewin.

change. Ideal conditions for change include openness, honesty, and mutual respect. This means that anyone affected by the change should be allowed to ask questions to which management honestly responds and through which mutual respect can be gained. Participants usually have a right to know what is going to happen. Resistance by the participants may mean something is wrong with the proposed change. The reasons for resistance should be investigated in order to eliminate the causes.

The moving phase identifies and removes interference. Interference consists of forces that impede progress toward change but are not directly concerned with the change. Some examples might be lack of information, lack of resources, lack of necessary skills, and a limited time for implementation of the change. Some methods for removing interference include interacting with the group to clarify information, correcting rumors, and providing training in new or required skills and knowledge, or providing necessary resources.

Groups have a vested interest in the status quo. Change threatens cohesiveness, norms, roles, and communication patterns. Too much change can result in confusion and disorientation, since it disturbs order. The last phase, or *refreezing phase,* is an attempt to stabilize the change and prevent reversion back to old methods. The period of stability should be longer than the period of change. The manager's role includes refining procedures so that new behaviors become routine—supporting and reinforcing desired behaviors, maintaining stability, providing a positive model of new behavior and attitudes, monitoring progress, revising procedures where necessary, and obtaining support of informal leaders.

Approaches to Change

Change can be approached in a variety of ways in the organization. Greiner identified several of the most common methods.

1. *The decree approach:* a unilateral authoritative announcement issued by a powerful person with formal authority;

2. *The replacement approach:* key organizational personnel are replaced with new people who believe in the desired change;

3. *The structural approach:* a change in the organization chart and the subsequent relationship of who is working for whom;

4. *The group decision approach:* emphasizes group participation and agreement on a predetermined course;

5. *The data discussion approach:* change data are presented as a catalyst and clients are urged to discuss the changes;

6. *The group problem-solving approach:* problem identification and problem solving are accomplished through group discussion.[7]

In addition to these approaches, current literature discusses team building, quality circles, the grid approach, and transactional analysis. Some of the latter approaches are actually specialized techniques employing the approaches outlined by Greiner in steps 4, 5, and 6. The following section describes several of these approaches.

The Decree Approach

Decrees are *authority decisions* made by individuals appointed by the system to act in assigned roles. Presidents, chairpersons of boards, and heads of departments have decision-making authority. Those in positions that report to them are bound by their decisions.

Ellingsworth states, and rightly so, that authority is the most rapid and predominant method of decision making. Its downfall occurs when individuals who must implement the decision fail to adopt the idea and show commitment; actual implementation may vary or fail. The paradox is that while decisions made by a "boss" or "chief" are efficient, individual decision making allows greater commitment and adaptation to individual needs.

The Replacement Approach

New administrations frequently bring with them major changes in staff assignments. One of the first tasks of a new President or governor is to make appointments in key positions that are politically and strategically critical for implementation of the administration's philosophy and policies.

The disadvantage of this approach is the loss of expertise in the layers of personnel at the top of the organizational structure. The new administrators must learn the system, a time-consuming task, before policy can be implemented. Since the new administration's philosophy may mean major changes in personnel or job assignments, it is likely to encounter strong resistance.

The Structural Approach

Earlier in the text we reviewed a variety of organizational structures and the effect that structure has on organizational communication. When structure is manipulated, the power to wield positive or negative sanctions is altered. In defining the subordinate's position, the manager also defines the accepted or formally recognized communication channels, role limitations, and sanctions for enforcement.

The Data Discussion Approach

Survey feedback has become a major tool in organizational change. Carefully designed questionnaires gather information from areas needing analysis. Based on the data generated, problems are diagnosed, and plans are developed for their resolution. While the research instrument may be tailored to the organization, many standardized questionnaires are available that include training programs for their use. Most questionnaires provide information on leadership, organizational climate, and worker satisfaction with pay, task, supervisor, or work group. Once the data is collected and analyzed, an external consultant presents and interprets it for the organization using the problem-solving and team-building approaches to diagnose and integrate change.

The Group Decision and Problem-Solving Approaches

The group decision approach relies on participation and consensus in decision making. Its benefits are a greater pooling of knowledge and a greater acceptance of the decision by participants, which enhances (1) the quality of the solution and (2) the implementation phase of the desired change. Chapters 9 and 13 provide in-depth coverage of groups, decision making, and problem solving.

Team Building

Team building has become a popular approach to facilitating change because it incorporates the process objectives of interpersonal training but maintains a task orientation, making it immediately useful to the organization. Effective for task forces as well as for regular work or family groups, its primary goals are (1) task completion, (2) building interpersonal relations, (3) utilizing effective processes (such as decision making and problem solving), (4) role clarification, and (5) role negotiation.

One of the techniques that has traditionally advocated a complete team-building approach using a specialized instrument is the grid approach, developed by Robert R. Blake and Jane S. Mouton in the 1960s.

Team Building and the Managerial Grid

In an attempt to measure perception, Blake and Mouton developed attitude scales to judge change (see Figure 15.4). While the program appears

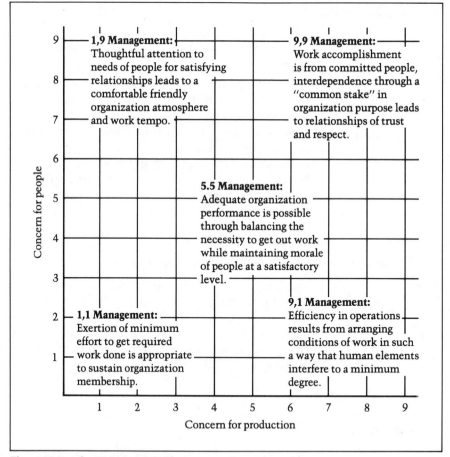

Figure 15.4 • The Managerial Grid

Source: The Managerial Grid figure from *The Managerial Grid III*, by Robert R. Blake and Jane Srygley Mouton (Houston: Gulf Publishing Company, 1985), p. 12. Copyright © 1985. Reproduced by permission.

similar to sensitivity training, it is not. It emphasizes team development rather than individual development. The focus is placed on managerial styles in place of interpersonal relationships. Emphasis is on decision making as a team.

The grid is set up so that the horizontal axis, numbered 1 through 9, represents concern for productivity. The vertical axis on a 1 through 9 basis represents concern for people. The object is for managers to work for a 9,9 organizational climate, or maximum concern for people and maximum concern for production.

The second phase of the managerial development section is team development. This is an extension on-the-job of phase I, where team members apply grid concepts to their own managerial culture. Ground rules and relationships for 9,9 management in individual groups are decided on.

Organizational development as opposed to managerial development composes a second part of the program. There are four phases involved. First, there is intergroup development where an attempt is made to build maximum concern for production and maximum concern for people beyond the single work group. Operating tensions are explored with the purpose of going beyond win/lose relationships into problem solving.

The second phase of organizational development is organizational goal setting. Problems involved at this level are important to all groups within the company, such as cost control, union/management relations, safety, promotion policies, and overall profit improvement. Goal attainment or major organizational concerns, in which stakes are real, are attacked. Teams must define and assess the problem and their goals and then put their plan to work.

Finally, a stabilization phase works to support the entire program. Changes are measured and reinforced to withstand pressures that may cause a "slip back" or regression. This phase also serves to evaluate the program's consistency with company goals. Blake had startling results that showed a positive change in every quantitative measure taken after the program had been in effect for one year.

The steps in the managerial grid and its implementation are similar to the organizational development steps of (1) diagnosis, (2) intervention, and (3) maintenance. In other words, management must first recognize that a problem exists, analyze it, then act to resolve it. The managerial grid provides a systematic method whereby the analysis can occur on an individual group basis as well as an organizational basis. It incorporates an essential quality of team building: recognizing the strengths and weaknesses of each team member and then placing each member in a role that capitalizes on his or her strengths and interests.

Quality Circles

Quality control circles were developed in Japan in the early 1960s as voluntary problem-solving groups. Workers met to study and discuss work-related problems. The resulting impact on Japanese quality and productivity has been phenomenal. As a result, the study and transfer of the techniques associated with quality circles became a primary concern of organizations in the U.S. in the late 1970s and early 1980s.

The quality circle leader is usually a person trained in group participation skills who acts as a focal point for the best interests of the workers as well as the organization. Tasks are delegated to group members to allow information flow and participation, which aid in the problem-solving process. Ideas and innovation are encouraged. Final proposals are presented by the group to top management for consideration.

Since the workers who are concerned about the problem actually participate in the problem-solving process, resistance to implementation is minimized and commitment to the solution is enhanced. In addition to being concerned, these participants usually have the most experience with causes and symptoms that affect the resolution of the problem. As a result of their familiarity with the problem, they are able to propose effective solutions that affect the overall productivity of the organization. Japanese organizations such as Sony are strong testimonies to the effectiveness of this approach.

One of the major problems associated with transferring the concept of quality circles to the United States has been overlooking the cultural differences between the two countries. While some U.S. organizations such as IBM and Hewlett-Packard share common traits with Japanese corporations, interpersonal skills are more consistently rewarded in Japanese organizations, which cultivate the basic leadership, problem-solving, decision-making, and supervisory skills that are essential for the facilitation of quality circles. The circles themselves do not develop leadership skills, yet they rely on these skills for effectiveness.

As an approach to implementing change, quality circles have been proven valuable. However, their success is based on the premise that participants—particularly the group facilitator—have acquired basic knowledge and skills in group decision making, group discussion, leadership, and supervision.

Organizational development can be facilitated by any of the approaches reviewed here: They all aim at improving an organization's problem solving and renewal processes. Regardless of the method chosen, however, the change should be planned, involve the total organization, emphasize work groups, and have long-range results. The next section explores the change agent's role in this process.

The Change Agent's Role

Regardless of organizational title or educational expertise, change agents are individuals who work to analyze needs as well as plan and implement changes. They specialize in overcoming resistance to change, have learned the art of persuasion, and recognize the need to establish credibility. They have the ability to develop specific change strategies and tactics to make the change work. Whether an outside consultant or full-time staff member, the change agent has five key tasks:

1. Establish credibility with the organizational members affected by the change;
2. Gather information necessary for identifying and solving the problem;
3. Establish a supportive environment for change;
4. Implement the approaches necessary to achieve the desired change;
5. Establish procedures for stabilizing, evaluating, and monitoring the change.

Credibility

When confronted by a change agent, an employee's typical response will be to question, "Who is this person, and why should I trust him or her?" Credibility is one of the primary keys to persuasion. Current research has identified the following sources of credibility:

1. Competence: knowledge and expertise;
2. Character: trustworthiness, honesty;
3. Composure: confidence, poise;
4. Extroversion: dynamism, personality, outgoingness;
5. Sociability: likability.[8]

An individual achieves credibility through other people's perceptions. In other words, a person may be an expert but may not be perceived as such by others. Certain sources of credibility may be perceived, while others are not. For example, one may appear trustworthy but incompetent. Finally, one person may perceive credibility where another does not.

Credibility, therefore, varies depending on the receiver, the situation, and the problem. To establish credibility before attempting to implement change, one must have proven credentials and references and be able to establish trust. Personal appearance and enthusiasm are critical.

Fact Gathering

In Chapter 13 we discussed the importance of fact gathering as a part of the problem-solving process. Two points need to be clarified here as they relate to the change agent. First, the change agent must have all the pieces of the puzzle before devising a plan. If a part is missing, the change may not be effective. Jerry Harvey described a consultant who conducted a companywide organizational development program because morale and productivity were low and conflict between employees had increased. He selected team building as an intervention and skillfully trained all employees. Yet there seemed to be little improvement in productivity. A visiting engineer noticed that the major drive shaft at the main mill was faulty. The company replaced the drive shaft; productivity jumped, and morale improved.[9] While all solutions may not be this simple, this example vividly points out the need for thorough research.

Second, willingness to listen to employees and gain insight into their perceptions of the problem—the process of fact gathering in itself—is important, since it lends credibility to the consultant's role. How many times have you heard someone say, "Nobody asked me, why should I get involved?" Having the opportunity to voice concerns, share information, and express conflicting points of view to a third party results in commitment and participation in the change process.

Supportive Environment

The discussion of group dynamics in Chapter 8 emphasized the importance of participation and commitment, and the concept of quality circles is based on these principles. A climate supportive of change encompasses broad agreement on organizational goals, trust between organization members, individual initiative and responsibility, participation in decision making, availability of accurate information on organizational conditions, and openness in organizational communication.

The consultant strives for co-orientation of all employees toward the change goal. To attain co-orientation, or a common belief or point of view, there must be understanding of the problems necessitating change, the risks generated, the actions and activities required, and their resulting effect on jobs and roles. Participation of employees in the process contributes to their recognition of the need for change, better planning, implementation, co-orientation, and positive attitudes. The following questions can help managers determine whether the organization is conducive to change:

1. *Will the organization commit to complete intervention?* We have already pointed out the importance of a thorough investigation of the problem. Consultants must have the support of top management to conduct interviews, review reports, evaluate policies, analyze procedures, and observe behavior in order to determine the most effective intervention. They must also have the freedom to implement broad changes that may range from training to structural reorganization.

2. *Does the organization want a "quick fix"?* Workshops and short courses usually focus on particular techniques or skills and leave it up to the participants to apply the concepts to their jobs. Training often motivates people and reviews or exposes them to principles and concepts that can be applied on the job. If the technique or skill is the cause of a problem, training may be sufficient. In many cases, however, it is aimed at symptoms and becomes a "quick fix" requested by management for selected employees. Training may be only one part of a comprehensive approach to change. Effective change eliminates the cause(s) of the problem and is based on thorough analysis.

3. *Are the contacts in the organization in a position to eliminate change?* There must be commitment and support from top management. Without this support, it won't matter whether the consultant's investigative efforts were thorough or whether the intervention is comprehensive. The plan will probably be put on the shelf. Top management must be exposed to the problem and its effect on the organization. The consultant must keep open lines of communication and, best of all, have top management participate in the change effort.

4. *Will top management participate and encourage participation on all levels of the organization?* Commitment can receive no greater testimony than having employees see their bosses involved and participating with them on all phases of the change effort. Participation of top management is a testimony to commitment and lends authority to the change effort. It also prepares management to fully understand the change and will lend stability to the final stages.

Approaches

A number of approaches to organizational change were summarized earlier in this chapter. Persuasion and communication skills are necessary for implementing these approaches. The ability of the change agent to analyze the audience, clarify and communicate purpose, gather information, apply sound problem-solving skills, and plan and act skillfully are critical to each approach. Communication is persuasion. You must choose the argument best suited to the occasion to convince others to act.

Lewis suggests the following guidelines:

1. *Explain the action to be implemented and the reasons for it.* This will combat rumors and minimize disruptive behavior.

2. *Prepare employees for major changes, and alert them to difficulties.* Sudden changes in the organization may result in fear and anxiety.

3. *Identify informal leaders in the organization, and explain management's objectives.* If top management is supportive, the informal leaders will encourage other group members to be cooperative.

4. *Repeat important information and techniques.* This is the most effective communication technique to increase memory. Repeat information and procedures three to five times.

5. *Allow people time to adjust to the change.* Recognize that conflict is healthy if it airs opinions and ideas that need to be resolved in the long run. Encourage employees who are doing well by recognizing their performance.[10]

Stabilizing, Evaluating, and Monitoring the Change

Employees cannot effectively implement change without understanding their roles, the steps involved in the change, and the time frames attached to these steps. Therefore, it is essential that you think through and communicate the procedures to them along with the means of evaluating and monitoring the change. In addition to knowing what to do, employees will want to know management's expectations. How will the change be evaluated? What factors will indicate that the change worked? Who will determine this? How will employees be evaluated? How will the change be stabilized? Without these questions answered, the organization is likely to return to the status quo.

The change agent acts as the guide and stabilizing influence in this process. Clear policies and procedures, and a system for program evaluation, are essential to the ongoing success of the change.

Summary

A variety of forces work to alter the behavior patterns of individuals in the organization. Some forces arouse greater concern than others because of their great effect on the productivity of the organization. All change, however, affects the role of each organization.

Healthy organizations must have the ability to anticipate, execute, and adapt to change. There are ways to marshal the forces of change in order to improve an organization's problem-solving and renewal processes. A thorough understanding of the change phase of problem solving is essential. Participation in the selection of the solution enhances commitment to the implementation of the change. The plan should include specific steps, time frames, assigned duties, and clearly delegated levels of authority. Reviewing and monitoring the change assists in stabilizing the organization and prevents slippage back to the status quo.

Effective change involves the total organization. It is planned, is comprehensive, emphasizes co-orientation of work groups, and requires the participation of a change agent.

The change agent can use a variety of approaches for implementing change and, after a thorough analysis of information, may need to combine several approaches. Finally, success will be based on credibility, effective problem identification, supportive climate, long-range planning, and a system of program evaluation.

Key Words

innovation	unfreezing phase	structural approach
change agent	moving phase	data discussion
change phase	refreezing phase	approach
delegated authority	decree approach	team building
driving forces	replacement	managerial grid
restraining forces	approach	quality circles
stationary		
equilibrium		

Review Questions

1. Review the approaches to change presented in this chapter. Which require the least investment of time and effort? the most?
2. Define credibility. Why is it important to the change agent? What are some methods that individuals and organizations use to enhance their credibility? Give examples.
3. When should a company hire an external consultant? When should a company use an internal consultant?

Exercises

1. Hold interviews with the following individuals:
   a. A communication consultant;
   b. A manager who has employed a communication consultant.
   Ask them to describe the relationship between the manager and the consul-

tant, the intervention they participated in, and the methods used to stabilize the change. What were their responses?

2. Analyze a major change implemented in your community. Describe the climate that existed at the time the change was initiated. Describe specific change and resistance forces that were evident. What efforts did the initiators or implementors of change make to increase the strength of change forces and to minimize resistance and remove interference? Evaluate the validity of any resistance that you identified. What attempts were made to reform behavior and stabilize change?

3. Prepare a detailed change plan for a change that you will implement. Using the force-field analysis, analyze change and resistance forces that are presently operating. Identify any interference that you could encounter in attempting to implement your plan. Describe specific steps that you will take to prevent or remove interference. Also describe specific steps to take to manage the "moving" phase and to refreeze behavior and stabilize the change. Select indicators that you will use to evaluate the success of your change effort. Include a timetable for implementation of each major step or phase of the plan.

4. Implement your change plan for exercise 3. Wait at least *one month*, and then evaluate your plan using the indicators you selected. Identify the strengths and weaknesses of your change strategy in the "unfreezing," "moving," and "refreezing" stages.

<hr>

References

1. Huber W. Ellingsworth, "Innovation and Change," in James L. Owen, Paul A. Page, and Gordon I. Zimmerman, eds., *Communication in Organizations* (New York: West Publishing, 1976), p. 299.

2. *Ibid.,* p. 299.

3. Chris Argyris, "Today's Problems with Tomorrow's Organizations," *Journal of Management Studies* (Feb. 1967), p. 53.

4. "How to Manage Change," *Applied Management Newsletter* (July 1981), pp. 1–4.

5. Kurt Lewin, "Quasi-Stationary Social Equilibria and the Problem of Permanent Change," in W. G. Bennis, K. D. Benne, and R. Chin, eds., *The Planning of Change* (New York: Holt, Rinehart, and Winston, 1969), pp. 235–38.

6. Daniel Katz and Robert L. Kahn, *The Social Psychology of Organizations* (New York: John Wiley, 1966), pp. 263–64.

7. L. E. Greiner, "Organizational Change and Development," Ph.D. dissertation, Harvard University, 1965.

8. William J. Seiler, E. Scott Baudherin, and L. David Schuelke, *Communication in Business and the Professions* (Reading, Mass.: Addison-Wesley, 1982), p. 184.

9. William G. Dyer, "Selecting an Intervention for Organization Change," *Training and Development Journal* (April 1981), p. 62.

10. Phillip V. Lewis, *Organizational Communications: The Essence of Effective Management,* 5th ed. (Columbus, Ohio: Grid, 1975), p. 225.

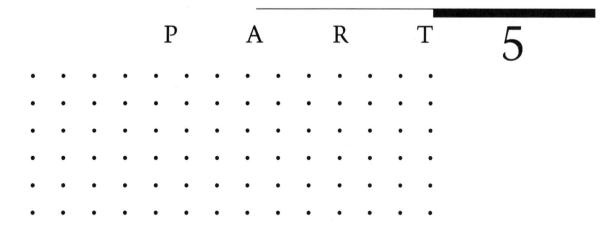

P A R T 5

Overview of the Chapters

There are extensive demands on managers to communicate effectively. It is their job to accomplish the goals of the organization by communicating and coordinating the tasks of employees. This chapter is an overview of the material contained in the first fifteen chapters on managerial communication.

Overview

There are extensive demands on managers to communicate effectively. It is their job to accomplish the goals of the organization by communicating and coordinating the tasks of employees, and by eliminating barriers to goal attainment. This requires knowledge of the job or *technical skills*, good interpersonal relations or *human skills*, and the ability to solve problems or *conceptual skills*.

Key Theories

Classical management theory is premised on establishing objective standards against which production can be measured. Its essential elements are *cooperation* and *scientific knowledge*. Fayol defined its functions as planning, organizing, commanding, controlling, and coordinating.

Human relations theory evolved because of the concern for people as resources. This theory focuses on working conditions. In Elton Mayo's experiment at Western Electric, informal communication systems and

421

social networks were observed. The work of Mayo and others in the human relations movement encouraged recognition of employees' needs.

Douglas McGregor enhanced the work of the human relations school by examining leadership roles. He described some managers as *autocratic* and labeled them *theory X* oriented. These managers assumed people were lazy, disliked work, and must be forced to take responsibility. *Theory Y* oriented managers assumed work was as natural as play and believed people would accept and seek responsibility.

Systems theory asserts that an organization is influenced by many interrelated parts: the environment, clients, the labor market, government regulations, and employees. Each part contributes to the overall purpose of the organization and exists as a subsystem. *Open systems* interact with their environment while *closed systems* do not.

Theory Z, developed in the last few years, assumes workers have a variety of social and economic bonds. In this theory employees need to have the total picture, clearly understand goals and objectives, participate in problem solving, be adaptable, and be innovative. Theory Z managers capitalize on the employees' strengths, promote an atmosphere conducive to productivity, incorporate a flexible structure, and encourage open communication.

It is true that managerial styles may vary within the organizational context, but communication is the foundation for practicing any and all styles.

Elements of Communication

Communication is defined as the sorting, selecting, forming, and transmitting of symbols to create meaning. The *source* initiates the message by *encoding* thoughts into *symbols* to form a *message* that conveys meaning to the listeners. The message is *transmitted* or sent out through a *channel* such as light, sound waves, or electrical impulses. The *receiver* or listener *decodes* the message to determine and *interpret* meaning. *Feedback*, or the response, can be a verbal statement, a letter, or merely a nod.

Communication is *dynamic* because it involves a continuous series of behavioral activities. It *cannot be reversed*, and it is *proactive*, involving the total person. Since communication involves two or more parties, it is *interactive*. Because it occurs in a certain set of circumstances, it is *contextual*. The accuracy of the message is affected by the communicator's knowledge, attitude, and social and cultural background.

Understanding communication is essential. Theories and models provide a framework from which to build this understanding. In addition, there are three major elements that can limit the development of communication skills: perceptual behavior, language barriers, and communication climate.

Perceptual Behavior

People, language, and organizational structure can limit the development of effective communication skills. One of the primary hurdles is the process of *perception*, or the filter through which we take in stimuli and understand our world. Through perception, using all of the five senses, we gain insight and knowledge about the world. Humans rely on sight and sound especially. When we communicate, we put our ideas into words or symbols to which a receiver can attach meaning. Our *references* include experience with past events, expectations of the present and future, current motivational state, knowledge, and sociocultural background. Misunderstanding often occurs in communication because of the differences in these references from one person to the next.

Our ability to perceive is limited and thus can complicate the communication process. Most objects are composed of elements we never see. In addition, most of our information about the world is gathered secondhand. What we do see is often distorted by our position, interfering factors, or another's interpretation.

Problems can often occur in perceiving people. They sometimes occur because of physical and/or mental proximity. The self-esteem of the source and receiver can also affect how the message is sent and received. Each interaction carries rewards and costs. Discrepancies can occur between how people view themselves and how they are viewed by others. The perceived intent of a person's actions determine future actions. The more accurate the perceptual process, the more effective the relationship.

A better understanding of our *self concept* will help us correct our perception-based problems. Practicing *self-disclosure*, sharing information about our thoughts and feelings, is also important. Finally, as managers, we encourage high performance from our employees by possessing and demonstrating *high expectations* of our own behavior, and theirs. Managers are many-faceted when their expectations of their employees are a key factor in the growth and success of the employees themselves, management, and the organization as a whole.

Language Barriers

Language affects perception, communication patterns, and interpersonal behavior. It is the second hurdle one must overcome to be an effective communicator. It focuses on the field of social semantics, evolved from research in the disciplines of science, linguistics, psychology, and sociology. Language is actually the study of meanings as transmitted by *symbols*. Mankind's superiority and uniqueness have contributed to the availability of a wider range of *signals*, or the ability to use signs to indicate and represent things. Signs can serve as symbols for the past, present, or future.

For humans, communication occurs in two ways—verbally and nonverbally. Nonverbal communication includes environmental signals, social symbols, human gestures, and signs used in the transfer of message and meaning. The symbols most used by humans are *words*. One word can have several meanings; two or more words can describe one thought or feeling. Words can be technical or non-technical, have regional meanings or usages, and their meanings can often change.

Social semanticists have examined problems in the use of words. *Allness* is indicative of people who only perceive a portion of what is going on in the world. They are intolerant of other viewpoints and think they know all there is to know about a subject. *Bypassing* occurs when senders and receivers miss each other with the meaning of their words.

Managers must remember that people have meaning, words do not. Words are incomplete. They are in a sense a map of our mental territory that we wish to share with others. People who are *intentionally* oriented first perceive and inspect the real world or territory and then construct a verbal map that corresponds to it.

In summary, the human nervous system is incapable of obtaining all the details on or about any problem. Hence, we must *abstract* some details and omit an infinite number of others. The words we use depend on how we conceive and understand an object. We can then decide to communicate our understanding of the real world to others.

Often in the process of observing our world, we draw *inferences* when we don't have all the necessary facts. *Factual statements* are based on what we observe, know, or experience with our senses. All statements about the future are based on inferences. Anything that cannot be observed is an inference. Inferences should be labeled as such to prevent miscommunication.

Effective managers avoid taking words for granted. Communication is accurate when it is preceded by a great deal of thought and reflection.

Communication Climate

The third hurdle a manager must overcome is to understand an organization's communication climate, flow, and loops. In the typical organization, communication occurs in a variety of oral, written, and nonverbal ways. This interaction may take the form of daily meetings, sales forecasts, manuals and documents, letters, or telephone conversations. Organizational communication is the sum of the communication networks relating to the major organizational goals.

The *communication climate* is the degree to which an organization allows and encourages a free flow of ideas and information between employees. This climate relies upon the *quality* of the communication content and the number of *channels* available for relaying information. Too little information or too much information may be a problem. Exchanging information too late can also create costly errors.

Formal communication flow occurs within the typical organization in three directions: downward, upward, and horizontal. *Downward communication* flows from top management to subordinates and usually includes goals, policies, directives, job descriptions, instructions, evaluations, and feedback.

Poor downward communication occurs when there is lack of growth, lack of clearly defined objectives, failure to audit communication techniques, confusion over the responsibility for communications, and segregation between supervisory and nonsupervisory personnel. Downward communication is improved by establishing clear objectives and taking specific care of the content of a message.

Upward communication flows from subordinates to superiors and includes reports on activities, resource requests, and feedback. Factors that lead to poor upward communication include the size and structure of the organization, unrealistic assumptions, filtering and distortion, fear of presenting bad news, poor superior/subordinate relations, and information bottlenecks. Upward communication is improved by encouraging feedback, both positive and negative, and by creating an open and receptive climate.

Horizontal communication is lateral or diagonal communication between employees on the same level in an organization. The interaction usually revolves around formal tasks and goals that are vital to the personnel occupying these positions. Horizontal communication assists in work coordination, problem solving, information sharing, conflict resolution, and covers such areas as production, sales, personnel, purchasing, and finance. Horizontal flow is also a means by which subordinates evaluate and critique their superiors' skills, attitudes, values, personalities, knowledge, and abilities. Horizontal communication is improved by constructing realistic organizational charts, providing accurate job descriptions, organizing and utilizing interdepartmental projects, encouraging regular meetings for communication, and modeling proper communication usage.

Informal Communication

The *grapevine* is a type of communication that flows informally within the organization. Referred to as a "rumor mill," it is a necessary network and is often a good source for information. Information is spread faster in the grapevine than in formal communication flows. Grapevines and the amount of influence they exude can be controlled, but they cannot be suppressed. Openness in handling problems, disproving rumors, being timely with information, and having an effective formal communications system can prevent the grapevine from being destructive. Employees should be educated as to its deleterious effects.

Communication loops depend upon personalities and the working relations of small groups for their existence. Loops are composed of people who are linked by the nature of their organizational tasks. Characteristics of communication loops are the size of the loop, the transmission technique, the immediate or delayed closure, and matching or mismatching of people and information.

Managers should examine the process of communication when they sense that a communication problem exists. This can be accomplished through various auditing techniques designed to test communication within the organization. Among the audit tests are employee surveys, the International Communication Audit (ICA Audit), the Organizational Communication Development Audit System (OCD), and the Episodic Communication Channels in Organizations Analysis (ECCO Analysis).

Managers need to develop five specific communications skills: nonverbal, listening, speaking, group leadership, and writing.

Nonverbal Communication

Nonverbal communication refers to human action and behavior and the corresponding meaning that is attached. Talking and writing are associated with the use of verbal symbols, or words that stand for facts, ideas, or other things. Nonverbal communication, however, includes gestures, facial expressions, vocal pauses, and body movement. These messages are often stronger than the verbal messages and occur more frequently. Nevertheless, we often ignore messages that are communicated nonverbally.

Communication is influenced by the *environment*. Within the environment *time, territory,* and *design and arrangement* contribute to communication messages. Time conveys messages depending upon its vantage point. The value of time can be based upon money, power, or status.

Humans are *territorial* creatures. We design, maintain, and use our territory for our safety and pleasure. The *design and arrangement* of our territory also communicates. Building design, office space design, room design, room color, and desk arrangement all send messages to receivers.

Social aspects of nonverbal communication send important messages concerning space and symbols. *Space,* and its impact on relationships with others, is classified as intimate, personal, social, or public. *Status* is conveyed by factors such as title, body language, assignment of a secretary or an assistant, or the ability of others to invade that space.

Our *physical* behavior also conveys nonverbal messages. Body movement, gestures, facial expressions, eye movement, vocal intonation, clothing, and touch send out messages to others. These messages tell whether we are happy, sad, angry, confused, trustworthy, irritated, organized, or disorganized.

Effective managers coordinate both their verbal and nonverbal messages. They are sensitive to what their peers, subordinates, and supervisors are nonverbally conveying.

Listening

Listening is composed of four stages: (1) *Hearing,* which uses sound waves and which is often a passive process; (2) *interpreting* the sounds and sights that we receive; (3) *evaluating* what we have heard and deciding how to use the information; (4) *reacting* to the entire process. Listening consumes the majority of our communication time and takes place in staff meetings, sales meetings, training sessions, telephone calls, conversations with superiors, discussions with peers, counseling, and attending speeches.

Feedback is the response to what a person sees, hears, reads, or feels. The knowledge gained by feedback is vital. It tells us when our instructions are misunderstood, if our comments lack relevance, and whether or not our behavior contradicts what we say. Effective feedback is clear, understood, accepted, and helpful when making changes.

Presentational Speaking

The professional presentation is a vital part of any business. Managers maximize the effectiveness of their presentations by employing a four-step process.

When *organizing* an oral presentation, one must know the basic steps and answer the questions of who, where, when, why, what, and how. Every group is different, and a speech needs to be designed for a particular *audience*. The *occasion* assists the speaker in determining the *purpose*. The place, date, and time of the presentation affects how well listeners receive it.

To answer the question of why, one must know the reason or purpose of the presentation. The two most common purposes for a business presentation are to *inform* and to *persuade*. A *pattern of organization* is the particular order in which supporting information is presented. The pattern should contribute to ease of listening and the accomplishment of desired results. Patterns can be chronological, spatial, topical, sequential, according to classification, comparative, problem-solution, advantage-disadvantage, or cause-effect.

Supporting material helps listeners picture the ideas by verifying, clarifying, and amplifying the main points. This may be accomplished by using a comparison or definition, providing an example or an illustration, presenting statistics, telling a story, or providing testimony. Visual aids such as charts, graphs, or filmstrips can also help the listener understand and retain the message.

A properly structured speech has three main parts: the *introduction*, the *body*, and a *conclusion*. Each part has a specific function. The *introduction* helps gain the audience's attention. It includes an attention-getting opening, a topic statement, and a preview of the presentation's main points. The *body* contains all of the major arguments and supporting evidence. The *conclusion* recaps the main ideas, emphasizes the message's importance, and ends with a statement of goodwill. Since the effectiveness of an oral presentation relies on the listener to remember the main points, the speaker must include simple words, key phrases, and signposts to indicate what parts of the presentation are most important.

The best speeches appear to be spontaneous no matter how detailed the preparation. Effective speakers know their material well, maintain eye contact with their audiences, add meaning and emphasis through nonverbal communication, and receive feedback from their listeners. Good speakers learn the skill of effective speaking by practice. Like any other musical, artistic, or athletic skill it can be learned and perfected.

Managing Small Groups

People on a management or staff level of an organization will testify to the large number of meetings which they attend daily and weekly. Meetings are one of the most effective communication devices used in business. They allow one person to give information to several receivers within a limited period of time. Meetings allow people to ask questions and give feedback in order to gain an understanding of the total message.

A *meeting* consists of two or more people who interact in an organized manner, face-to-face and over a period of time, and who feel a sense of common identity. They meet because of shared goals. In group meetings individual roles and leadership patterns emerge.

Meetings result in increased participation of employees in the decision-making process, better decisions because of the pooling of knowledge, and quicker implementation of ideas because participants accept the solution. Disadvantages of meetings are the amount of time they consume, the backing of the decision by management, and the often questionable quality of knowledge of the participants. Meetings can also be very expensive because of the time involved, especially if they are slow and poorly run.

The *objective* of all group meetings is to accomplish the end result as quickly and effectively as possible. Meetings have two functions: *task* and *maintenance*. The *task* function is to complete the goal that the group has identified. The *maintenance* function involves the interpersonal needs of the group members; i.e., morale, conflict, cooperation, and communication.

Writing

Managers compose letters, memoranda, and reports in order to accomplish specific purposes and to maintain goodwill. Written communication is most effective when properly combined with oral communication. Used alone, writers must carefully evaluate their situation and their audience in order to select the words and ideas that avoid misunderstanding.

Reports and documents written for the purpose of informing or persuading may present past events, new information, or recommendations. They may be sent upward to top management, horizontally to other departments, or radially within and outside the organization. Their objectives are usually *informational* and *analytical.* The data may be presented *formally* in a prescribed format or *informally* as in routine status and progress reports.

The traditional parts of a formal report include title page, authorization letter, transmittal letter, synopsis, table of contents, introduction, findings, conclusion, and any appended parts. An *inverted* approach puts the news up front and saves the reader time. It allows you to accomplish 100 percent readership at the start.

The ability to write an effective *business letter* is essential. A letter may be part of a daily routine, it may be used for emphasis or just to record an activity, or it may be used as a follow-up to a discussion.

Letters convey *good news* or *bad news,* and different approaches should be used for both. *Good news* requires little explanation and background. A *bad news* letter requires an indirect approach which provides reasons or details that convince the reader a decision was unavoidable. *Persuasive* letters overcome resistance by establishing a logical presentation of reasoning and a closing statement. *Application letters* summarize a person's achievements and interests and requests consideration for a specific job. *Memoranda* are informal messages that can be used to request information, reinforce agreements, clarify previous messages, or act as short reports about daily problems.

Editing is the polish and assures that oversights and errors are eliminated. Editing results in messages that are clear, concise, and correct in every detail. There are several methods to edit a written document:

1. eliminate unneeded words
2. explain abbreviations and acronyms
3. eliminate jargon
4. eliminate unnatural phrases
5. use smaller words
6. use active instead of passive verbs
7. use the readability index
8. use the right word
9. correct spelling and grammatical errors
10. correct sexist errors

Effective written communications reflect the sender. They are neat, well-organized, easily read, and follow an acceptable format. If properly edited, they are effective tools for achieving organizational goals.

Effective managers not only must understand the communication process, the hurdles to its effective use, and communication skills, but also must translate this information into specific managerial areas.

The Communicating Manager as an Interviewer

An interview is an interaction that occurs between two parties to accomplish a predetermined purpose essential to the welfare of the organization. The manager's responsibility as the interviewer is to make sure that the interviewee understands the purpose. The manager also brings the right parties together and plans the interview structure or format. Like a speech, the interview includes an opening to establish contact and set the tone, a body to gain the information necessary, and a close which summarizes and indicates when the interview is completed. Key *questioning techniques* are essential. *Closed questions* are used to limit response and gain information about attitudes and beliefs. *Mirror questions* help encourage further discussion. Managers should avoid leading questions since they assume agreement, or at the very least, presume to lead the interviewee to a predetermined response.

Managers are involved in several *types of interviews*, including the employment interview, the orientation interview, the counseling interview, and the disciplinary interview. Each of these requires specific techniques to enhance the effectiveness of the communication.

The Communicating Manager as a Leader

Managers accomplish, bring about, conduct or direct. To be effective they must be capable of leading motivated employees.

Leadership

Leadership *traits* have been identified by Davis as *intelligence, social maturity, breadth, inner motivation and achievement drives*, and *human relations attitudes.* Physical traits that have been associated with leaders are energy, appearance, and height. The study of traits, however, is not successful in explaining leadership since all leaders do not possess them.

Certain *leadership styles* have been identified that are appropriate in different situations, depending upon the people involved. The *authoritarian style* characterizes the manager who is directive, uses negative rewards and reprimands, and uses power to silence opposition. This leader demands results and rarely involves the group in decision making. The *democratic style* is used by a positive manager who emphasizes praise for a job well done, delegates projects, states expectations clearly, sets high standards, minimizes direct orders, uses authority to minimize obstacles, and assists in accomplishing goals. The *participative style* is placed somewhere between the autocratic and democratic approaches. It encourages participation and decision making but lacks complete confidence in a subordinate's ability to make decisions. The *laissez-faire style* describes a manager who leaves things alone. Employees have little input and receive little information. There is a lack of clear expectations and minimal direction.

While these are predominant styles, other leadership approaches are also used. *Functional leadership* derives from any group member that promotes the achievement of the group. In other words, leadership varies by function. *Situational leadership* is based on the dynamics of the business situation. Leadership is favorable if the leader is generally accepted by followers, the task is highly structured, and the leader has power through formal authority in the organization. *Path-goal leadership* relates the leader's behavior to employee motivation, satisfaction, and performance.

Motivation

Motivation consists of three interrelated elements: needs, drives, and goals. A lack or imbalance of motivation creates dissatisfaction or tension and creates a *need*. This creates a *drive* that makes the person try to resolve the need. The *goal* is the outcome that the person perceives will eliminate the need and restore the balance. *Motivation* is the reason behind the behavior or the action.

Symptoms of low motivation are easily observed and include apathy, boredom, inattention, lack of concentration, intentional resistance, and waste. Theories of motivation are insightful for managers when determining ways to motivate the individual. Maslow's *Hierarchy of Needs* is widely used. Maslow identifies the basic needs of *survival* and *safety*. Unless these basic needs are met, higher level or secondary needs are ignored. Among the secondary needs are *belonging, ego* or *esteem*, and *self-actualization.*

Herzberg's *Motivation-Hygiene Model* states that motivation to do a better job depends upon *growth* factors, or those actions that result in a sense of achievement to the worker. Herzberg's *hygiene* factors are working conditions, company policy and administration, and interpersonal relationships. Herzberg states that these factors may cause unhappy or dissatisfied workers, and rarely motivate.

McClelland's *Needs Theory* recognizes that *power, achievement*, and *affiliation* act as motivating forces. In addition, *expectancies* and *equity* also play a role in the motivation of employees.

Communication satisfaction is a desirable end result and is basic to the relationship between subordinates and supervisors. It is a major factor in job satisfaction. Job satisfaction is dependent upon the communication *climate, personal feedback,* and the *relationship with the superior.*

The Communicating Manager as a Decision Maker and Problem Solver

All managers are concerned with finding the right solutions for problems in order to reach organizational goals. Being effective as a decision maker depends upon the *quality* and *acceptance* of the solution. There are three types of decision making. Managers may make the decision *alone*, with a *group*, or by hiring a *consultant*. Which method to use depends upon the nature of the *task*, the importance of the *acceptance* of the decision, the value placed on the *quality* of the decision, the *competency* of each person involved, and the anticipated operating effectiveness of the *group*.

If *consensus* is desired, everyone in the group agrees to live with the solution. There is no voting or compromise. Effective decision making is both creative and analytical. The creative problem solver has *flexibility*, *fluency* or the ability to recall ideas and associations, and *originality*. In order to generate ideas, *brainstorming, synectics, forcing*, and *nominal techniques* are helpful. Whichever technique is selected, a six-step problem-solving and decision-making model is followed:

1. defining the problem
2. analyzing the problem
3. generating alternative solutions
4. choosing a solution or course of action
5. implementing the solution
6. evaluating the effectiveness of the solution

Creativity assists in idea generation and is associated with the first three steps. Idea analysis is deduction: all facts and information are presented, and the participant clarifies, evaluates, or eliminates solutions.

The Communicating Manager as a Conflict Resolver

Conflict adds to a greater understanding and identification of problems as well as increasing alternatives and involvement. Conflict is restrictive when it encourages hostility. The organizational structure, performance measures, ambiguity, and conflicting reality perceptions serve as sources of conflict. If conflict is recognized in its early *stages*, it is managed effectively. A conflict episode usually includes *latent* conflict, *perceived* conflict, *felt* conflict, *manifest* conflict, and conflict *aftermath*.

Strategies are *outcome directed* (who gets what) or *goal directed* (what would benefit both). They are classified as *win/lose, lose/lose, win/win*. Both the win/lose and the lose/lose strategies are outcome directed. The atmosphere is one of victory or defeat. *Win/win* is the most desirable because all parties agree upon a solution. It requires a consensus and an approach that stresses goals and values while deemphasizing solutions and win/lose tactics.

Managers may find themselves involved in conflict intervention from three different perspectives. As *negotiators,* they will be involved in the process of conferring with others to arrive at a settlement. As *mediators,* they intervene or act as a neutral third party to promote reconciliation or to act as interpreter. As *arbitrators,* they hear and determine the case in question as an appointed statutory authority. The arbitrator acts as a judge and has the power to decide.

Conflict is a natural phenomenon that can be managed. Its absence is not necessarily good. Conflict encourages sounder decision making and stimulates interest.

The Communicating Manager as a Change Agent

Organizations, like individuals, are in a constant state of change. The change process includes the elements of innovation, messages about innovation, the passage of time from the first exposure until the innovation is no longer new, a group of people or a social system, and some observable response to the innovation. Change relies upon communication as an integral part of the process.

People resist change because it threatens the *status quo.* Change brings uncertainty and anxiety. In reality, change is a natural evolution of the problem-solving process. Change is the phase where the solution is put in place.

The person or group who is given the responsibility of implementing the change is called the *change agent. Change forces* include any aspects of the situation which increase willingness to change. The *driving forces* encourage the members of the organization to accept the solution. *Restraining forces* include any aspects of the situation which reduce the willingness to change from the *equilibrium.* Alternatives include increasing the strength of the driving forces, decreasing the strength of the restraining forces, or combining both of these approaches.

Healthy organizations have the ability to anticipate, execute, and adapt to change. Effective change involves the total organization and is planned, is comprehensive, emphasizes co-orientation of work groups, and requires participation of a change agent. Success of the change is based on the change agent's credibility, effective problem identification, supportive climate, long-range planning, and a system of program evaluation.

Sample Speeches

This appendix presents eight sample speeches, each with a different pattern of organization (see discussion on pages 180–183 of Chapter 8). All present a variety of types of verbal supporting material (pages 183–187).

```
         Topic:  THE AMAZING TELEPHONE
       Purpose:  To inform (chronological pattern)
Specific purpose:  To describe the importance of the telephone as a
                   communication instrument


                        Introduction


    A. Telephone conversation is initiated with Alex.
    B. The history of the telephone has provided a foundation for its
       present and future development.
    C. The new priority calling service provides freedom from inter-
       ruption.


                            Body


  I. About the past
     A. It all started with Alexander Graham Bell in 1876.
     B. A lot of developments have occurred between Bell's time and
        now:
        1. Digital computer switching in 1937
        2. Transistor invented in 1947
        3. Micro-processor chip of the 1970s
     C. Today's electronics have turned the evolution of the telephone
        into a revolution of new services.

 II. About the present
     A. New services include custom calling.
        1. Call waiting
        2. Call forwarding
     B. Touch-A-Matic dialing operates with one touch of a button.
     C. Machine talk can function at 75,000 words per minute.

III. And the future
     A. Sand, not copper, will be used for cables.
     B. At a busy signal, automatic callback will come to the rescue.
     C. Split connection and transmission lines provide benefits such
        as built-in answering machines.


                         Conclusion


     A. From the liquid phone to the wireless, that's progress.
     B. America has the best telephone service in the world.
     C. Telephone conversation is closed.
```

Source: A speech outline prepared by Martin Cominsky for BA 6113, "Effective Speaking," in the Edwin L. Cox School of Business, Southern Methodist University, Dallas, Tex., Nov. 9, 1977.

```
              Topic: DIAMONDS
            Purpose: To inform (comparative pattern)
   Specific purpose: To explain the different comparisons that must be
                     made when buying a diamond.


                         Introduction

     A. You've heard that diamonds are a girl's best friend. Most women
        hope to someday have a diamond. Today I am here to tell both you
        men and women what to consider when buying a diamond.
     B. This information is important so you will get the most for your
        money.
     C. Since many of us are seniors and may be contemplating marriage
        in the near future, I will tell you some of the comparisons to
        make as you consider this important investment.


                            Body


   I. Definition of a diamond: hardest known mineral, formed of crys-
      talline carbon, transparent and colorless, valued as a precious
      stone

  II. Compare shape and size
      A. Round
      B. Marquis
      C. Pear
      D. Square
      E. Oval
      F. Heart
      G. Large
      H. Small

 III. Compare color
      A. Top silver cape
      B. Fine top silver cape
      C. Very fine top silver cape
      D. No color
      E. Blue white

  IV. Compare flaws
      A. Bubble
      B. Ice
      C. Hairlike cracks
      D. Feathers
      E. Carbon spots
      F. Clouds
```

(continued)

```
    V. Compare weight
       A. Until 1913, no two countries had exactly the same measure for
          measuring the weight of diamonds.
       B. A carat weighs exactly one-fifth of a gram, as standardized by
          the United States. There are 100 points to the carat.

   VI. Compare price
       A. Don't be swayed by the ''good investment'' argument.
       B. Anxiety over debt at the outset of a marriage is one sure hin-
          drance to a good start.
       C. Average-size engagement ring of good quality runs $1,000 and
          up.


                               Conclusion


       A. I have given you a brief explanation of the five comparisons
          that should be made when buying a diamond. Remember, the dia-
          mond you select must be considered in relation to how much you
          can spend. Compromises usually must be made. Good luck and
          happy diamond buying.
```

Source: A speech outline prepared by Julie Jordin for BA 3303, "Business Communications," in the Edwin L. Cox School of Business, Southern Methodist University, Dallas, Tex., Nov. 15, 1977.

```
           Topic: THE TRADING OF COMMODITY FUTURES
         Purpose: To inform (topical pattern)
Specific purpose: To explain the different positions a trader can take
                  in the futures market


                          Introduction


  A. I will tell you how to triple your money in a matter of weeks.
  B. Commodity futures trading is a speculative investment to some
     traders. To other traders, it is a hedge against rising prices
     on the commodity they use in their business.
  C. There are three basic positions a trader can take in trading
     futures.


                             Body


  I. Long position
     A. Definition of going long
     B. When to go long
     C. What factors influence a trader to go long
     D. Receiving the commodity

 II. Short position
     A. Definition of going short
     B. When to go short
     C. What factors influence a trader to go short
     D. Delivering the commodity

III. Hedging
     A. Definition of a hedge
     B. Uses of hedging
     C. Receiving the commodity


                          Conclusion


  A. I have described the positions a trader can take in the commod-
     ity futures market.
  B. It is possible to triple your money in the futures market. How-
     ever, the odds are far greater that you will not. Unless you are
     a person who is willing to chance your money at 20 to 1 odds, you
     should not speculate in the commodity futures market. But if
     you are willing to take that chance, commodities can be a fast
     way to get rich.
```

Source: A speech outline prepared by Michael Merriman for BA 3303, "Business Communications," in the Edwin L. Cox School of Business, Southern Methodist University, Dallas, Tex. Nov. 6, 1979.

Topic: ENERGY CONSERVATION EFFORTS
Purpose: To inform (classification pattern)
Specific purpose: To explain the different categories of energy efficiency

Introduction

A. Energy conservation is an activity that affects every aspect of our lives.
B. This presentation will increase your awareness of the categories of conservation. Discussion will be centered around conservation efforts in the home, on the road, in offices, and in industrial facilities.

Body

I. Conservation in the home
   A. Solar heating
      1. Construction
      2. Feasibility
   B. Wood-burning fireplace and stove
   C. Insulation
   D. Additional techniques
      1. Caulking
      2. Home maintenance
      3. Using resources efficiently

II. Conservation on the road
   A. Popular conservation programs
      1. 55 mile per hour speed limit
      2. Carpooling
   B. New conservation programs being explored
      1. Increasing parking costs
      2. Utilizing existing railroad tracks
      3. Park and ride
      4. Future plans for Dallas transit bus service
   C. 1990 plans for North Texas region

III. Office buildings
   A. Existing conservation programs
      1. Adjusting thermostats
      2. Window shades
      3. Insulation
   B. Technologically available energy-saving designs
      1. Sunshades—inside and out
      2. Reflective glass
      3. Insulated windows
      4. Partitions
      5. Extended building usage

(continued)

```
      C.  Examples of conservation efforts in Dallas area
          1.  Dallas Fire Department
          2.  North Hampton Park Recreation and Health Center
          3.  La Quinta Motor Inn

  IV.  Industrial conservation
       A.  Current regulation
           1.  Department of Energy
           2.  MECA
       B.  Internal efforts
           1.  Vanpooling
           2.  Staggered work hours
           3.  Energy management centers
       C.  Alternate sources
           1.  Solar heating and cooling
           2.  Photovoltaic


                          Conclusion


       A.  Tremendous potential exists
       B.  Necessity for awareness
```

Source: A group presentation outline prepared by Walt Lammert for BA 6113, "Effective Speaking," in the Edwin L. Cox School of Business, Southern Methodist University, Dallas, Tex. March 10, 1980.

```
           Topic:  PROPER TABLE ETIQUETTE AT A FORMAL DINNER
         Purpose:  To inform (sequential pattern)
Specific purpose:  To explain proper table etiquette, which can prevent
                   embarrassing situations at a formal dinner setting


                         Introduction


    A.  The story is told of an executive who was embarrassed once at a
        formal dinner because he did not know how to use the dining
        utensils properly.
    B.  To prevent you from making the same mistake, I will explain
        proper etiquette and the sequence of a formal dinner. You are
        encouraged to use good etiquette as we play a ''pretend'' game
        where I am your boss.
        1.  You are my employees and are invited to dinner in my home.
        2.  You are confronted with a very formal place setting.
```

(continued)

Body

I. First, this is what you should do before eating.
 A. The ladies should all be seated first.
 B. The napkin should be placed in the lap.
 C. The service plate should be used for decoration and to receive smaller dishes from courses preceding the main course.

II. The first course is served.
 A. The guest is unsure of which dining utensil to use.
 B. The small fork is used for the appetizer.

III. The second course is served.
 A. Assume that this course is soup.
 B. The soup spoon on the far right side of the plate is used.

IV. The third course is served.
 A. The piece of silverware farthest from the plate is always used first.
 B. A salad fork is used for this course.

V. The fourth course is served.
 A. Assume that this course is fish.
 B. A knife and fork are used.
 C. The white wine is poured.

VI. The fifth course is served.
 A. Assume that this is the meat entree.
 B. The service plate is removed.
 C. The remaining knife and fork are used.
 D. The red wine is poured.

VII. The final course is served.
 A. Assume this includes dessert, coffee, or an after dinner drink.
 B. The few remaining pieces of silverware are used.

Conclusion

A. By following and practicing these guidelines you can avoid an embarrassing situation at a formal dinner setting.
B. By using good table etiquette, you can make a favorable impression on the boss and thus secure a promising future with the company.

Source: A speech outline prepared by Brad Kelly for BA 6113, "Effective Speaking," in the Edwin L. Cox School of Business, Southern Methodist University, Dallas, Tex. Feb. 6, 1979.

```
              Topic: MONEY MARKET MUTUAL FUNDS
            Purpose: To persuade (advantage/disadvantage pattern)
   Specific purpose: To define the money market mutual fund phenomenon,
                     explain how it works, and list its advantages over
                     regular savings accounts


                            Introduction


        A. I can tell you how to earn twice as much interest on your sav-
           ings.
        B. The Federal Reserve prohibits your bank from paying you more
           than 5 ½% interest on passbook savings.
        C. A money market mutual fund can earn you 13.8% on your savings.



                               Body


    I. Money market mutual fund defined
        A. It is a trust established by an investment company.
        B. A mutual fund allows investment in high-yield securities.
        C. It is an old stock market practice for inactive holdings.
        D. A large amount is typically needed for eligibility ($500–
           $5,000).

   II. New interest
        A. Presently seventy-five funds hold approximately $40 billion.
        B. $175 million go into the funds each day.
        C. Even such high interest as 13.8% cannot keep up with inflation.

  III. Disadvantages
        A. Many money market funds require $5,000 to invest.
        B. Inflation is still well above 13%.
        C. The attractiveness of these funds has shifted money out of
           banks and savings and loans.

   IV. Advantages
        A. Maximum return on your savings: as high as 13.8%.
        B. You invest in high-quality paper and Treasury bills: low risk.
        C. The investor is given exceptional liquidity.


                            Conclusion


        A. If you are looking for an investment with high returns and lit-
           tle or no risk, then I suggest money market mutual funds.
```

Source: A speech outline prepared by Todd Winter for BA 3303, "Business Communications," in the Edwin L. Cox School of Business, Southern Methodist University, Dallas, Tex., Nov. 7, 1979.

```
        Topic:  MINIMIZING ANXIETY
      Purpose:  To persuade (cause/effect pattern)
Specific purpose:  To prove the need for recreation to help minimize
                   anxiety
```

Introduction

A. "What is the greatest need of the human mind today?" The answer
   is "relaxation."
B. Anxiety is a prevalent problem in our society.
C. I will prove why anxiety needs to be minimized, how recreation
   can minimize it, and how to best utilize recreation.

Body

I. Anxiety needs to be minimized.
   A. Anxiety is suffered increasingly in our fast-paced modern
      world.
   B. Excessive anxiety is a major symptom of neurosis.
   C. Anxiety can get you into a rut.

II. Recreation helps minimize anxiety.
   A. *Recreation:* the word means re-creation.
   B. Recreation is a "tactical retreat."
   C. Recreation relaxes you and enables you to have fun.

III. Recreation is best utilized the following ways.
   A. Relearn to play.
   B. Do things you like to do.
   C. Develop work/play contingencies.
   D. Set reasonable goals.

Conclusion

A. I hope you realize that excessive anxiety is definitely a problem in our fast-paced society and must be curbed.
B. Recreation is one easy and fun way to minimize anxiety, allowing you to escape work and return to it feeling refreshed and
   more productive.

Source: A speech outline prepared by Diane Reddington for BA 3303, "Business Communications," in the Edwin L. Cox School of Business, Southern Methodist University, Dallas, Tex., Nov. 6, 1979.

```
            Topic:  BANKING FOCUS
          Purpose:  To persuade (problem/solution pattern)
 Specific purpose:  To show how your problems as a banker can be resolved
                    by a subscription to Banking Focus


                              Introduction

     A.  Bank officers and directors need to be informed about what is
         happening in the financial industry.
     B.  A wealth of literature is available to keep them informed.
     C.  There are problems with this approach to keeping informed.
     D.  There is an alternative: Banking Focus.


                                 Body

   I.  What can Banking Focus tell you about the competition?
       A.  It tells you what Savings and Loan Associations and Credit
           Unions are doing in the areas of lending and savings.
       B.  This information helps you determine strategies and policies
           to enable your bank to compete effectively.

  II.  What can Banking Focus tell you about legislative and regulatory
       developments?
       A.  It describes proposed Federal Reserve rulings and therefore
           Reserve requirements.
       B.  It describes new policies from the Comptroller's Office and the
           FDIC regarding reporting requirements and performance stan-
           dards.
       C.  It can tell you about proposed congressional legislation.
       D.  With this information you can respond to legislative and regu-
           latory bodies with recommendations and suggestions regarding
           proposed laws.

 III.  What can Banking Focus tell you about trends and developments in
       banking?
       A.  It predicts what the demands for credit will be in the automo-
           bile, agriculture, and housing markets.
       B.  It projects what the market conditions will be like for raising
           capital.
       C.  It forecasts where interest rates are headed—up, down, or
           holding steady.
       D.  This information helps you know where the greatest demand for
           your bank's funds will be, where the highest profits can be
           made, and what constraints your bank will be operating under.

  IV.  Your cost is minimal.
       A.  The first one-year subscription is $30.
       B.  The next nine subscriptions are $12 per year.
       C.  Any additional subscriptions are $9 per year.
```

(continued)

```
                            Conclusion

     A. For as low as $30 per year you can be a better-informed banker.
     B. Subscribe today, and you will gain both the information and the
        time you need to be a more effective banker.
```

Source: A speech outline prepared by Cathy Bell for BA 6113, "Effective Speaking," in the Edwin L. Cox School of Business, Southern Methodist University, Dallas, Tex., March 13, 1979.

A P P E N D I X B

Writing Materials That Help Build Important Writing Skills

The materials contained in this appendix serve as examples of typical writing assignments, checklists, and exercises designed to guide you as you acquire the expertise in writing skills that you will need throughout your lifetime.

Sample Pages from a Model Report

IMPROVING WRITTEN COMMUNICATION SKILLS

THROUGH PROGRAMMED INSTRUCTION

FINAL REPORT

SUBMITTED TO:

THE BOARD OF EXECUTIVES

PRESENTED BY:

MARY M. RYDESKY

CUSTOMER SERVICE DEPARTMENT

LONE STAR BANK

June 29, 1986

Exhibit B.1 • Model Report—Title Page

LONE STAR BANK
2000 Commerce Street
Dallas, Texas 75220
214-695-0000

June 29, 1986

The Board of Executives
Lone Star Bank
2000 Commerce Street
Dallas, TX 75220

Ladies and Gentlemen:

Enclosed is the final report on an exciting in-company educational
program that you authorized in April of this year.

The program, Improving Written Communications Skills: Punctuation
Module, has been developed and tested, and the results are presented for
your consideration. The program was low cost for Lone Star, took no on-
the-job time since it was designed as programmed instruction for home
use, and resulted in a significant level of reduced errors in writing.

The report gives a background of the study, describes the method of
instruction, and makes recommendations for further development.

Respectfully,

Mary M. Rydesky, Director
Customer Service Department

Exhibit B.2 • Model Report—Transmittal Letter

SYNOPSIS

This report describes the development and testing of programmed instruction materials for teaching punctuation in the Customer Service Department of Lone Star Bank. The report presents the initial problem, background information that led to the study, the method of research undertaken through testing and training, and the findings of the research after training was performed.

The appendixes contain several items that support and add information to the report: a sample page of instruction, pre- and post-test scores, and selected employee comments on the instruction. The major conclusions drawn from the study are that programmed instruction meets five criteria for Lone Star Bank:

1. It allows employees to work at self-determined paces;

2. It allows employees to study at home rather than on the job;

3. It reinforces learning immediately so that the employee can use each lesson as it is covered, rather than waiting until the course is completed;

4. It reinforces the Lone Star style of correspondence; and

5. It minimizes the costs and time loss while achieving the desired goal of improved performance.

(continued)

Recommendations for further development are:

1. Transfer Ann Ford to Customer Service so she may develop additional programmed instruction modules.

2. Create modules on dictation skills, spelling, and proofreading during the next six months. Test each module immediately after development.

3. Fund Ann Ford to present Lone Star's Improved Written Communication Skills services at the 1986 American Society for Training and Development annual conference.

4. Fund Rydesky to write an article for *Banking Management.* The article would compare Lone Star's new program with competitor's methods.

Exhibit B.3 · Model Report—Synopsis

TABLE OF CONTENTS

(continued)

Exhibit B.4 • Model Report—Table of Contents

INTRODUCTION

Purpose

    This report describes a new training process, programmed instruc-
tion, developed and tested at the Lone Star Bank. The report will examine the background of the problem, research methods employed, the formation of the Improving Written Communication Skills: Punctuation
Module, the findings following the training, and recommendations for
future training.

(continued)

Problem Statement

The Customer Service Department needed instruction in how to correct punctuation errors. To find the right educational process the
department investigated materials and tested a programmed instruction
package.

Background

For some time a high incidence of punctuation errors has been noted
by the Customer Service Department staff. The director investigated
methods used within the banking industry to improve writing skills.
They were found to be time consuming and costly to develop or purchase.
A comparison of costs was presented in the April 15, 1986, proposal,
which is reproduced in Appendix A of this report. While several of the
methods resulted in improved writing skills, the costs outweighed the
benefits.

Programmed instruction, which is an educational method of presentation that reinforces the student's learning throughout the course,
was then investigated. This approach to instruction is organized in a
psychologically coherent sequence rather than in a logical sequence.
The ideas flow one to another rather than being divided into a logical
introduction, body, and summary. Self-instruction and self-testing are
incorporated in programmed instruction to decrease reliance on a live
instructor in a formal classroom. Because material is presented in
small increments punctuated by test questions that require the student
to practice the new knowledge, it can be studied during spare moments
without compromising the student's attention to the content.

(continued)

Programmed instruction meets five criteria for Lone Star:

1. It allows employees to work at self-determined paces;

2. It allows employees to study at home rather than on the job;

3. It reinforces learning immediately so that the employee can use each
   lesson as it is covered, rather than waiting until the course is
   completed;

4. It reinforces the Lone Star style of correspondence;

5. It minimizes the costs and time loss while achieving the desired goal
   of improved performance.

In addition, the programmed instruction workbooks can be given to
the employees to use as reference texts after the initial study period.
(A copy of the workbook can be found in Appendix B.)

The methodology for testing was:

1. Customer Service staff was tested on punctuation skills and then
   divided into two groups of thirty-two. Each group was ''matched'' by
   test scores so that neither would be more knowledgeable about punctuation prior to the program.

2. The experimental group used programmed instruction workbooks at
   home.

3. The control group received a classroom lecture during business
   hours.

4. Both groups were tested prior to instruction and then again following instruction. (Pre-test and post-test scores were recorded
   and compared.)

(continued)

The chronology of the testing was:

May 7, 1986   Pre-tests given; groups assigned.

May 10, 1986 Ford meets with experimental group for a thirty-min-
ute briefing. Employees are asked to complete workbooks at home.

May 11, 1986 Control group receives instruction; lecture takes
sixty minutes to deliver.

FINDINGS

As a result of the testing the following findings were revealed:

May 15, 1986 Both groups tested; scores are compared with pre-test
scores:

	Pre	Post	Change
A. Experimental group programmed instruction	25.9	34.9	+9.0
B. Control group classroom instruction	25.7	33.2	+7.5

(See Appendix C for complete statistics.) Programmed instruction
effects the greater change. Results are subjected to statistical
testing; validity is verified.

June 10, 1986 Groups are recalled for a surprise retest to see
whether retention of information is related to method of presentation:

A. Experimental group   31.3

B. Control group   28.9

(continued)

The employees who used the programmed instruction materials re-
tained more knowledge. Employees' comments about programmed
instruction are collected.

June 11, 1986 Employees' comments are collated:

A. 98% are favorable and indicate interest in having more programmed instruction materials.

B. 2% disliked doing the study at home.

June 29, 1986 Report of results submitted to the Committee of Executives. Major recommendation is to continue the development of
programmed instruction materials on writing skills.

CONCLUSION

Summary

The programmed method of instruction is by far the most cost effective and beneficial for Lone Star Bank. The greatest contribution of
this study is the reduction in errors in correspondence prepared by
employees in the Customer Service Department. A comparison of letters
written last December with those written in May shows 46% to 75% fewer
errors. In addition, fewer letters have been received from customers
who request explanations of materials sent to them. If a customer's case
can be handled through one piece of correspondence instead of several,
the savings for Lone Star are large.

(continued)

Recommendations

    Because the scores indicate that programmed instruction is effective in teaching writing skills, and because Lone Star employees react favorably to this method of instruction, development of additional packages is warranted. Recommendations are:

1. Transfer Ann Ford to Customer Service so she may develop additional programmed instruction modules.

2. Create modules on dictation skills, spelling, and proofreading during the next six months. Test each module immediately after development.

3. Fund Ann Ford to present Lone Star's Improving Written Communication Skills series at the 1986 American Society for Training and Development annual conference.

4. Fund Rydesky to write an article for *Banking Management* magazine. The article would compare Lone Star's new program with competitors' methods.

Exhibit B.5 • Model Report—Text

Source: Mary M. Rydesky, "Lone Star Bank Report," prepared for this book.

Letter Writer's Checklists

Table B.1 • Letter Checklist: Direct Approach

I. Get letter under way quickly.
    A. Place key question in the first line of the letter, or
    B. Start with a general question, and place more specific questions later in letter.

II. Give adequate explanation.
    A. Tailor message to reader.
    B. Place general explanatory material following the direct opening sentence.
    C. Include explanatory material with questions where needed.
    D. Ask the minimum number of questions to get necessary information.

III. Structure questions carefully.
    A. Ask directly for information; do not hint.
    B. Avoid "loaded" questions.
    C. Word questions carefully to get necessary information.
    D. Itemize questions when necessary.
    E. Vary sentence form and length to avoid singsong effect.

IV. End with goodwill.
    A. Refer to reader's next action.
    B. Express appreciation.
    C. Avoid trite expressions.

V. Take care in word choice.

VI. Use correct emphasis.

Source: Adapted from C. W. Wilkinson, Peter B. Clark, Dorothy C. M. Wilkinson, *Communicating through Letters and Reports* (Homewood, Ill.: Richard D. Irwin, 1980), p. 101.

Table B.2 • Letter Checklist: Indirect Approach

I. Use indirect approach.
    A. Use friendly, neutral talk to establish common ground.
    B. Start with comments that set up the following strategy.

II. Present the explanation and the refusal.
    A. Give justifying reasons prior to refusal.
    B. Have reasoning flow logically to refusal.
    C. State refusal positively.

III. Close with a feeling of goodwill.
    A. Use last words to give a forward look.
    B. Show how the reader benefits.

IV. Take care in word choice; avoid negatives.

V. Use correct emphasis.

VI. Avoid critical or patronizing tone.

Source: Adapted from C. W. Wilkinson, Peter B. Clark, Dorothy C. M. Wilkinson, *Communicating through Letters and Reports* (Homewood, Ill.: Richard D. Irwin, 1980), p. 211.

Table B.3 · Letter Checklist: Persuasive Approach

    I. *Start with attention-getting opening.*
        A. Begin with an attention-getting sentence.
        B. Avoid negative tone.
        C. Establish common ground.

   II. *Present reasoning in systematic order.*
        A. Use indirect approach.
        B. Avoid overlap and repetition.
        C. Establish case through specific information and sound reasoning.
        D. Avoid leading statements or loaded words.
        E. Begin with arguments that will have greatest impact or success.
        F. Label opinions, and support them with facts.

  III. *End with an action-getting close.*
        A. Present desired action to the reader.
        B. Emphasize benefits of action.
        C. Convey goodwill.

  IV. *Avoid negative language.*

   V. *Use correct emphasis.*

  VI. *Avoid trite expressions.*

Letter Formats

KEYSTONE LTD.
4332 Amherst Ave.
Baton Rouge, LA 70811

February 22, 1986

Ms. B. A. Buckman
Box 1113
Dallas, TX 75275

Dear Ms. Buckman:

This is an example of a semiblock-style letter. Its appearance is balanced because of the indented paragraphs and placement of the date and salutation. It is a traditional style still preferred by many people.

The first line of each paragraph is indented five spaces. The date line and the close begin at the center of the page.

You may desire to use this style for more formal occasions.

Sincerely,

Lynn Harris

Lynn Harris

Exhibit B.6 • The Modified Block Format

KEYSTONE LTD.
4332 Amherst Ave.
Baton Rouge, LA 70811

February 22, 1986

Ms. B. A. Buckman
Box 1113
Beaumont, TX 77705

Dear Ms. Buckman:

This is an example of a block—style letter, which has become common in many organizations. It is efficient because it saves time and energy for the typist.

The block style has no indentions. All parts of the letter begin at the left margin, including the date, salutation, and signature block.

You will find this is a convenient, time—saving format.

Sincerely,

Lynn Harris

Lynn Harris

Exhibit B.7 • The Block Format

```
                              KEYSTONE LTD.
                              4332 Amherst Ave.
                              Lake City, LA 71327
                              (318) 932-7619


February 22, 1986




Ms. B. A. Buckman
Box 1113
Dallas, TX 75275

THE AMS STYLE

This is an example of the AMS style. You'll note the elimination of the
salutation and close. There will be times when you will not address your
letter to a specific person and the AMS style will be an excellent
choice.

As in the block style, all parts of the letter begin at the left margin.
It has the same time-saving features with the added simplicity of elimi-
nating the formalities.

Your letter can be direct, yet friendly, with this format. Use it to
adapt to your specific letter-writing needs.

LYNN HARRIS

Lynn Harris
```

Exhibit B.8 • The AMS Format

Answers to Exercises in Chapter 10

The Convention Travel Report Errors (page 275)

1. <u>Sir</u>: There are many different formats for memoranda, but in formal correspondence, a colon should follow *sir*, not a comma.

2. <u>In compliance with</u>: This is an overused expression that can be stated much more succinctly—that is, *as directed* or *as requested*.
3. <u>I have attended</u>: The simple past tense should be used here.
4. <u>Memorandum is submitted</u>: Using the passive voice robs good writing of forcefulness.
5. <u>For your perusal</u>: Another trite expression that should be eliminated. The boss already knows the memorandum was written for him to read.
6. <u>Convention discussed</u>: Things do not discuss; people discuss.
7. <u>Three main topics</u>: Use a colon instead of a dash to introduce a series.
8. <u>DIA's</u>: Acronyms can be very confusing; they should be spelled on first use in a body of writing.
9. <u>Interferance</u>: Misspelled.
10. <u>Companies</u>: This word is the possessive of *programs* and should be followed by an apostrophe. Another way to correct this is to use an *of* phrase rather than an apostrophe, as is shown in the corrected draft.
11. <u>OSHA's</u>: Another unexplained acronym. Although her boss would probably understand, it is better to spell it out the first time.
12. <u>The fact that</u>: This phrase is always unnecessary.
13. <u>Rivetting</u>: Misspelled.
14. <u>For quality control purposes and</u>: "To make sure it meets their requirements" restates "quality control."
15. <u>First off</u>: This phrase is grammatically incorrect and unnecessary.
16. <u>Fed's</u>: The recipient of this report is not the Godfather. Slang has no place in business writing.
17. <u>Full of baloney</u>: Archaic slang is even worse!
18. <u>One hundred and fifty million</u>: Do not use "and" between the parts of a large whole number. Also, when referring to dollars, figures and the "$" sign are preferred (that is, $150,000,000 or $150 million).
19. <u>Were stolen</u>: The subject of this phrase, *equipment*, requires a singular verb.
20. <u>And</u>: Do not begin a sentence with a conjunction.
21. <u>More was destroyed</u>: "More" what? The reference here is unclear.
22. <u>I know</u>: Personal references have no place in formal memo-

randa. The boss may not care about the opinion of an uninformed junior executive.

23. <u>More strict</u>: This comparative expression is unclear. As used, it could mean either more standards or stricter standards.
24. <u>Never</u>: Double negative.
25. <u>Deleteriously</u>: Use a shorter, more common word if no sense of meaning is lost.
26. <u>Impact on</u>: Unless the writer thinks the standards will physically collide with the plans, she should delete the superfluous *on*.
27. <u>Their</u>: A common misuse of the intended *they're*. Writing out the contraction can avoid this mistake. Better yet, make the reference clearer as in the corrected example.
28. <u>dBh</u>: An unexplained abbreviation.
29. <u>Has me worried; </u>: The writer injects a personal opinion again. Also, the following conjunction, *but*, requires a comma, not a semicolon.
30. <u>About it</u>: This phrase is unnecessary.
31. <u>To much</u>: This is a common mistake—using a preposition when an adverb is intended. This is also the wrong form of the word *to*.
32. <u>Point in time</u>: Made popular several years ago in the Watergate proceedings, this phrase is ridiculously superfluous.
33. <u>Rivets is</u>: The verb must agree with the subject.
34. <u>Though</u>: When used as conjunction, *though* should introduce a dependent clause.
35. <u>Principle problem</u>: The word *principle* is a noun meaning a fundamental truth, rule of conduct, source, origin. The word *principal* can be a noun or an adjective; as the latter it means chief, leading, highest in rank or importance. *Principal*, the adjective, should be used here.
36. <u>Inspect everyone</u>: The reference of *everyone* is vague and needs to be more defined.
37. <u>Aeorospace Industry</u>: There are two errors here: *aerospace* is misspelled, and the words do not need to be capitalized.
38. <u>We're</u>: By using *we* instead of *they*, the writer shifts her point of view from *everyone* and implies an improper meaning.
39. <u>Our men and girls</u>: These are sexist terms and should be made neutral.
40. <u>Backing, during</u>: This comma is unnecessary.
41. <u>Affects</u>: The noun should be *effects*. *Affect* is a verb.
42. <u>Disasterous</u>: Misspelled.

43. <u>Well</u>: Use of *well* in this sense is too informal.
44. <u>After rivets</u>: This is poor construction. The writer means to say "after the subject of rivets was discussed."
45. <u>Completely finished</u>: The word *completely* is superfluous.
46. <u>For the purpose of</u>: Trite expression.
47. <u>Quantifying</u>: Improper use of an impressive-sounding verb.
48. <u>Goals and objectives</u>: Superfluous.
49. <u>Viable alternatives</u>: Overused expression.
50. <u>Resounding success</u>: This is a weak and overused phrase.
51. <u>Respectively</u>: A misused word. The writer means to say *Respectfully*.

To: George Harris,
           Vice-President in Charge of Policy

From: Beth Williams,
           Government Relations Division

Subject: Convention Report

Sir:

As directed, I recently attended the convention "Government Regulations in the Aerospace Industry." The discussion involved three main
topics: interference of the Defense Intelligence Agency in the internal
security programs of companies, noise exposure standards of the Occupational Safety and Health Administration (OSHA), and the U.S. government's quality control inspections of the new Teflon riveting technique.

The federal delegate's presentation on internal security was illumi-
nating. He stated that last year spies stole microprocessing equipment
worth $150,000,000. Even more equipment was destroyed by espionage.

OSHA's decision to impose stricter noise exposure standards could se-
verely impact our production plans. OSHA is considering requiring 90
decibels per hour exposure limits, which, according to our production
planners, could be a long-range problem for us.

The special rivets are another matter, however. The principal problem
with the rivets is that they shear off at high altitudes, so to insure
safety the government plans to inspect all companies in the aerospace
industry. Federal stress engineers propose our workers reinforce their
rivets with a steel backing during airframe assembly. Otherwise, the
effects on high-altitude test flights could be disastrous.

The discussion concerning rivets concluded the convention. All the
delegates agreed the goal of improving industry relations with the
government was achieved.

Respectfully,

The Corrected Travel Report Memo

Source: Timothy Riggins.

Eliminate Unneeded Words Exercise (pages 292–293)

Practice 1 (48 words)

In order to keep you informed of the results of the sales meeting held on August 13 to consider ways and means of reducing the cost of the proposed spring sales campaign, we are submitting herewith a brief resume and the procedure outlined for the cost reduction plans.

Sample Answer (21 words)

Here is a resume of plans, drawn at the August 13 meeting, for cutting costs on the proposed spring sales campaign.

Practice 2 (36 words)

Memoranda intended for internal distribution should be written just as carefully as those to be distributed outside of the division, and, actually, they serve as an excellent opportunity for developing an individual's proficiency in writing.

Sample Answer (24 words)

Write memoranda for use within a division as carefully as those sent outside. They give you a good chance to build your writing skill.

Active Voice Exercise (page 293)

1. (Passive) A sharp decrease in sales was noted.
   (Active) Sales decreased sharply.
2. (Passive) The department is dependent on our aid for its success.
   (Active) The department's success depends on our aid.
3. (Passive) It is desired by the president that this problem be brought before the board of directors.
   (Active) The president desires that this problem be brought before the board of directors.

Answers to Misused Words Exercise (page 293)

1. We shall be seriously <u>effected</u> by the new corporate policy.
   The verb should be *affected*. Effect, as a verb, means to bring about. When used as a noun it means result. The word affect means to influence.
2. The <u>amount</u> of conventioners who come to New York City varies with the season.
   The correct word is *number*, which refers to countable units. The word amount refers to general quantity.
3. We shall appreciate your <u>advising</u> us of your decision.
   The proper word is *notifying*. Advising means to give advice.
4. The estate was divided <u>between</u> the millionaire's three sons.
   The correct word is *among*, which refers to three or more units. *Between* is used when referring to only two units.
5. <u>Can</u> we have your permission to proceed with the instructions outlined in this letter?
   The correct word is *may*. *May* denotes permission; *can* denotes ability.

Answers to Problem Sentences Exercises (page 293)

1. Divided into two sections, the accountant balances the accounts more readily.
   <u>Error</u>: Dangling participle
   <u>Corrected</u>: Divided into two sections, the accounts are more readily balanced by the accountant.
2. Depreciation accounting is not a system of valuation but of allocation.
   <u>Error</u>: Misplaced modifier
   <u>Corrected</u>: Depreciation accounting is a system not of valuation but of allocation.
3. To form an opinion as to the collectibility of the accounts, they were reviewed with the credit manager.
   <u>Error</u>: Dangling infinitive
   <u>Corrected</u>: To form an opinion as to the collectibility of the accounts, we reviewed them with the credit manager.
4. This problem can only be alleviated by a change in policy
   <u>Error</u>: Misplaced modifier
   <u>Corrected</u>: This problem can be alleviated only by a change in policy.
5. Bob Smith's interest and devotion to his work are not to be questioned.
   <u>Error</u>: Omission of a preposition
   <u>Corrected</u>: Bob Smith's interest in and devotion to his work are not to be questioned.

Answers to Spelling Errors Exercise (pages 293–294)

1.	semi–annual	incorrect	semiannual
2.	occurrance	incorrect	occurrence
3.	facimile	incorrect	facsimile
4.	supercede	incorrect	supersede
5.	government	correct	
6.	disasterous	incorrect	disastrous
7.	proceedure	incorrect	procedure
8.	defecit	incorrect	deficit
9.	permissable	incorrect	permissible
10.	prevalant	incorrect	prevalent
11.	irrelevant	correct	
12.	questionaire	incorrect	questionnaire
13.	promissary	incorrect	promissory
14.	preferance	incorrect	preference
15.	maintainence	incorrect	maintenance

Writing and Grammar Examples

INSENSITIVE COMMUNICATION

Dear Mr. Sorrento:

   We are sorry to hear that your wife recently died. Thanks for letting us know about it.

   The AmericanMoneycard account in her name has been cancelled. Also, we require that you destroy all AmericanMoneycards in your possession that were issued in her name.
   Now that you have enjoyed the benefits of an AmericanMoneycard, you will no doubt wish to have an account opened in your own name, so we are enclosing an application form for you to fill out.
   As you will discover, the AmericanMoneycard will help you in managing your money. Every month you will receive an itemized statement with a record showing each charge transaction. In addition, the AmericanMoneycard will always be there to provide you with convenient and secure financial protection.
   So fill out your application and send it in to us today!

(continued)

IMPERSONAL COMMUNICATION

NOTICE OF TERMINATION OF AUTOMOBILE INSURANCE

Applicable paragraphs are checked.

☐ This communication serves to notify you herewith that your above numbered Automobile Policy is being cancelled, effective on the date given above.

☐ This communication serves to notify you herewith that your above numbered Automobile Policy, which expires on the date given above, will not be renewed or continued.

☑ Your above numbered Automobile Policy is being terminated because you failed to discharge when due your obligations regarding payment of premiums on the above numbered policy or any installment thereof, payable either directly to this Company or indirectly under a finance plan or credit extension.

☑ You have the right to request that the Company provide you with a written explanation of its reason for terminating your policy, provided that your request is mailed or delivered to the Company no less than __7__ days prior to the effective date of the termination given above.

INCOMPREHENSIBLE COMMUNICATION

Company Policy Handbook: Incentive Compensation of Company's Sales Volume

The key aspect of the method of relating the previous year to the current year compensation opportunity is as follows: The selling task requires equal output for the goal achievement. Analysis of the market, price increases, or if any decreases, must be made. Using this reference point, sales volume bracket levels make up the entering point for incentive earnings. The sales goal would be represented by the highest bracket level above the sales reference point. The complete compensation control limit and base salary range allow flexibility in the area of the incentive portion of total compensation.

Exhibit B.9

471

OLD POLICY 1980

SECTION I — LIABILITY

1. **Coverage A — Bodily Injury Liability;** **Coverage C — Property Damage Liability:** To pay on behalf of the insured all sums which the insured shall become legally obligated to pay as damages because of

    The insura
    sured agai

Coverage A bodily injury, sickness or disease, including
therefrom, hereinafter called "
any person;

Coverage C injury

NEW POLICY 1981

PART A — LIABILITY COVERAGE

INSURING AGREEMENT

We will pay damages for bodily injury or property damage for becomes legally responsible because of an auto accident. Propert of the damaged property. We will settle or defend, as we conside asking for these damages. In addition to our limit of liability, w incur. Our duty to settle or defend ends when our limit of lia exhausted.

"Covered person" as used in this Part means:

1. You or any family member for the ownership, maintenar
2. Any person using your covered auto.
3. For your covered auto, any person or organizatic for acts or omissions of a person for wh
covered auto

Figure B.1

Source: Rich Waechter, "New Insurance Form Takes It Easy." *Dallas Morning News*, Aug. 21, 1980, p. 1C.

The 100+ Words Most Frequently Misspelled

accommodate	achievement	acquire	all right
among	apparent	argument	arguing
belief*	believe*	beneficial	benefited
bookkeeper	category	coming	comparative
conscious	controversy	controversial	deficit
definitely	definition	define	describe
description	disastrous	effect	embarrass
environment	exaggerate	existence*	existent*
experience	explanation	facsimile	fascinate
government	height	indispensable	interest
irrelevant	irresponsibility	its, it's	judgment
lose	losing	maintenance	led
mere	necessary	occasion*	marriage
occurring	occurrence	opinion	occurred
paid	particular	performance	opportunity
personal	personnel	possession	permissible
practical	precede*	preference	possible
prepare	prevalent	principal	prejudice
privilege*	probably	proceed	principle
professor	profession	prominent	procedure
pursue	questionable	questionnaire	promissory
receive*	receiving*	recommend	quiet
repetition	rhythm	semiannual	referring*
separate*	separation*	shining	sense
studying	succeed	succession	similar*
technique	than	then	surprise
there*	they're*	thorough	their*
transferred	unforeseen	unnecessary	to,* too,* two*
woman	write	writing	villain

*most frequently misspelled words among the first hundred

Examples of Ways to Eliminate Age and Sex Connotations

The following suggestions are in line with revisions of the Dictionary of Occupational Titles by the U.S. Department of Labor in 1975 to eliminate age and sex connotations.

A. *Edit to Eliminate Unnecessary Gender Pronouns.*

No	Yes
If credit management is too lax, the seller maximizes sales volume, *but he reduces* the percentage of accounts receivable *he collects.*	If credit management is too lax, the seller maximizes sales volume *but reduces* the percentage of accounts *receivable collected.*

No	**Yes**
The individual student is to determine which keystrokes *give him the most difficulty* and then practice them.	The individual student is to determine which keystrokes *give the most difficulty* and then practice them.
The bailee has a duty to do only the work agreed on; *he has no right* to use the car *for his own personal purposes.*	The bailee has a duty to do only the work agreed on *and has no right* to use the car *for personal purposes.*

B. Recast into the Plural.

No	**Yes**
When *an individual* travels by mass transit, *he* is confronted with a user charge.	When *individuals* travel by mass transit, *they are confronted* with a user charge.
Another type of conditional gift is made when the donor expects that *he* may die imminently. *He* may take *his* gifts back if *he* survives or changes *his* mind before *he* dies.	Another type of conditional gift is made when a donor expects to die imminently. *Donors* who survive may take *their* gifts back or change *their* minds before *they* die.
Such participation aids the *student* in developing *his* ability to communicate.	Such participation aids the *students* in developing *their* abilities to communicate.

C. Avoid Using Special Female-Gender Word Forms.

No	**Yes**
the *girls* or the *ladies* (meaning adult females)	the women
girl, as in, I'll have my girl check that	I'll have my secretary (or my assistant or my associate or the person's name) check that
lady used as a modifier, as in *lady* lawyer	lawyer (when you must modify, use *woman* or *female*, as in: a course on women writers, or the airline's first female pilot)

D. Substitute Alternatives to the Generic Use of the Word Man.

No	**Yes**
man, men, mankind	human(s), human being(s), person(s), people, individuals, humanity, human race, women and men, men and women
men (as in men, machines, money)	labor, human resources
Forty miles an hour, under the conditions described, was faster than an ordinary, *prudent man* would have driven his own car.	Forty miles an hour, under the conditions described, was faster than an ordinary, *prudent person* would have been driving.
By environment we mean simply the sum total of all the resources *available to man* by which he seeks to maintain himself as a species.	By environment we mean simply the sum total of all the available *resources by which people* seek to maintain themselves as a species.

E. Substitute Nonsexist Words for Man *Suffixes and Prefixes.*

No	Yes
businessman	businessperson, business executive, merchant, industrialist, entrepreneur, manager
businessmen	businesspeople, people in business
chairman	chairperson, moderator, chair, group leader, presiding officer
congressmen	members of Congress, congressional representatives, congressmen and congresswomen
manmade	manufactured, hand-built, handmade, machinemade
manpower	human resources, human energy, work-force personnel
salesmen	salespeople, salespersons, sales agents, sales associates, sales representatives, sales force
spokesman	representative, spokesperson, advocate, proponent
statesman	political leader, public servant
workmen	workers

F. Use Up-to-Date Occupational Titles.

No	Yes
cameraman	camera operator
deliveryman	delivery driver, delivery clerk, deliverer
draftsman	drafter
foreman	supervisor
maid	houseworker
pressman	press operator
repairman	repairer
salesman	sales agent, sales associate, sales representative, salesperson
serviceman	servicer
stock boy, stock man	stock clerk
yardman	yard worker

Index